Revenue Statistics 2018

1965-2017

OECD
BETTER POLICIES FOR BETTER LIVES

This work is published under the responsibility of the Secretary-General of the OECD. The opinions expressed and arguments employed herein do not necessarily reflect the official views of OECD member countries.

This document, as well as any data and any map included herein, are without prejudice to the status of or sovereignty over any territory, to the delimitation of international frontiers and boundaries and to the name of any territory, city or area.

Please cite this publication as:
OECD (2018), *Revenue Statistics 2018*, OECD Publishing, Paris.
https://doi.org/10.1787/rev_stats-2018-en

ISBN 978-92-64-30878-7 (print)
ISBN 978-92-64-30879-4 (pdf)

Annual: Revenue Statistics
ISSN 2522-7696 (print)
ISSN 2522-770X (online)

The statistical data for Israel are supplied by and under the responsibility of the relevant Israeli authorities. The use of such data by the OECD is without prejudice to the status of the Golan Heights, East Jerusalem and Israeli settlements in the West Bank under the terms of international law.

Photo credits: Cover © some of the graphic elements in the main cover illustration were adapted from Freepik.com.

Corrigenda to OECD publications may be found on line at: *www.oecd.org/publishing/corrigenda*.

Foreword

This annual publication provides information on tax levels and tax structures in OECD countries. It was prepared under the auspices of the Working Party on Tax Policy Analysis and Tax Statistics of the Committee on Fiscal Affairs and is published under the responsibility of the Secretary-General of the OECD.

In Memoriam

This edition is dedicated to the memory of Michel Lahittete who passed away on 11 July 2018.

Michel was a valued friend and colleague of the staff at the Centre for Tax Policy and Administration (CTPA). Michel's contribution to *Revenue Statistics* and to CTPA was invaluable. His brilliant mind, technical expertise and sense of humour will be deeply missed.

We thank all those who contributed to finalising this year's edition in his absence.

Acknowledgements

Revenue Statistics 2018 has been produced by the Organisation for Economic Cooperation and Development (OECD)'s Centre for Tax Policy and Administration (CTPA) under the auspices of Working Party No.2 on Tax Policy Analysis and Tax Statistics (WP2) of the Committee on Fiscal Affairs. The authors of this edition were Michel Lahittete, Michelle Harding, Jose René Orozco, Bethany Millar-Powell and Michael Sharratt.

The authors would like to thank colleagues in the OECD for their invaluable comments and practical support in finalising the publication, including Leonie Beisemann, Bert Brys, David Bradbury, Karena Garnier, Emmanuelle Modica, Dominique Paturot, Violet Sochay, Carrie Tyler and Talita Yamashiro Fordelone in CTPA; Nadim Ahmad, Helen Beilby-Orrin, Frederic Parrot and Peter Van de Ven in the Statistics and Data Directorate and the Statistical Editors and Content Management Team in the Press and Communications Directorate. Alexandra Le Cam and Marie-Aurélie Elkurd at CTPA assisted with the production and publication of this report and Stephanie Coic in the Development Cooperation Directorate (DCD) designed the cover. The authors would also like to thank WP2 delegates and their colleagues working in national administrations for their input and comments.

Table of contents

Additional chapters

Two additional chapters are available on line only at: https://doi.org/10.1787/rev_stats-2018-en

- Chapter 5. Detailed country tables, 1965-2016
- Chapter 6. Tax revenues by subsectors of general government

Tables

Figures

Executive Summary

Since 1995, tax levels and tax structures in OECD countries have converged around a higher average tax-to-GDP ratio and an average tax structure that is more reliant on value-added taxes, social security contributions, and corporate income taxes, while less reliant on personal income taxes and other forms of taxes and goods and services. In 2017, these trends continued, with the OECD average tax-to-GDP ratio continuing its steady increase to a high of 34.2%.

Taxes are defined as compulsory, unrequited payments to general government. They are unrequited in that the benefits provided by governments to taxpayers are not normally allocated in proportion to their payments. Taxes are classified by their base: income, profits and capital gains; payroll; property; goods and services; and other taxes. Compulsory social security contributions (SSCs) paid to general government are also treated as taxes. Revenues are analysed by level of government: federal or central; state; local; and social security funds. Detailed information on the classifications applied is set out in the Interpretative Guide in Annex A.

Tax levels in 2017

Across OECD countries, tax-to-GDP ratios in 2017 ranged from 16.2% in Mexico to 46.2% in France, with 20 countries within five percentage points of the OECD average of 34.2%. Between 2016 and 2017, the OECD average tax-to-GDP ratio has increased 0.2 percentage points, from 34.0% to 34.2%. This continues the consistent increase in the average OECD tax-to-GDP ratio since the financial crisis.

An increase in tax-to-GDP ratios from 2016 to 2017 is also observed in 19 of the 34 countries for which preliminary 2017 data is available. In all of these countries, the increase was due to nominal tax revenues increasing more than the nominal increases in GDP. The increase in the tax-to-GDP ratio was largest in Israel, due to higher revenues from taxes on income, and the United States, due to higher property tax revenues, with no other increases above one percentage point in this period.

Fifteen countries experienced a decrease in tax-to-GDP ratios in 2016 relative to 2015. The falls were also typically small, with a decrease exceeding one percentage point in only Iceland and Hungary. In Iceland, the fall was due to the impact of one-off stability contributions in 2016; whereas in Hungary, the fall was due to decreases in taxes on income and profits and a decrease in taxes on goods and services . Decreases were also seen in Chile, Sweden, Denmark, Italy, Turkey, Slovenia, Austria, Mexico, Norway, Canada, Ireland, Finland and Estonia; and in all cases were due to tax revenues increasing less than GDP.

Twenty-two OECD countries reported tax-to-GDP ratios in 2017 that were higher than those in 2007, with the greatest increases seen in Greece and Mexico. Among the remaining 12 countries, tax levels in 2016 remained more than three percentage points lower in Ireland and Norway.

Tax structure in 2016

In 2016, SSCs amounted to the largest share of tax revenues in the OECD, at just over one-quarter (26.0%) of total revenues, and together with personal income taxes (23.5%) the two categories amounted to nearly one-half of tax revenues in OECD countries on average. Value-added taxes accounted for a further one-fifth of total revenues (20.0%). Other consumption taxes and taxes on corporate income accounted for smaller shares of tax revenues (12.5% and 9% respectively), with property taxes (6.5%) and residual taxes accounting for the remaining share.

Since 2015, the biggest change in the tax structure occurred in the composition of taxes on income and profits, where the share of personal income taxes decreased by 0.3 percentage points (from 24.1 to 23.8 of total revenues) and the share of corporate income taxes increased by 0.2 percentage points (from 8.8 to 9.0% of total revenues). Changes in other categories were all less than 0.1 percentage point, with the result that the OECD average structure stayed relatively constant in 2016, with the exception of the shift away from personal toward corporate income taxes.

Changes by level of government

Tax revenues at different levels of government remained stable in 2016 relative to 2015, both on an OECD average basis and in individual countries. The federal share of revenues in 2015 remained at 53.2% of general government revenue in federal countries and at 63.5% in unitary countries. In federal countries, 25.4% of revenues were received at subnational level on average (ranging from 4.6% in Austria to 50.2% in Canada), with roughly two-thirds of revenues being received by state governments and one-third by local governments. In unitary countries, the share of local government revenues was 11.4% on average, ranging from less than 1.5% in the Czech Republic, Estonia and Lithuania, to 35.4% in Sweden.

Convergence in OECD tax levels and structures

A special feature in this report measures the convergence of tax levels and tax structures in OECD countries, demonstrating that the OECD average tax-to-GDP ratio in 2016 is more representative than it has been at any point in the last twenty years. Since 1995, the longest period for which data is available for all OECD countries, the OECD average tax-to-GDP ratio has increased from 33.0% to 34.0% in 2016, while dispersion of country tax-to-GDP ratios around this mean has decreased.

Similarly, tax structures in most OECD countries have converged toward the OECD average tax structure, which has become more reliant on value-added taxes, social security contributions, and corporate income taxes; and which has moved away from taxes on personal income and other forms of taxes on goods and services. In 2016, the countries with the greatest difference in tax structures from the OECD average were Chile, New Zealand, Denmark, Australia and the United States; whereas the smallest differences were observed in Portugal, Norway, Finland, Luxembourg and Spain.

Introduction

The purpose of this annual publication is to provide internationally comparative data on tax levels and tax structures in member countries of the OECD. The taxes imposed in each country are presented in a standardised framework based upon the OECD classification of taxes and its Interpretative Guide as contained in Annex A to this Report.

Starting in 2004, the data for recent years in this publication are mainly reported on an accrual basis, rather than the cash basis that was used in previous editions. The reasons for this change were discussed in Special Feature S.2 of the 2003 edition. Details of the practical implementation of this change were given in Special Feature S.1 of the 2004 edition.

The data for the Report has, for the most part, been provided by Delegates to Working Party No.2 on Tax Policy Analysis and Tax Statistics of the Committee on Fiscal Affairs. The OECD acknowledges the co-operation of the International Monetary Fund, whose classification of tax revenues — although in a number of respects less detailed — is in many respects similar to that of the OECD.[1] The most important of the other classifications currently in use is the System of National Accounts (henceforth referred to as SNA) and the European System of Integrated Economic Accounts of EU member states (henceforth referred to as ESA), which is primarily an elaboration of SNA, though differing from it in certain respects. Subject to a few exceptions, SNA/ESA figures can be reconciled with the figures in the present Report, since SNA criteria and definitions have been adopted unless the contrary is specifically indicated.

The material is organised in six chapters. Chapter 1 summarises tax trends of the past 50 years focusing in turn on tax-to-GDP ratios (section 1.1), tax structures (section 1.2) and taxes by level of government (section 1.3). Section 1.4 discusses the impact of alternate treatments of non-wastable tax credits. This year's issue also carries in Chapter 2 a special feature on "Convergence of tax levels and tax structures in OECD countries". Chapter 3 contains a set of comparative statistical tables for years 1965-2017. Chapter 4 provides country tables with tax revenue and tax-to-GDP ratios broken down by selected tax categories and by level of government for years between 1990 and 2016 (section 4.1).[2] Two memorandum tables show how countries finance their social benefits, and report taxes and social security contributions paid by general government (section 4.2). Chapter 5, which is available on line only provides statistical tables with a detailed breakdown of tax revenues by country for years between 1965 and 2016 (section 5.1). Two memorandum tables show how countries finance their social benefits, and report taxes and social security contributions paid by general government (section 5.2). Chapter 6, which is also only available on line, attributes tax revenues to general government by the following sub-sectors: central, state; local and social security funds. It contains a set of comparative statistical tables for years 1975-2016 (section 6.1) and a second series of tables with a detailed breakdown of tax revenues by country for years between 1975 and 2016 (section 6.2).

Notes

1 See IMF, *Government Finance Statistics Manual 2014 (Washington D.C.*: International Monetary Fund, 2014).

2 Because of space limitations data are shown for selected years between 1965 and 2016. Data for years not shown are available online.

Chapter 1. Tax revenue trends 1965-2017

Chapter 1 provides information on trends in tax revenues in OECD countries from 1965 to 2017, including changes in tax-to-GDP ratios, tax structures, taxes by level of government and non-wastable tax credits.

Revenue Statistics 2018 presents detailed internationally comparable data on tax revenues of OECD countries for all levels of government. The latest edition provides final data on tax revenues in 1965-2016. In addition, provisional estimates of tax revenues in 2017 are included for almost all OECD countries.[1]

Box 1.1. Revenue Statistics in OECD Countries – definitions & classifications

In *Revenue Statistics 2018*, taxes are defined as compulsory, unrequited payments to general government. Taxes are unrequited in the sense that benefits provided by government are not normally in proportion to their payments.

In the OECD classification, taxes are classified by the base of the tax:

- Income and profits (heading 1000)
- Compulsory social security contributions paid to general government, which are treated as taxes (heading 2000)
- Payroll and workforce (heading 3000)
- Property (heading 4000)
- Goods and services (heading 5000)
- Other (heading 6000)

Much greater detail on the tax concept, the classification of taxes and the accrual basis of reporting is set out in the OECD Interpretative Guide at annex A of *Revenue Statistics 2018.*

All of the averages presented in this summary are unweighted.

1.1. Tax-to-GDP ratios

1.1.1. Tax ratios for 2017 (provisional data)

New OECD data in the annual *Revenue Statistics 2018* publication show that tax revenues as a percentage of GDP (i.e. the tax-to-GDP ratio) have continued to increase since the low-point experienced in almost all countries in 2008 and 2009 as a result of the financial and economic crisis. The average tax-to-GDP ratio in OECD countries was 34.2%[2] in 2017 compared with 34.0% in 2016 and 33.7% in 2015. The 2017 figure is the highest recorded OECD average tax-to-GDP ratio since records began in 1965 (Figure 1.1).

Figure 1.1. Trends in tax-to-GDP ratios, 1965-2017p (as % of GDP)

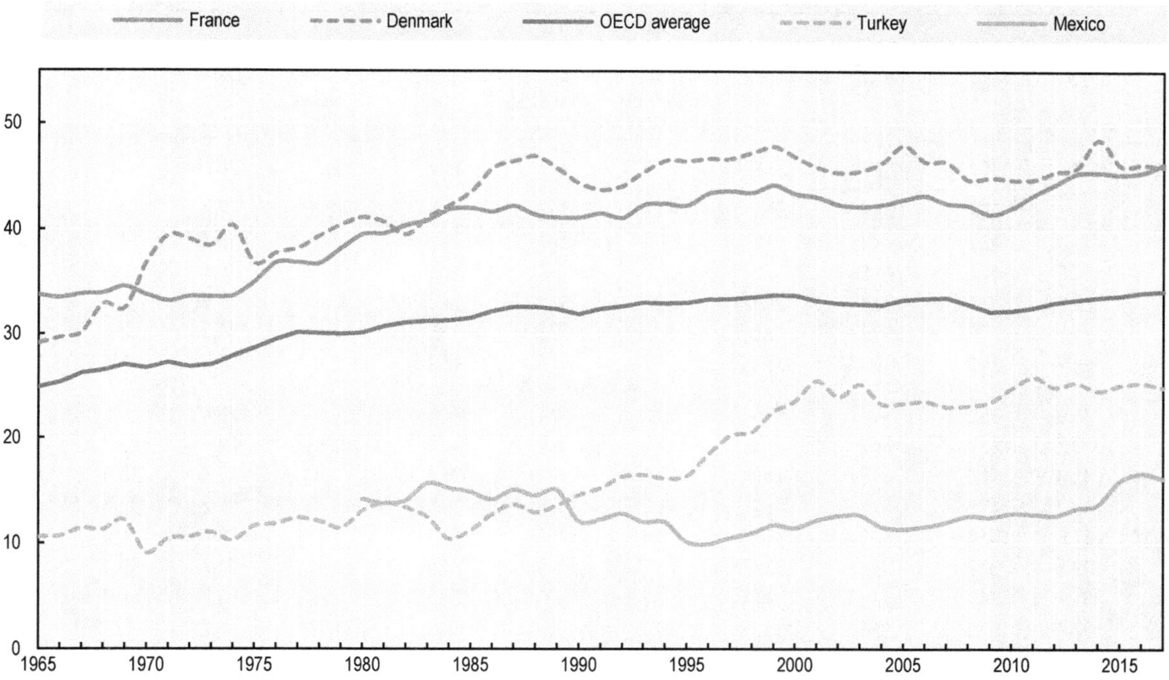

1. Data for 2017 are preliminary. The OECD average in 2017 is calculated by applying the unweighted average percentage change for 2017 in the 33 countries providing data for that year to the overall average tax to GDP ratio in 2016.
2. The 2016 OECD average tax-to-GDP ratio excludes the one-off revenues from stability contributions in Iceland.
Source: Table 3.1.

StatLink http://dx.doi.org/10.1787/888933858867

Table 1.1. Revenue Statistics: overview

	Tax revenue as % of GDP				Tax revenue as % of total tax revenue in 2016						
	2017p	2016	2015	2000	1100 Taxes on income, individuals (PIT)	1200 Taxes on income, corporates (CIT)	2000 Social security contributions (SSC)	4000 Taxes on property	5111 Value added taxes	Other consumption taxes[6]	All other taxes[7]
OECD - Average[1]	34.2	34.0	33.7	33.8	23.8	9.0	26.2	5.7	20.2	12.5	2.6
Australia	..	27.8	27.9	30.5	40.8	16.5	0.0	10.8	12.9	14.2	4.9
Austria	41.8	42.2	43.1	42.3	21.6	5.6	34.7	1.3	18.3	10.0	8.5
Belgium	44.6	44.1	44.8	43.5	27.7	7.8	31.1	8.0	15.4	9.1	0.9
Canada	32.2	32.7	32.7	34.8	36.3	10.5	14.9	12.0	13.5	9.7	3.2
Chile	20.2	20.2	20.4	18.8	8.8	20.9	7.2	5.1	41.2	13.4	3.5
Czech Republic	34.9	34.2	33.3	32.4	11.2	11.0	42.9	1.4	21.7	11.3	0.5
Denmark[2]	46.0	46.2	46.1	46.9	53.5	5.8	0.1	4.0	20.4	11.6	4.5
Estonia	33.0	33.7	33.3	31.1	17.2	5.0	33.2	0.8	27.0	16.3	0.5
Finland	43.3	44.0	43.9	45.8	29.6	5.0	29.1	3.2	20.7	12.1	0.3
France[2]	46.2	45.5	45.3	43.4	18.8	4.5	36.8	9.4	15.2	9.2	6.2
Germany[3]	37.5	37.4	37.0	36.2	26.6	5.2	37.6	2.8	18.5	8.6	0.6
Greece[2]	39.4	38.8	36.6	33.4	15.2	6.5	28.5	8.1	21.2	18.4	2.1
Hungary	37.7	39.2	38.7	38.5	13.3	6.0	33.2	2.8	23.7	18.6	2.3
Iceland	37.7	51.6	36.3	36.3	26.7	4.9	6.7	34.2	16.2	7.1	4.1
Ireland	22.8	23.3	23.1	30.8	31.6	11.5	16.8	6.0	20.1	12.6	1.4
Israel[4]	32.7	31.3	31.3	34.9	19.8	9.9	16.6	10.3	24.1	13.7	5.6
Italy	42.4	42.6	43.1	40.6	25.8	5.0	30.1	6.6	14.4	13.8	4.4
Japan	..	30.6	30.6	25.8	18.6	12.0	40.4	8.3	13.3	7.1	0.3
Korea	26.9	26.2	25.2	21.5	17.6	13.6	26.2	11.6	15.8	12.3	2.9
Latvia	30.4	30.4	29.2	29.1	21.0	5.6	27.3	3.5	26.8	15.1	0.7
Lithuania	29.8	29.8	28.9	30.8	13.4	5.4	40.8	1.1	26.2	12.2	0.8
Luxembourg	38.7	38.1	37.1	36.9	24.7	12.2	28.5	9.3	16.7	8.5	0.3
Mexico[5]	16.2	16.6	15.9	11.5	20.4	21.0	13.0	1.9	23.7	15.1	5.0
Netherlands	38.8	38.4	37.0	36.9	18.5	8.7	38.2	4.0	17.6	11.9	1.1
New Zealand	32.0	31.6	31.6	32.5	36.8	15.5	0.0	6.1	29.8	8.5	3.2
Norway	38.2	38.7	38.4	41.9	27.6	10.4	27.4	3.3	22.3	9.1	0.0
Poland	33.9	33.4	32.4	32.9	14.5	5.5	38.1	4.1	21.1	15.3	1.4
Portugal	34.7	34.3	34.4	31.1	19.8	8.9	26.6	3.7	24.8	14.8	1.4
Slovak Republic	32.9	32.4	32.2	33.6	10.2	10.8	43.5	1.3	20.6	12.4	1.2
Slovenia	36.0	36.5	36.4	36.6	14.4	4.4	39.7	1.7	22.5	16.8	0.5
Spain[2]	33.7	33.2	33.6	33.2	21.4	6.8	34.2	7.7	19.1	10.3	0.5
Sweden	44.0	44.0	43.1	49.0	29.8	6.2	22.6	2.4	20.9	7.2	10.9
Switzerland	28.5	27.8	27.6	27.6	31.0	11.3	24.3	7.3	12.2	9.2	4.7
Turkey	24.9	25.3	25.1	23.6	14.6	6.5	28.8	4.8	19.8	23.8	1.6
United Kingdom	33.3	32.7	32.2	32.9	27.4	8.3	18.9	12.6	20.8	11.5	0.5
United States	27.1	25.9	26.2	28.2	40.3	7.6	24.0	11.1	0.0	16.9	0.0

1. 2017 provisional average calculated by applying the unweighted average percentage change for 2017 in the 34 countries providing data for that year to the overall average tax to GDP ratio in 2016. The 2016 OECD average tax-to-GDP ratio excludes the one-off revenues from stability contributions in Iceland.

2. The total tax revenue has been reduced by the amount of any capital transfer that represents uncollected taxes.

3. From 1991 the figures relate to the united Germany.

4. The data for Israel are supplied by and under the responsibility of the relevant Israeli authorities. The use of such data by the OECD is without prejudice to the status of the Golan Heights, East Jerusalem and Israeli settlements in the West Bank under the terms of international law.

5. 2017 provisional: Secretariat estimate, including expected revenues collected by state and local governments.

6. Calculated as 5000 Taxes on goods and services less 5111 Value added taxes.

7. Includes 1300 Unallocable between personal and corporate income tax, 3000 Taxes on payroll and workforce and 6000 Other taxes.

StatLink http://dx.doi.org/10.1787/888933858886

Country tax-to-GDP ratios in 2017 varied considerably (Table 1.1), both across countries and since 2016. Key observations include:

- France had the highest tax-to-GDP ratio in 2017 (46.2%). Denmark, which had the highest tax-to-GDP ratio of OECD countries from 2002 to 2016, had the second-highest tax-to-GDP ratio in 2017 (46.0%). Mexico had the lowest tax-to-GDP ratio (16.2%).
- Of the 34 countries for which data for 2017 are available, the ratio of tax revenues to GDP compared to 2016 rose in 19 and fell in 15.
- Between 2016 and 2017, the largest tax ratio increases were in Israel and the United States. Israel introduced a number of policy changes which impacted revenues from taxes on income and profits – including a reduced basic tax credit for personal income taxes, increased employer SSCs, and changes to corporate taxation – which together contributed to an increase in its tax-to-GDP ratio of 1.4 percentage points. The tax-to-GDP ratio in the United States increased by 1.3 percentage points, partly due to the one-off deemed repatriation tax on foreign earnings under the Tax Cuts and Jobs Act. No other country experienced an increase of more than one percentage point in their tax-to-GDP ratio between 2016 and 2017 (Figure 1.2).
- The largest falls in the tax-to-GDP ratio between 2016 and 2017 were in Iceland (13.9 percentage points, due to one-off stability contributions in 2016) and Hungary (1.5 percentage points, due to lower revenues from taxes on income and profits and from taxes in goods and services following a package of reforms in 2016). There were no other decreases of over one percentage point.

In 2016, Iceland received revenues from one-off stability contributions from entities that previously operated as commercial or savings banks and were concluding operations. The stability contributions aimed to liberalise the capital controls that were imposed following the 2007-08 crisis, while preserving Iceland's economic stability. The revenue from these contributions led to unusually high tax revenues for a single year.

The one-off stability contributions raised nearly ISK 385 000 million, equivalent to 15.7% of Iceland's GDP in 2016. Iceland's tax-to-GDP ratio rose from 36.3% in 2015 to 51.6% in 2016, before dropping 13.9 percentage points to 37.7% in 2017 (provisional). Due to the exceptional nature of the stability contributions, they are not representative of trends in tax levels across OECD countries and have been excluded from the calculation of the OECD average in 2016.

Figure 1.2. Changes in tax-to-GDP ratios, p.p., 2016-17p and 2007-17p

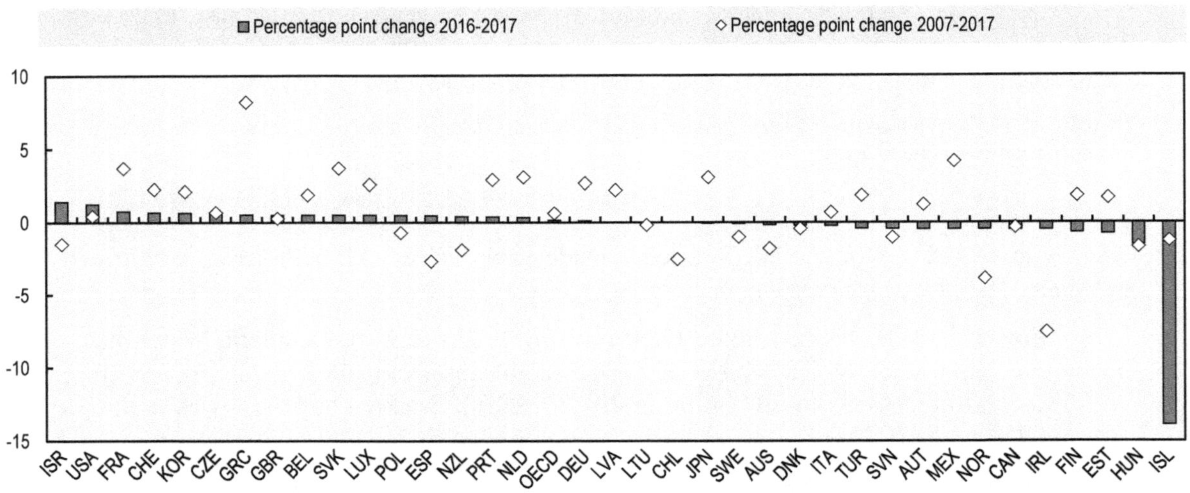

1. Preliminary data for 2017 was not available for Australia and Japan. For these countries the comparison shown is 2015-2016 and 2007-2016 data.
2. The 2016 OECD average tax-to-GDP ratio excludes the one-off revenues from stability contributions in Iceland.
Source: Secretariat calculations based on Table 3.1.

StatLink http://dx.doi.org/10.1787/888933858905

Although the OECD average tax-to-GDP ratio was higher in 2017 than in 2007 (pre-crisis), this was not the case in 15 OECD countries[3], which had lower tax-to-GDP ratios in 2017 than in 2007. In particular, the ratio in 2017 remains at least 3 percentage points lower in two countries; Ireland and Norway. The biggest fall has been in Ireland, from 30.4% in 2007 to 22.8% of GDP in 2017, largely due to the exceptional increase in GDP in 2015. Excluding Ireland, the largest fall has been in Norway, from 42.1% of GDP in 2007 to 38.2% in 2017 (Figure 1.2). In contrast, the strongest increase over this period was in Greece (8.2 percentage points, from 31.2% to 39.4% between 2007 and 2017). Five other countries, France, Japan, Mexico, the Netherlands and the Slovak Republic, experienced increases of 3 percentage points or more over the same period.

Box 1.2. Methodology: the tax-to-GDP ratio

The tax-to-GDP ratios shown in *Revenue Statistics 2018* express aggregate tax revenues as a percentage of GDP. The value of this ratio depends on its denominator (GDP) as well as its numerator (tax revenue), and that the denominator – GDP – is subject to historical revision.

The numerator (tax revenue)

- For the numerator, the OECD Secretariat uses revenue figures that are submitted annually by correspondents from national Ministries of Finance, Tax Administrations or National Statistics Offices. Although provisional figures for most countries become available with a lag of about six months, finalised data become available with a lag of around one and a half years. Final revenue data for 2016 were received during the period May-August 2018.
- In thirty-three OECD countries the reporting year coincides with the calendar year. Three countries — Australia, Japan and New Zealand — have different reporting years. Reporting year 2015 includes Q2/2015–Q1/2016 (Japan) and Q3/2015–Q2/2016 (Australia, New Zealand) respectively (Q = quarter).

The denominator (GDP)

- For the denominator, the GDP figures used for *Revenue Statistics 2018* are the most recently available in September 2018. By that time, the 2016 and 2017 GDP figures were available for all OECD countries.
- Using these GDP figures ensures a maximum of consistency and international comparability for the reported tax-to-GDP ratios.
- The GDP figures are based on the OECD Annual National Accounts (ANA – SNA) for the thirty-two OECD countries where the reporting year is the actual calendar year.
- Where the reporting year differs from the calendar year, the annual GDP estimates are obtained by aggregating quarterly GDP estimates provided by the OECD Statistics Directorate for those quarters corresponding to each country's fiscal (tax) year. For example, in the case of Japan Q2/2016–Q1/2017.

Changes in the tax-to-GDP ratio are driven by the relative changes in nominal tax revenues and in nominal GDP. From one year to the next, if tax revenues rise more than GDP (or fall less than GDP) the tax-to-GDP ratio will increase. Conversely, if tax revenues rise less than GDP, or fall further, the tax-to-GDP ratio will go down. Therefore, the tax-to-GDP ratio does not necessarily mean that the amount of tax revenues have increased in nominal, or even real, terms.

In 2017, 19 OECD countries had an increase in their tax-to-GDP ratio relative to 2016. In all of these countries, GDP growth was positive, although to a lesser degree than tax revenue growth. Of the fifteen OECD countries that experienced a decline in their tax-to-GDP ratio in 2017, thirteen had higher levels of tax revenues, although to a lesser degree than growth in nominal GDP levels. Two countries (Iceland and Mexico) had positive nominal GDP growth and negative tax revenue growth; no countries experienced declines in nominal GDP (Figure 1.3). In Figure 1.3, changes between 2015 and 2016 are shown for Australia and Japan, where the tax-to-GDP ratio is not available in 2017. In both countries, GDP grew faster than nominal tax revenues, leading to decreases in the tax-to-GDP ratio.

Figure 1.3. Relative changes in nominal tax revenues and nominal GDP, percentage, 2016-17p

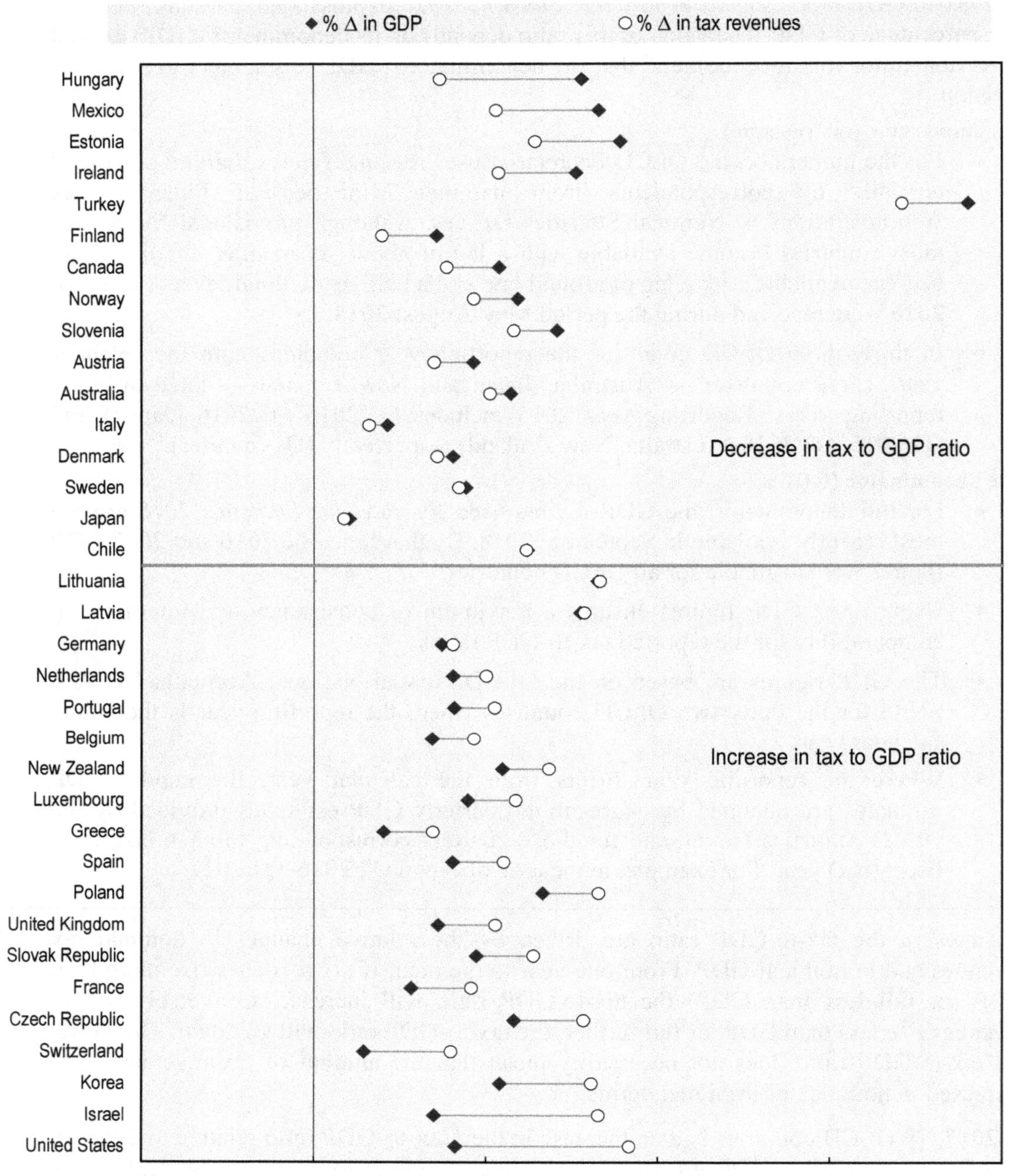

1. Data for Australia and Japan show the change between 2015 and 2016, as preliminary data for 2017 was not available for Australia and Japan. Data for Mexico in 2017 show a Secretariat estimate, including expected revenues collected by state and local governments.
2. Iceland's tax-to-GDP dropped 24% from 2016 to 2017, due to large one-off revenues from stability contributions in 2016. To improve readability of the graph, Iceland has not been included.
Source: Secretariat calculations based on chapter 4 (tax revenues) and table 3.19 (GDP).

StatLink http://dx.doi.org/10.1787/888933858924

Figure 1.4. Tax to GDP ratios in 2016 and 2017p (as % of GDP)

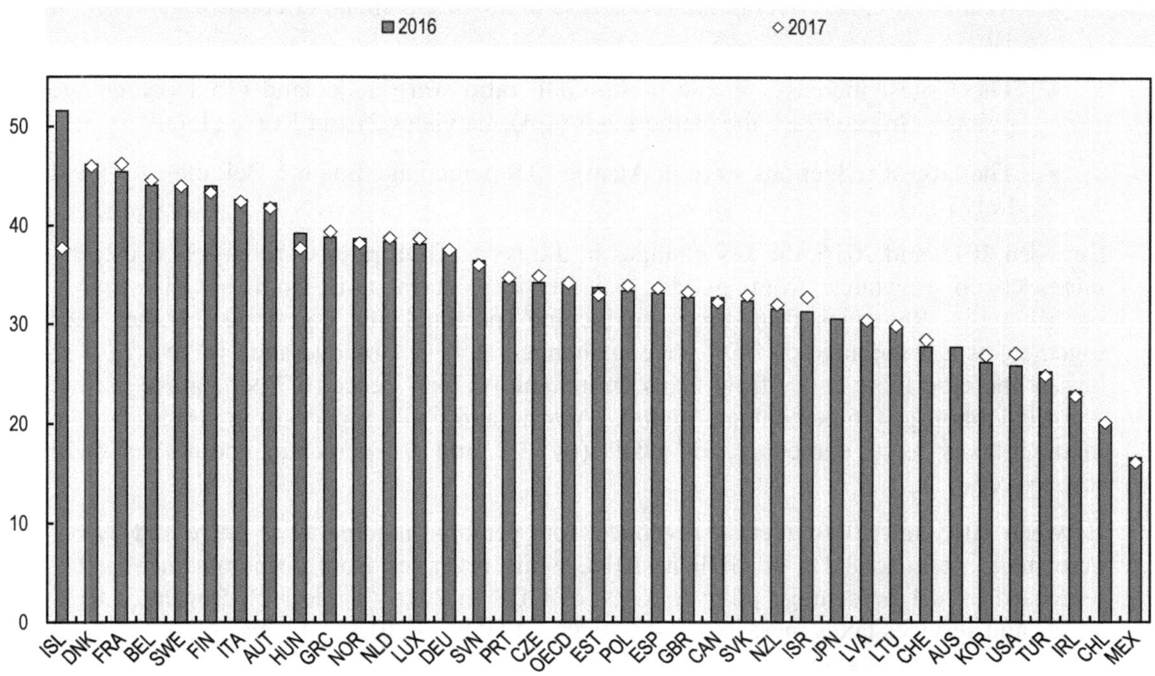

1. Preliminary data for 2017 was not available for Australia and Japan.
2. The 2016 OECD average tax-to-GDP ratio excludes the one-off revenues from stability contributions in Iceland. These stability contributions caused a large increase in Iceland's tax-to-GDP ratio in 2016, after which the tax-to-GDP ratio returned to more typical levels.
Source: Secretariat calculations based on Table 3.1

StatLink http://dx.doi.org/10.1787/888933858943

1.1.2. Tax-to-GDP ratios for 2016 (final data)

The latest year for which tax-to-GDP ratios are based on final revenue data and available for all OECD countries is 2016 (Figure 1.4). These data show that tax ratios vary considerably across countries:

- In 2016, Iceland had the highest tax-to-GDP ratio (51.6%), due to one-off stability contributions in that year. Excluding Iceland, Denmark (46.2%), France (45.5%), Belgium (44.1) and Sweden (44.0%) had the highest tax-to-GDP ratios in the OECD in 2016.
- Mexico had the lowest ratio at 16.6% followed by Chile (20.2%), Ireland (23.3%), Turkey (25.3%) and the United States (25.9%).
- Eight countries – Austria, Belgium, Denmark, Finland, France, Iceland, Italy and Sweden – had tax-to-GDP ratios of above 40%.
- In contrast, nine countries – Australia, Chile, Ireland, Korea, Lithuania, Mexico, Switzerland, Turkey and the United States – had tax-to-GDP ratios below 30%.

- The tax-to-GDP ratio in the OECD area as a whole (un-weighted average) was 34.0% in 2016 and rose by 0.3 percentage points from 2015.
- Relative to 2015, overall tax ratios rose in 26 OECD member countries and fell in 10.
- The largest increases in the tax-to-GDP ratio were in Iceland (15.3 percentage points), Greece (2.3), the Netherlands (1.4), Latvia (1.2) and Korea (1.1).
- The largest reductions were in Austria (0.9 percentage points), Belgium (0.7) and Italy (0.5).

Between 2015 and 2016, the key changes in the tax-to-GDP ratio were largely driven by increases in revenues from goods and services taxes and from social security contributions. Revenues from taxes on income (personal and corporate income taxes together) as a percentage of GDP were unchanged at 11.3% on average (Table 1.2). The largest increase in revenues from taxes on income was in Greece (0.7 percentage points) and Luxembourg (0.6 percentage points). Austria and Chile reported the largest falls in income taxes as a percentage of GDP (by 1.2 and 0.7 percentage points of GDP respectively).

Between 2015 and 2016, average revenues from personal income taxes decreased by 0.1 percentage point to 8.2% of GDP in 2016, while revenues from corporate income tax increased by 0.1 percentage point to 2.9% of GDP in 2016 (Table 1.2). Revenues from goods and services taxes increased from 10.8% of GDP in 2015 to 11.0% in 2016. Social security contributions also increased from 9.0% of GDP in 2015 to 9.2% in 2016. The other ratios were largely unchanged between 2015 and 2016.

Table 1.2. Tax structures in the OECD area, selected years (unweighted average as % of GDP)

Per cent

	1965	1990	2000	2007	2010	2012	2014	2015	2016
Total tax revenue	24.9	31.9	33.8	33.6	32.3	33.1	33.6	33.7	34.0
1000 Taxes on income, profits and capital gains	8.7	12.2	11.9	12.1	10.6	11.0	11.2	11.3	11.3
of which:									
1100 Taxes on income, profits and capital gains of individuals	6.8	9.7	8.7	8.2	7.6	7.9	8.2	8.3	8.2
1200 Taxes on income, profits and capital gains of corporates	2.1	2.5	3.2	3.6	2.7	2.8	2.8	2.8	2.9
2000 Social security contributions (SSC)	4.5	7.3	8.6	8.4	8.9	9.0	9.0	9.0	9.2
3000 Taxes on payroll and workforce	0.3	0.3	0.4	0.3	0.3	0.4	0.4	0.4	0.4
4000 Taxes on property	1.9	1.8	1.8	1.8	1.7	1.8	1.9	1.9	1.9
5000 Taxes on goods and services	9.4	10.0	10.9	10.6	10.6	10.7	10.8	10.8	11.0
of which:									
5111 Value added taxes	0.7	5.2	6.4	6.5	6.5	6.6	6.7	6.7	6.8
5121 Excises	3.5	2.6	2.9	2.6	2.7	2.7	2.6	2.6	2.6
6000 Other Taxes	0.1	0.3	0.2	0.2	0.2	0.2	0.2	0.2	0.2

Note: Percentage share of major tax categories in GDP. Data are included from 1965 onwards for Australia, Austria, Belgium, Canada, Denmark, Finland, France, Germany, Greece, Iceland, Ireland, Italy, Japan, Luxembourg, the Netherlands, New Zealand, Norway, Portugal, Spain, Sweden, Switzerland, Turkey, United Kingdom and United States; from 1972 for Korea; from 1980 for Mexico; from 1990 for Chile; from 1991 for Hungary and Poland; from 1993 for the Czech Republic and from 1995 for Estonia, Israel, Latvia, the Slovak Republic and Slovenia. The figures for the 2016 OECD average exclude the one-off revenues from stability contributions in Iceland.

Source: OECD (2018), "Revenue Statistics: Comparative tables", OECD Tax Statistics (database).

StatLink http://dx.doi.org/10.1787/888933858962

1.1.3. Tax ratio changes between 1965 and 2016

Between 1965 and 2016, the average tax-to-GDP ratio in the OECD area increased from 24.9% to 34.0% (an increase of 9.1 percentage points) (Figure 1.1).

Before the first oil shock (1973 to 1974), strong, almost uninterrupted income growth enabled tax levels to rise in all OECD countries. In part, tax levels rose automatically through the effect of fiscal drag on personal income tax schedules. From 1975 to 1985, the tax burden in the OECD area increased by 2.9 percentage points. After the mid-1970s, the combination of slower real income growth and higher levels of unemployment apparently limited the revenue raising capacity of governments. But during and after the deep recession following the second oil shock (1980), countries in Europe saw tax levels rise further, to finance higher spending on social security and rein in budget deficits.

After the mid-1980s, most OECD countries substantially reduced the statutory rates of their personal and corporate income tax, but the negative revenue impact of widespread tax reforms was often offset by reducing or abolishing tax reliefs. By 1999, the average OECD tax-to-GDP ratio had risen to 33.8%, the highest recorded level at that time. It fell back slightly between 2001 and 2004, but then rose again between 2005 and 2007 before falling back following the crisis. Taking these changes together the average tax level in the OECD area increased by 1.0 percentage points between 1995 and 2016 (Figure 1.1).

The OECD average conceals the great variety in national tax-to-GDP ratios. In 1965, tax-to-GDP ratios in OECD countries ranged from 10.6% in Turkey to 33.7% in France. By 2016 the corresponding range was from 16.6% in Mexico to 51.6% in Iceland, the latter due to exceptional revenues from one-off stability contributions in 2016. Without this one-off increase in tax revenues in Iceland, the tax-to-GDP ratio in OECD countries in 2016 ranged from 16.6% in Mexico to 46.2% in Denmark. The trend towards higher tax levels over this period reflects the need to finance a significant increase of public sector outlays in almost all OECD countries.

1.2. Tax structures

Tax structures are measured by the share of major taxes in total tax revenue. In 2016, the tax structures of OECD countries varied. Sixteen countries raised the largest part of their revenues from income taxes (both corporate and personal), eleven countries raised the largest part of their revenues from SSCs, and eight countries raised the largest part of their revenues from consumption taxes (including VAT). Taxes on property and payroll taxes played a smaller role in the revenue systems of OECD countries in 2016, both on average and within most countries (Figure 1.5).

Figure 1.5. Tax structures in 2016 (as % of total tax revenue)

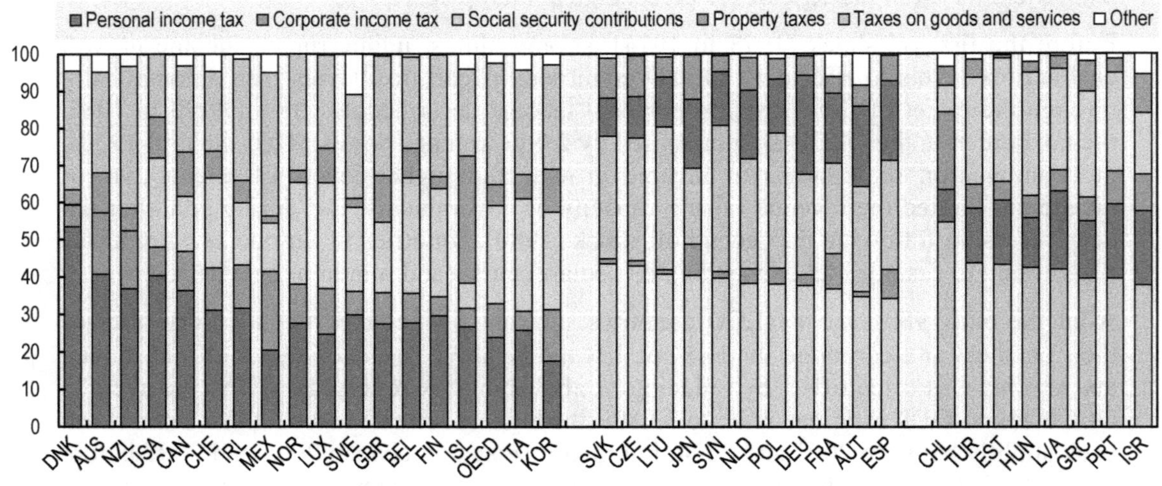

1. Countries are grouped and ranked by those where income tax revenues (personal and corporate) form the highest share of total tax revenues, followed by those where social security contributions, or taxes on goods and services, form the highest share.
2. The OECD average tax structure excludes the one-off revenues from stability contributions in Iceland.
3. The one-off revenues raised by stability contributions in Iceland in 2016 are classified as property taxes. Without these exceptional revenues, personal income taxes would have been the largest source of tax revenues in Iceland in 2016.
Source: Secretariat calculations based on data in chapter 4.

StatLink http://dx.doi.org/10.1787/888933858981

While on average tax levels have generally been rising, the tax structure or tax 'mix' has been remarkably stable over time. Nevertheless, several trends have emerged up to 2016 – the latest year for which data is available for all 36 OECD countries.

1.2.1. Taxes on income and profits

On average, in 2016, OECD countries collected 33.6% of their tax revenues through taxes on income and profits (personal and corporate income taxes taken together). Taxes on personal and corporate incomes remain the most important source of revenues used to finance public spending in 16 OECD countries, and in eight of them – Australia, Canada, Denmark, Ireland, Mexico, New Zealand, Switzerland and the United States – the share of income taxes in the tax mix in 2016 exceeded 40%.

Figure 1.6. Trends in tax structures (1965-2016, as % of total tax revenue)

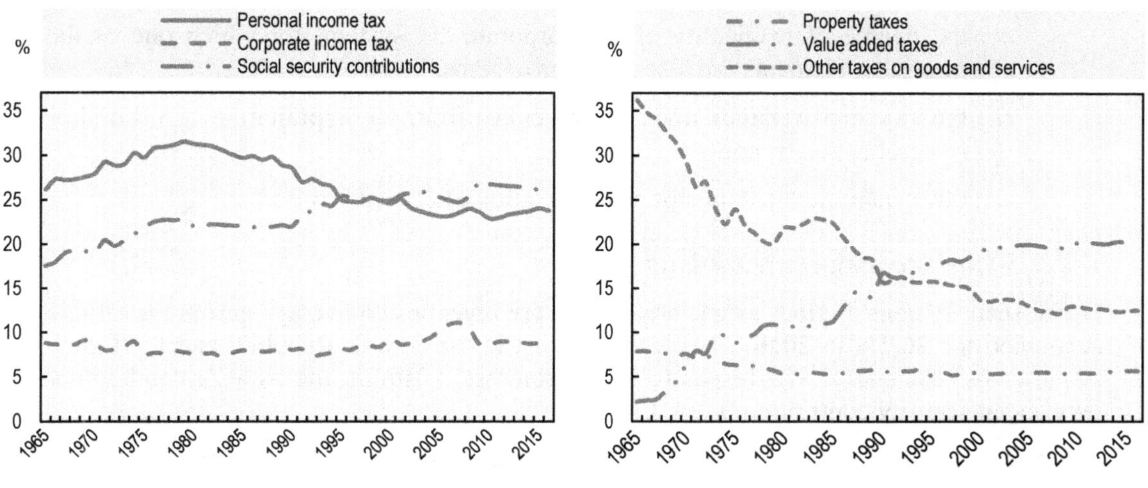

1. The OECD average tax revenue in 2016 from main categories excludes the one-off revenues from stability contributions in Iceland.

Source: Secretariat calculations based on tables 3.8 to 3.14.

StatLink http://dx.doi.org/10.1787/888933859000

Within taxes on income and profits, the share of PIT and CIT varies:

- Revenues from personal income taxes are 23.8% of total taxes on average in 2016 compared with around 30% in the 1980s. About two percentage points of this reduction can be attributed to the impact on the average of a number of relatively new entrants to the OECD from Eastern Europe for which tax revenue data is only available from the 1990s onwards. These countries tend to have relatively low personal income tax revenues and high revenues from social security contributions, but this impact is observed in the post 1990 data only.
- The variation in the share of the personal income tax between countries is considerable. In 2016, it ranged from a low of 8.8% and 10.2% in Chile and the Slovak Republic to 40.8% in Australia and 53.5% in Denmark (Figure 1.5).
- The sharp fall in the share of revenues from corporate income taxes in total taxation in 2008 and 2009 did not continue into 2011 and 2012, but the share of these taxes in total revenues remains at 9.0% of total tax revenues in 2016, below its 11.1% share in 2007.
- The share of the corporate income tax in total tax revenues varied considerably across countries from less than 5% (France, Iceland and Slovenia) to 21.0% (Mexico) and 20.9% (Chile) in 2016. Apart from the spread in statutory rates of the corporate income tax, these differences are at least partly explained by institutional and country specific factors, for example:
    - o the degree to which firms in a country are incorporated,

- o the breadth of the corporate income tax base, for example some narrowing may occur as a consequence of generous depreciation schemes and of tax incentives,
- o the degree of cyclicality of the corporate tax system, for which one of the important elements are loss offset provisions,
- o the extent of reliance upon tax revenues from the exploitation of oil and/or mineral deposits, and
- o other instruments to postpone the taxation of earned profits.

1.2.2. Social security contributions

Social security contributions as a share of total tax revenues on average across the OECD accounted for 26.2% in 2016. They were highest in the Slovak Republic and the Czech Republic (43.5% and 42.9%, respectively). In contrast, Australia and New Zealand do not levy social security contributions.

There is also wide variation across OECD countries in the relative proportions of social security contributions paid by employees and employers (Figure 1.7):

- Seven countries (Chile, Greece, Israel, Luxembourg, the Netherlands, Poland, and Slovenia) raise more revenues from employee SSCs, whereas the remainder raise more from employer SSCs.
- The highest share of employee SSC revenues are found in Slovenia, at 20.5% of total revenues. Germany, Greece, Japan, the Netherlands and Slovenia also have employee SSC revenues of over 15% of total tax revenues. Denmark had the lowest share, at 0.1% of total revenues. Apart from Denmark, only Estonia had revenues from employee SSCs of less than 5% of total revenues.
- The highest share of employer social security contribution revenues are found in Estonia, at 31.5% of total revenues. Lithuania and the Czech Republic also had employer SSC revenues of over 25% of total tax revenues, at 27.6% and 27.2% respectively. Denmark and Chile had the lowest shares, at 0.05% and 0.2% of total revenues respectively.
- The highest share of self-employed or non-employed social security contribution revenues are found in the Netherlands and the Slovak Republic, at 9.3% and 8.8% of total revenues respectively.

Figure 1.7. Composition of social security contributions, as % of total social security contributions, 2016

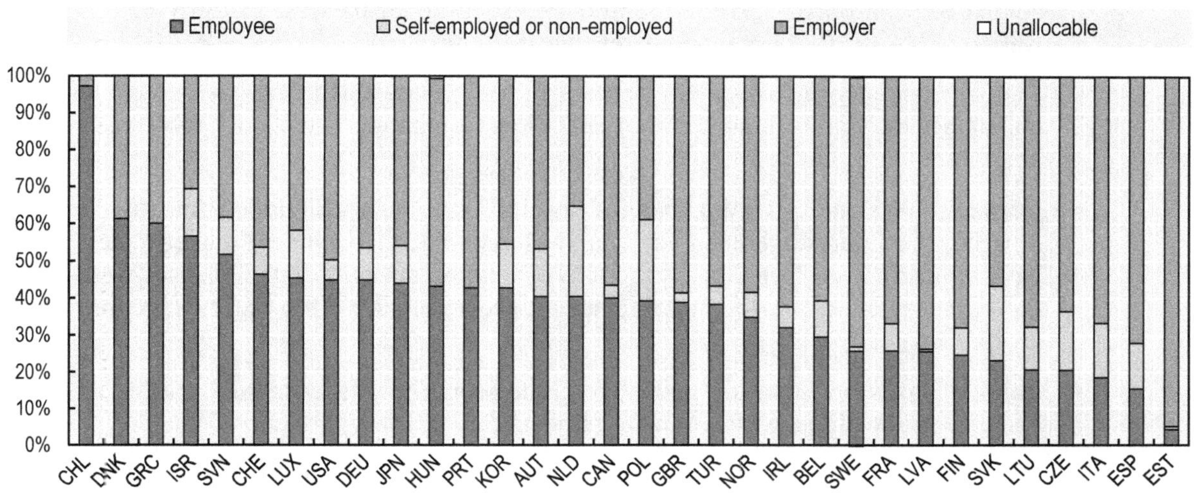

1. Australia, Iceland, Mexico and New Zealand are not included within figure 1.7.Although Iceland and Mexico collect social security contributions, disaggregated data is not available. New Zealand and Australia do not levy social security contributions.

Source: Secretariat calculations based on data in chapter 4.

StatLink http://dx.doi.org/10.1787/888933859019

1.2.3. Property taxes

Between 1965 and 2016, the share of taxes on property fell from 7.9% to 5.7% of total tax revenues on average across the OECD (Figure 1.6). Iceland had the highest share of revenue from property taxes in 2016 (34.2%) although this was due to one-off stability contributions that applied in that year, followed by the United Kingdom (12.6%) and Canada (12.0%). Property taxes accounted for 0.8% of total revenues in Estonia, the lowest of OECD countries:

- Property taxes accounted for more than 10% of total tax revenue in seven countries in 2016 (Australia, Canada, Iceland, Israel, Korea, the United Kingdom and the United States).
- Property taxes account for less than 2% of total revenue in seven countries (Austria, Czech Republic, Estonia, Lithuania, Mexico, Slovenia and the Slovak Republic).

1.2.4. Consumption taxes

- The share of taxes on consumption (general consumption taxes plus specific consumption taxes) fell from 38.4% to 32.7% between 1965 and 2016 (Figure 1.6).
- During this period, the composition of taxes on goods and services has fundamentally changed. A fast-growing revenue source has been general

consumption taxes, especially the value-added tax (VAT) which is now imposed in thirty-five of the thirty-six OECD countries.[4]

- General consumption taxes presently account for 20.8% of total tax revenue, compared with only 11.9% in the mid-1960s. In 2016, the vast majority of this was from VAT (20.2% of total tax revenues) (Figure 1.6)
- The substantially increased importance of the value-added tax has served to counteract the diminishing share of specific consumption taxes, such as excises and custom duties.
- Between 1975 and 2016 the share of specific taxes on consumption (mostly on tobacco, alcoholic drinks and fuels, as well as some environment-related taxes) have almost halved from 17.7% to 9.8% of total revenues. In 2016, excises were the largest single category of total revenues, accounting for 7.8% of total revenues (Figure 1.8).
- Rates of taxes on imported goods were considerably reduced across all OECD countries, reflecting a global trend to remove trade barriers.
- Nevertheless, countries such as Estonia, Mexico, Poland, and Slovenia (around 14%) and Turkey (around 22%) still collect a relatively large proportion of their tax revenues through taxes on specific goods and services.

Figure 1.8. Share of general consumption tax revenues (left panel) and specific consumption revenues (right panel) as % of total revenues, 1975-2016

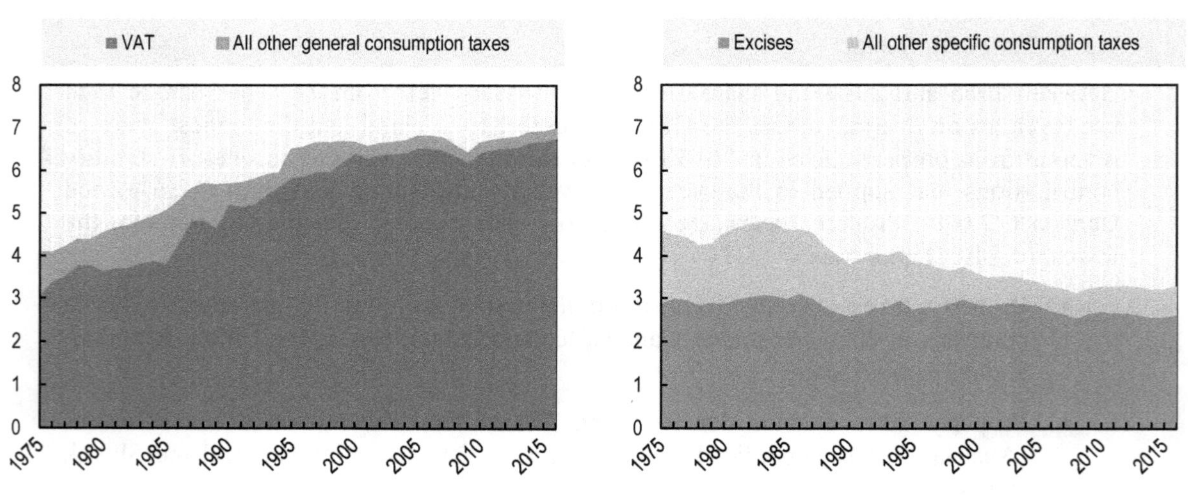

1. The unweighted average for each year includes all countries which report revenue in the categories shown in that year. The OECD averages for 2016 OECD exclude the one-off revenues from stability contributions in Iceland.

Source: Secretariat calculations based on chapter 4.

StatLink http://dx.doi.org/10.1787/888933859038

1.3. Taxes by level of government

This section discusses the relative share of tax revenues attributed to the various sub-sectors of general government in 2016. The different sub-sectors are:

- Central government
- State government (federal and regional countries only)
- Local government
- Social security funds
- Supranational (EU countries only)

The guidelines for attributing these revenue shares to the different levels of government are based on the final version of the 2008 System of National Accounts. These guidelines are discussed in the special feature S.1 in the 2011 edition of OECD *Revenue Statistics*.

1.3.1. Revenues of sub-national governments

Eight OECD countries have a federal structure. Among these countries, central governments received 53.2% of total revenues in 2016 on average. The second-highest share of revenues on average was received by social security funds, which are a sub-sector of general government, at 21.2% of total revenues, followed by 17.6% at the state level and 7.8% at the local level (Table 1.3). However, within countries there was considerable variation around these means:

- In 2016, the share of central government receipts in the eight federal OECD countries varied from 29.7% in Germany to 79.5% in Australia.
- In 2016, the share of the states varied from 1.6% in Austria, 4.0% in Mexico and 10.7% in Belgium to 39.9% in Canada. The share of local government varied from 1.5% in Mexico to 15.6% in Switzerland.
- Between 1975 and 2016 the share of federal government revenues declined by nearly fifteen percentage points in Belgium and to a lesser extent in Canada, Germany and the United States.
- The share of federal government revenues increased in Austria and Switzerland by around 15 and five percentage points respectively. There was little change in Australia and Mexico.
- Of the seven federal countries with social security funds, five increased the share of revenue between 1975 and 2016. The exceptions were Canada and Mexico, where the share slightly declined between 1975 (1980 for Mexico due to data availability) and 2016.

Spain is classified as a regional rather than a unitary country because of its highly decentralised political structure. In 2016 the share of central government receipts was 41.6% compared with 14.7% for the regional government. Between 1975 and 2016, the share of local government receipts increased from around 4% to 10% and the share of social security funds declined from 47.5% to 33.2%.

Table 1.3. Attribution of tax revenues to sub-sectors of general government as % of total tax revenue, federal countries

	Supranational			Central government			State or Regional government			Local government			Social Security Funds		
	1975	1995	2016	1975	1995	2016	1975	1995	2016	1975	1995	2016	1975	1995	2016
Federal countries															
Australia	..	..	..	80.1	77.5	79.5	15.7	19.0	16.9	4.2	3.4	3.6	0.0	0.0	0.0
Austria	..	0.0	0.4	51.7	65.1	66.0	10.6	1.8	1.6	12.4	4.1	3.0	25.3	29.0	28.9
Belgium	1.4	1.0	1.0	65.3	60.1	50.7	..	1.8	10.7	4.4	4.8	5.0	28.8	32.2	32.6
Canada	..	..	..	47.6	39.1	40.7	32.5	37.1	39.9	9.9	9.8	10.3	10.0	14.0	9.1
Germany	1.2	0.6	0.6	33.5	31.4	29.7	22.3	21.6	23.6	9.0	7.4	8.5	34.0	39.0	m37.6
Mexico	..	..	..	..	73.9	81.5	..	2.8	4.0	..	1.5	1.5	..	21.8	13.0
Switzerland	..	..	..	30.7	31.4	35.2	27.0	24.2	25.0	20.3	17.6	15.6	22.0	26.8	24.3
United States	..	..	..	45.4	41.4	42.1	19.5	20.0	19.4	14.7	13.3	14.5	20.5	25.2	24.0
Unweighted average	1.3	0.6	0.7	50.6	52.5	53.2	21.3	16.0	17.6	10.7	7.7	7.8	20.1	23.5	21.2
Regional country															
Spain[1,2]	..	0.5	0.5	48.2	51.3	41.6	..	4.8	14.7	4.3	8.8	9.9	47.5	34.6	33.2

1. Spain is constitutionally a non-federal country but has a highly decentralised political structure.

2. The total tax revenue has been reduced by the amount of any capital transfer that represents uncollected taxes.

StatLink http://dx.doi.org/10.1787/888933859057

The remaining twenty-seven OECD countries have a unitary structure. In these countries, an average of 63.5% of revenues were derived at the central level, with 24.8% accounted for by social security funds. A further 11.4% were raised by local governments. Among unitary OECD countries:

- The share of central government receipts in 2016 varied from 33.4% in France and 35.2% in Switzerland to 93.3% in New Zealand.
- The local government share varied from 1.0% in Estonia to 35.4% in Sweden.
- Between 1975 and 2016 there have been shifts to local government of 5 percentage points or more in five countries – France, Italy, Korea, Portugal and Sweden and a smaller increase in the Netherlands. Shifts of 5 percentage points or more in the other direction occurred in three countries – Ireland, Norway and the United Kingdom.[5]
- Between 1975 and 2016, there were increases in the share of social security funds of 7 or more percentage points in four countries – Finland, France, Japan and Korea and corresponding decreases in four other countries – Italy, Norway, Portugal and Sweden.

Table 1.4. Attribution of tax revenues to sub-sectors of general government as % of total tax revenue, unitary countries

	Supranational			Central government			State or Regional government			Local government			Social Security Funds		
	1975	1995	2016	1975	1995	2016	1975	1995	2016	1975	1995	2016	1975	1995	2016
Unitary countries															
Chile	..	..	..	..	89.9	86.4	..	..	..	..	6.5	7.8	..	3.6	5.7
Czech Republic	..	..	0.5	..	57.7	55.5	..	..	..	..	0.9	1.1	..	41.4	42.9
Denmark[1]	1.1	0.5	0.3	68.9	68.2	72.6	..	..	..	30.0	31.3	27.0	0.1	0.0	0.0
Estonia	..	..	0.5	..	84.3	82.4	..	..	..	..	0.8	1.0	..	14.9	16.1
Finland	..	0.4	0.3	56.0	46.6	47.6	..	..	..	23.5	22.3	23.1	20.4	30.8	29.0
France[1]	0.7	0.4	0.4	51.2	42.6	33.4	..	..	..	7.6	11.0	13.5	40.6	46.0	52.8
Greece[1]	..	0.6	0.3	67.1	66.9	69.6	..	..	..	3.4	0.9	2.4	29.5	31.6	27.7
Hungary	..	..	0.3	..	63.8	60.6	..	..	..	..	2.5	5.8	..	33.6	33.3
Iceland	..	..	..	81.3	79.2	81.4	..	..	..	18.7	20.8	18.6	0.0	0.0	0.0
Ireland	2.3	1.5	1.0	77.4	83.1	82.2	..	..	..	7.3	2.7	2.3	13.1	12.7	14.5
Israel	..	..	..	..	79.6	75.5	..	..	..	..	6.4	7.9	..	14.0	16.6
Italy	..	0.4	0.4	53.2	62.7	54.4	..	..	..	0.9	5.4	15.0	45.9	31.5	30.1
Japan	..	..	..	45.5	41.2	35.7	..	..	..	25.6	25.2	23.9	29.0	33.6	40.4
Korea	..	..	..	89.0	69.2	56.3	..	..	..	10.1	18.7	17.5	0.9	12.1	26.2
Latvia	..	..	0.7	..	43.5	52.5	..	..	..	..	19.5	19.5	..	36.9	27.3
Lithuania	..	..	0.9	..	71.7	57.1	..	..	..	..	2.3	1.3	..	26.1	40.8
Luxembourg	0.8	0.4	0.5	63.6	66.5	68.0	..	..	..	6.7	6.5	3.9	29.0	26.6	27.6
Netherlands	1.5	1.3	1.1	58.9	56.0	57.6	..	..	..	1.2	3.1	3.1	38.4	39.5	38.2
New Zealand	..	..	..	92.3	94.7	93.3	..	..	..	7.7	5.3	6.7	0.0	0.0	0.0
Norway	..	..	..	50.6	58.4	83.8	..	..	..	22.4	19.6	16.2	27.0	22.0	0.0
Poland	..	..	0.5	..	61.2	48.5	..	..	..	..	8.5	12.9	..	30.3	38.1
Portugal	..	0.8	0.5	65.4	72.3	72.8	..	..	..	0.0	5.4	7.3	34.6	21.5	19.4
Slovak Republic	..	..	0.6	..	62.5	55.0	..	..	..	..	1.3	2.0	..	36.2	42.5
Slovenia	..	..	0.4	..	51.8	50.8	..	..	..	..	6.3	9.5	..	41.9	39.2
Sweden	..	0.4	0.3	51.3	46.9	52.3	..	..	..	29.2	30.9	35.4	19.5	21.8	12.1
Turkey	..	..	..	..	75.1	61.5	..	..	..	..	12.8	9.7	..	12.1	28.8
United Kingdom	1.0	1.0	0.5	70.5	77.5	75.7	..	..	..	11.1	3.7	4.9	17.5	17.8	18.9
Unweighted average	1.2	0.7	0.5	65.1	65.7	63.5	..	..	..	12.8	10.4	11.4	21.6	23.6	24.8

1. The total tax revenue has been reduced by the amount of any capital transfer that represents uncollected taxes.

StatLink http://dx.doi.org/10.1787/888933859076

The 'supranational' column of Table 1.3 and Table 1.4 report taxes collected on behalf of the European Union (EU) by the twenty-three EU member states that are members of the OECD. For years prior to 1998, customs duties collected on behalf of the EU by national tax administrations of the EU member states are included under heading 5123.[6] From 1998 onwards they are shown as a memorandum item since they represent a tax imposed by the EU and collected by national administrations.

Table 1.5. Customs duties collected on behalf of the European Union

	2000	2005	2007	2009	2011	2013	2014	2015	2016	2017p
Austria[1]	356	325	397	320	378	328	369	415	449	464
Belgium[1]	960	1 208	1 388	1 147	1 285	1 185	1 250	1 367	1 575	1 622
Czech Republic	..	5 586	6 443	5 548	6 961	5 556	6 970	7 912	8 033	8 271
Denmark	2 325	2 833	3 282	2 647	3 177	2 824	3 001	3 285	3 069	3 136
Estonia[1]	..	22	35	20	29	29	30	34	34	38
Finland[1]	129	148	199	152	189	166	170	165	163	174
France[1]	1 513	1 583	1 657	1 461	1 866	1 842	1 827	1 932	1 819	1 908
Germany[1]	3 394	3 433	3 972	3 778	4 556	4 251	4 608	5 195	5 089	5 043
Greece[1]	210	262	307	252	186	148	163	181	197	268
Hungary	..	26 572	27 981	25 657	27 462	26 337	31 947	38 960	41 620	45 403
Ireland[1]	208	226	273	208	240	247	275	327	311	334
Italy[1]	1 536	1 785	2 261	2 008	2 319	1 890	2 022	2 246	2 270	2 293
Latvia[1]	..	26	37	21	31	28	36	40	47	46
Lithuania	..	44	61	51	59	68	86	99	96	101
Luxembourg[1]	27	21	23	13	17	15	19	23	25	27
Netherlands[1]	1 310	1 265	1 679	1 518	1 889	1 756	2 046	2 266	2 353	2 436
Poland	..	1 098	1 760	1 589	1 859	1 977	2 316	2 823	3 292	..
Portugal[1]	204	145	185	154	168	144	149	158	174	187
Slovak Republic[1]	..	75	136	111	157	115	127	119	126	134
Slovenia[1]	..	34	85	57	62	52	52	52	53	54
Spain[1]	971	1 436	1 722	1 328	1 553	1 315	1 512	1 754	1 879	1 917
Sweden	3 450	4 327	5 099	4 764	5 399	4 976	5 737	6 243	6 044	6 225
United Kingdom	1 800	1 908	2 074	2 435	2 925	2 914	2 949	3 077	3 318	3 419

Note: p: provisional.

1. For euro area countries, the figures are in euros for all years.

StatLink http://dx.doi.org/10.1787/888933859095

1.3.2. Composition of central and sub central revenues

Figure 1.9 shows the revenues from each major category of tax revenue for central and sub central governments. For federal and regional countries, the sub central level includes revenues received by both state and local governments. Figure 1.9 demonstrates that:

- Central government revenues in almost all OECD countries are predominantly derived from income and goods and services taxes, with a negligible share from property taxes.
- At the subnational level, revenue from property taxes provides a much larger share of revenues than at the central level, and accounts for over 90% of revenues in four countries (Israel, Ireland, Greece and the United Kingdom).
- By contrast, the share of income taxes and goods and services taxes is lower at the sub-central level, the exceptions being Finland, Luxembourg and Sweden, where over 90% of sub-central revenues are derived from income taxes.

Figure 1.9. Composition of revenues of federal or central government (left) and sub-national government (right), 2016

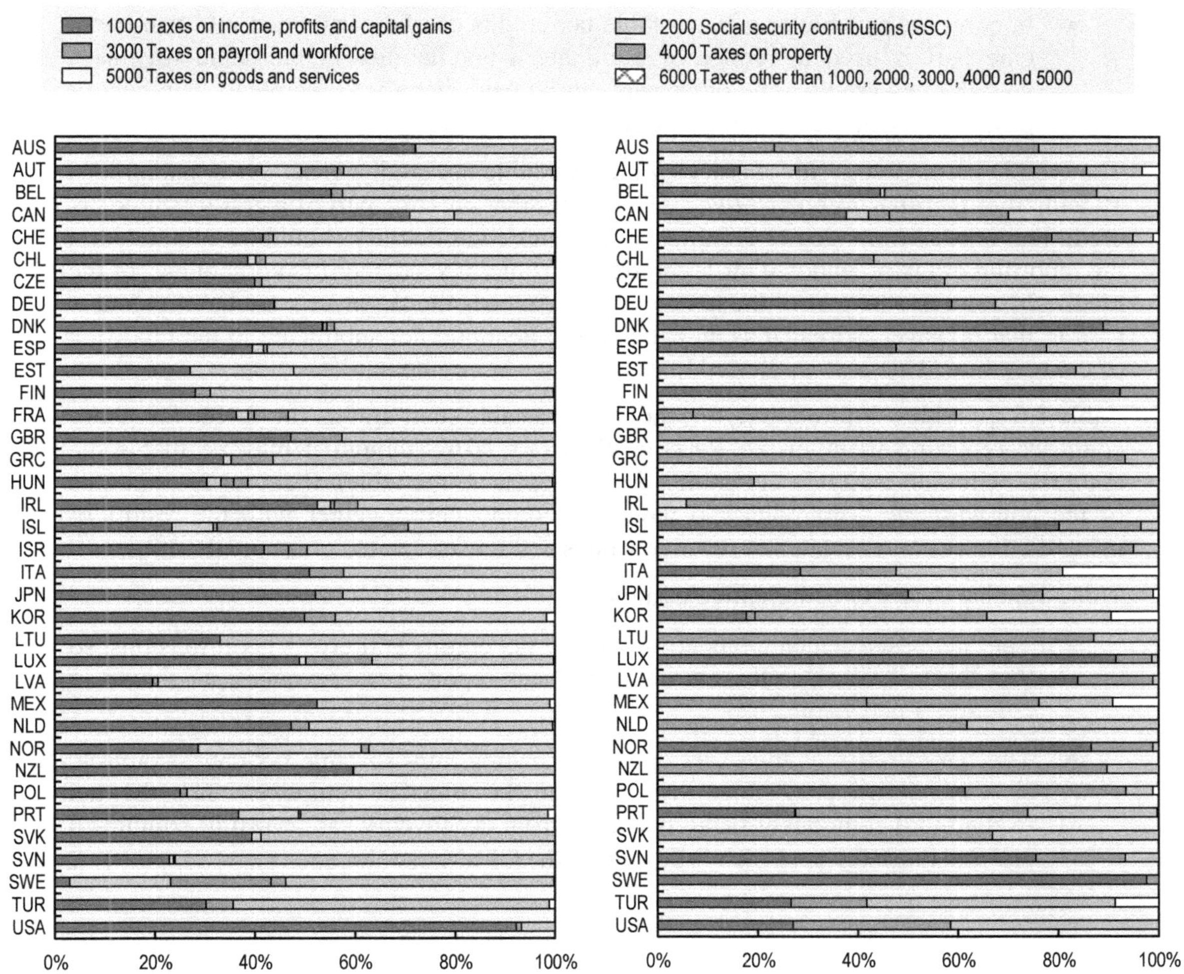

1. The left-hand panel (a) refers to only those taxes which are classified as central government taxes. Social security contributions paid to social security funds are excluded. The right-hand panel (b) refers only to those taxes which are classified as sub-central taxes (local and (where relevant) state taxes). Social security contributions paid to social security funds are excluded.
2. The one-off revenues raised by stability contributions in Iceland in 2016 are classified as property taxes collected by the central government. Without these exceptional revenues, personal income taxes would have been the largest source of revenues for Iceland's central government in 2016.
Source: Secretariat calculations based on tables 3.16 to 3.18.

StatLink http://dx.doi.org/10.1787/888933859114

1.4. Non-wastable tax credits

There are two kinds of tax credits that apply to income taxes (both personal and corporate):

- Non-payable or wastable tax credits are those that can only ever be used to reduce or eliminate a tax liability. They cannot be paid out to either taxpayers or non-tax payers as a benefit. They are, therefore, the same as a tax allowance or relief.
- In contrast, payable or non-wastable tax credits can be partitioned into two parts. One part is used to reduce or eliminate a tax liability in the same way as a wastable tax credit. The other part can be paid directly to recipients as a benefit payment, when the benefit exceeds the tax liability.

The OECD methodology for classifying non-wastable tax credits is set out in paragraphs 19 and 20 of the *Interpretative Guide*. This states that only the part of a non-wastable tax credit that is used to reduce or eliminate a taxpayer's tax liability should be subtracted in the reporting of tax revenues. This is referred to as the 'tax expenditure component' of the credit. In contrast, the part of the tax credit that exceeds the taxpayer's tax liability and is paid to that taxpayer is treated as an expenditure item and not subtracted in the reporting of tax revenues. This part is referred to as the 'transfer component'.

Table 1.6 provides information on the non-wastable tax credits in 2016 for those countries reporting them in the *Revenue Statistics 2018* (though it may be that some countries with non-wastable tax credits do not appear in the table). It shows the amounts of the non-wastable tax credits and their two components together with the results of using the figures to calculate tax revenue values and the associated tax-to-GDP ratios.

Table 1.6 also shows two alternative treatments:

- The 'net basis' which treats non-wastable tax credits entirely as tax provisions, so that the full value of the tax credit reduces reported tax revenues, as shown in columns 4 and 7.
- The 'gross basis' is the exact opposite, treating non-wastable tax credits entirely as expenditure provisions, with neither the transfer component nor the tax expenditure component being deducted from tax revenue, as shown in columns 6 and 9. This is the approach followed by the GFSM and the SNA.

Table 1.6. Effect of alternative treatments of non-wastable tax credits, 2016

	Non-wastable tax credits in billlions of national currency			Total tax revenue in millions of national currency			Total tax revenue as a percentage of GDP		
	Total value	Transfer component	Tax expenditure component	Net basis	Split basis (per current guidance)	Gross basis	Net basis	Split basis (per current guidance)	Gross basis
Australia	9.1	6.7	2.4	480.4	487.1	489.5	27.4	27.8	27.9
Austria[1]	0.5	0.3	0.2	148.9	149.2	149.4	42.1	42.2	42.3
Belgium	0.8	0.3	0.5	186	186.3	186.8	44	44.1	44.2
Canada[2]	10.9	10	1	655.9	665.9	666.8	32.2	32.7	32.8
Chile[3]	179.6	129.6	50.1	34 129.3	34 258.9	34 308.9	20.2	20.2	20.3
Czech Republic	32.8	8.6	24.3	1 623.9	1 632.4	1 656.7	34.1	34.2	34.7
Denmark[4]	4.2	0.2	4	954	954.2	958.2	46.2	46.2	46.4
France[4]	25.9	11.6	14.3	1 001.5	1 013.1	1 027.4	44.9	45.5	46.1
Germany	42.9	15.7	27.3	1 167.1	1 182.7	1 210.0	36.9	37.4	38.3
Iceland	1.4	1.2	0.2	1 264.4	1 265.6	1 265.8	51.5	51.6	51.6
Ireland	0.5	..	0.5	..	63.7	64.3	..	23.3	23.5
Israel[5]	1.3	1.2	0.1	380.6	381.8	381.9	31.2	31.3	31.3
Italy	12.6	3.7	8.9	712.6	716.2	725.2	42.4	42.6	43.1
Luxembourg[6]	0.2	..	..	..	..	20.2	..	..	38.1
Mexico	44.9	1.1	43.7	3 342.2	3 343.3	3 387.0	16.6	16.6	16.9
New Zealand	2.3	1.1	1.2	85.5	86.6	87.8	31.2	31.6	32
Norway	3.6	3	0.6	1 204.1	1 207.1	1 207.8	38.6	38.7	38.7
Slovak Republic[6]	0.3	..	..	..	..	26.3	..	..	32.4
Spain[4]	1.8	0.9	0.9	370.3	371.2	372.1	33.1	33.2	33.3
United Kingdom	30.1	26.7	3.4	618	644.7	648.1	31.4	32.7	32.9
United States	165.6	121.1	44.6	4 700.5	4 821.5	4 866.1	25.2	25.9	26.1

Note: In *Revenue Statistics*, the tax revenue data are reported on a split basis, unless indicated otherwise.

1. The children's tax credit is not regarded as a tax credit in the *Revenue Statistics 2018* and is treated entirely as an expenditure provision.
2. Some non-wastable tax credits cannot be split into the transfer and tax expenditure components. Their total values have been added to the transfer component.
3. In *Revenue Statistics*, the tax revenue data for Chile are reported on a net basis.
4. The total tax revenue has been reduced by the amount of any capital transfer that represents uncollected taxes.
5. The data for Israel are supplied by and under the responsibility of the relevant Israeli authorities. The use of such data by the OECD is without prejudice to the status of the Golan Heights, East Jerusalem and Israeli settlements in the West Bank under the terms of international law.
6. In *Revenue Statistics 2018*, the tax revenue data for Luxembourg and Slovak Republic are reported on a gross basis.

StatLink http://dx.doi.org/10.1787/888933859133

Table 1.6 shows that, with some exceptions, the choice of method for reporting non-wastable tax credits has only a small impact on the ratio of total tax revenue to GDP. For the countries with available data, the differences between the ratios on a net basis and on a gross basis are one percentage point or more in only France, Germany and the United Kingdom, and between half a percentage point and one percentage point in Australia, Canada, Czech Republic, Italy, New Zealand and the United States.

Notes

1 Provisional 2017 figures are not available for Australia and provisional figures on social security contributions in Japan are also not available as at the time *Revenue Statistics 2018* was published.

2 Calculated by applying the unweighted average percentage change for 2017 in the 34 countries providing data for that year to the overall average tax-to-GDP ratio in 2016.

3 As provisional 2017 figures are not available for Australia and Japan, the change in the tax-to-GDP ratio is calculated between 2007 and 2016.

4 The terms "value added tax" and "VAT" are used to refer to any national tax that embodies the basic features of a value added tax by whatever name or acronym it is known e.g. "Goods and Services Tax" ("GST").

5 For 1975, please see table 1.4 of *Revenue Statistics 2018*.

6 From 1998 onwards, these custom duties are shown as a 'memorandum' item since they represent a tax imposed by the EU and collected by national administrations. However, they continue to be part of the aggregate revenue figures that represent all taxes imposed within the territory of EU member states. This approach ensures consistency of the time series, and ensures that the tax-to-GDP ratio measures are immune to changes in the relative share of customs duties in (1) the composition of EU financing resources and (2) national tax mixes of EU member states.

Chapter 2. Special feature: Convergence of tax levels and tax structures in OECD countries

This chapter provides a special study on the convergence of tax-to-GDP ratios and of tax structures in OECD countries from 1995-2016.

2.1. Introduction

Tax levels, measured by the tax-to-GDP ratio, and tax structures, measured by tax categories as a share of total tax revenues, vary across OECD countries for a variety of historical, economic and political reasons, including choices on how to develop and fund the welfare state. However, since 1995, the trend of the OECD average[1] tax-to-GDP ratio has shown similarity to that of many countries: dipping following the financial crisis before resuming a slow and long-running increase. Similarly, over this period a number of tax policy changes have impacted tax structures in OECD countries, including the introduction of value-added taxes in all but one OECD country, and the developing consensus around the impact of different taxes on growth and the consequent effort of many countries to implement these recommendations (OECD, 2010[1]).

This chapter explores the impact of these and other changes on the distribution of tax levels and tax structures in OECD countries, with particular attention to whether the OECD average is becoming more or less representative of the underlying distribution over time. The chapter considers sigma measures of convergence to examine the dispersion of the tax-to-GDP ratio in member countries in the years from 1995 to 2016 before examining intra-OECD groups at different levels of tax revenues. It then calculates an index of the similarity of all countries to the OECD average tax structure, assessing changes in tax structures across the period. The paper concludes by examining the combined changes in the dispersion of tax levels and structures around the OECD average.

2.2. OECD countries have higher and more similar tax levels in 2016 relative to 1995

Since 1995, the OECD average tax-to-GDP ratio has increased from 33.0% to 34.0% in 2016, with the lowest point of the period (32.2%) occurring in 2009 following the financial crisis. In this time, the highest tax-to-GDP ratio was seen in Sweden, at 49.0% in 2000[2], although for most of the period, the highest tax rate in each year was observed in Denmark (ranging from a low of 44.8% to a high of 48.6%). The lowest tax-to-GDP ratio was consistently seen in Mexico (ranging between 9.9% and 16.6% across the period).

Across the OECD, the dispersion of tax-to-GDP ratios decreased between 1995 and 2016, with a brief interruption in 2009, a period which coincided with the lowest average OECD tax-to-GDP ratio in the period. Figure 2.1 illustrates that the dispersion of tax-to-GDP ratios decreased around the OECD average tax-to-GDP ratio (standard deviation and coefficient of variation) as well as around the median (absolute deviation) and when country pairs are considered (Gini coefficient); with these measures of dispersion showing similar trends across the period. An analysis of year-on-year growth rates for these indicators supports this.

Figure 2.1. Dispersion of tax-to-GDP ratios in OECD countries, 1995-2016

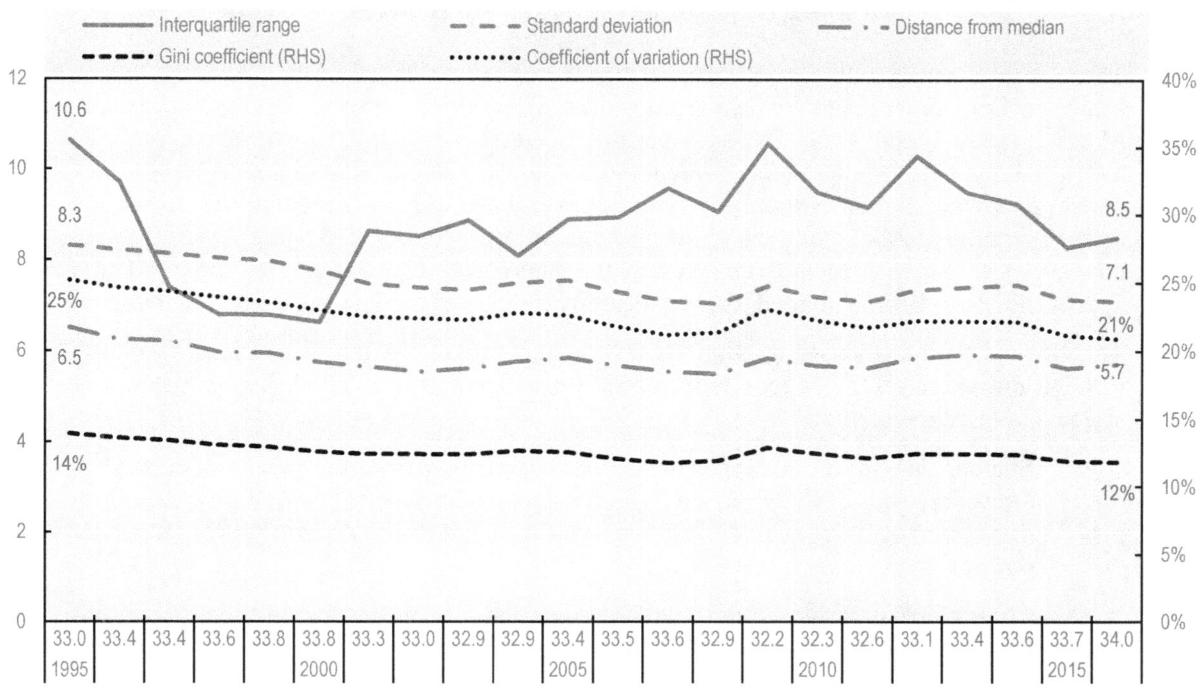

Note: The figures on the horizontal axis (above the years) show the OECD average tax-to-GDP ratio in each year.
Source: Authors' calculations based on OECD *Revenue Statistics (2017)* (OECD, 2017[2]).

StatLink http://dx.doi.org/10.1787/888933859152

The interquartile range shows a different trend over this period, due to changes in the tax levels of the top quartile of OECD countries. Conceptually, movements of the interquartile range and the other indicators in opposite directions can be explained if one of the outer quartiles is moving away from the other while converging among itself. This occurred, for example, between 2005 and 2008, where all other indicators showed decreased dispersion and the interquartile range increased. In these years, the threshold for the upper quartile increased, moving further away from the main distribution, but at the same time there was a decrease in the ratios of the four countries with the very highest tax levels (and a particularly sharp decrease in the two top countries). The combined impact of the increasing threshold for the top quartile, together with the reductions in the tax-to-GDP ratios of the highest countries, decreased dispersion around both the OECD average and median even as the interquartile range increased. A similar phenomenon occurred in 2000, where the threshold for the lower quartile decreased even as countries with the lowest tax-to-GDP ratios increased these.

2.3. Groups within the OECD are emerging

In 2016, OECD countries fell into four groups with different tax levels: low (tax-to-GDP ratios less than 30%)[3]; low-mid (tax-to-GDP ratios between 30 and 35%); high-mid (tax-to-GDP ratios between 35 and 40%) and high (tax-to-GDP ratios greater than 40%) (Figure 2.2).[4]

Box 2.1. Measuring convergence of tax levels

There is an extensive discussion of convergence of tax revenues in the literature, which has been born out of neoclassical frameworks of economic growth (Barro and Sala-I-Martin, 1992[31]) and (Mankiw, Romer and Weil D., 1992[4]). Convergence may be measured by beta convergence, which measures the rate at which poorer economies converge toward richer economies; sigma convergence, which measures the dispersion across a cross-section of economies using a variety of indicators; and gamma convergence, which measures changes in the ranking of economies over time. These approaches have been extended to estimate convergence of tax levels across countries.[5]

This special feature focuses on sigma convergence, measuring the dispersion of the tax-to-GDP ratio across OECD economies in the years from 1995 to 2016. Key indicators of sigma convergence include:

- Standard deviation: a simple measure of dispersion from the mean, calculated as the square root of the variance (which averages the sum of squared residuals from the mean) and is measured in the same unit as the variable. It is affected by outliers.
- Coefficient of variation: the standard deviation as a percentage of the mean. It has the advantage of standardising across data with different means, but is exposed to outliers as they affect both the standard deviation and the mean. It is also driven by the value of the mean in the denominator, e.g. very large values of the mean can lower the coefficient of variation while keeping the SD constant.
- Absolute deviation from the average: the sum of the absolute distance of each country from the average (either mean or median), divided by the total number of countries. This indicator is measured in the same unit as the data. If the median is used as the central point, the indicator is outlier-resistant.
- Gini coefficient: calculates the distance between all country pairs and therefore is a better measure for inter-country dispersion. It is normalised by dividing by twice the number of data points and the mean and is expressed as a number between 0 and 1, with 0 indicating no dispersion. It can also be displayed in a Lorenz curve. It is less affected by outliers due to the use of country pairs.
- Range measures: the difference between two points in the distribution. The interquartile range is commonly used, which measures the difference between the upper (Q3) and the lower quartiles (Q1). Half of the data falls within this range. This measure is also resistant to outliers and avoids bias inherent in the mean.

Figure 2.2. Distribution of tax-to-GDP ratios in OECD countries, 2016

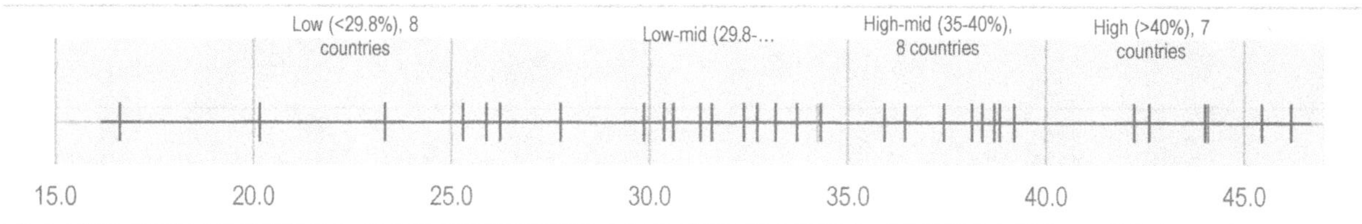

Note: Each + represents the tax-to-GDP ratio of an OECD country in 2016.
Source: Authors' calculations based on OECD *Revenue Statistics (2017)*.

StatLink http://dx.doi.org/10.1787/888933859171

If these groups are considered across the period from 1995 to 2016, the composition of the upper and lower groups was relatively stable. Among the countries with low tax-to-GDP ratios in 2016, only Ireland did not have a tax-to-GDP ratio under the threshold of 30% in 1995, but did from 2001 onwards with a brief exception in 2006 and 2007. In the countries with high tax-to-GDP ratios in 2016, all countries in that group also had tax-to-GDP ratios above 40 in 1995, and only one country fell below this threshold at any point during the period (Italy, in 2002 and 2004-5).

There was more change across the period for the two middle groups, with the composition of both groups becoming more stable after around 2000. For the low-mid tax-to-GDP ratio group (30-35% of GDP in 2016), all but three countries had tax-to-GDP ratios within the thresholds by 2000: each of these three countries saw an increasing tax-to-GDP ratio throughout the period, with Japan's tax-to-GDP ratio increasing above the threshold in 2014 and Latvia's in 2016; Lithuania in 2016 had a tax-to-GDP ratio of 29.9%. After 2000, a few of the other countries spent brief periods outside the thresholds: Estonia, Israel, Portugal and Spain had tax-to-GDP ratios below the threshold for this group in one year, and the Slovak Republic for seven; and Estonia and New Zealand briefly exceeded the upper threshold (from 2005-2007 in Estonia and 2005-2006 in New Zealand).

The high-mid group, comprised of countries with tax-to-GDP ratios of between 35% and 40% in 2016, also had all but two countries within this range from 1999[6]: until 2012, Greece's tax-to-GDP ratio was below 35% and prior to 1998, it was below 30%. Norway initially had a tax-to-GDP ratio over 40% but this dropped under the upper threshold for this group in 2013. After 1999, a few other countries in this group had tax-to-GDP ratios briefly outside the thresholds, including the Netherlands, Germany and Iceland, all prior to 2012.

The movement of countries' tax-to-GDP ratios across the period is indicated in Figure 2.3, which shows tax-to-GDP ratios in 1995 and 2016, as well as the minimum and maximum tax-to-GDP ratio for each country, regardless of year (in the shaded area).

Figure 2.3. Tax-to-GDP ratios in OECD countries: 1995, 2016; minimum and maximums between these dates

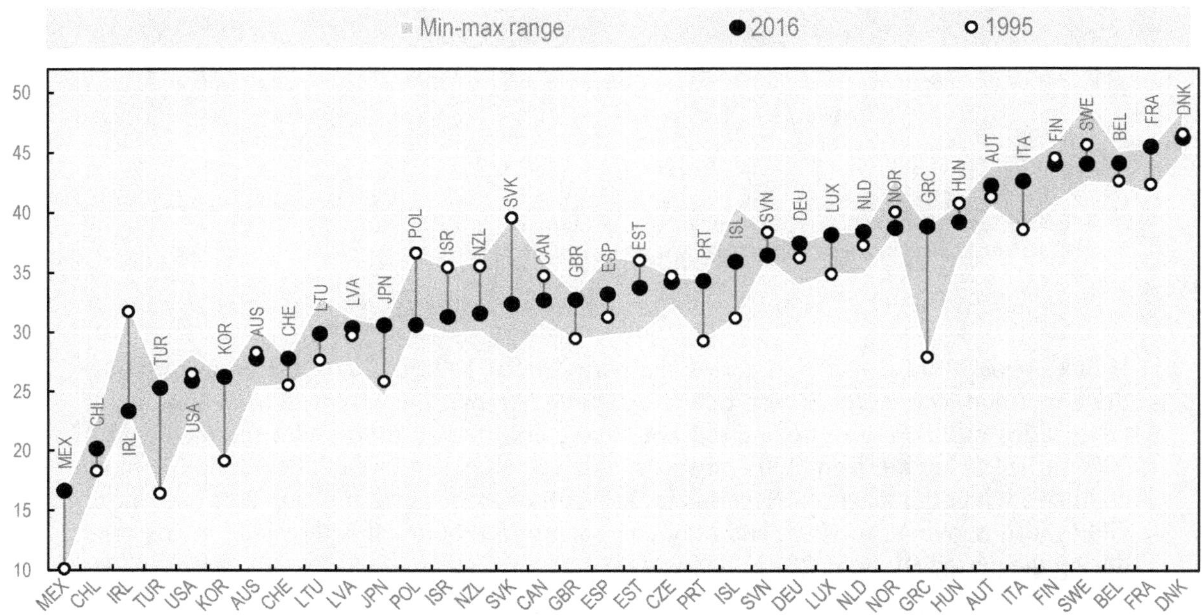

Note: Figures shown for Iceland in 2016 exclude the one-off revenues from the stability contributions. If included, the tax-to-GDP ratio for Iceland in 2016 would be 51.6%, as shown in the first chapter.
Source: Authors' calculations based on OECD *Revenue Statistics (2017)*.

StatLink http://dx.doi.org/10.1787/888933859190

Throughout the period, divergence within these four groups was highest in the group with the lowest tax-to-GDP ratios, although dispersion in this group narrowed considerably across the period. Another strong decrease in dispersion was seen in the high-mid tax-to-GDP ratio countries from 2010 to 2015, concurrently with an increase in its mean tax-to-GDP ratio (Figure 2.4). This increase was partially explained by increases in the tax-to-GDP ratios in Greece and Iceland, which initially had lower tax-to-GDP ratios, and smaller increases in most other countries in the group, with the exception of Norway.

With one exception, tax-to-GDP ratios in each of the four groups became less dispersed around a higher mean tax-to-GDP ratio in 2016 than in 1995. The exception was the group with low-mid tax-to-GDP ratios, where although divergence decreased, the mean tax-to-GDP ratio has not yet recovered from its drop during the financial crisis and remains lower than in 1995 (Figure 2.4), despite the fact that the two countries initially below the threshold had by 2016 increased their tax-to-GDP ratios past 30%. Of the thirteen countries in this group, seven had lower tax-to-GDP ratios in 2016 than in 1995; by contrast, only nine countries in the rest of the OECD experienced falls in this timeframe.

Figure 2.4. Dispersion and mean tax-to-GDP ratios by intra-OECD groups, 1995-2016

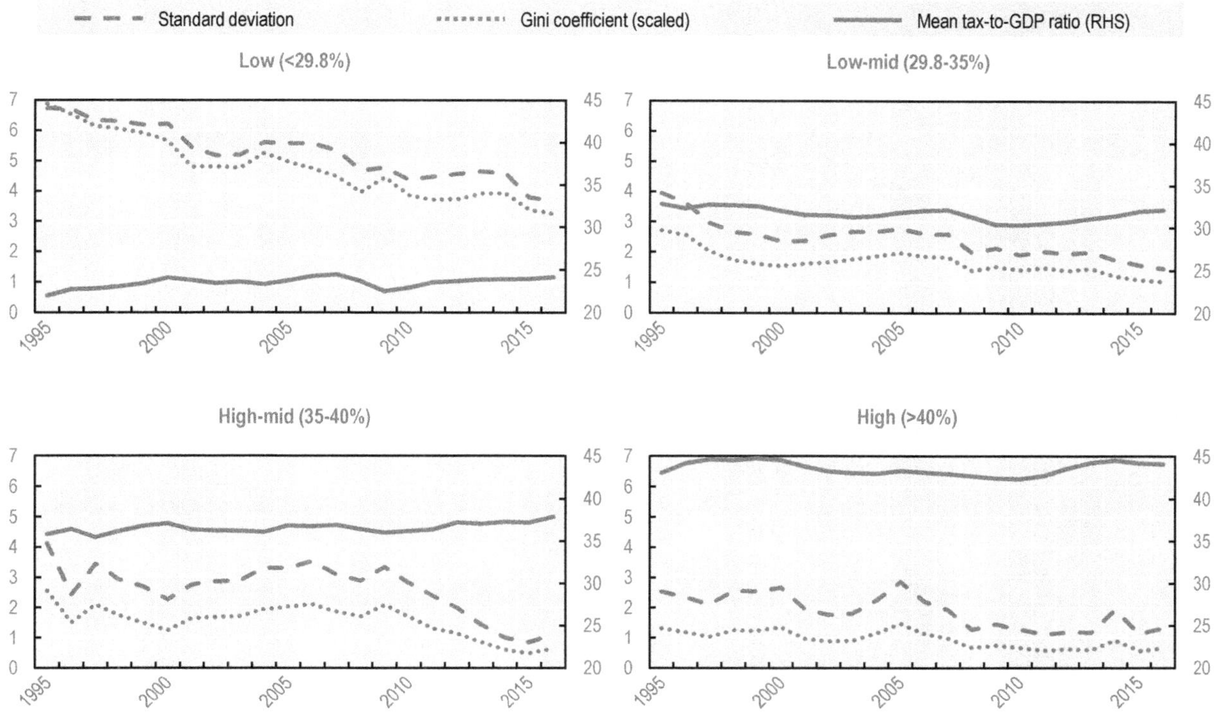

Note: Top-left: countries with a tax-to-GDP ratio of less than 30% in 2016 (8 countries); top-right, countries with a tax-to-GDP ratio of between 30% and 35% in 2016 (12 countries); bottom- left, 35-40% (8 countries) and bottom-right, greater than 40% (7 countries). Standard deviation and Gini coefficients are shown on the left hand axis (the Gini is scaled by a factor of 40 for comparability) and the mean tax-to-GDP ratio is on the right-hand axis.
Source: Authors' calculations based on OECD *Revenue Statistics (2017)*.

StatLink http://dx.doi.org/10.1787/888933859209

Dividing the OECD into these groups also demonstrates why dispersion for the OECD as a whole increased in 2005. This was due to an increase in dispersion among countries with high tax-to-GDP ratios: in 2005, the ratios of the two highest countries (Sweden and Denmark) increased sharply relative to 2004, before falling back in 2006. At the same time, Austria's tax-to-GDP ratio, one of four situated in the middle of this range, fell in 2005 before being caught up to in 2006 by Italy, the country with the lowest tax-to-GDP ratio in this group.

The combination of these trends meant that by 2016, countries with high and high-mid tax levels had converged towards each other and away from low and low-mid countries, which also became less divergent and moved away from the group of countries with higher tax-to-GDP ratios. Most of the movement in tax levels occurred between 1995 and 2009, when the gap between countries with high and high-mid ratios and countries with low and low-mid ratios widened. The two lower groups were also more impacted by falls in the tax-to-GDP ratio during the financial crisis. The difference between the group means has since stayed relatively constant: since 2009, all groups have increased their mean tax-to-GDP ratios at similar rates except for the high ratio group, where it has been decreasing slowly since 2014 (Figure 2.5).

Figure 2.5. Mean tax-to-GDP ratios across countries with low, low-mid, high-mid and high levels, 1995-2016

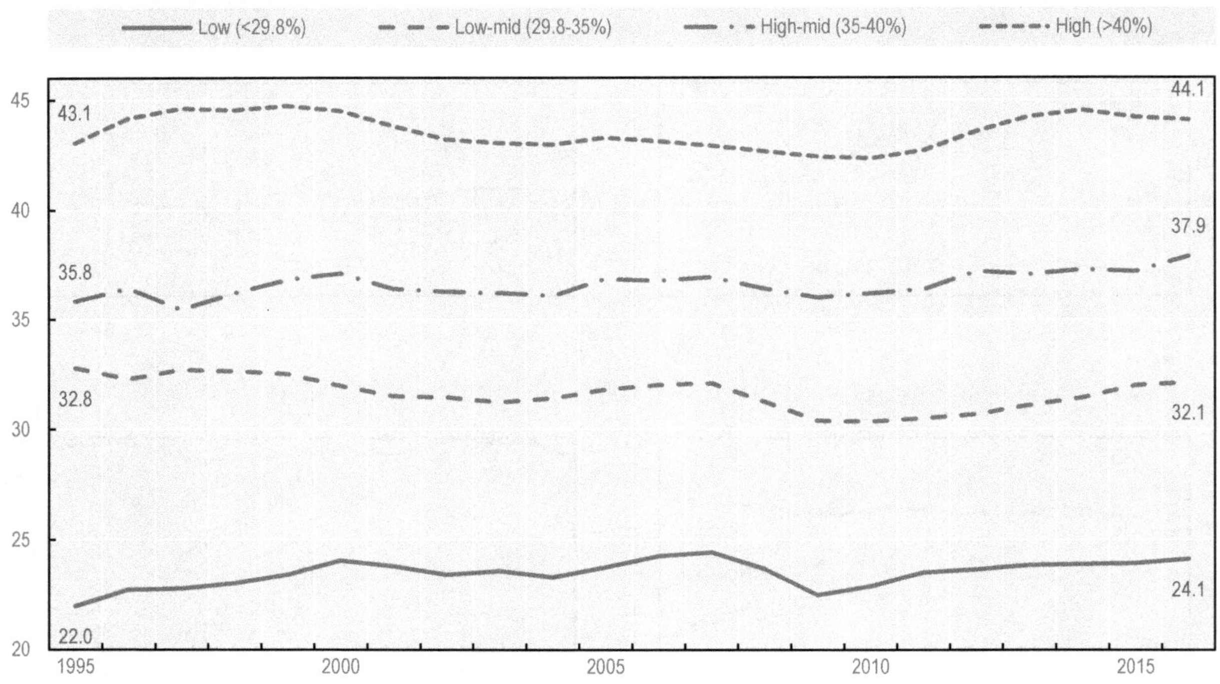

Source: Authors' calculations based on OECD *Revenue Statistics (2017)*.

StatLink http://dx.doi.org/10.1787/888933859228

2.4. Tax structures converge toward higher shares of VAT, SSCs and CIT in total taxes

Across the same period there has been a large amount of change in the tax structures of OECD countries and the OECD average, measured as the decomposition of total tax revenue by eight major tax categories (Box 2.2). Across the period, there has been a shift away from personal income taxes and non-VAT consumption taxes, toward higher social

In 1995, the predominant shares of the OECD tax structure were social security contributions and personal income taxes (26.2% and 25.0% of total tax revenues, respectively) with corporate income taxes at 8.1% of total tax revenue. Value-added taxes were already the predominant share of consumption tax revenues (at 18.1% of total tax revenues) but taxes on imports and exports, and other consumption taxes continued to play a significant role (15.8% of total tax revenue, combined).

security contributions and VAT.

Box 2.2. Measuring convergence of tax structures

Tax structures are measured by a second key indicator in *Revenue Statistics*: a tax category as a share of total revenue. The OECD Interpretative Guide provides a highly-detailed breakdown of tax revenues into different tax categories. This special feature divides tax revenues into eight categories as set out in Table 2.1.

Table 2.1. Disaggregation of tax structures used to construct D-index

Detailed tax types	Acronym	Corresponding *Revenue Statistics* code	Share in 1995	Share in 2016
1. Personal income tax	PIT	1100 Personal income tax	25.0	23.8
2. Corporate income tax	CIT	1200 Corporate income tax	8.1	9.0
3. Social security contributions & payroll taxes	SSC	2000 Social security contributions, 3000 Payroll taxes	26.2	27.2
4. Property taxes	PROP	4000 Taxes on property	5.2	5.7
5. VAT	VAT	5111 Value-added taxes	18.1	20.2
6. Taxes on imports & exports	TIE	5123 Customs & import duties; 5124 Taxes on exports; 5127 Other taxes on international trade & transactions, Customs duties collected for the EU	2.3	0.7
7. Other consumption taxes	OCT	All other taxes under 5000 (consumption taxes): 5112, 5113, 5121, 5122, 5125, 5126, 5128, 5130, 5200, 5300	13.5	11.8
8. Residual taxes	RT	1300 Unallocable between 1100 & 1200; Taxes on payroll & workforce; 6000 Other taxes	1.6	1.5

Source: Authors' calculations based on OECD *Revenue Statistics (2018)*.

Capturing the similarity of tax structures comprised of a number of parts in a single indicator is difficult. However, composite indices can be used to aggregate the different tax categories that make up total tax revenue and provide a single indication of similarity. These include:

- The D-index (Delgado, 2013[51]): this calculates the absolute difference for the share of each tax category in a country from its share in the OECD and sums it, providing an indicator of the difference of that country's tax structure from the OECD average tax structure. Consequently, a value of 0 indicates that the country's tax structure is the same as the OECD average structure.
- The structural similarity index (Becker and Elsayyad, 2009[61]): this calculates the minimum share of each tax category for every country pair in the OECD and, to generate the indicator for an individual country, averages it for the number of pairs. Consequently, a value of 0 indicates that there are no similarities between that country and any other country.

This special feature focuses on the D-index, which measures the distance of each country's tax structure from the OECD average.

By 2016, personal income taxes and social security contributions continued to be the two most significant sources of revenue, on average, but the importance of social security contributions had grown and personal income taxes fallen (to 27.2% and 23.8%, respectively). The share of value-added taxes (VAT) also increased (to 20.2%) whereas other consumption taxes, and particularly taxes on imports and exports, fell. The fall in non-VAT goods and services taxes was not quite offset by the increase in VAT.

The direction of these changes is not sensitive to the start- or end-year within a five-year period in either direction, although the magnitudes differ depending on the start and end-point. However, although the share of corporate income taxes was higher in 2016 than in 1995, the trend across the period was less clear as corporate income taxes were more volatile across the period than the other categories: starting at 8.1% of total revenues in 1995, and increasing to between 8.5% and 8.7% from 1997 to 2003, before peaking at 11.1% in 2007 and falling back to between 8.6 and 9.0% from 2009 to 2016.

Tax structures across individual OECD countries became closer to the OECD average structure across the period 1995 to 2016, as measured by the D-index (Box 2.2). The mean country distance from the OECD average tax structure declined constantly between 1995 and 2004, with a particularly steep decrease in the first few years, partially impacted by the introduction of VAT in Slovenia (1999) and Australia (2000). Tax structures diverged from the OECD average before and immediately after the financial crisis (Figure 2.6) before resuming (in 2011) a descent towards their lowest level of divergence across the period in 2016.

Figure 2.6. Mean difference of country tax structures to OECD average structure (D-index), 1995-2016

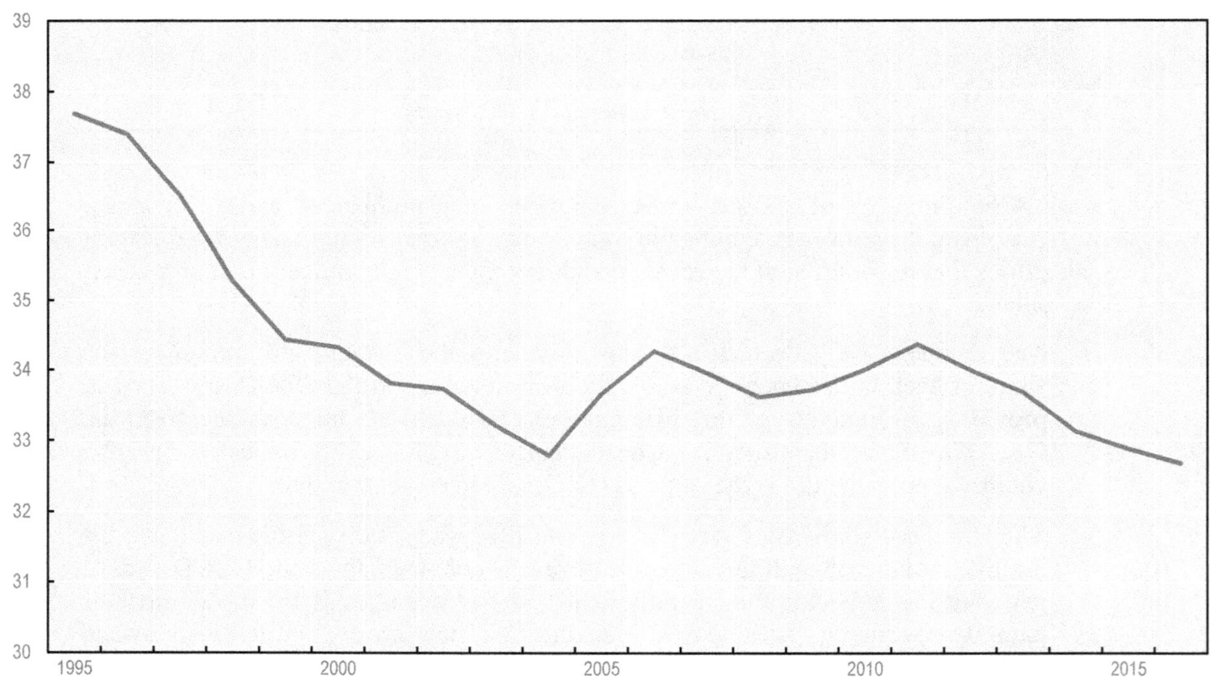

Source: Authors' calculations based on OECD *Revenue Statistics (2017)*.

StatLink http://dx.doi.org/10.1787/888933859247

All but eight OECD countries were more similar to the OECD average tax structure in 1995 than in 2016 (Figure 2.7). These countries were Lithuania, Poland, the United States, Italy, Mexico, New Zealand, Hungary and Estonia:

- in Lithuania, where the largest change in the D-index was observed, this was caused by a sharp increase in the share of social security contributions between 1995 and 2016 and a fall in personal income taxes, which in both cases were significantly greater than the corresponding change in the OECD average;
- in Poland this was due to an increase in VAT (measured either as a share of tax revenue or of GDP) that was higher than the change for the OECD on average. This also mechanically decreased the share of personal income taxes away from the OECD average share;
- in Italy, where corporate income taxes fell as a share of total tax revenue and GDP, countering the increase seen for the OECD average;
- in Mexico, where increases in personal and corporate income taxes as a percentage of GDP meant that the share of social security contributions in total tax revenues fell away from the average OECD share; the increase in corporate income taxes also moved further away from the OECD average, whereas the increase in personal income taxes approached the OECD average;
- in the United States, where personal income taxes increased as a share of total tax revenues, and further away from the OECD average; and the increase in VAT in the OECD average structure also widened the difference;
- in Estonia, where personal income taxes fell more quickly than the OECD average share between 1995 and 2016, and where the share of corporate income taxes decreased (as opposed to the increase in the OECD average share);
- in New Zealand, where a sharp fall in the share of personal income taxes toward the OECD average was more than offset by an increase in corporate income taxes and VAT, away from the OECD average share; and
- in Switzerland, where the D-index increased slightly as a result of higher growth of the share of corporate income taxes in Switzerland than in the OECD average, but no change in the share of VAT in Switzerland when it increased for the average.

Figure 2.7. Distance from the OECD average tax structure (D-index), 1995 and 2016

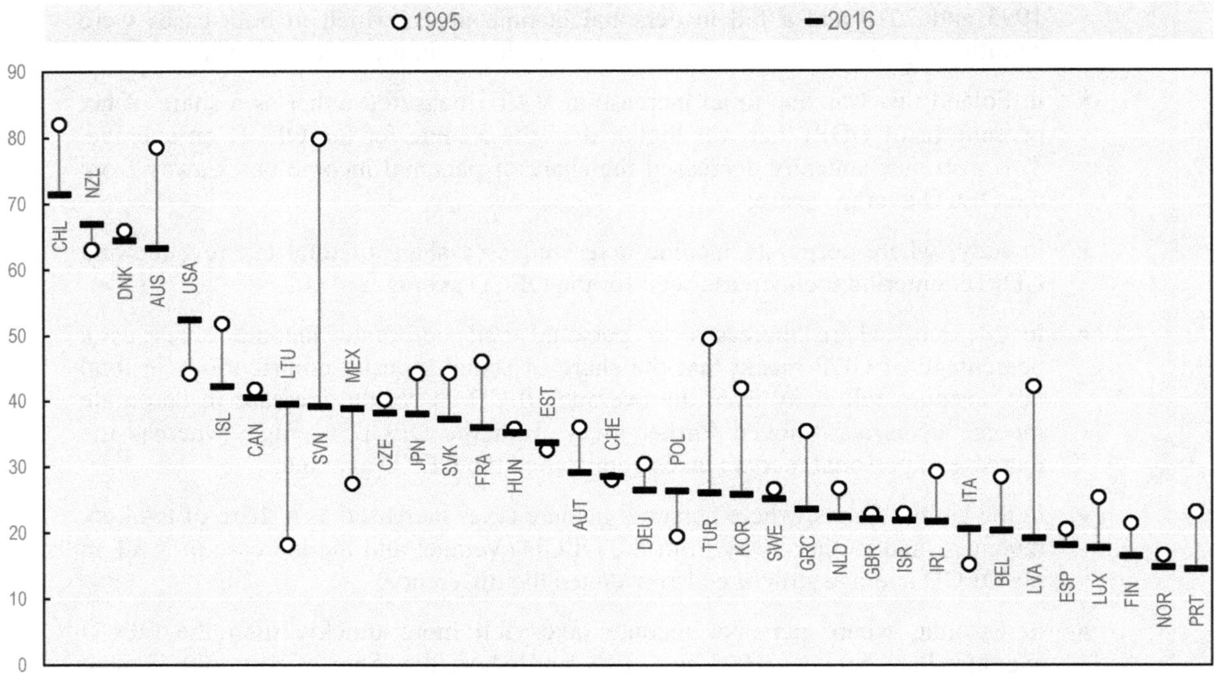

Source: Authors' calculations based on OECD *Revenue Statistics (2017)*.

StatLink http://dx.doi.org/10.1787/888933859266

Countries that increased their similarity to the OECD average the most were those that introduced VAT (Slovenia and Australia) or that made large changes in social security contributions (e.g. in Latvia where they fell as a percentage of GDP and total taxes, or in Korea, where they increased strongly in both) that drew the share of these revenues toward the OECD average.

Similarly, of the five countries where the distance from the OECD average is the highest (Figure 2.8), four do not levy taxes in one of the major categories: Australia and New Zealand do not levy social security contributions and in Denmark, revenues from social security contributions are less than 1% of total tax revenue; the United States does not have a VAT. However, the country least similar to the mean in 2016 was Chile.[7] The differences were due to higher shares of corporate income tax and VAT revenues (20.9% and 41.2% of total revenues, respectively, although the differences as a percentage of GDP were more comparable) and a corresponding low share of personal income taxes and social security contributions (8.8% and 7.2%, respectively, with both also lower than the OECD average as a percentage of GDP).

Across the OECD, there are six countries in 2016 with tax structures that differ by less than 20% from the OECD average structure (Figure 2.7and Figure 2.8). These are all EU countries with the exception of Norway.

Figure 2.8. Tax structures in the OECD ordered by proximity to the OECD average, 2016

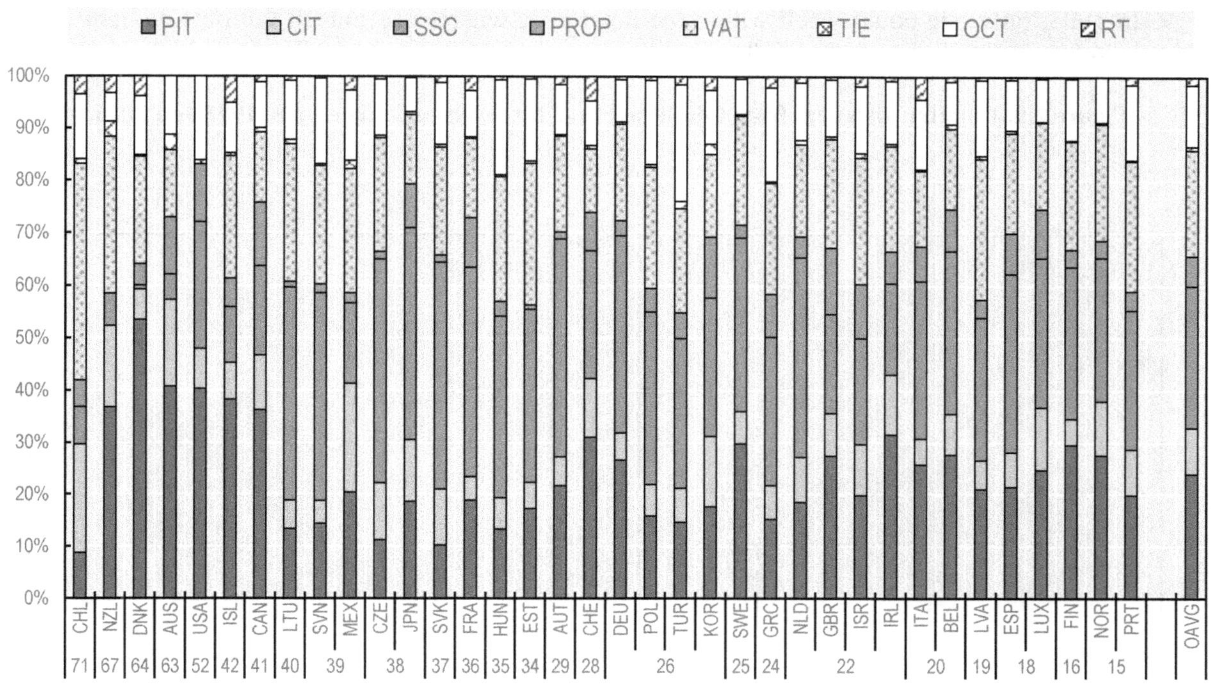

Note: Countries are ordered by increasing proximity to the OECD average structure (right). Numbers underneath the country names show the D-index for each country in 2016.
Source: Authors' calculations based on OECD *Revenue Statistics (2017)*.

StatLink http://dx.doi.org/10.1787/888933859285

2.5. OECD average tax level and structure are more representative

The combined impact of these changes means that the OECD average tax-to-GDP ratio and the OECD average tax structure are more representative in 2016 than they were in 1995. Dispersions of tax-to-GDP ratios from the OECD average (whether measured by standard deviations, coefficient of variation, or absolute deviations from the mean), are currently at a comparatively low level and near their lowest level across the period. Similarly, the mean distance of OECD countries from the OECD average tax structure is at its lowest level since 1995 (Figure 2.6).

This is illustrated in Figure 2.9, which shows the distribution of all OECD countries by reference to the OECD average. Each country is placed along the horizontal axis by their tax-to-GDP ratios in 1995 (left-hand panel) and 2016 (right-hand panel). Along the vertical axis, the graphs show the position of each country on the D-index in each year, with proximity to zero indicating proximity to the OECD average. The OECD average tax-to-GDP ratio is shown on the horizontal axis with a D-index of zero. The inner squares shown on each graph include countries that are located within five percentage points of the OECD average tax-to-GDP ratio in each year as well as having a D-index of less than 20. The outer square is set at the boundary of plus or minus ten percentage points of the OECD tax-to-GDP ratio and a D-index of less than 40.

Although these boundaries are arbitrary, they serve to highlight the increasing convergence of OECD countries towards the OECD average tax level and tax structure. In 1995, only one country fell within the inner box; whereas seventeen fell outside both boxes. In 2016, five countries fell within the inner box; and only ten fell outside both.

Figure 2.9. Country distances from OECD average tax levels and structures, 1995 and 2016

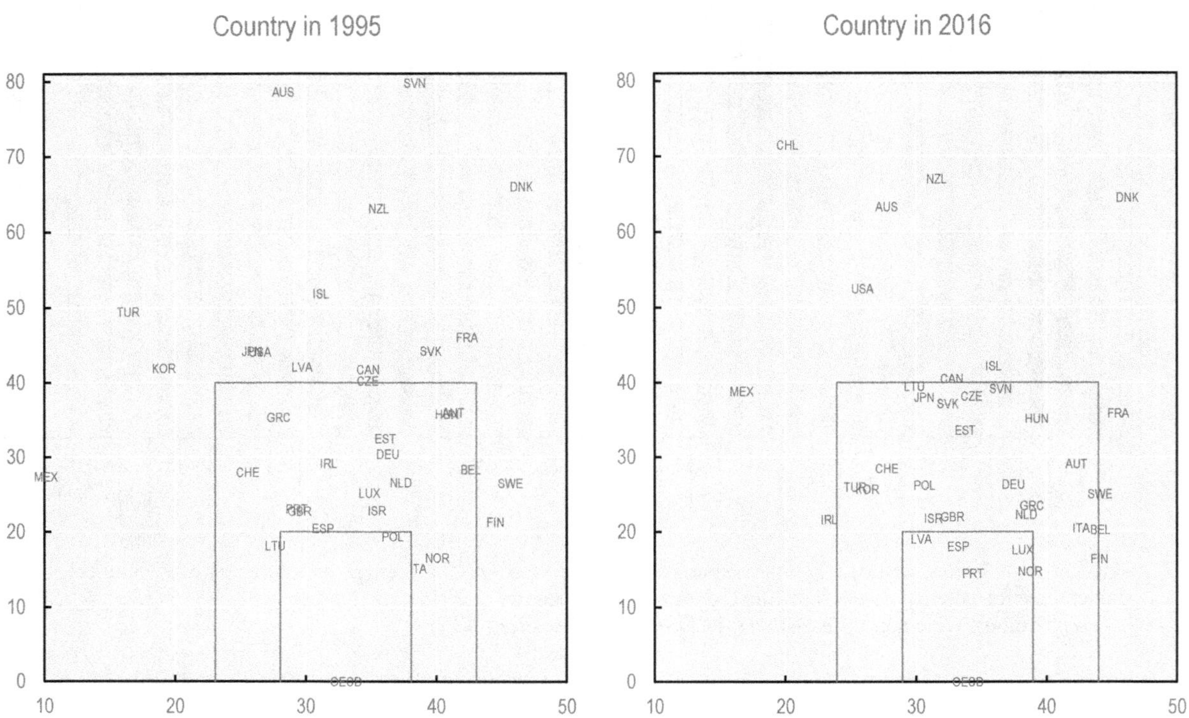

Note: The boxes show an arbitrary indication of proximity to the OECD average in each year: +/- 5 percentage points and a D-index of less than 20; and +/-10 percentage points and a D-index of less than 40.
Source: Authors' calculations based on OECD *Revenue Statistics 2017*.

StatLink http://dx.doi.org/10.1787/888933859304

2.6. Conclusions

From 1995 to 2016, the distribution of countries around the OECD average tax-to-GDP ratio and average tax structure has become more similar and in 2016, the OECD average was more representative of the underlying distribution than at any point in the preceding 20 years. OECD countries have converged around a higher level of taxation: as the dispersion of tax-to-GDP levels in the OECD has decreased, the levels of the tax-to-GDP ratio have also increased and were one percentage point higher in 2016 than in 1995.

Among OECD countries, however, there remains considerable heterogeneity of tax levels, and in 2016, four main groups of OECD countries were evident: those with low, low-mid, high-mid, and high tax-to-GDP ratios. Within these four groups, countries with low tax-to-GDP ratios have the greatest divergence in tax-to-GDP ratios, but their differences have narrowed considerably and their tax-to-GDP ratios increased quickly across the period. In the high-mid group, by contrast, the mean tax-to-GDP ratio has increased slowly but converged quickly since 2010. All of the four intra-OECD groups have become more similar across the period and have higher tax-to-GDP ratios than in 1995, with the exception of the low-mid group, where the tax-to-GDP ratio has not yet recovered to pre-crisis peaks and in 2016, remains lower than it was in 1995.

In 2016, the gap between countries with high and high-mid, and with low and low-mid, tax-to-GDP ratios was higher than it was in 1995, in part because tax levels in countries with lower tax-to-GDP ratios were more impacted by the financial crisis in 2008. Between 1995 and 2007, the gap in the mean tax levels of countries with high & high-mid ratios and countries with low and low-mid ratios widened, and has since stayed relatively constant. Since 2009, all groups have increased their mean tax-to-GDP ratios at similar rates except for the high ratio group, where it has been decreasing slowly since 2014, although it remains above 1995 levels.

OECD countries have also converged towards a tax structure that places more emphasis on value-added taxes, social security contributions, and, to a lesser extent, on corporate income taxes; while moving away from personal income taxes and non-VAT forms of consumption taxes. In 1995, the mean D-index score across OECD countries was 37.7, compared to 32.8 in 2016, indicating a higher degree of convergence of OECD countries with the OECD average. Only eight countries have moved further away from the OECD average structure over the period (Lithuania, Poland, the United States, Italy, Mexico, New Zealand, Hungary and Estonia). For almost all countries, and on average, the OECD average tax level and tax structure is therefore now more representative than it has been at any point in the last 21 years.

Individual countries differ in their distance from the OECD average, with six countries having a D-index of under 20, indicating proximity to the OECD average tax structure: Portugal, Norway, Finland, Luxembourg, Spain and Latvia. By contrast, the countries with the most different tax structures to the OECD average were Chile, New Zealand, Denmark, Australia and the United States, each with a D-index greater than 50.

Future analysis could explore links between tax structures and tax levels and whether the intra-OECD groups seen by tax level also have characteristic structures or have been converging internally towards more similar tax structures. This analysis could also seek to understand the drivers of different tax levels and structures in OECD countries: for example, the link between social benefit systems and the level of social security contributions, or the impact of the privatisation of infrastructure spending on revenue needs and structure. Similarly, exploring the structural similarity index could allow relationships between the tax structures of country pairs to be examined and could lead to the development of country groups by reference to the composition of tax revenues.

Notes

1 In this special feature, as in the rest of the publication, the term "OECD average" refers only to the unweighted mean of OECD countries and specifically to the two key indicators used throughout the publication: i.e. the OECD average tax-to-GDP ratio or the OECD average tax structure. Otherwise, the term "average" is avoided and reference is instead made to the mean or median for clarity. All means presented are unweighted.

2 In 2016, Iceland received revenues from one-off stability contributions that increased its tax-to-GDP ratio by 15.7 percentage points, to 51.6% of GDP. As the special feature considers trends over time, these one-off revenues have not been included in the analysis. For the purposes of this special

feature, the tax level and structure in Iceland has been calculated exclusive of the revenues from these one-off contributions.

3 Lithuania, with a tax-to-GDP ratio of 29.9% in 2016, has been included in the low-mid group for this analysis. The country with the next highest ratio is Switzerland, with a ratio of 27.8% in 2016, which has been included in the group of countries with low tax-to-GDP ratios in 2016. Future analysis could consider whether it would be more appropriate to further divide the lowest group, particularly if additional countries were to be included.

4 Had the groups been constructed on the basis of data for 2015 they would have been the same, with two exceptions. Both Latvia and Lithuania would have been included in the low group rather than the low-mid group, as their tax-to-GDP ratios were 28.9% and 29.2% in 2015.

5 See for example (Delgado and Presno, 2011[7]); (Dvorokova, 2014[11]); (Young, Higgins and Levy, 2008[10]); (Gemmell and Kneller, 2003[9]); (Tibulca, 2015[8]).

6 Iceland was below the thresholds for this group from 2001-2002 and 2009-2011 and above them in 2006; and Germany had a tax-to-GDP ratio of below 35% from 2002 to 2007.

7 Although Chile, and to a lesser extent New Zealand, Denmark and Australia are outliers, they do not affect the overall trend of the indicator, although do increase the average distance. When Chile is excluded from the calculation, the OECD-35 average D-index in 1995 was 36.4 and in 2016 it was 31.6 (compared to 37.7 and 32.7 with Chile included). The trend over time is also similar.

References

Barro, R. and X. Sala-I-Martin (1992), "Convergence", *Journal of Political Economy*, Vol. 100, pp. 223-251, http://dx.doi.org/10.1086/261816. [3]

Becker, J. and M. Elsayyad (2009), "The evolution and convergence of OECD tax systems", *Intereconomics*, Vol. 44, pp. 105-113, http://dx.doi.org/10.1007/s10272-009-0284-0. [6]

Delgado, F. (2013), "Are Taxes Converging in Europe? Trends and Some Insights into the Effect of Economic Crisis", *Journal of Global Economics*, Vol. 1, pp. 1-3, http://dx.doi.org/10.4172/2375-4389.1000102. [5]

Delgado, F. and M. Presno (2011), "Convergence of fiscal pressure in the EU: a time series approach", *Applied Economics*, Vol. 43, pp. 4257-4267, http://dx.doi.org/10.1080/00036846.2010.491449. [7]

Dvorokova, K. (2014), "Sigma Versus Beta-convergence in EU28: do they lead to different results?", *Mathematical Methods in Finance and Business Administration*, pp. 88-94, http://www.wseas.us/e-library/conferences/2014/Tenerife/ECONMATH/ECONMATH-13.pdf. [11]

Gemmell, N. and R. Kneller (2003), "Fiscal Policy, Growth and Convergence in Europe", *New Zealand Treasury Working Paper*, Vol. 14, pp. 1-28, https://treasury.govt.nz/sites/default/files/2007-09/twp03-14.pdf. [9]

Mankiw, G., D. Romer and Weil D. (1992), "A contribution to the empirics of economic growth", *The Quarterly Journal of Economics*, Vol. 107, pp. 407-37, https://eml.berkeley.edu/~dromer/papers/MRW_QJE1992.pdf. [4]

OECD (2017), *Revenue Statistics 1965-2016*, OECD Publishing, Paris, http://dx.doi.org/10.1787/10.1787/9789264283183-en. [2]

OECD (2010), *Tax Policy Reform and Economic Growth*, OECD Publishing, Paris, http://dx.doi.org/10.1787/9789264091085-en. [1]

Tibulca, I. (2015), "Is there Evidence of Tax Convergence in the European Union?", *Procedia Economics and Finance*, Vol. 32, pp. 194-199, https://doi.org/10.1016/S2212-5671(15)01382-9. [8]

Young, A., M. Higgins and D. Levy (2008), "Sigma Convergence versus Beta Convergence: Evidence from U.S. County-Level Data", *Journal of Money, Credit and Banking*, Vol. 40, pp. 1083-1093, https://www.biu.ac.il/soc/ec/d_levy/wp/jmcb5.pdf. [10]

Chapter 3. Tax Levels and Tax Structures, 1965-2017

Chapter 3 provides an overview of tax levels and tax structures in OECD countries from 1965-2017.

In all of the following tables the symbol (…) indicates not available/or not applicable. The main series in this chapter cover the years 1965 to 2016. A selection of years are shown in this chapter because of lack of space. The complete series is available on line. Data for 1955 and 1960 (for nineteen OECD countries) are provided in part V of the 1998 edition of this Report.

The Gross Domestic Product (GDP) figures are based on the 2008 System of National Accounts (SNA) for all OECD countries.

In this chapter, the OECD average for 2016 in all tables has been calculated excluding the one-off revenues from stability contributions in Iceland.

Box 3.1. Treatment of capital transfers

Footnotes to Tables 3.1 to 3.18 refer to the treatment of the capital transfers that some countries make to account for taxes that have been assessed but not collected. The capital transfer has been subtracted from the total tax revenue and this reduction has been allocated between tax headings in proportion to their tax revenues.

This applies to the following countries:

- Denmark from 1971.
- France from 1992.
- Greece for 1999 and 2000.
- Lithuania from 1999.
- Spain from 1995.

Table 3.1. Total revenue as % of GDP

	1965	1990	2000	2007	2010	2012	2014	2015	2016	2017p
Australia	20.6	28.1	30.5	29.6	25.3	27.0	27.3	27.9	27.8	..
Austria	33.5	39.3	42.3	40.5	41.0	41.8	42.7	43.1	42.2	41.8
Belgium	30.6	41.2	43.5	42.7	42.6	44.2	45.1	44.8	44.1	44.6
Canada	25.1	35.2	34.8	32.6	31.1	31.3	31.3	32.7	32.7	32.2
Chile	..	16.9	18.8	22.7	19.6	21.3	19.6	20.4	20.2	20.2
Czech Republic	..	..	32.4	34.2	32.5	33.7	33.1	33.3	34.2	34.9
Denmark[1]	29.1	44.4	46.9	46.4	44.8	45.5	48.5	46.1	46.2	46.0
Estonia	..	..	31.1	31.3	33.3	31.7	32.3	33.3	33.7	33.0
Finland	30.0	42.9	45.8	41.5	40.8	42.7	43.8	43.9	44.0	43.3
France[1]	33.7	41.2	43.4	42.5	42.1	44.4	45.4	45.3	45.5	46.2
Germany[2]	31.6	34.8	36.2	34.9	35.0	36.4	36.7	37.0	37.4	37.5
Greece[1]	17.1	25.2	33.4	31.2	32.0	35.5	35.7	36.6	38.8	39.4
Hungary	..	..	38.5	39.4	37.3	38.4	38.0	38.7	39.2	37.7
Iceland	26.1	30.9	36.3	38.9	33.2	35.0	38.3	36.3	51.6	37.7
Ireland	24.5	32.4	30.8	30.4	27.0	27.6	28.4	23.1	23.3	22.8
Israel	..	..	34.9	34.2	30.7	30.0	31.2	31.3	31.3	32.7
Italy	24.7	36.4	40.6	41.7	41.9	43.9	43.5	43.1	42.6	42.4
Japan	17.6	28.2	25.8	27.5	26.5	28.2	30.3	30.6	30.6	..
Korea	..	18.8	21.5	24.8	23.4	24.8	24.6	25.2	26.2	26.9
Latvia	..	..	29.1	28.2	28.2	28.6	29.0	29.2	30.4	30.4
Lithuania	..	..	30.8	30.0	28.3	27.0	27.5	28.9	29.8	29.8
Luxembourg	26.4	33.5	36.9	36.1	37.4	38.4	37.4	37.1	38.1	38.7
Mexico	..	12.1	11.5	12.0	12.8	12.6	13.7	15.9	16.6	16.2
Netherlands	30.5	39.7	36.9	35.7	35.7	35.6	37.0	37.0	38.4	38.8
New Zealand	24.5	36.2	32.5	33.9	30.3	31.6	31.2	31.6	31.6	32.0
Norway	29.4	40.2	41.9	42.1	41.9	41.5	38.8	38.4	38.7	38.2
Poland	..	..	32.9	34.6	31.4	32.1	31.9	32.4	33.4	33.9
Portugal	15.7	26.5	31.1	31.8	30.4	31.8	34.3	34.4	34.3	34.7
Slovak Republic	..	..	33.6	29.2	28.1	28.3	31.1	32.2	32.4	32.9
Slovenia	..	..	36.6	37.1	36.9	36.8	36.2	36.4	36.5	36.0
Spain[1]	14.3	31.6	33.2	36.4	31.2	32.1	33.6	33.6	33.2	33.7
Sweden	31.4	49.5	49.0	45.0	43.2	42.6	42.6	43.1	44.0	44.0
Switzerland	16.5	23.7	27.6	26.2	26.6	26.9	26.9	27.6	27.8	28.5
Turkey	10.6	14.5	23.6	23.1	24.8	24.9	24.6	25.1	25.3	24.9
United Kingdom	30.1	32.9	32.9	33.0	32.3	32.4	31.8	32.2	32.7	33.3
United States	23.5	26.0	28.2	26.7	23.5	24.1	26.0	26.2	25.9	27.1
Unweighted average										
OECD Average[3]	**24.9**	**31.9**	**33.8**	**33.6**	**32.3**	**33.1**	**33.6**	**33.7**	**34.0**	**34.2**

.. Not available

Note: Full time series can be accessed at http://oe.cd/full-time-series.

1. The total tax revenue has been reduced by the amount of any capital transfer that represents uncollected taxes. The capital transfer has been allocated between tax headings in proportion to the reported tax revenue.
2. From 1991 the figures relate to the united Germany.
3. 2017: calculated by applying the unweighted average percentage change for 2017 in the 34 countries providing data for that year to the overall average tax to GDP ratio in 2016. The 2016 OECD average tax-to-GDP ratio excludes the one-off revenues from stability contributions in Iceland.

StatLink http://dx.doi.org/10.1787/888933859323

Table 3.2. Total tax revenue in billions of US dollars at market exchange rates

	1965	1990	2000	2007	2010	2012	2014	2015	2016	2017p
Australia	5.6	90.9	124.4	290.8	328.3	428.0	399.3	348.2	362.0	..
Austria	..	68.6	83.2	157.6	160.5	171.1	188.7	164.7	165.0	174.1
Belgium	..	89.4	103.6	201.6	206.1	220.0	239.2	204.0	206.0	219.8
Canada	14.2	209.2	262.8	477.2	501.4	570.1	564.6	510.0	502.4	532.8
Chile	..	5.8	14.7	39.4	42.8	57.0	51.1	49.7	50.4	55.9
Czech Republic	..	..	20.0	64.8	67.4	70.0	68.8	62.3	66.8	75.3
Denmark[1]	3.0	61.4	76.9	148.3	144.2	149.0	171.1	139.0	141.8	149.7
Estonia	..	..	1.8	7.0	6.5	7.3	8.6	7.6	8.1	8.8
Finland	..	49.6	57.5	106.0	101.1	109.6	119.4	102.1	105.2	109.4
France[1]	..	550.7	591.8	1 130.7	1 113.7	1 191.0	1 296.4	1 104.3	1 120.4	1 194.3
Germany[2]	..	577.4	706.9	1 200.4	1 196.2	1 290.1	1 431.0	1 251.1	1 307.9	1 387.0
Greece[1]	..	14.6	43.4	99.3	95.9	87.2	84.7	71.6	74.8	78.9
Hungary	..	..	18.2	55.1	48.8	49.1	53.2	47.6	49.3	52.5
Iceland	0.1	2.0	3.2	8.3	4.4	5.0	6.6	6.2	10.5	9.0
Ireland	0.7	15.6	30.7	82.0	60.0	62.0	73.6	67.3	70.5	75.7
Israel	..	..	46.2	61.2	72.0	77.4	96.1	93.6	99.4	114.8
Italy	..	336.6	463.6	918.8	889.5	910.2	935.5	790.4	792.1	820.3
Japan	17.1	903.6	1 263.4	1 242.0	1 509.6	1 749.1	1 482.2	1 351.5	1 516.2	..
Korea	..	52.6	120.5	278.2	256.2	303.2	347.0	347.9	371.1	411.7
Latvia	..	..	1.8	8.7	6.7	8.0	9.1	7.9	8.4	9.2
Lithuania	..	..	3.8	11.9	10.5	11.6	13.3	12.0	12.8	14.1
Luxembourg	..	4.7	7.9	18.4	19.9	21.8	24.8	21.4	22.4	24.1
Mexico	..	35.9	81.2	126.5	135.9	152.2	179.9	186.1	179.5	..
Netherlands	..	132.6	153.7	302.5	301.9	298.7	330.1	283.3	300.8	322.0
New Zealand	1.4	16.4	18.0	47.1	44.9	56.1	63.5	56.8	60.3	65.7
Norway	2.4	48.2	71.8	168.9	179.9	211.7	193.7	148.6	143.7	152.7
Poland	..	..	56.6	148.7	150.6	160.7	173.8	154.5	157.4	177.8
Portugal	..	18.8	36.8	76.4	72.5	68.8	78.7	68.7	70.4	75.5
Slovak Republic	..	..	9.8	25.2	25.1	26.5	31.4	28.2	29.1	31.5
Slovenia	..	..	6.4	17.8	17.7	17.1	18.1	15.7	16.3	17.6
Spain[1]	..	131.6	197.9	538.0	446.8	429.4	462.6	402.5	410.5	441.5
Sweden	7.8	127.7	127.3	219.4	211.2	231.7	244.4	214.7	226.7	236.6
Switzerland	2.6	61.3	75.1	125.8	155.3	179.8	190.9	187.5	185.7	193.2
Turkey	1.3	30.2	64.5	156.2	192.0	218.6	229.6	215.5	218.4	211.8
United Kingdom	30.6	359.5	542.9	1 016.8	792.2	870.1	966.4	931.4	870.1	874.0
United States	167.0	1 552.4	2 900.5	3 867.4	3 515.8	3 888.5	4 526.9	4 754.0	4 821.5	5 263.3
Unweighted average										
OECD Average	..	**205.5**	**233.0**	**373.5**	**363.4**	**398.8**	**426.5**	**400.2**	**409.7**	..

.. Not available

Note: Full time series can be accessed at http://oe.cd/full-time-series.

1. The total tax revenue has been reduced by the amount of any capital transfer that represents uncollected taxes. The capital transfer has been allocated between tax headings in proportion to the reported tax revenue.
2. From 1991 the figures relate to the united Germany.

StatLink http://dx.doi.org/10.1787/888933859342

Table 3.3. Tax revenue of main headings as % of GDP, 2016

	1000 Income & profits	2000 Social security	3000 Payroll	4000 Property	5000 Goods and services	6000 Others	EU Custom Duties
Australia	15.9	0.0	1.4	3.0	7.5	0.0	..
Austria	11.8	14.6	2.9	0.6	11.9	0.2	0.1
Belgium	15.7	13.7	0.0	3.5	10.8	0.0	0.4
Canada	15.6	4.9	0.7	3.9	7.6	0.0	..
Chile	6.8	1.4	0.0	1.0	11.0	-0.1	..
Czech Republic	7.6	14.7	0.0	0.5	11.3	0.0	0.2
Denmark[1]	29.0	0.1	0.3	1.9	14.8	0.0	0.1
Estonia	7.5	11.2	0.0	0.3	14.6	0.0	0.2
Finland	15.2	12.8	0.0	1.4	14.4	0.0	0.1
France[1]	10.6	16.7	1.6	4.3	11.1	1.2	0.1
Germany[2]	11.9	14.1	0.0	1.1	10.1	0.1	0.2
Greece	9.1	11.1	0.0	3.2	15.4	0.0	0.1
Hungary	7.6	13.0	0.6	1.1	16.6	0.1	0.1
Iceland	17.5	3.5	0.3	17.6	12.1	0.6	..
Ireland	10.1	3.9	0.1	1.4	7.6	0.0	0.1
Israel	9.9	5.2	1.2	3.2	11.8	0.0	..
Italy	13.6	12.8	0.0	2.8	12.0	1.2	0.1
Japan	9.4	12.4	0.0	2.6	6.3	0.1	..
Korea	8.2	6.9	0.1	3.0	7.4	0.7	..
Latvia	8.1	8.3	0.0	1.1	12.8	0.0	0.2
Lithuania	5.6	12.2	0.0	0.3	11.5	0.0	0.2
Luxembourg	14.0	10.9	0.0	3.5	9.6	0.1	0.0
Mexico	7.1	2.2	0.4	0.3	6.4	0.2	..
Netherlands	10.4	14.7	0.0	1.5	11.3	0.1	0.3
New Zealand	17.6	0.0	0.0	1.9	12.1	0.0	..
Norway	14.7	10.6	0.0	1.3	12.1	0.0	..
Poland	6.7	12.7	0.2	1.4	12.2	0.1	0.2
Portugal	9.9	9.1	0.0	1.3	13.6	0.4	0.1
Slovak Republic	7.0	14.1	0.0	0.4	10.7	0.0	0.2
Slovenia	6.8	14.5	0.0	0.6	14.3	0.0	0.1
Spain[1]	9.3	11.3	0.0	2.6	9.8	0.0	0.2
Sweden	15.9	10.0	4.6	1.1	12.4	0.0	0.1
Switzerland	12.9	6.7	0.0	2.0	5.9	0.1	..
Turkey	5.4	7.3	0.0	1.2	11.0	0.4	..
United Kingdom	11.7	6.2	0.0	4.1	10.6	0.0	0.2
United States	12.4	6.2	0.0	2.9	4.4	0.0	..
Unweighted average							
OECD Average	**11.3**	**9.2**	**0.4**	**1.9**	**11.0**	**0.2**	**0.2**

.. Not available

1. The total tax revenue has been reduced by the amount of any capital transfer that represents uncollected taxes. The capital transfer has been allocated between tax headings in proportion to the reported tax revenue.
2. From 1991 the figures relate to the united Germany.

StatLink http://dx.doi.org/10.1787/888933859361

Table 3.4. Tax revenue of main headings as % of total tax revenue, 2016

	1000 Income & profits	2000 Social security	3000 Payroll	4000 Property	5000 Goods and services	6000 Others	EU Custom Duties
Australia	57.2	0.0	4.9	10.8	27.1	0.0	..
Austria	28.0	34.7	7.0	1.3	28.3	0.5	0.3
Belgium	35.6	31.1	0.0	8.0	24.5	0.0	0.8
Canada	47.8	14.9	2.1	12.0	23.2	0.1	..
Chile	33.5	7.2	0.0	5.1	54.6	-0.3	..
Czech Republic	22.2	42.9	0.0	1.4	33.0	0.0	0.5
Denmark[1]	62.8	0.1	0.6	4.0	32.1	0.0	0.3
Estonia	22.3	33.2	0.0	0.8	43.3	0.0	0.5
Finland	34.6	29.1	0.0	3.2	32.8	0.1	0.2
France[1]	23.3	36.8	3.4	9.4	24.4	2.6	0.2
Germany[2]	31.9	37.6	0.0	2.8	27.1	0.2	0.4
Greece	23.5	28.5	0.0	8.1	39.6	0.0	0.3
Hungary	19.3	33.2	1.6	2.8	42.4	0.4	0.3
Iceland	33.9	6.7	0.6	34.2	23.4	1.2	..
Ireland	43.1	16.8	0.6	6.0	32.7	0.0	0.5
Israel	31.6	16.6	3.7	10.3	37.8	0.0	..
Italy	32.0	30.1	0.0	6.6	28.1	2.9	0.3
Japan	30.6	40.4	0.0	8.3	20.4	0.3	..
Korea	31.2	26.2	0.3	11.6	28.1	2.6	..
Latvia	26.6	27.3	0.0	3.5	42.0	0.0	0.6
Lithuania	18.9	40.8	0.0	1.1	38.5	0.0	0.8
Luxembourg	36.8	28.5	0.0	9.3	25.2	0.2	0.1
Mexico	42.7	13.0	2.3	1.9	38.8	1.4	..
Netherlands	27.2	38.2	0.0	4.0	29.5	0.3	0.9
New Zealand	55.6	0.0	0.0	6.1	38.3	0.0	..
Norway	38.0	27.4	0.0	3.3	31.4	0.0	..
Poland	20.0	38.1	0.7	4.1	36.4	0.1	0.5
Portugal	28.7	26.6	0.0	3.7	39.6	1.1	0.3
Slovak Republic	21.7	43.5	0.0	1.3	33.1	0.0	0.5
Slovenia	18.8	39.7	0.1	1.7	39.3	0.0	0.4
Spain[1]	28.2	34.2	0.0	7.7	29.4	0.0	0.5
Sweden	36.0	22.6	10.5	2.4	28.1	0.1	0.3
Switzerland	46.5	24.3	0.0	7.3	21.4	0.5	..
Turkey	21.1	28.8	0.0	4.8	43.6	1.6	..
United Kingdom	35.7	18.9	0.0	12.6	32.3	0.0	0.5
United States	48.0	24.0	0.0	11.1	16.9	0.0	..
Unweighted average							
OECD Average	**33.6**	**26.2**	**1.1**	**5.7**	**32.7**	**0.5**	**0.4**

.. Not available

1. The total tax revenue has been reduced by the amount of any capital transfer that represents uncollected taxes. The capital transfer has been allocated between tax headings in proportion to the reported tax revenue.
2. From 1991 the figures relate to the united Germany.

StatLink http://dx.doi.org/10.1787/888933859380

Table 3.5. Tax revenue of main headings as % of GDP, 2017p

	1000 Income & profits	2000 Social security	3000 Payroll	4000 Property	5000 Goods and services	6000 Others	EU Custom Duties
Australia	..	..	..	..	..	..	..
Austria	11.8	14.5	2.8	0.5	11.8	0.2	0.1
Belgium	16.3	13.6	0.0	3.5	10.8	0.0	0.4
Canada	15.4	4.6	0.7	3.8	7.7	0.0	..
Chile	7.0	1.5	0.0	1.1	11.0	-0.4	..
Czech Republic	7.7	15.0	0.0	0.5	11.5	0.0	0.2
Denmark[1]	29.1	0.0	0.3	1.8	14.6	0.0	0.1
Estonia	7.2	11.2	0.0	0.2	14.2	0.0	0.2
Finland	15.4	12.1	0.0	1.5	14.2	0.0	0.1
France[1]	10.9	16.8	1.6	4.4	11.3	1.2	0.1
Germany[2]	12.2	14.2	0.0	1.0	9.9	0.1	0.2
Greece	9.0	11.7	0.0	3.2	15.4	0.0	0.2
Hungary	6.9	12.8	0.7	1.1	16.0	0.1	0.1
Iceland	18.6	3.5	0.3	2.0	12.6	0.7	..
Ireland	9.9	3.9	0.1	1.3	7.4	0.0	0.1
Israel	11.6	5.3	1.2	3.3	11.3	0.0	..
Italy	13.4	12.9	0.0	2.6	12.0	1.3	0.1
Japan	9.7	..	0.0	2.5	6.1	0.1	..
Korea	8.6	6.9	0.1	3.1	7.5	0.7	..
Latvia	8.2	8.4	0.0	1.0	12.6	0.0	0.2
Lithuania	5.4	12.3	0.0	0.4	11.5	0.0	0.2
Luxembourg	14.4	11.1	0.0	3.7	9.4	0.1	0.0
Mexico	7.2	2.1	..	..	..	..	..
Netherlands	11.6	13.8	0.0	1.6	11.3	0.1	0.3
New Zealand	17.8	0.0	0.0	1.9	12.3	0.0	..
Norway	14.6	10.4	0.1	1.3	11.9	0.0	..
Poland	6.9	12.9	0.0	1.2	11.7	1.2	..
Portugal	9.8	9.3	0.0	1.4	13.8	0.3	0.1
Slovak Republic	6.8	14.5	0.0	0.4	11.0	0.0	0.2
Slovenia	6.9	14.4	0.0	0.6	13.9	0.0	0.1
Spain[1]	9.7	11.5	0.0	2.5	9.8	0.0	0.2
Sweden	15.8	9.7	5.1	1.0	12.3	0.0	0.1
Switzerland	13.2	6.7	0.0	2.0	6.4	0.1	..
Turkey	5.3	7.3	0.0	1.1	10.8	0.3	..
United Kingdom	11.9	6.4	0.1	4.2	10.5	0.0	0.2
United States	12.4	6.3	0.0	4.2	4.3	0.0	..

.. Not available

1. The total tax revenue has been reduced by the amount of any capital transfer that represents uncollected taxes. The capital transfer has been allocated between tax headings in proportion to the reported tax revenue.
2. From 1991 the figures relate to the united Germany.

StatLink http://dx.doi.org/10.1787/888933859399

Table 3.6. Tax revenue of main headings as % of total tax revenue, 2017p

	1000 Income & profits	2000 Social security	3000 Payroll	4000 Property	5000 Goods and services	6000 Others	EU Custom Duties
Australia	..	..	..	..	..	..	..
Austria	28.3	34.8	6.6	1.3	28.2	0.5	0.3
Belgium	36.5	30.5	0.0	7.9	24.3	0.0	0.8
Canada	47.6	14.3	2.1	11.9	24.0	0.1	..
Chile	34.5	7.3	0.0	5.4	54.8	-2.0	..
Czech Republic	22.2	43.0	0.0	1.4	32.9	0.1	0.5
Denmark[1]	63.2	0.1	0.6	4.0	31.9	0.0	0.3
Estonia	22.0	33.9	0.0	0.7	42.9	0.0	0.5
Finland	35.5	27.9	0.0	3.6	32.8	0.1	0.2
France[1]	23.6	36.4	3.4	9.5	24.4	2.5	0.2
Germany[2]	32.6	37.9	0.0	2.7	26.2	0.2	0.4
Greece	22.8	29.6	0.0	8.1	39.1	0.0	0.4
Hungary	18.3	33.9	1.9	2.8	42.5	0.3	0.3
Iceland	49.5	9.3	0.8	5.4	33.3	1.7	..
Ireland	43.6	17.0	0.6	5.6	32.5	0.0	0.5
Israel	35.6	16.2	3.7	10.0	34.7	0.0	..
Italy	31.7	30.4	0.0	6.0	28.4	3.1	0.3
Japan	..	..	..	..	..	..	..
Korea	32.1	25.7	0.3	11.7	27.7	2.5	..
Latvia	27.0	27.7	0.0	3.3	41.4	0.0	0.6
Lithuania	18.1	41.4	0.0	1.3	38.5	0.0	0.8
Luxembourg	37.2	28.6	0.0	9.6	24.3	0.1	0.1
Mexico	..	..	..	..	..	..	..
Netherlands	30.1	35.7	0.0	4.0	29.1	0.3	0.9
New Zealand	55.6	0.0	0.0	6.0	38.4	0.0	..
Norway	38.3	27.1	0.2	3.3	31.1	0.0	..
Poland	20.5	37.9	0.0	3.6	34.4	3.7	..
Portugal	28.2	26.8	0.0	4.0	39.8	0.9	0.3
Slovak Republic	20.7	44.1	0.0	1.3	33.4	0.0	0.5
Slovenia	19.1	40.0	0.1	1.8	38.6	0.0	0.3
Spain[1]	28.7	34.2	0.0	7.5	29.1	0.0	0.5
Sweden	35.9	22.0	11.5	2.2	28.0	0.1	0.3
Switzerland	46.5	23.6	0.0	7.1	22.3	0.5	..
Turkey	21.4	29.3	0.0	4.5	43.4	1.3	..
United Kingdom	35.9	19.2	0.3	12.6	31.5	0.0	0.5
United States	45.7	23.1	0.0	15.4	15.9	0.0	..

.. Not available
1. The total tax revenue has been reduced by the amount of any capital transfer that represents uncollected taxes. The capital transfer has been allocated between tax headings in proportion to the reported tax revenue.
2. From 1991 the figures relate to the united Germany.

StatLink http://dx.doi.org/10.1787/888933859418

Table 3.7. Taxes on income and profits (1 000) as % of GDP and as % of total tax revenue

	% of GDP					% of total tax revenue				
	1990	2000	2010	2015	2016	1990	2000	2010	2015	2016
Australia	16.1	17.7	14.3	15.8	15.9	57.1	57.9	56.5	56.6	57.2
Austria	10.0	12.0	11.5	13.0	11.8	25.5	28.3	28.1	30.2	28.0
Belgium	15.2	16.8	14.6	16.0	15.7	36.9	38.6	34.2	35.7	35.6
Canada	17.1	17.4	14.5	15.8	15.6	48.6	50.1	46.6	48.3	47.8
Chile	3.9	4.4	7.5	7.4	6.8	23.2	23.3	38.1	36.4	33.5
Czech Republic	..	7.4	6.6	7.2	7.6	..	22.8	20.2	21.5	22.2
Denmark[1]	27.2	28.8	27.5	29.3	29.0	61.2	61.5	61.5	63.5	62.8
Estonia	..	7.7	6.6	7.8	7.5	..	24.8	19.8	23.4	22.3
Finland	16.8	19.7	14.5	15.4	15.2	39.2	43.1	35.5	35.2	34.6
France[1]	6.6	10.8	9.5	10.6	10.6	16.1	24.8	22.6	23.4	23.3
Germany[2]	11.3	10.9	10.0	11.5	11.9	32.4	30.1	28.5	31.2	31.9
Greece[1]	5.0	9.0	7.0	8.5	9.1	19.9	26.9	22.0	23.1	23.5
Hungary	..	9.3	7.7	7.1	7.6	..	24.3	20.7	18.3	19.3
Iceland	9.2	14.5	14.7	17.0	17.5	29.7	39.9	44.4	46.9	33.9
Ireland	12.3	13.4	10.5	9.9	10.1	38.0	43.6	38.7	42.9	43.1
Israel	..	13.8	9.0	9.8	9.9	..	39.6	29.1	31.2	31.6
Italy	13.3	13.5	13.7	13.7	13.6	36.5	33.2	32.6	31.8	32.0
Japan	14.2	9.0	8.0	9.5	9.4	50.2	34.8	30.2	31.2	30.6
Korea	6.2	6.2	6.6	7.6	8.2	32.8	28.8	28.0	30.3	31.2
Latvia	..	7.0	7.2	7.5	8.1	..	24.1	25.5	25.8	26.6
Lithuania	..	8.3	4.6	5.4	5.6	..	27.0	16.2	18.6	18.9
Luxembourg	13.5	13.5	13.6	13.5	14.0	40.2	36.5	36.4	36.3	36.8
Mexico	4.1	4.1	5.1	6.6	7.1	34.0	36.0	39.8	41.7	42.7
Netherlands	12.8	9.6	9.9	10.3	10.4	32.3	25.9	27.9	27.7	27.2
New Zealand	21.6	19.5	16.3	17.3	17.6	59.6	60.0	53.8	54.9	55.6
Norway	14.2	18.8	19.7	15.2	14.7	35.2	45.0	47.1	39.7	38.0
Poland	..	6.7	6.3	6.5	6.7	..	20.4	20.0	20.1	20.0
Portugal	6.8	9.1	8.1	10.4	9.9	25.7	29.3	26.8	30.3	28.7
Slovak Republic	..	6.9	5.3	7.0	7.0	..	20.5	19.0	21.8	21.7
Slovenia	..	6.8	7.4	6.6	6.8	..	18.5	20.1	18.0	18.8
Spain[1]	9.7	9.4	8.7	9.5	9.3	30.6	28.3	27.8	28.4	28.2
Sweden	20.6	20.0	15.3	15.5	15.9	41.6	40.8	35.5	35.9	36.0
Switzerland	11.2	12.2	12.1	12.8	12.9	47.0	44.1	45.5	46.4	46.5
Turkey	4.9	7.0	5.3	5.1	5.4	33.5	29.5	21.3	20.3	21.1
United Kingdom	12.9	13.1	12.1	11.3	11.7	39.3	39.6	37.6	35.2	35.7
United States	11.7	14.1	10.0	12.7	12.4	45.2	50.1	42.4	48.6	48.0
Unweighted average										
OECD Average	**12.2**	**11.9**	**10.6**	**11.3**	**11.3**	**37.5**	**34.8**	**32.8**	**33.6**	**33.6**

.. Not available

Note: Full time series can be accessed at http://oe.cd/full-time-series.

1. The total tax revenue has been reduced by the amount of any capital transfer that represents uncollected taxes. The capital transfer has been allocated between tax headings in proportion to the reported tax revenue.
2. From 1991 the figures relate to the united Germany.

StatLink http://dx.doi.org/10.1787/888933859437

Table 3.8. Taxes on personal income (1 100) as % of GDP and as % of total tax revenue

	% of GDP					% of total tax revenue				
	1990	2000	2010	2015	2016	1990	2000	2010	2015	2016
Australia	12.1	11.5	9.8	11.6	11.3	43.0	37.7	38.6	41.4	40.8
Austria	8.2	9.3	9.2	10.4	9.1	21.0	22.0	22.4	24.1	21.6
Belgium	13.2	13.7	12.0	12.6	12.2	32.0	31.4	28.2	28.2	27.7
Canada	14.4	12.8	10.9	12.0	11.9	40.8	36.8	35.0	36.9	36.3
Chile	0.9	1.4	1.3	2.0	1.8	5.6	7.6	6.8	9.8	8.8
Czech Republic	..	4.2	3.3	3.6	3.8	..	12.9	10.2	10.7	11.2
Denmark[1]	24.0	24.7	23.3	25.5	24.7	54.1	52.7	52.0	55.2	53.5
Estonia	..	6.8	5.3	5.7	5.8	..	22.0	15.9	17.2	17.2
Finland	14.9	14.0	12.1	13.3	13.0	34.7	30.6	29.5	30.2	29.6
France[1]	4.4	7.8	7.2	8.5	8.6	10.7	17.9	17.0	18.8	18.8
Germany[2]	9.6	9.2	8.5	9.8	10.0	27.6	25.3	24.3	26.6	26.6
Greece[1]	3.6	4.8	4.0	5.8	5.9	14.1	14.5	12.4	15.7	15.2
Hungary	..	7.2	6.5	5.3	5.2	..	18.6	17.4	13.7	13.3
Iceland	8.3	12.6	12.1	13.3	13.8	26.9	34.8	36.5	36.7	26.7
Ireland	10.7	9.8	8.1	7.3	7.4	33.1	31.9	30.0	31.6	31.6
Israel	..	10.1	5.5	6.1	6.2	..	29.1	18.0	19.4	19.8
Italy	9.6	10.1	11.2	11.2	11.0	26.3	24.8	26.8	26.0	25.8
Japan	7.8	5.4	4.9	5.8	5.7	27.8	21.1	18.6	18.9	18.6
Korea	3.8	3.1	3.3	4.3	4.6	20.0	14.6	14.2	17.2	17.6
Latvia	..	5.5	6.2	5.9	6.4	..	18.8	22.1	20.3	21.0
Lithuania	..	7.6	3.6	3.8	4.0	..	24.8	12.7	13.3	13.4
Luxembourg	8.1	6.8	7.9	9.1	9.4	24.1	18.5	21.0	24.4	24.7
Mexico	..	..	2.3	3.3	3.4	..	..	18.3	20.6	20.4
Netherlands	9.8	5.6	7.7	7.6	7.1	24.7	15.1	21.5	20.5	18.5
New Zealand	17.4	14.0	11.4	11.7	11.6	48.0	43.1	37.7	37.2	36.8
Norway	10.5	10.1	9.9	10.8	10.7	26.2	24.1	23.6	28.0	27.6
Poland	..	4.3	4.4	4.7	4.8	..	13.2	13.9	14.4	14.5
Portugal	4.2	5.4	5.4	7.3	6.8	15.9	17.4	17.6	21.2	19.8
Slovak Republic	..	3.3	2.6	3.1	3.3	..	9.9	9.4	9.7	10.2
Slovenia	..	5.5	5.6	5.1	5.2	..	15.0	15.1	14.0	14.4
Spain[1]	6.9	6.4	6.8	7.2	7.1	21.7	19.1	21.7	21.4	21.4
Sweden	19.1	16.3	12.0	12.5	13.1	38.5	33.2	27.9	29.1	29.8
Switzerland	7.7	8.2	8.4	8.5	8.6	32.5	29.6	31.7	31.0	31.0
Turkey	3.9	5.2	3.5	3.7	3.7	26.8	22.2	14.0	14.6	14.6
United Kingdom	9.7	9.6	9.3	8.9	9.0	29.4	29.0	28.7	27.7	27.4
United States	9.8	11.9	8.2	10.6	10.4	37.7	42.2	34.8	40.5	40.3
Unweighted average										
OECD Average	**9.7**	**8.7**	**7.6**	**8.3**	**8.2**	**28.6**	**24.6**	**22.9**	**24.1**	**23.8**

.. Not available

Note: Full time series can be accessed at http://oe.cd/full-time-series.

1. The total tax revenue has been reduced by the amount of any capital transfer that represents uncollected taxes. The capital transfer has been allocated between tax headings in proportion to the reported tax revenue.
2. From 1991 the figures relate to the united Germany.

StatLink http://dx.doi.org/10.1787/888933859456

Table 3.9. Taxes on corporate income (1 200) as % of GDP and as % of total tax revenue

	% of GDP					% of total tax revenue				
	1990	2000	2010	2015	2016	1990	2000	2010	2015	2016
Australia	4.0	6.2	4.5	4.3	4.6	14.1	20.2	17.9	15.2	16.5
Austria	1.4	1.9	1.9	2.2	2.4	3.6	4.6	4.6	5.2	5.6
Belgium	2.0	3.1	2.5	3.3	3.5	4.8	7.2	5.9	7.4	7.8
Canada	2.5	4.2	3.3	3.4	3.4	7.0	12.2	10.5	10.4	10.5
Chile	2.1	2.1	4.0	4.3	4.2	12.4	11.2	20.4	21.0	20.9
Czech Republic	..	3.2	3.2	3.6	3.7	..	9.9	10.0	10.8	11.0
Denmark[1]	1.7	3.2	2.3	2.7	2.7	3.8	6.8	5.0	5.9	5.8
Estonia	..	0.9	1.3	2.1	1.7	..	2.8	4.0	6.2	5.0
Finland	1.9	5.7	2.4	2.2	2.2	4.5	12.5	6.0	4.9	5.0
France[1]	2.2	3.0	2.3	2.1	2.0	5.3	6.9	5.5	4.6	4.5
Germany[2]	1.7	1.8	1.5	1.7	2.0	4.8	4.8	4.3	4.6	5.2
Greece[1]	1.4	4.0	2.5	2.2	2.5	5.5	12.0	7.9	5.9	6.5
Hungary	..	2.2	1.2	1.8	2.3	..	5.7	3.3	4.6	6.0
Iceland	0.9	1.2	0.9	2.4	2.5	2.8	3.3	2.7	6.5	4.9
Ireland	1.6	3.6	2.4	2.6	2.7	4.9	11.7	8.7	11.3	11.5
Israel	..	3.3	2.6	3.0	3.1	..	9.6	8.6	9.5	9.9
Italy	3.7	2.8	2.3	2.0	2.1	10.0	6.9	5.5	4.7	5.0
Japan	6.3	3.5	3.1	3.8	3.7	22.4	13.7	11.6	12.3	12.0
Korea	2.4	3.0	3.2	3.3	3.6	12.8	14.1	13.8	13.1	13.6
Latvia	..	1.5	1.0	1.6	1.7	..	5.3	3.5	5.5	5.6
Lithuania	..	0.7	1.0	1.5	1.6	..	2.2	3.5	5.3	5.4
Luxembourg	5.4	6.6	5.8	4.4	4.6	16.1	18.0	15.4	11.9	12.2
Mexico	..	..	1.8	3.2	3.5	..	..	14.4	20.1	21.0
Netherlands	3.0	4.0	2.3	2.7	3.3	7.5	10.9	6.4	7.2	8.7
New Zealand	2.3	4.0	3.7	4.4	4.9	6.5	12.4	12.2	14.0	15.5
Norway	3.6	8.8	9.9	4.5	4.0	9.0	20.9	23.5	11.7	10.4
Poland	..	2.4	1.9	1.8	1.8	..	7.3	6.2	5.7	5.5
Portugal	2.1	3.7	2.7	3.1	3.1	8.0	11.9	9.0	9.1	8.9
Slovak Republic	..	2.6	2.5	3.7	3.5	..	7.7	8.7	11.5	10.8
Slovenia	..	1.1	1.8	1.5	1.6	..	3.1	5.0	4.0	4.4
Spain[1]	2.8	3.0	1.9	2.4	2.2	8.8	9.1	6.1	7.0	6.8
Sweden	1.5	3.7	3.3	3.0	2.7	3.1	7.5	7.6	6.8	6.2
Switzerland	1.8	2.4	2.7	3.0	3.1	7.4	8.9	10.0	10.7	11.3
Turkey	1.0	1.7	1.8	1.4	1.6	6.7	7.3	7.3	5.7	6.5
United Kingdom	3.3	3.5	2.9	2.4	2.7	9.9	10.6	8.9	7.5	8.3
United States	2.0	2.2	1.8	2.1	2.0	7.5	7.9	7.6	8.1	7.6
Unweighted average										
OECD Average	**2.5**	**3.2**	**2.7**	**2.8**	**2.9**	**8.1**	**9.3**	**8.6**	**8.8**	**9.0**

.. Not available

Note: Full time series can be accessed at http://oe.cd/full-time-series.

1. The total tax revenue has been reduced by the amount of any capital transfer that represents uncollected taxes. The capital transfer has been allocated between tax headings in proportion to the reported tax revenue.
2. From 1991 the figures relate to the united Germany.

StatLink http://dx.doi.org/10.1787/888933859475

Table 3.10. Social security contributions (2 000) as % of GDP and as % of total tax revenue

	% of GDP					% of total tax revenue				
	1990	2000	2010	2015	2016	1990	2000	2010	2015	2016
Australia	0.0	0.0	0.0	0.0	0.0	0.0	0.0	0.0	0.0	0.0
Austria	12.9	14.3	14.0	14.5	14.6	32.9	33.8	34.2	33.6	34.7
Belgium	13.7	13.4	13.8	14.3	13.7	33.2	30.8	32.4	31.9	31.1
Canada	4.3	4.7	4.6	4.8	4.9	12.1	13.6	14.9	14.8	14.9
Chile	1.5	1.4	1.3	1.4	1.4	9.0	7.3	6.8	6.9	7.2
Czech Republic	..	14.4	14.5	14.4	14.7	..	44.3	44.8	43.0	42.9
Denmark[1]	0.0	0.6	0.1	0.1	0.1	0.0	1.4	0.2	0.1	0.1
Estonia	..	10.9	12.8	11.1	11.2	..	35.1	38.4	33.3	33.2
Finland	11.0	11.6	12.1	12.7	12.8	25.6	25.2	29.7	28.9	29.1
France[1]	18.1	15.6	16.1	16.7	16.7	44.1	35.8	38.2	36.9	36.8
Germany[2]	13.0	14.1	13.7	13.9	14.1	37.5	39.0	39.2	37.7	37.6
Greece[1]	7.6	10.1	10.9	10.7	11.1	30.2	30.2	34.2	29.2	28.5
Hungary	..	11.3	11.7	12.5	13.0	..	29.3	31.4	32.3	33.2
Iceland	1.0	2.8	3.9	3.6	3.5	3.1	7.7	11.8	9.8	6.7
Ireland	4.6	3.6	5.0	3.9	3.9	14.1	11.8	18.6	16.8	16.8
Israel	..	5.1	5.2	5.1	5.2	..	14.6	16.9	16.4	16.6
Italy	12.0	11.6	13.0	13.0	12.8	32.9	28.5	31.1	30.1	30.1
Japan	7.5	9.1	10.9	12.1	12.4	26.5	35.2	41.1	39.4	40.4
Korea	1.9	3.6	5.5	6.7	6.9	10.1	16.7	23.3	26.6	26.2
Latvia	..	9.8	8.7	8.3	8.3	..	33.5	30.7	28.6	27.3
Lithuania	..	9.9	11.6	11.5	12.2	..	32.2	41.1	40.0	40.8
Luxembourg	9.2	9.6	10.8	10.7	10.9	27.5	26.1	29.0	29.0	28.5
Mexico	2.0	2.1	2.1	2.2	2.2	16.8	18.0	16.2	13.9	13.0
Netherlands	14.9	14.3	12.9	14.0	14.7	37.4	38.7	36.3	37.8	38.2
New Zealand	0.0	0.0	0.0	0.0	0.0	0.0	0.0	0.0	0.0	0.0
Norway	10.6	8.8	9.4	10.4	10.6	26.3	20.9	22.4	27.2	27.4
Poland	..	12.9	10.8	12.4	12.7	..	39.2	34.4	38.4	38.1
Portugal	7.2	7.9	8.6	9.0	9.1	27.2	25.5	28.3	26.1	26.6
Slovak Republic	..	14.0	12.1	13.8	14.1	..	41.5	43.0	42.8	43.5
Slovenia	..	13.9	14.8	14.4	14.5	..	38.0	40.2	39.7	39.7
Spain[1]	11.2	11.6	11.9	11.4	11.3	35.4	34.9	38.1	33.8	34.2
Sweden	13.5	12.9	10.9	9.6	10.0	27.2	26.3	25.3	22.4	22.6
Switzerland	5.5	6.7	6.3	6.7	6.7	23.3	24.1	23.6	24.4	24.3
Turkey	2.9	4.4	6.2	7.3	7.3	19.7	18.7	24.9	29.0	28.8
United Kingdom	5.6	5.5	6.1	6.0	6.2	17.0	16.8	19.0	18.7	18.9
United States	6.6	6.6	6.1	6.2	6.2	25.6	23.6	26.1	23.7	24.0
Unweighted average										
OECD Average	**7.3**	**8.6**	**8.9**	**9.0**	**9.2**	**22.0**	**25.0**	**26.8**	**26.2**	**26.2**

.. Not available

Note: Full time series can be accessed at http://oe.cd/full-time-series.

1. The total tax revenue has been reduced by the amount of any capital transfer that represents uncollected taxes. The capital transfer has been allocated between tax headings in proportion to the reported tax revenue.
2. From 1991 the figures relate to the united Germany.

StatLink http://dx.doi.org/10.1787/888933859494

Table 3.11. Taxes on payroll and workforce (3 000) as % of GDP and as % of total tax revenue

	% of GDP					% of total tax revenue				
	1990	2000	2010	2015	2016	1990	2000	2010	2015	2016
Australia	1.7	1.4	1.3	1.4	1.4	6.1	4.5	5.2	5.0	4.9
Austria	2.4	2.7	2.8	2.9	2.9	6.0	6.4	6.9	6.8	7.0
Belgium	0.0	0.0	0.0	0.0	0.0	0.0	0.0	0.0	0.0	0.0
Canada	0.8	0.7	0.6	0.7	0.7	2.3	2.1	2.1	2.0	2.1
Chile	0.0	0.0	0.0	0.0	0.0	0.0	0.0	0.0	0.0	0.0
Czech Republic	..	0.0	0.0	0.0	0.0	..	0.0	0.0	0.0	0.0
Denmark[1]	0.3	0.2	0.2	0.3	0.3	0.7	0.4	0.5	0.6	0.6
Estonia	..	0.0	0.0	0.0	0.0	..	0.0	0.0	0.0	0.0
Finland	0.0	0.0	0.0	0.0	0.0	0.0	0.0	0.0	0.0	0.0
France[1]	0.8	1.0	1.3	1.6	1.6	1.9	2.3	3.2	3.5	3.4
Germany[2]	0.0	0.0	0.0	0.0	0.0	0.0	0.0	0.0	0.0	0.0
Greece[1]	0.2	0.0	0.0	0.0	0.0	0.7	0.0	0.0	0.0	0.0
Hungary	..	1.4	0.4	0.6	0.6	..	3.6	1.1	1.5	1.6
Iceland	1.1	0.0	0.2	0.3	0.3	3.5	0.1	0.5	0.8	0.6
Ireland	0.4	0.0	0.2	0.1	0.1	1.3	0.0	0.7	0.6	0.6
Israel	..	1.3	1.2	1.2	1.2	..	3.6	3.8	3.8	3.7
Italy	0.1	0.0	0.0	0.0	0.0	0.3	0.0	0.0	0.0	0.0
Japan	0.0	0.0	0.0	0.0	0.0	0.0	0.0	0.0	0.0	0.0
Korea	0.1	0.0	0.1	0.1	0.1	0.4	0.2	0.2	0.3	0.3
Latvia	..	0.0	0.0	0.0	0.0	..	0.0	0.1	0.0	0.0
Lithuania	..	0.0	0.0	0.0	0.0	..	0.0	0.0	0.0	0.0
Luxembourg	0.0	0.0	0.0	0.0	0.0	0.0	0.0	0.0	0.0	0.0
Mexico	0.2	0.2	0.3	0.4	0.4	1.8	1.5	2.2	2.4	2.3
Netherlands	0.0	0.0	0.0	0.0	0.0	0.0	0.0	0.0	0.0	0.0
New Zealand	0.0	0.0	0.0	0.0	0.0	0.0	0.0	0.0	0.0	0.0
Norway	0.0	0.0	0.0	0.0	0.0	0.0	0.0	0.0	0.0	0.0
Poland	..	0.2	0.3	0.2	0.2	..	0.7	0.8	0.7	0.7
Portugal	0.0	0.0	0.0	0.0	0.0	0.0	0.0	0.0	0.0	0.0
Slovak Republic	..	0.0	0.0	0.0	0.0	..	0.0	0.0	0.0	0.0
Slovenia	..	1.5	0.1	0.1	0.0	..	4.2	0.2	0.1	0.1
Spain[1]	0.0	0.0	0.0	0.0	0.0	0.0	0.0	0.0	0.0	0.0
Sweden	1.2	2.1	3.1	4.6	4.6	2.5	4.3	7.1	10.7	10.5
Switzerland	0.0	0.0	0.0	0.0	0.0	0.0	0.0	0.0	0.0	0.0
Turkey	0.0	0.0	0.0	0.0	0.0	0.0	0.0	0.0	0.0	0.0
United Kingdom	0.0	0.0	0.0	0.0	0.0	0.0	0.0	0.0	0.0	0.0
United States	0.0	0.0	0.0	0.0	0.0	0.0	0.0	0.0	0.0	0.0
Unweighted average										
OECD Average	**0.3**	**0.4**	**0.3**	**0.4**	**0.4**	**1.0**	**0.9**	**1.0**	**1.1**	**1.1**

.. Not available

Note: Full time series can be accessed at http://oe.cd/full-time-series.

1. The total tax revenue has been reduced by the amount of any capital transfer that represents uncollected taxes. The capital transfer has been allocated between tax headings in proportion to the reported tax revenue.
2. From 1991 the figures relate to the united Germany.

StatLink http://dx.doi.org/10.1787/888933859513

Table 3.12. Taxes on property (4 000) as % of GDP and as % of total tax revenue

	% of GDP					% of total tax revenue				
	1990	2000	2010	2015	2016	1990	2000	2010	2015	2016
Australia	2.5	2.7	2.4	3.0	3.0	9.0	8.8	9.4	10.7	10.8
Austria	1.1	0.6	0.5	0.6	0.6	2.7	1.3	1.3	1.3	1.3
Belgium	1.6	2.0	3.1	3.5	3.5	3.8	4.7	7.2	7.8	8.0
Canada	3.5	3.3	3.8	3.9	3.9	10.0	9.5	12.3	11.8	12.0
Chile	1.0	1.3	0.8	0.9	1.0	6.2	7.0	4.1	4.4	5.1
Czech Republic	..	0.5	0.4	0.5	0.5	..	1.4	1.3	1.4	1.4
Denmark[1]	1.9	1.6	1.8	1.9	1.9	4.3	3.3	4.1	4.2	4.0
Estonia	..	0.4	0.3	0.3	0.3	..	1.2	1.0	0.8	0.8
Finland	1.1	1.1	1.1	1.4	1.4	2.4	2.4	2.7	3.3	3.2
France[1]	2.6	3.1	3.7	4.2	4.3	6.3	7.2	8.7	9.3	9.4
Germany[2]	1.2	0.8	0.8	1.0	1.1	3.4	2.3	2.3	2.8	2.8
Greece[1]	1.2	2.0	1.7	3.1	3.2	4.6	6.1	5.2	8.4	8.1
Hungary	..	0.7	1.1	1.3	1.1	..	1.7	3.1	3.3	2.8
Iceland	2.6	2.8	2.3	1.9	17.6	8.4	7.9	7.0	5.4	34.2
Ireland	1.5	1.8	1.4	1.5	1.4	4.6	5.7	5.3	6.5	6.0
Israel	..	3.1	3.3	3.3	3.2	..	9.0	10.7	10.6	10.3
Italy	0.8	1.9	2.0	2.8	2.8	2.3	4.6	4.8	6.5	6.6
Japan	2.7	2.7	2.6	2.5	2.6	9.4	10.5	9.7	8.2	8.3
Korea	2.2	2.7	2.6	3.1	3.0	11.8	12.4	11.3	12.4	11.6
Latvia	..	1.1	0.9	1.0	1.1	..	3.8	3.1	3.4	3.5
Lithuania	..	0.5	0.4	0.3	0.3	..	1.5	1.3	1.2	1.1
Luxembourg	2.8	3.9	2.6	3.3	3.5	8.4	10.7	7.1	8.9	9.3
Mexico	0.2	0.2	0.3	0.3	0.3	1.9	1.8	2.3	2.0	1.9
Netherlands	1.5	1.9	1.4	1.4	1.5	3.7	5.3	3.8	3.8	4.0
New Zealand	2.5	1.7	2.0	2.0	1.9	6.8	5.3	6.6	6.2	6.1
Norway	1.2	1.0	1.2	1.1	1.3	2.9	2.3	2.8	3.0	3.3
Poland	..	1.4	1.3	1.4	1.4	..	4.3	4.2	4.2	4.1
Portugal	0.7	1.1	1.1	1.3	1.3	2.7	3.7	3.5	3.7	3.7
Slovak Republic	..	0.6	0.4	0.4	0.4	..	1.8	1.5	1.3	1.3
Slovenia	..	0.6	0.6	0.6	0.6	..	1.7	1.7	1.7	1.7
Spain[1]	1.7	2.2	2.1	2.6	2.6	5.5	6.5	6.7	7.7	7.7
Sweden	1.7	1.7	1.0	1.0	1.1	3.5	3.4	2.4	2.4	2.4
Switzerland	2.1	2.7	2.0	2.0	2.0	8.9	9.6	7.6	7.2	7.3
Turkey	0.3	0.7	1.0	1.2	1.2	2.3	3.2	4.1	4.9	4.8
United Kingdom	2.7	3.8	3.9	4.0	4.1	8.2	11.5	12.0	12.6	12.6
United States	3.0	2.9	3.1	2.8	2.9	11.6	10.2	13.1	10.8	11.1
Unweighted average										
OECD Average	**1.8**	**1.8**	**1.7**	**1.9**	**1.9**	**5.8**	**5.4**	**5.4**	**5.7**	**5.7**

.. Not available

Note: Full time series can be accessed at http://oe.cd/full-time-series.

1. The total tax revenue has been reduced by the amount of any capital transfer that represents uncollected taxes. The capital transfer has been allocated between tax headings in proportion to the reported tax revenue.
2. From 1991 the figures relate to the united Germany.

StatLink http://dx.doi.org/10.1787/888933859532

Table 3.13. Taxes on goods and services (5 000) as % of GDP and as % of total tax revenue

	% of GDP					% of total tax revenue				
	1990	2000	2010	2015	2016	1990	2000	2010	2015	2016
Australia	7.8	8.8	7.3	7.7	7.5	27.8	28.8	29.0	27.6	27.1
Austria	12.4	12.2	11.6	11.8	11.9	31.5	28.9	28.4	27.4	28.3
Belgium	10.7	10.9	10.8	10.7	10.8	26.1	25.0	25.3	23.8	24.5
Canada	9.1	8.4	7.4	7.5	7.6	25.8	24.2	24.0	23.0	23.2
Chile	10.6	12.0	10.0	11.0	11.0	62.9	63.8	51.2	54.1	54.6
Czech Republic	..	10.2	10.8	11.2	11.3	..	31.5	33.2	33.5	33.0
Denmark[1]	15.0	15.5	14.9	14.4	14.8	33.8	33.1	33.2	31.2	32.1
Estonia	..	12.1	13.4	14.0	14.6	..	38.8	40.2	42.0	43.3
Finland	14.0	13.3	13.0	14.2	14.4	32.5	29.0	31.8	32.4	32.8
France[1]	11.7	11.2	10.5	11.0	11.1	28.4	25.8	24.8	24.2	24.4
Germany[2]	9.3	10.2	10.3	10.3	10.1	26.7	28.1	29.5	27.8	27.1
Greece[1]	11.2	12.1	12.3	14.3	15.4	44.5	36.4	38.3	39.1	39.6
Hungary	..	15.6	16.0	17.0	16.6	..	40.5	42.9	43.9	42.4
Iceland	15.9	16.0	11.7	11.8	12.1	51.3	44.1	35.2	32.4	23.4
Ireland	13.6	11.7	9.8	7.5	7.6	41.9	38.2	36.2	32.6	32.7
Israel	..	11.6	12.1	11.9	11.8	..	33.1	39.4	38.0	37.8
Italy	10.2	11.3	11.0	11.8	12.0	28.0	27.9	26.3	27.3	28.1
Japan	3.9	5.0	5.0	6.4	6.3	13.7	19.3	18.7	21.0	20.4
Korea	8.3	8.2	7.9	7.1	7.4	44.3	38.4	33.7	28.0	28.1
Latvia	..	11.2	11.3	12.2	12.8	..	38.6	40.2	41.6	42.0
Lithuania	..	12.1	11.5	11.4	11.5	..	39.4	40.8	39.3	38.5
Luxembourg	7.9	9.7	10.2	9.5	9.6	23.6	26.3	27.3	25.6	25.2
Mexico	5.3	4.8	4.9	6.2	6.4	44.0	41.7	38.0	38.6	38.8
Netherlands	10.5	10.7	11.0	11.0	11.3	26.4	28.9	30.8	29.6	29.5
New Zealand	12.1	11.3	12.0	12.3	12.1	33.6	34.7	39.6	38.9	38.3
Norway	14.3	13.3	11.6	11.6	12.1	35.5	31.8	27.7	30.2	31.4
Poland	..	11.6	12.6	11.7	12.2	..	35.3	40.1	36.0	36.4
Portugal	11.7	12.5	12.2	13.3	13.6	44.2	40.3	40.2	38.5	39.6
Slovak Republic	..	12.2	10.1	10.8	10.7	..	36.2	35.8	33.6	33.1
Slovenia	..	13.8	13.8	14.6	14.3	..	37.6	37.3	40.0	39.3
Spain[1]	9.0	10.0	8.4	9.9	9.8	28.4	30.0	26.8	29.6	29.4
Sweden	12.4	12.1	12.7	12.1	12.4	25.0	24.8	29.3	28.1	28.1
Switzerland	4.9	6.1	6.1	6.0	5.9	20.6	21.9	22.9	21.6	21.4
Turkey	4.1	9.9	11.8	11.1	11.0	27.9	42.0	47.7	44.3	43.6
United Kingdom	10.2	10.4	10.0	10.6	10.6	31.0	31.6	30.9	33.0	32.3
United States	4.6	4.6	4.3	4.4	4.4	17.6	16.1	18.3	16.9	16.9
Unweighted average										
OECD Average	**10.0**	**10.9**	**10.6**	**10.8**	**11.0**	**32.5**	**33.1**	**33.2**	**32.6**	**32.7**

.. Not available

Note: Full time series can be accessed at http://oe.cd/full-time-series.

1. The total tax revenue has been reduced by the amount of any capital transfer that represents uncollected taxes. The capital transfer has been allocated between tax headings in proportion to the reported tax revenue.
2. From 1991 the figures relate to the united Germany.

StatLink http://dx.doi.org/10.1787/888933859551

Table 3.14. Value added taxes (5 111) as % of GDP and as % of total tax revenue

	% of GDP					% of total tax revenue				
	1990	2000	2010	2015	2016	1990	2000	2010	2015	2016
Australia	0.0	3.4	3.4	3.6	3.6	0.0	11.1	13.4	13.0	12.9
Austria	8.2	7.9	7.7	7.6	7.7	20.8	18.7	18.7	17.7	18.3
Belgium	6.8	7.0	6.9	6.7	6.8	16.4	16.1	16.2	15.0	15.4
Canada	0.0	3.2	4.3	4.3	4.4	0.0	9.2	13.7	13.2	13.5
Chile	6.3	7.9	7.5	8.3	8.3	37.4	41.8	38.5	40.8	41.2
Czech Republic	..	5.9	6.6	7.3	7.4	..	18.3	20.5	21.7	21.7
Denmark[1]	8.4	9.1	9.4	9.1	9.4	18.8	19.5	21.0	19.8	20.4
Estonia	..	8.4	8.5	9.1	9.1	..	27.1	25.7	27.2	27.0
Finland	8.3	8.0	8.3	9.1	9.1	19.3	17.4	20.4	20.6	20.7
France[1]	7.6	7.2	6.8	6.9	6.9	18.4	16.7	16.1	15.2	15.2
Germany[2]	5.8	6.7	7.0	7.0	6.9	16.6	18.4	20.0	18.8	18.5
Greece[1]	6.2	7.0	7.1	7.3	8.2	24.6	20.9	22.0	20.0	21.2
Hungary	..	8.6	8.5	9.6	9.3	..	22.4	22.9	24.9	23.7
Iceland	8.8	10.4	7.5	8.2	8.4	28.5	28.5	22.7	22.6	16.2
Ireland	6.6	7.1	6.0	4.6	4.7	20.4	22.9	22.2	19.7	20.1
Israel	..	7.4	7.5	7.8	7.5	..	21.1	24.4	25.0	24.1
Italy	5.3	6.3	6.1	6.1	6.1	14.7	15.4	14.5	14.2	14.4
Japan	1.2	2.3	2.5	4.2	4.1	4.4	9.1	9.6	13.7	13.3
Korea	3.5	3.7	4.1	3.8	4.2	18.7	17.0	17.5	15.3	15.8
Latvia	..	7.0	6.7	7.7	8.2	..	23.9	23.7	26.4	26.8
Lithuania	..	7.5	7.8	7.7	7.8	..	24.4	27.5	26.7	26.2
Luxembourg	4.0	4.9	6.4	6.5	6.4	12.1	13.4	17.0	17.6	16.7
Mexico	3.2	2.8	3.8	3.8	3.9	26.1	24.7	29.4	23.9	23.7
Netherlands	6.5	6.4	6.7	6.5	6.8	16.5	17.3	18.7	17.6	17.6
New Zealand	8.1	8.1	9.3	9.5	9.4	22.4	24.9	30.7	30.2	29.8
Norway	7.6	8.2	7.8	8.2	8.6	18.8	19.7	18.5	21.3	22.3
Poland	..	6.9	7.6	7.0	7.0	..	21.0	24.2	21.6	21.1
Portugal	5.2	7.6	7.5	8.5	8.5	19.6	24.4	24.7	24.8	24.8
Slovak Republic	..	6.9	6.2	6.9	6.7	..	20.4	22.0	21.3	20.6
Slovenia	..	8.5	8.1	8.3	8.2	..	23.3	21.9	22.8	22.5
Spain[1]	5.0	5.9	5.2	6.3	6.3	15.7	17.6	16.6	18.9	19.1
Sweden	7.4	8.3	9.2	9.0	9.2	14.9	16.9	21.2	20.9	20.9
Switzerland	2.8	3.6	3.4	3.4	3.4	11.6	13.1	12.7	12.4	12.2
Turkey	2.7	5.7	5.4	5.2	5.0	18.3	24.2	21.7	20.6	19.8
United Kingdom	5.5	5.9	6.0	6.8	6.8	16.9	17.9	18.7	21.2	20.8
United States	0.0	0.0	0.0	0.0	0.0	0.0	0.0	0.0	0.0	0.0
Unweighted average										
OECD Average	**5.2**	**6.4**	**6.5**	**6.7**	**6.8**	**16.7**	**19.4**	**20.3**	**20.2**	**20.2**

.. Not available

Note: Full time series can be accessed at http://oe.cd/full-time-series.

1. The total tax revenue has been reduced by the amount of any capital transfer that represents uncollected taxes. The capital transfer has been allocated between tax headings in proportion to the reported tax revenue.
2. From 1991 the figures relate to the united Germany.

StatLink http://dx.doi.org/10.1787/888933859570

Table 3.15. Tax revenues of sub-sectors of general government as % of total tax revenue

	Supranational			Central government			State or Regional government			Local government			Social Security Funds		
	1975	1995	2016	1975	1995	2016	1975	1995	2016	1975	1995	2016	1975	1995	2016
Federal countries															
Australia	..	..	..	80.1	77.5	79.5	15.7	19.0	16.9	4.2	3.4	3.6	0.0	0.0	0.0
Austria	..	0.0	0.4	51.7	65.1	66.0	10.6	1.8	1.6	12.4	4.1	3.0	25.3	29.0	28.9
Belgium	1.4	1.0	1.0	65.3	60.1	50.7	..	1.8	10.7	4.4	4.8	5.0	28.8	32.2	32.6
Canada	..	..	..	47.6	39.1	40.7	32.5	37.1	39.9	9.9	9.8	10.3	10.0	14.0	9.1
Germany	1.2	0.6	0.6	33.5	31.4	29.7	22.3	21.6	23.6	9.0	7.4	8.5	34.0	39.0	37.6
Mexico	..	..	..	..	73.9	81.5	..	2.8	4.0	..	1.5	1.5	..	21.8	13.0
Switzerland	..	..	..	30.7	31.4	35.2	27.0	24.2	25.0	20.3	17.6	15.6	22.0	26.8	24.3
United States	..	..	..	45.4	41.4	42.1	19.5	20.0	19.4	14.7	13.3	14.5	20.5	25.2	24.0
Unweighted average	1.3	0.6	0.7	50.6	52.5	53.2	21.3	16.0	17.6	10.7	7.7	7.8	20.1	23.5	21.2
Regional country															
Spain[1,2]	..	0.5	0.5	48.2	51.3	41.6	..	4.8	14.7	4.3	8.8	9.9	47.5	34.6	33.2
Unitary countries															
Chile	..	..	..	..	89.9	86.4	..	..	..	..	6.5	7.8	..	3.6	5.7
Czech Republic	..	..	0.5	..	57.7	55.5	..	..	..	..	0.9	1.1	..	41.4	42.9
Denmark[2]	1.1	0.5	0.3	68.9	68.2	72.6	..	..	..	30.0	31.3	27.0	0.1	0.0	0.0
Estonia	..	..	0.5	..	84.3	82.4	..	..	..	..	0.8	1.0	..	14.9	16.1
Finland	..	0.4	0.3	56.0	46.6	47.6	..	..	..	23.5	22.3	23.1	20.4	30.8	29.0
France[2]	0.7	0.4	0.4	51.2	42.6	33.4	..	..	..	7.6	11.0	13.5	40.6	46.0	52.8
Greece[2]	..	0.6	0.3	67.1	66.9	69.6	..	..	..	3.4	0.9	2.4	29.5	31.6	27.7
Hungary	..	..	0.3	..	63.8	60.6	..	..	..	..	2.5	5.8	..	33.6	33.3
Iceland	..	..	..	81.3	79.2	81.4	..	..	..	18.7	20.8	18.6	0.0	0.0	0.0
Ireland	2.3	1.5	1.0	77.4	83.1	82.2	..	..	..	7.3	2.7	2.3	13.1	12.7	14.5
Israel	..	..	..	..	79.6	75.5	..	..	..	..	6.4	7.9	..	14.0	16.6
Italy	..	0.4	0.4	53.2	62.7	54.4	..	..	..	0.9	5.4	15.0	45.9	31.5	30.1
Japan	..	..	..	45.5	41.2	35.7	..	..	..	25.6	25.2	23.9	29.0	33.6	40.4
Korea	..	..	..	89.0	69.2	56.3	..	..	..	10.1	18.7	17.5	0.9	12.1	26.2
Latvia	..	..	0.7	..	43.5	52.5	..	..	..	..	19.5	19.5	..	36.9	27.3
Lithuania	..	..	0.9	..	71.7	57.1	..	..	..	..	2.3	1.3	..	26.1	40.8
Luxembourg	0.8	0.4	0.5	63.6	66.5	68.0	..	..	..	6.7	6.5	3.9	29.0	26.6	27.6
Netherlands	1.5	1.3	1.1	58.9	56.0	57.6	..	..	..	1.2	3.1	3.1	38.4	39.5	38.2
New Zealand	..	..	..	92.3	94.7	93.3	..	..	..	7.7	5.3	6.7	0.0	0.0	0.0
Norway	..	..	..	50.6	58.4	83.8	..	..	..	22.4	19.6	16.2	27.0	22.0	0.0
Poland	..	..	0.5	..	61.2	48.5	..	..	..	..	8.5	12.9	..	30.3	38.1
Portugal	..	0.8	0.5	65.4	72.3	72.8	..	..	..	0.0	5.4	7.3	34.6	21.5	19.4
Slovak Republic	..	..	0.6	..	62.5	55.0	..	..	..	..	1.3	2.0	..	36.2	42.5
Slovenia	..	..	0.4	..	51.8	50.8	..	..	..	..	6.3	9.5	..	41.9	39.2
Sweden	..	0.4	0.3	51.3	46.9	52.3	..	..	..	29.2	30.9	35.4	19.5	21.8	12.1
Turkey	..	..	..	..	75.1	61.5	..	..	..	..	12.8	9.7	..	12.1	28.8
United Kingdom	1.0	1.0	0.5	70.5	77.5	75.7	..	..	..	11.1	3.7	4.9	17.5	17.8	18.9
Unweighted average	1.2	0.7	0.5	65.1	65.7	63.5	..	..	..	12.8	10.4	11.4	21.6	23.6	24.8

.. Not available

1. Spain is constitutionally a non-federal country but has a highly decentralised political structure.
2. The total tax revenue has been reduced by the amount of any capital transfer that represents uncollected taxes.

StatLink http://dx.doi.org/10.1787/888933859589

Table 3.16. Main central government taxes as % of total tax revenues of central government, 2016

	1000 Income & profits	2000 Social security[2]	3000 Payroll	4000 Property	5000 Goods and services	6000 Others
Federal countries						
Australia	72.0	0.0	0.2	0.0	27.9	0.0
Austria	41.3	7.9	7.2	1.2	41.8	0.5
Belgium	55.1	0.1	0.0	2.2	42.6	0.0
Canada	70.9	8.9	0.0	0.0	20.3	0.0
Germany	43.7	0.0	0.0	0.1	56.2	0.0
Mexico	52.4	0.0	0.0	0.0	46.6	1.1
Switzerland	41.6	0.0	0.0	2.0	56.3	0.1
United States	92.3	0.0	0.0	1.0	6.8	0.0
Unweighted average	58.7	2.1	0.9	0.8	37.3	0.2
Regional country						
Spain[1]	39.5	2.2	0.0	0.7	57.5	0.1
Unitary countries						
Chile	38.8	1.6	0.0	2.0	58.0	-0.4
Czech Republic	39.9	0.0	0.0	1.4	58.6	0.1
Denmark[1]	53.4	0.1	0.8	1.5	44.1	0.0
Estonia	27.0	20.8	0.0	0.0	52.2	0.0
Finland	28.0	0.0	0.0	3.1	68.7	0.2
France[1]	36.3	2.4	1.2	6.8	53.1	0.2
Greece	33.7	1.6	0.0	8.4	56.4	0.0
Hungary	30.3	2.9	2.5	2.8	61.0	0.5
Iceland	23.4	8.3	0.7	38.3	27.9	1.4
Ireland	52.5	2.6	0.7	4.7	39.4	0.0
Israel	41.8	0.0	4.9	3.7	49.6	0.0
Italy	50.9	0.0	0.0	6.8	42.3	0.0
Japan	52.1	0.0	0.0	5.4	42.4	0.0
Korea	49.9	0.0	0.0	6.1	42.2	1.7
Latvia	19.5	0.0	0.1	1.1	79.4	0.0
Lithuania	33.0	0.0	0.0	0.0	66.9	0.0
Luxembourg	48.9	1.2	0.0	13.2	36.4	0.2
Netherlands	47.2	0.0	0.0	3.6	48.7	0.5
New Zealand	59.6	0.0	0.0	0.1	40.3	0.0
Norway	28.6	32.7	0.0	1.5	37.2	0.0
Poland	25.0	0.0	1.4	0.0	73.6	0.0
Portugal	36.8	12.0	0.0	0.4	49.3	1.5
Slovak Republic	39.4	1.8	0.0	0.0	58.8	0.0
Slovenia	22.8	0.8	0.3	0.1	76.0	0.0
Sweden	2.9	20.2	20.1	3.0	53.7	0.2
Turkey	30.2	0.0	0.0	5.5	63.1	1.2
United Kingdom	47.1	0.0	0.0	10.2	42.6	0.0
Unweighted average	37.5	4.2	1.2	3.4	53.3	0.3

Note: Excluding social security contributions accruing to social security funds.

1. The total tax revenue has been reduced by the amount of any capital transfer that represents uncollected taxes. The capital transfer has been allocated between tax headings in proportion to the reported tax revenue.
2. These comprise only social security contributions accruing to central government.

StatLink http://dx.doi.org/10.1787/888933859608

Table 3.17. Main state government taxes as % of total tax revenues of state government, 2016

	1000 Income & profits	2000 Social security	3000 Payroll	4000 Property	5000 Goods and services	6000 Others
Federal countries						
Australia	0.0	0.0	28.2	42.7	29.1	0.0
Austria[1]	47.4	20.8	8.8	1.8	17.0	4.1
Belgium[1]	48.4	1.1	0.0	35.5	14.9	0.0
Canada	47.5	5.5	5.2	4.8	37.0	0.0
Germany[1]	51.2	0.0	0.0	6.9	41.9	0.0
Mexico	0.0	0.0	57.7	17.8	19.5	5.1
Switzerland	76.7	0.0	0.0	16.6	6.2	0.5
United States	42.7	0.0	0.0	2.2	55.1	0.0
Unweighted average	39.2	3.4	12.5	16.0	27.6	1.2
Regional country						
Spain[1,2,3]	69.0	0.0	0.0	19.8	11.2	0.0
Unitary countries						
Chile	..	..	..	..	..	..
Czech Republic	..	..	..	..	..	..
Denmark	..	..	..	..	..	..
Estonia	..	..	..	..	..	..
Finland	..	..	..	..	..	..
France	..	..	..	..	..	..
Greece	..	..	..	..	..	..
Hungary	..	..	..	..	..	..
Iceland	..	..	..	..	..	..
Ireland	..	..	..	..	..	..
Israel	..	..	..	..	..	..
Italy	..	..	..	..	..	..
Japan	..	..	..	..	..	..
Korea	..	..	..	..	..	..
Latvia	..	..	..	..	..	..
Lithuania	..	..	..	..	..	..
Luxembourg	..	..	..	..	..	..
Netherlands	..	..	..	..	..	..
New Zealand	..	..	..	..	..	..
Norway	..	..	..	..	..	..
Poland	..	..	..	..	..	..
Portugal	..	..	..	..	..	..
Slovak Republic	..	..	..	..	..	..
Slovenia	..	..	..	..	..	..
Sweden	..	..	..	..	..	..
Turkey	..	..	..	..	..	..
United Kingdom	..	..	..	..	..	..
Unweighted average	..	..	..	..	..	..

.. Not available

1. Payments to the European Union are excluded from these comparisons.
2. The total tax revenue has been reduced by the amount of any capital transfer that represents uncollected taxes. The capital transfer has been allocated between tax headings in proportion to the reported tax revenue.
3. Spain is constitutionally a non-federal country but has a highly decentralised political structure.

StatLink http://dx.doi.org/10.1787/888933859627

Table 3.18. Main local government taxes as % of total tax revenues of local government, 2016

	1000 Income & profits	2000 Social security	3000 Payroll	4000 Property	5000 Goods and services	6000 Others
Federal countries						
Australia	0.0	0.0	0.0	100.0	0.0	0.0
Austria[1]	0.0	5.8	68.2	15.1	7.8	3.0
Belgium[1]	35.8	0.2	0.0	57.1	6.9	0.0
Canada	0.0	0.0	0.0	97.3	1.7	1.0
Germany[1]	79.9	0.0	0.0	13.6	6.3	0.2
Mexico	0.0	0.0	0.0	77.8	2.6	19.6
Switzerland	81.9	0.0	0.0	15.5	0.5	2.1
United States	6.1	0.0	0.0	70.6	23.3	0.0
Unweighted average	25.5	0.8	8.5	55.9	6.1	3.2
Regional country						
Spain[1,2]	15.9	0.0	0.0	45.3	38.7	0.1
Unitary countries						
Chile	0.0	0.0	0.0	43.1	56.9	0.0
Czech Republic[1]	0.0	0.0	0.0	57.3	42.7	0.0
Denmark[1,3]	89.0	0.0	0.0	11.0	0.0	0.0
Estonia[1]	0.0	0.0	0.0	83.5	16.5	0.0
Finland[1]	92.3	0.1	0.0	7.6	0.0	0.0
France[1,3]	0.0	0.0	7.1	52.6	23.2	17.1
Greece[1]	0.0	0.0	0.0	93.4	6.6	0.0
Hungary[1]	0.0	0.0	0.0	19.3	80.7	0.0
Iceland	80.2	0.0	0.0	16.3	3.5	0.0
Ireland[1]	0.0	5.7	0.0	94.3	0.0	0.0
Israel	0.0	0.0	0.0	95.0	5.0	0.0
Italy[1]	28.6	0.0	0.0	19.0	33.3	19.1
Japan	50.1	0.0	0.0	26.8	22.1	1.1
Korea	17.7	0.0	1.7	46.3	24.8	9.4
Latvia[1]	84.0	0.0	0.0	14.9	1.1	0.0
Lithuania	0.0	0.0	0.0	87.2	12.8	0.0
Luxembourg[1]	91.5	0.0	0.0	7.1	1.2	0.1
Netherlands[1]	0.0	0.0	0.0	61.8	38.2	0.0
New Zealand	0.0	0.0	0.0	89.8	10.2	0.0
Norway	86.6	0.0	0.0	12.2	1.2	0.0
Poland[1]	61.4	0.0	0.0	32.1	5.3	1.2
Portugal[1]	27.4	0.2	0.0	46.3	25.8	0.3
Slovak Republic[1]	0.0	0.0	0.0	66.9	33.1	0.0
Slovenia[1]	75.5	0.0	0.0	17.9	6.6	0.0
Sweden[1]	97.6	0.0	0.0	2.4	0.0	0.0
Turkey	26.6	0.0	0.0	15.1	49.7	8.6
United Kingdom[1]	0.0	0.0	0.0	100.0	0.0	0.0
Unweighted average	33.6	0.2	0.3	45.2	18.5	2.1

1. Payments to the European Union are excluded from these comparisons.
2. Spain is constitutionally a non-federal country but has a highly decentralised political structure.
3. The total tax revenue has been reduced by the amount of any capital transfer that represents uncollected taxes. The capital transfer has been allocated between tax headings in proportion to the reported tax revenue.

StatLink http://dx.doi.org/10.1787/888933859646

Table 3.19. Gross domestic product for tax reporting years at market prices, in billions of national currency

		1965	1990	2000	2007	2010	2012	2014	2015	2016	2017p
Australia[1]	AUD	24.3	414.5	704.8	1 175.7	1 414.2	1 533.9	1 621.4	1 659.6	1 754.7	1 855.3
Austria	EUR	18.5	137.5	213.6	284.0	295.9	318.7	333.1	344.5	353.3	369.7
Belgium	EUR	21.0	171.0	258.2	344.7	365.1	387.5	400.1	410.3	422.7	437.2
Canada	CAD	61.1	693.6	1 121.7	1 573.5	1 662.1	1 822.8	1 990.2	1 994.9	2 035.5	2 145.2
Chile	CLP	..	10 522.7	42 005.2	90 702.9	111 508.6	129 947.3	148 623.7	159 605.9	169 263.9	179 776.2
Czech Republic	CZK	..	726.7	2 379.4	3 840.1	3 962.5	4 059.9	4 313.8	4 595.8	4 768.0	5 045.2
Denmark	DKK	71.5	855.6	1 326.9	1 738.8	1 810.9	1 895.0	1 981.2	2 027.1	2 066.0	2 149.6
Estonia	EUR	..	..	6.2	16.2	14.7	17.9	20.1	20.7	21.7	23.6
Finland	EUR	4.5	91.0	136.3	186.6	187.1	199.8	205.5	209.6	216.1	223.8
France	EUR	76.4	1 053.5	1 478.6	1 941.4	1 995.3	2 088.8	2 149.8	2 198.4	2 228.6	2 291.7
Germany	EUR	234.8	1 306.7	2 116.5	2 513.2	2 580.1	2 758.3	2 938.6	3 048.9	3 159.8	3 277.3
Greece	EUR	0.7	45.5	141.2	232.7	226.0	191.2	178.7	176.3	174.2	177.7
Hungary	HUF	..	..	13 350.1	25 680.2	27 224.6	28 781.1	32 591.7	34 324.1	35 420.3	38 183.3
Iceland	ISK	0.2	371.4	701.8	1 365.6	1 627.1	1 787.7	2 020.5	2 235.0	2 453.0	2 554.6
Ireland	EUR	1.3	37.9	108.4	197.2	167.7	175.2	195.3	262.5	273.2	294.1
Israel	ILS	..	118.9	539.6	734.1	873.5	992.1	1 103.5	1 162.5	1 220.3	1 262.9
Italy	EUR	22.3	728.5	1 239.3	1 609.6	1 604.5	1 613.3	1 621.8	1 652.6	1 680.9	1 716.9
Japan[1]	JPY	35 100.0	463 919.2	528 512.7	530 997.3	499 281.0	494 478.1	518 468.6	533 894.9	539 373.2	548 664.8
Korea	KRW	831.3	197 712.3	635 184.6	1 043 257.8	1 265 308.0	1 377 456.7	1 486 079.3	1 564 123.9	1 641 786.0	1 730 398.5
Latvia	EUR	..	..	6.9	22.6	17.9	21.9	23.6	24.3	24.9	26.9
Lithuania	EUR	..	..	13.4	29.0	28.0	33.3	36.6	37.4	38.7	41.9
Luxembourg	EUR	1.0	11.0	23.1	37.2	40.2	44.1	50.0	52.1	53.0	55.4
Mexico	MXN	..	843.6	6 693.7	11 504.1	13 366.4	15 817.8	17 471.5	18 536.5	20 099.6	21 766.9
Netherlands	EUR	35.6	263.0	452.0	619.2	639.2	653.0	671.6	690.0	708.3	737.0
New Zealand[1]	NZD	4.1	75.9	122.2	189.1	205.8	218.8	245.4	258.2	274.3	289.3
Norway	NOK	57.2	749.9	1 507.9	2 351.0	2 593.7	2 968.3	3 146.7	3 118.1	3 119.3	3 304.4
Poland	PLN	..	62.7	747.0	1 187.6	1 445.3	1 629.4	1 719.8	1 799.4	1 858.5	1 982.1
Portugal	EUR	0.6	56.0	128.5	175.5	179.9	168.4	173.1	179.8	185.5	193.1
Slovak Republic	EUR	..	10.0	31.6	63.1	67.6	72.7	76.1	78.9	81.2	85.0
Slovenia	EUR	..	0.9	18.9	35.2	36.3	36.1	37.6	38.8	40.4	43.3
Spain	EUR	8.7	327.8	646.3	1 080.8	1 080.9	1 039.8	1 037.8	1 080.0	1 118.5	1 163.7
Sweden	SEK	127.5	1 528.0	2 380.4	3 297.1	3 520.0	3 684.8	3 936.8	4 199.9	4 404.8	4 599.6
Switzerland	CHF	68.1	358.5	459.4	576.1	608.8	626.4	649.7	653.7	659.0	668.5
Turkey	TRY	0.0	0.5	170.7	880.5	1 160.0	1 569.7	2 044.5	2 338.6	2 608.5	3 104.9
United Kingdom	GBP	36.4	615.7	1 089.3	1 541.4	1 587.5	1 694.4	1 844.3	1 895.8	1 969.5	2 040.7
United States	USD	710.7	5 979.6	10 284.8	14 477.6	14 964.4	16 155.3	17 427.6	18 120.7	18 624.5	19 390.6

.. Not available

1. GDP is fiscal year. The year Y is calculated (at annual rate) as the average of: Q2(Y) to Q1(Y+1) for Japan; and Q3(Y) to Q2(Y+1) for Australia and New Zealand.

Source: OECD National Accounts.

StatLink http://dx.doi.org/10.1787/888933859665

Table 3.20. Exchange rates used, national currency per US dollar at market exchange rates

		1965	1990	2000	2007	2010	2012	2014	2015	2016	2017p
Australia	AUD	0.893	1.282	1.727	1.195	1.090	0.966	1.109	1.331	1.345	1.305
Austria	EUR	..	0.788	1.085	0.730	0.755	0.778	0.754	0.901	0.904	0.887
Belgium	EUR	..	0.788	1.085	0.730	0.755	0.778	0.754	0.901	0.904	0.887
Canada	CAD	1.078	1.167	1.485	1.074	1.030	0.999	1.105	1.278	1.325	1.298
Chile	CLP	0.003	304.903	539.388	522.228	509.982	485.984	570.636	654.322	676.541	648.677
Czech Republic	CZK	..	..	38.637	20.289	19.080	19.538	20.758	24.593	24.441	23.385
Denmark	DKK	6.915	6.186	8.088	5.443	5.622	5.790	5.619	6.725	6.731	6.602
Estonia	EUR	..	..	1.085	0.730	0.755	0.778	0.754	0.901	0.904	0.887
Finland	EUR	..	0.788	1.085	0.730	0.755	0.778	0.754	0.901	0.904	0.887
France	EUR	..	0.788	1.085	0.730	0.755	0.778	0.754	0.901	0.904	0.887
Germany	EUR	..	0.788	1.085	0.730	0.755	0.778	0.754	0.901	0.904	0.887
Greece	EUR	..	0.788	1.085	0.730	0.755	0.778	0.754	0.901	0.904	0.887
Hungary	HUF	..	..	282.286	183.595	207.764	224.823	232.619	279.194	281.521	274.476
Iceland	ISK	0.431	58.378	78.845	64.075	122.242	125.118	116.688	131.896	120.835	106.823
Ireland	EUR	0.454	0.788	1.085	0.730	0.755	0.778	0.754	0.901	0.904	0.887
Israel	ILS	0.000	2.016	4.077	4.109	3.731	3.850	3.577	3.887	3.839	3.599
Italy	EUR	..	0.788	1.085	0.730	0.755	0.778	0.754	0.901	0.904	0.887
Japan	JPY	361.491	144.796	107.835	117.755	87.761	79.814	105.848	121.002	108.803	112.183
Korea	KRW	266.250	707.995	1 130.640	929.450	1 155.431	1 125.935	1 053.064	1 131.309	1 160.589	1 130.635
Latvia	EUR	..	..	1.085	0.730	0.755	0.778	0.754	0.901	0.904	0.887
Lithuania	EUR	..	..	1.085	0.730	0.755	0.778	0.754	0.901	0.904	0.887
Luxembourg	EUR	..	0.788	1.085	0.730	0.755	0.778	0.754	0.901	0.904	0.887
Mexico	MXN	0.013	2.841	9.453	10.929	12.632	13.150	13.305	15.874	18.627	18.871
Netherlands	EUR	..	0.788	1.085	0.730	0.755	0.778	0.754	0.901	0.904	0.887
New Zealand	NZD	0.722	1.678	2.205	1.361	1.388	1.235	1.206	1.434	1.437	1.407
Norway	NOK	7.151	6.258	8.797	5.858	6.042	5.815	6.302	8.064	8.400	8.271
Poland	PLN	..	..	4.346	2.765	3.015	3.252	3.154	3.770	3.944	3.779
Portugal	EUR	..	0.788	1.085	0.730	0.755	0.778	0.754	0.901	0.904	0.887
Slovak Republic	EUR	..	..	1.085	0.730	0.755	0.778	0.754	0.901	0.904	0.887
Slovenia	EUR	..	..	1.085	0.730	0.755	0.778	0.754	0.901	0.904	0.887
Spain	EUR	..	0.788	1.085	0.730	0.755	0.778	0.754	0.901	0.904	0.887
Sweden	SEK	5.158	5.918	9.161	6.758	7.202	6.769	6.860	8.429	8.556	8.547
Switzerland	CHF	4.328	1.389	1.688	1.200	1.043	0.937	0.915	0.962	0.985	0.985
Turkey	TRY	0.000	0.003	0.624	1.300	1.499	1.792	2.189	2.723	3.022	3.649
United Kingdom	GBP	0.358	0.563	0.661	0.500	0.647	0.631	0.607	0.654	0.741	0.777
United States	USD	1.000	1.000	1.000	1.000	1.000	1.000	1.000	1.000	1.000	1.000

.. Not available

Source: OECD Financial indicators data.

StatLink http://dx.doi.org/10.1787/888933859684

Chapter 4. Country tables, 1990-2016

Chapter 4 provides a summary of tax revenues by category and by level of government for each OECD country from 1990-2016.

4.1. Tax revenue and % of GDP by selected tax category and by level of government

In all of the following tables the symbol (…) indicates not available/or not applicable. The main series in this chapter cover the years 1990 to 2016. Figures referring to 1965-1989, 1991-1999, 2001-2009 and 2011-2014 have been omitted because of lack of space. A complete series is, however, available on line. Data for 1955 and 1960 (for nineteen OECD countries) are provided in part V of the 1998 edition of this Report.

The Gross Domestic Product (GDP) figures are based on the 2008 System of National Accounts (SNA) for all OECD countries.

Box 4.1. Treatment of capital transfers

Some tables refer to the treatment of the capital transfers that some countries make to account for taxes that have been assessed but not collected. The capital transfer has been subtracted from the total tax revenue and this reduction has been allocated between tax headings in proportion to their tax revenues.

This applies to the following countries:

- Denmark from 1971.
- France from 1992.
- Greece for 1999 and 2000.
- Lithuania from 1999.
- Spain from 1995.

Table 4.1. Australia, tax revenue and % of GDP by selected tax category

	Billion AUD					% of GDP				
	1990	2000	2010	2015	2016	1990	2000	2010	2015	2016
Total tax revenue	**116.5**	**214.8**	**358.0**	**463.4**	**487.1**	**28.1**	**30.5**	**25.3**	**27.9**	**27.8**
1000 Taxes on income, profits and capital gains	**66.5**	**124.4**	**202.2**	**262.4**	**278.8**	**16.1**	**17.7**	**14.3**	**15.8**	**15.9**
1100 Of individuals	50.1	81.0	138.2	191.7	198.5	12.1	11.5	9.8	11.6	11.3
1200 Corporate	16.5	43.4	64.0	70.6	80.2	4.0	6.2	4.5	4.3	4.6
1300 Unallocable between 1100 and 1200	0.0	0.0	0.0	0.0	0.0	0.0	0.0	0.0	0.0	0.0
2000 Social security contributions	**0.0**	**0.0**	**0.0**	**0.0**	**0.0**	**0.0**	**0.0**	**0.0**	**0.0**	**0.0**
2100 Employees	0.0	0.0	0.0	0.0	0.0	0.0	0.0	0.0	0.0	0.0
2200 Employers	0.0	0.0	0.0	0.0	0.0	0.0	0.0	0.0	0.0	0.0
2300 Self-employed or non-employed	0.0	0.0	0.0	0.0	0.0	0.0	0.0	0.0	0.0	0.0
2400 Unallocable between 2100, 2200 and 2300	0.0	0.0	0.0	0.0	0.0	0.0	0.0	0.0	0.0	0.0
3000 Taxes on payroll and workforce	**7.1**	**9.6**	**18.5**	**23.4**	**23.8**	**1.7**	**1.4**	**1.3**	**1.4**	**1.4**
4000 Taxes on property	**10.4**	**18.8**	**33.5**	**49.6**	**52.6**	**2.5**	**2.7**	**2.4**	**3.0**	**3.0**
4100 Recurrent taxes on immovable property	6.1	9.1	19.9	27.1	29.2	1.5	1.3	1.4	1.6	1.7
4200 Recurrent taxes on net wealth	0.0	0.0	0.0	0.0	0.0	0.0	0.0	0.0	0.0	0.0
4300 Estate, inheritance and gift taxes	0.0	0.0	0.0	0.0	0.0	0.0	0.0	0.0	0.0	0.0
4400 Taxes on financial and capital transactions	4.3	9.8	13.6	22.5	23.4	1.0	1.4	1.0	1.4	1.3
4500 Non-recurrent taxes	0.0	0.0	0.0	0.0	0.0	0.0	0.0	0.0	0.0	0.0
4600 Other recurrent taxes on property	0.0	0.0	0.0	0.0	0.0	0.0	0.0	0.0	0.0	0.0
5000 Taxes on goods and services	**32.4**	**61.9**	**103.8**	**128.0**	**131.9**	**7.8**	**8.8**	**7.3**	**7.7**	**7.5**
5100 Taxes on production, sale, transfer, etc	27.2	56.2	92.0	110.2	113.2	6.6	8.0	6.5	6.6	6.4
5110 General taxes	9.4	25.8	49.3	61.8	64.3	2.3	3.7	3.5	3.7	3.7
5111 Value added taxes	0.0	23.9	48.1	60.3	62.7	0.0	3.4	3.4	3.6	3.6
5120 Taxes on specific goods and services	17.8	30.3	42.7	48.4	48.9	4.3	4.3	3.0	2.9	2.8
5121 Excises	12.0	19.8	26.7	22.5	22.8	2.9	2.8	1.9	1.4	1.3
5200 Taxes on use of goods and perform activities	5.2	5.7	11.7	17.8	18.8	1.3	0.8	0.8	1.1	1.1
5300 Unallocable between 5100 and 5200	0.0	0.0	0.0	0.0	0.0	0.0	0.0	0.0	0.0	0.0
6000 Other taxes	**0.0**	**0.0**	**0.0**	**0.0**	**0.0**	**0.0**	**0.0**	**0.0**	**0.0**	**0.0**
Non-wastable tax credits										
Non-wastable tax credits against 1000	..	0.2	6.7	9.4	9.1	..	0.0	0.5	0.6	0.5
Transfer component	..	0.0	4.4	6.7	6.7	..	0.0	0.3	0.4	0.4
Tax expenditure component	..	0.2	2.4	2.8	2.4	..	0.0	0.2	0.2	0.1

.. Not available

Note: More detailed country data and country notes are available in online chapter 5 "Country Tables, 1965-2016": http://dx.doi.org/10.1787/rev_stats-2018-en. Full time series can be accessed at http://oe.cd/full-time-series.

Source: Australian Bureau of Statistics.

StatLink http://dx.doi.org/10.1787/888933859703

Table 4.2. Australia, tax revenue and % of GDP by level of government and main taxes

	Billion AUD					% of GDP				
	1990	2000	2010	2015	2016	1990	2000	2010	2015	2016
Federal or Central government										
Total tax revenue	**92.6**	**175.7**	**287.1**	**367.6**	**387.4**	**22.3**	**24.9**	**20.3**	**22.2**	**22.1**
1000 Taxes on income, profits and capital gains	66.5	124.4	202.2	262.4	278.8	16.1	17.7	14.3	15.8	15.9
2000 Social security contributions	0.0	0.0	0.0	0.0	0.0	0.0	0.0	0.0	0.0	0.0
3000 Taxes on payroll and workforce	1.3	0.1	0.5	0.7	0.6	0.3	0.0	0.0	0.0	0.0
4000 Taxes on property	0.2	0.0	0.0	0.0	0.0	0.1	0.0	0.0	0.0	0.0
5000 Taxes on goods and services	24.5	51.1	84.4	104.6	108.0	5.9	7.3	6.0	6.3	6.2
6000 Other taxes	0.0	0.0	0.0	0.0	0.0	0.0	0.0	0.0	0.0	0.0
State/Regional										
Total tax revenue	**19.7**	**32.7**	**58.4**	**79.1**	**82.3**	**4.7**	**4.6**	**4.1**	**4.8**	**4.7**
1000 Taxes on income, profits and capital gains	0.0	0.0	0.0	0.0	0.0	0.0	0.0	0.0	0.0	0.0
2000 Social security contributions	0.0	0.0	0.0	0.0	0.0	0.0	0.0	0.0	0.0	0.0
3000 Taxes on payroll and workforce	5.8	9.5	18.0	22.7	23.2	1.4	1.3	1.3	1.4	1.3
4000 Taxes on property	6.0	12.4	21.1	33.0	35.2	1.4	1.8	1.5	2.0	2.0
5000 Taxes on goods and services	7.9	10.8	19.3	23.4	23.9	1.9	1.5	1.4	1.4	1.4
6000 Other taxes	0.0	0.0	0.0	0.0	0.0	0.0	0.0	0.0	0.0	0.0
Local government										
Total tax revenue	**4.2**	**6.4**	**12.4**	**16.6**	**17.4**	**1.0**	**0.9**	**0.9**	**1.0**	**1.0**
1000 Taxes on income, profits and capital gains	0.0	0.0	0.0	0.0	0.0	0.0	0.0	0.0	0.0	0.0
2000 Social security contributions	0.0	0.0	0.0	0.0	0.0	0.0	0.0	0.0	0.0	0.0
3000 Taxes on payroll and workforce	0.0	0.0	0.0	0.0	0.0	0.0	0.0	0.0	0.0	0.0
4000 Taxes on property	4.2	6.4	12.4	16.6	17.4	1.0	0.9	0.9	1.0	1.0
5000 Taxes on goods and services	0.0	0.0	0.0	0.0	0.0	0.0	0.0	0.0	0.0	0.0
6000 Other taxes	0.0	0.0	0.0	0.0	0.0	0.0	0.0	0.0	0.0	0.0
Social Security Funds										
Total tax revenue	**0.0**	**0.0**	**0.0**	**0.0**	**0.0**	**0.0**	**0.0**	**0.0**	**0.0**	**0.0**
1000 Taxes on income, profits and capital gains	0.0	0.0	0.0	0.0	0.0	0.0	0.0	0.0	0.0	0.0
2000 Social security contributions	0.0	0.0	0.0	0.0	0.0	0.0	0.0	0.0	0.0	0.0
3000 Taxes on payroll and workforce	0.0	0.0	0.0	0.0	0.0	0.0	0.0	0.0	0.0	0.0
4000 Taxes on property	0.0	0.0	0.0	0.0	0.0	0.0	0.0	0.0	0.0	0.0
5000 Taxes on goods and services	0.0	0.0	0.0	0.0	0.0	0.0	0.0	0.0	0.0	0.0
6000 Other taxes	0.0	0.0	0.0	0.0	0.0	0.0	0.0	0.0	0.0	0.0

Note: More detailed country data and country notes are available in online chapter 6 "Tax revenues by sub-sectors of general government": http://dx.doi.org/10.1787/rev_stats-2018-en. Full time series can be accessed at http://oe.cd/full-time-series.
Source: Australian Bureau of Statistics.

StatLink http://dx.doi.org/10.1787/888933859722

Table 4.3. Austria, tax revenue and % of GDP by selected tax category

	Billion EUR					% of GDP				
	1990	2000	2010	2015	2016	1990	2000	2010	2015	2016
Total tax revenue	**54.0**	**90.3**	**121.2**	**148.5**	**149.2**	**39.3**	**42.3**	**41.0**	**43.1**	**42.2**
1000 Taxes on income, profits and capital gains	**13.8**	**25.6**	**34.0**	**44.8**	**41.8**	**10.0**	**12.0**	**11.5**	**13.0**	**11.8**
1100 Of individuals	11.3	19.9	27.1	35.8	32.3	8.2	9.3	9.2	10.4	9.1
1200 Corporate	1.9	4.2	5.5	7.7	8.4	1.4	1.9	1.9	2.2	2.4
1300 Unallocable between 1100 and 1200	0.5	1.5	1.4	1.3	1.1	0.4	0.7	0.5	0.4	0.3
2000 Social security contributions	**17.8**	**30.5**	**41.4**	**49.9**	**51.7**	**12.9**	**14.3**	**14.0**	**14.5**	**14.6**
2100 Employees	7.5	12.5	16.8	20.1	20.9	5.5	5.8	5.7	5.8	5.9
2200 Employers	8.8	14.7	19.4	23.3	24.2	6.4	6.9	6.6	6.8	6.8
2300 Self-employed or non-employed	1.5	3.4	5.2	6.5	6.6	1.1	1.6	1.7	1.9	1.9
2400 Unallocable between 2100, 2200 and 2300	0.0	0.0	0.0	0.0	0.0	0.0	0.0	0.0	0.0	0.0
3000 Taxes on payroll and workforce	**3.3**	**5.8**	**8.4**	**10.0**	**10.4**	**2.4**	**2.7**	**2.8**	**2.9**	**2.9**
4000 Taxes on property	**1.5**	**1.2**	**1.6**	**2.0**	**2.0**	**1.1**	**0.6**	**0.5**	**0.6**	**0.6**
4100 Recurrent taxes on immovable property	0.4	0.5	0.7	0.8	0.8	0.3	0.2	0.2	0.2	0.2
4200 Recurrent taxes on net wealth	0.6	0.0	0.0	0.0	0.0	0.5	0.0	0.0	0.0	0.0
4300 Estate, inheritance and gift taxes	0.1	0.1	0.0	0.0	0.0	0.1	0.1	0.0	0.0	0.0
4400 Taxes on financial and capital transactions	0.4	0.6	0.8	1.1	1.1	0.3	0.3	0.3	0.3	0.3
4500 Non-recurrent taxes	0.0	0.0	0.0	0.1	0.1	0.0	0.0	0.0	0.0	0.0
4600 Other recurrent taxes on property	0.0	0.0	0.0	0.0	0.0	0.0	0.0	0.0	0.0	0.0
5000 Taxes on goods and services	**17.0**	**26.1**	**34.4**	**40.6**	**42.2**	**12.4**	**12.2**	**11.6**	**11.8**	**11.9**
5100 Taxes on production, sale, transfer, etc	16.2	24.3	31.8	37.2	38.7	11.8	11.4	10.7	10.8	10.9
5110 General taxes	11.2	16.9	22.7	26.3	27.3	8.2	7.9	7.7	7.6	7.7
5111 Value added taxes	11.2	16.9	22.7	26.3	27.3	8.2	7.9	7.7	7.6	7.7
5120 Taxes on specific goods and services	4.9	7.4	9.1	10.9	11.3	3.5	3.4	3.1	3.2	3.2
5121 Excises	3.3	5.5	6.9	7.7	7.9	2.4	2.6	2.3	2.2	2.2
5200 Taxes on use of goods and perform activities	0.9	1.9	2.6	3.4	3.5	0.6	0.9	0.9	1.0	1.0
5300 Unallocable between 5100 and 5200	0.0	0.0	0.0	0.0	0.0	0.0	0.0	0.0	0.0	0.0
6000 Other taxes	**0.7**	**0.8**	**1.1**	**0.7**	**0.8**	**0.5**	**0.4**	**0.4**	**0.2**	**0.2**
Non-wastable tax credits										
Non-wastable tax credits against 1000	..	0.7	0.7	0.5	0.5	..	0.3	0.2	0.2	0.2
Transfer component	..	0.1	0.2	0.2	0.3	..	0.0	0.1	0.1	0.1
Tax expenditure component	..	0.6	0.4	0.3	0.2	..	0.3	0.1	0.1	0.1

.. Not available

Note: More detailed country data and country notes are available in online chapter 5 "Country Tables, 1965-2016": http://dx.doi.org/10.1787/rev_stats-2018-en. Full time series can be accessed at http://oe.cd/full-time-series.

Source: Statistics Austria.

StatLink http://dx.doi.org/10.1787/888933859741

Table 4.4. Austria, tax revenue and % of GDP by level of government and main taxes

	Billion EUR					% of GDP				
	1990	2000	2010	2015	2016	1990	2000	2010	2015	2016
Federal or Central government										
Total tax revenue	**27.2**	**60.5**	**80.7**	**99.6**	**98.5**	**19.8**	**28.3**	**27.3**	**28.9**	**27.9**
1000 Taxes on income, profits and capital gains	8.6	24.9	33.1	43.7	40.6	6.3	11.7	11.2	12.7	11.5
2000 Social security contributions	2.4	5.1	6.3	7.5	7.8	1.7	2.4	2.1	2.2	2.2
3000 Taxes on payroll and workforce	2.6	3.9	5.8	6.9	7.1	1.9	1.8	1.9	2.0	2.0
4000 Taxes on property	0.9	0.7	0.9	1.2	1.2	0.6	0.3	0.3	0.4	0.3
5000 Taxes on goods and services	12.3	25.3	33.7	39.7	41.2	8.9	11.8	11.4	11.5	11.7
6000 Other taxes	0.5	0.6	0.9	0.5	0.5	0.4	0.3	0.3	0.2	0.1
State/Regional										
Total tax revenue	**5.8**	**1.4**	**2.0**	**2.3**	**2.4**	**4.2**	**0.7**	**0.7**	**0.7**	**0.7**
1000 Taxes on income, profits and capital gains	2.8	0.6	0.9	1.1	1.1	2.0	0.3	0.3	0.3	0.3
2000 Social security contributions	0.2	0.4	0.5	0.5	0.5	0.2	0.2	0.2	0.1	0.1
3000 Taxes on payroll and workforce	0.0	0.1	0.2	0.2	0.2	0.0	0.1	0.1	0.1	0.1
4000 Taxes on property	0.1	0.0	0.0	0.0	0.0	0.0	0.0	0.0	0.0	0.0
5000 Taxes on goods and services	2.7	0.2	0.3	0.4	0.4	2.0	0.1	0.1	0.1	0.1
6000 Other taxes	0.0	0.1	0.1	0.1	0.1	0.0	0.0	0.0	0.0	0.0
Local government										
Total tax revenue	**6.1**	**3.2**	**3.8**	**4.4**	**4.5**	**4.4**	**1.5**	**1.3**	**1.3**	**1.3**
1000 Taxes on income, profits and capital gains	2.4	0.0	0.0	0.0	0.0	1.8	0.0	0.0	0.0	0.0
2000 Social security contributions	0.2	0.3	0.3	0.3	0.3	0.1	0.1	0.1	0.1	0.1
3000 Taxes on payroll and workforce	0.7	1.8	2.4	3.0	3.1	0.5	0.8	0.8	0.9	0.9
4000 Taxes on property	0.5	0.5	0.6	0.7	0.7	0.4	0.2	0.2	0.2	0.2
5000 Taxes on goods and services	2.1	0.6	0.4	0.4	0.4	1.5	0.3	0.1	0.1	0.1
6000 Other taxes	0.2	0.1	0.1	0.1	0.1	0.1	0.0	0.0	0.0	0.0
Social Security Funds										
Total tax revenue	**15.0**	**24.8**	**34.4**	**41.6**	**43.2**	**10.9**	**11.6**	**11.6**	**12.1**	**12.2**
1000 Taxes on income, profits and capital gains	0.0	0.0	0.0	0.0	0.0	0.0	0.0	0.0	0.0	0.0
2000 Social security contributions	15.0	24.8	34.4	41.6	43.2	10.9	11.6	11.6	12.1	12.2
3000 Taxes on payroll and workforce	0.0	0.0	0.0	0.0	0.0	0.0	0.0	0.0	0.0	0.0
4000 Taxes on property	0.0	0.0	0.0	0.0	0.0	0.0	0.0	0.0	0.0	0.0
5000 Taxes on goods and services	0.0	0.0	0.0	0.0	0.0	0.0	0.0	0.0	0.0	0.0
6000 Other taxes	0.0	0.0	0.0	0.0	0.0	0.0	0.0	0.0	0.0	0.0

Note: More detailed country data and country notes are available in online chapter 6 "Tax revenues by sub-sectors of general government": http://dx.doi.org/10.1787/rev_stats-2018-en. Full time series can be accessed at http://oe.cd/full-time-series.

Source: Statistics Austria.

StatLink http://dx.doi.org/10.1787/888933859760

Table 4.5. Belgium, tax revenue and % of GDP by selected tax category

	Billion EUR					% of GDP				
	1990	2000	2010	2015	2016	1990	2000	2010	2015	2016
Total tax revenue	**70.4**	**112.4**	**155.6**	**183.9**	**186.3**	**41.2**	**43.5**	**42.6**	**44.8**	**44.1**
1000 Taxes on income, profits and capital gains	**26.0**	**43.4**	**53.2**	**65.6**	**66.2**	**15.2**	**16.8**	**14.6**	**16.0**	**15.7**
1100 Of individuals	22.5	35.3	44.0	51.9	51.6	13.2	13.7	12.0	12.6	12.2
1200 Corporate	3.4	8.1	9.2	13.6	14.6	2.0	3.1	2.5	3.3	3.5
1300 Unallocable between 1100 and 1200	0.0	0.1	0.0	0.1	0.1	0.0	0.0	0.0	0.0	0.0
2000 Social security contributions	**23.4**	**34.6**	**50.4**	**58.6**	**57.9**	**13.7**	**13.4**	**13.8**	**14.3**	**13.7**
2100 Employees	7.2	10.9	15.0	17.0	17.1	4.2	4.2	4.1	4.1	4.0
2200 Employers	14.7	20.8	30.8	36.2	35.2	8.6	8.1	8.4	8.8	8.3
2300 Self-employed or non-employed	1.5	2.9	4.6	5.5	5.7	0.9	1.1	1.3	1.3	1.3
2400 Unallocable between 2100, 2200 and 2300	0.0	0.0	0.0	0.0	0.0	0.0	0.0	0.0	0.0	0.0
3000 Taxes on payroll and workforce	**0.0**	**0.0**	**0.0**	**0.0**	**0.0**	**0.0**	**0.0**	**0.0**	**0.0**	**0.0**
4000 Taxes on property	**2.7**	**5.3**	**11.3**	**14.4**	**14.9**	**1.6**	**2.0**	**3.1**	**3.5**	**3.5**
4100 Recurrent taxes on immovable property	0.6	1.2	4.6	5.4	5.6	0.4	0.5	1.3	1.3	1.3
4200 Recurrent taxes on net wealth	0.0	0.1	0.2	0.7	1.0	0.0	0.0	0.1	0.2	0.2
4300 Estate, inheritance and gift taxes	0.5	1.1	2.3	3.0	2.9	0.3	0.4	0.6	0.7	0.7
4400 Taxes on financial and capital transactions	1.5	2.7	3.5	4.4	4.5	0.9	1.0	1.0	1.1	1.1
4500 Non-recurrent taxes	0.0	0.1	0.3	0.6	0.4	0.0	0.0	0.1	0.2	0.1
4600 Other recurrent taxes on property	0.1	0.2	0.3	0.3	0.4	0.1	0.1	0.1	0.1	0.1
5000 Taxes on goods and services	**18.4**	**28.1**	**39.4**	**43.8**	**45.7**	**10.7**	**10.9**	**10.8**	**10.7**	**10.8**
5100 Taxes on production, sale, transfer, etc	17.4	26.0	37.0	41.4	43.2	10.2	10.1	10.1	10.1	10.2
5110 General taxes	11.6	18.2	25.5	27.8	29.0	6.8	7.1	7.0	6.8	6.9
5111 Value added taxes	11.5	18.1	25.3	27.6	28.7	6.8	7.0	6.9	6.7	6.8
5120 Taxes on specific goods and services	5.8	7.8	11.5	13.6	14.3	3.4	3.0	3.1	3.3	3.4
5121 Excises	3.5	5.7	7.8	8.6	9.4	2.0	2.2	2.1	2.1	2.2
5200 Taxes on use of goods and perform activities	1.0	2.1	2.4	2.5	2.5	0.6	0.8	0.7	0.6	0.6
5300 Unallocable between 5100 and 5200	0.0	0.0	0.0	0.0	0.0	0.0	0.0	0.0	0.0	0.0
6000 Other taxes	**0.0**	**0.0**	**0.0**	**0.0**	**0.0**	**0.0**	**0.0**	**0.0**	**0.0**	**0.0**
Non-wastable tax credits										
Non-wastable tax credits against 1000	..	..	1.0	0.8	0.8	..	..	0.3	0.2	0.2
Transfer component	..	..	0.4	0.3	0.3	..	..	0.1	0.1	0.1
Tax expenditure component	..	..	0.6	0.5	0.5	..	..	0.2	0.1	0.1

.. Not available

Note: More detailed country data and country notes are available in online chapter 5 "Country Tables, 1965-2016": http://dx.doi.org/10.1787/rev_stats-2018-en. Full time series can be accessed at http://oe.cd/full-time-series.

Source: Federal Ministry of Finance.

StatLink http://dx.doi.org/10.1787/888933859779

Table 4.6. Belgium, tax revenue and % of GDP by level of government and main taxes

	Billion EUR					% of GDP				
	1990	2000	2010	2015	2016	1990	2000	2010	2015	2016
Federal or Central government										
Total tax revenue	**42.5**	**69.4**	**87.8**	**100.0**	**94.4**	**24.9**	**26.9**	**24.0**	**24.4**	**22.3**
1000 Taxes on income, profits and capital gains	23.9	39.6	49.3	57.1	52.0	13.9	15.3	13.5	13.9	12.3
2000 Social security contributions	0.9	1.3	2.5	2.3	0.1	0.5	0.5	0.7	0.6	0.0
3000 Taxes on payroll and workforce	0.0	0.0	0.0	0.0	0.0	0.0	0.0	0.0	0.0	0.0
4000 Taxes on property	1.1	2.3	0.9	1.9	2.1	0.6	0.9	0.3	0.5	0.5
5000 Taxes on goods and services	16.7	26.3	35.0	38.6	40.2	9.8	10.2	9.6	9.4	9.5
6000 Other taxes	0.0	0.0	0.0	0.0	0.0	0.0	0.0	0.0	0.0	0.0
State/Regional										
Total tax revenue	**1.2**	**2.4**	**8.1**	**14.1**	**19.9**	**0.7**	**0.9**	**2.2**	**3.4**	**4.7**
1000 Taxes on income, profits and capital gains	0.0	0.1	0.0	4.3	9.7	0.0	0.0	0.0	1.0	2.3
2000 Social security contributions	0.0	0.0	0.0	0.0	0.2	0.0	0.0	0.0	0.0	0.1
3000 Taxes on payroll and workforce	0.0	0.0	0.0	0.0	0.0	0.0	0.0	0.0	0.0	0.0
4000 Taxes on property	0.9	1.9	5.6	7.1	7.1	0.5	0.7	1.5	1.7	1.7
5000 Taxes on goods and services	0.2	0.5	2.4	2.7	3.0	0.1	0.2	0.7	0.7	0.7
6000 Other taxes	0.0	0.0	0.0	0.0	0.0	0.0	0.0	0.0	0.0	0.0
Local government										
Total tax revenue	**3.1**	**4.6**	**7.9**	**8.9**	**9.4**	**1.8**	**1.8**	**2.2**	**2.2**	**2.2**
1000 Taxes on income, profits and capital gains	2.1	3.1	2.9	3.1	3.3	1.2	1.2	0.8	0.7	0.8
2000 Social security contributions	0.1	0.0	0.0	0.0	0.0	0.1	0.0	0.0	0.0	0.0
3000 Taxes on payroll and workforce	0.0	0.0	0.0	0.0	0.0	0.0	0.0	0.0	0.0	0.0
4000 Taxes on property	0.6	1.0	4.4	5.1	5.3	0.3	0.4	1.2	1.3	1.3
5000 Taxes on goods and services	0.3	0.4	0.6	0.7	0.6	0.2	0.2	0.2	0.2	0.2
6000 Other taxes	0.0	0.0	0.0	0.0	0.0	0.0	0.0	0.0	0.0	0.0
Social Security Funds										
Total tax revenue	**22.7**	**34.9**	**50.6**	**59.3**	**60.8**	**13.3**	**13.5**	**13.9**	**14.4**	**14.4**
1000 Taxes on income, profits and capital gains	0.0	0.6	1.0	1.1	1.2	0.0	0.2	0.3	0.3	0.3
2000 Social security contributions	22.4	33.3	47.9	56.3	57.6	13.1	12.9	13.1	13.7	13.6
3000 Taxes on payroll and workforce	0.0	0.0	0.0	0.0	0.0	0.0	0.0	0.0	0.0	0.0
4000 Taxes on property	0.1	0.2	0.3	0.3	0.3	0.1	0.1	0.1	0.1	0.1
5000 Taxes on goods and services	0.2	0.8	1.3	1.6	1.6	0.1	0.3	0.4	0.4	0.4
6000 Other taxes	0.0	0.0	0.0	0.0	0.0	0.0	0.0	0.0	0.0	0.0

Note: More detailed country data and country notes are available in online chapter 6 "Tax revenues by sub-sectors of general government": http://dx.doi.org/10.1787/rev_stats-2018-en. Full time series can be accessed at http://oe.cd/full-time-series.
Source: Federal Ministry of Finance.

StatLink http://dx.doi.org/10.1787/888933859798

Table 4.7. Canada, tax revenue and % of GDP by selected tax category

	Billion CAD					% of GDP				
	1990	2000	2010	2015	2016	1990	2000	2010	2015	2016
Total tax revenue	**244.2**	**390.2**	**516.6**	**651.9**	**665.9**	**35.2**	**34.8**	**31.1**	**32.7**	**32.7**
1000 Taxes on income, profits and capital gains	**118.6**	**195.3**	**241.0**	**314.9**	**318.1**	**17.1**	**17.4**	**14.5**	**15.8**	**15.6**
1100 Of individuals	99.7	143.7	180.9	240.3	241.5	14.4	12.8	10.9	12.0	11.9
1200 Corporate	17.2	47.6	54.1	68.0	70.0	2.5	4.2	3.3	3.4	3.4
1300 Unallocable between 1100 and 1200	1.7	4.0	6.0	6.6	6.7	0.2	0.4	0.4	0.3	0.3
2000 Social security contributions	**29.7**	**53.1**	**76.8**	**96.4**	**98.9**	**4.3**	**4.7**	**4.6**	**4.8**	**4.9**
2100 Employees	10.6	21.4	30.6	38.7	39.6	1.5	1.9	1.8	1.9	1.9
2200 Employers	18.4	30.3	43.5	54.4	55.9	2.7	2.7	2.6	2.7	2.7
2300 Self-employed or non-employed	0.6	1.4	2.6	3.3	3.4	0.1	0.1	0.2	0.2	0.2
2400 Unallocable between 2100, 2200 and 2300	0.0	0.0	0.0	0.0	0.0	0.0	0.0	0.0	0.0	0.0
3000 Taxes on payroll and workforce	**5.5**	**8.0**	**10.8**	**13.3**	**13.9**	**0.8**	**0.7**	**0.6**	**0.7**	**0.7**
4000 Taxes on property	**24.5**	**37.2**	**63.7**	**76.9**	**79.7**	**3.5**	**3.3**	**3.8**	**3.9**	**3.9**
4100 Recurrent taxes on immovable property	20.2	30.2	51.7	62.3	64.2	2.9	2.7	3.1	3.1	3.2
4200 Recurrent taxes on net wealth	1.9	4.2	1.5	0.4	0.4	0.3	0.4	0.1	0.0	0.0
4300 Estate, inheritance and gift taxes	0.0	0.0	0.2	0.3	0.3	0.0	0.0	0.0	0.0	0.0
4400 Taxes on financial and capital transactions	0.0	0.0	3.1	4.9	6.1	0.0	0.0	0.2	0.2	0.3
4500 Non-recurrent taxes	2.4	2.7	7.3	9.1	8.7	0.3	0.2	0.4	0.5	0.4
4600 Other recurrent taxes on property	0.0	0.0	0.0	0.0	0.0	0.0	0.0	0.0	0.0	0.0
5000 Taxes on goods and services	**63.1**	**94.5**	**123.8**	**149.7**	**154.6**	**9.1**	**8.4**	**7.4**	**7.5**	**7.6**
5100 Taxes on production, sale, transfer, etc	59.6	88.9	116.2	140.2	145.1	8.6	7.9	7.0	7.0	7.1
5110 General taxes	34.5	55.3	72.1	90.1	93.0	5.0	4.9	4.3	4.5	4.6
5111 Value added taxes	0.0	35.9	70.7	86.0	89.9	0.0	3.2	4.3	4.3	4.4
5120 Taxes on specific goods and services	25.2	33.6	44.0	50.1	52.1	3.6	3.0	2.6	2.5	2.6
5121 Excises	14.5	18.4	23.3	25.2	26.0	2.1	1.6	1.4	1.3	1.3
5200 Taxes on use of goods and perform activities	3.5	5.6	7.6	9.5	9.4	0.5	0.5	0.5	0.5	0.5
5300 Unallocable between 5100 and 5200	0.0	0.0	0.0	0.0	0.0	0.0	0.0	0.0	0.0	0.0
6000 Other taxes	**2.9**	**2.2**	**0.6**	**0.7**	**0.7**	**0.4**	**0.2**	**0.0**	**0.0**	**0.0**
Non-wastable tax credits										
Non-wastable tax credits against 1000	..	3.4	11.1	11.2	10.9	..	0.3	0.7	0.6	0.5
Transfer component	..	3.1	10.2	10.3	10.0	..	0.3	0.6	0.5	0.5
Tax expenditure component	..	0.3	0.9	1.0	1.0	..	0.0	0.1	0.0	0.0

.. Not available

Note: More detailed country data and country notes are available in online chapter 5 "Country Tables, 1965-2016": http://dx.doi.org/10.1787/rev_stats-2018-en. Full time series can be accessed at http://oe.cd/full-time-series.

Source: Statistics Canada.

StatLink http://dx.doi.org/10.1787/888933859817

Table 4.8. Canada, tax revenue and % of GDP by level of government and main taxes

	Billion CAD					% of GDP				
	1990	2000	2010	2015	2016	1990	2000	2010	2015	2016
Federal or Central government										
Total tax revenue	**101.7**	**184.4**	**212.8**	**268.3**	**270.8**	**14.7**	**16.4**	**12.8**	**13.4**	**13.3**
1000 Taxes on income, profits and capital gains	73.6	126.3	148.7	191.5	191.9	10.6	11.3	8.9	9.6	9.4
2000 Social security contributions	0.0	18.8	17.9	23.7	24.0	0.0	1.7	1.1	1.2	1.2
3000 Taxes on payroll and workforce	0.0	0.0	0.0	0.0	0.0	0.0	0.0	0.0	0.0	0.0
4000 Taxes on property	0.0	0.0	0.0	0.0	0.0	0.0	0.0	0.0	0.0	0.0
5000 Taxes on goods and services	28.1	39.4	46.2	53.1	54.8	4.0	3.5	2.8	2.7	2.7
6000 Other taxes	0.0	0.0	0.0	0.0	0.0	0.0	0.0	0.0	0.0	0.0
State/Regional										
Total tax revenue	**89.3**	**148.2**	**201.1**	**257.8**	**265.9**	**12.9**	**13.2**	**12.1**	**12.9**	**13.1**
1000 Taxes on income, profits and capital gains	44.9	69.0	92.2	123.4	126.2	6.5	6.2	5.5	6.2	6.2
2000 Social security contributions	0.0	8.3	11.7	13.9	14.6	0.0	0.7	0.7	0.7	0.7
3000 Taxes on payroll and workforce	5.5	8.0	10.8	13.3	13.9	0.8	0.7	0.6	0.7	0.7
4000 Taxes on property	4.2	8.4	9.8	11.8	12.7	0.6	0.7	0.6	0.6	0.6
5000 Taxes on goods and services	34.6	54.5	76.7	95.5	98.5	5.0	4.9	4.6	4.8	4.8
6000 Other taxes	0.0	0.0	0.0	0.0	0.0	0.0	0.0	0.0	0.0	0.0
Local government										
Total tax revenue	**23.5**	**31.5**	**55.4**	**67.0**	**68.9**	**3.4**	**2.8**	**3.3**	**3.4**	**3.4**
1000 Taxes on income, profits and capital gains	0.0	0.0	0.0	0.0	0.0	0.0	0.0	0.0	0.0	0.0
2000 Social security contributions	0.0	0.0	0.0	0.0	0.0	0.0	0.0	0.0	0.0	0.0
3000 Taxes on payroll and workforce	0.0	0.0	0.0	0.0	0.0	0.0	0.0	0.0	0.0	0.0
4000 Taxes on property	20.3	28.8	53.9	65.1	67.0	2.9	2.6	3.2	3.3	3.3
5000 Taxes on goods and services	0.4	0.6	0.9	1.2	1.2	0.1	0.1	0.1	0.1	0.1
6000 Other taxes	2.9	2.2	0.6	0.7	0.7	0.4	0.2	0.0	0.0	0.0
Social Security Funds										
Total tax revenue	**29.7**	**26.0**	**47.2**	**58.9**	**60.3**	**4.3**	**2.3**	**2.8**	**3.0**	**3.0**
1000 Taxes on income, profits and capital gains	0.0	0.0	0.0	0.0	0.0	0.0	0.0	0.0	0.0	0.0
2000 Social security contributions	29.7	26.0	47.2	58.9	60.3	4.3	2.3	2.8	3.0	3.0
3000 Taxes on payroll and workforce	0.0	0.0	0.0	0.0	0.0	0.0	0.0	0.0	0.0	0.0
4000 Taxes on property	0.0	0.0	0.0	0.0	0.0	0.0	0.0	0.0	0.0	0.0
5000 Taxes on goods and services	0.0	0.0	0.0	0.0	0.0	0.0	0.0	0.0	0.0	0.0
6000 Other taxes	0.0	0.0	0.0	0.0	0.0	0.0	0.0	0.0	0.0	0.0

Note: More detailed country data and country notes are available in online chapter 6 "Tax revenues by sub-sectors of general government": http://dx.doi.org/10.1787/rev_stats-2018-en. Full time series can be accessed at http://oe.cd/full-time-series.

Source: Statistics Canada.

StatLink http://dx.doi.org/10.1787/888933859836

Table 4.9. Chile, tax revenue and % of GDP by selected tax category

	Billion CLP					% of GDP				
	1990	2000	2010	2015	2016	1990	2000	2010	2015	2016
Total tax revenue	**1 777.2**	**7 902.0**	**21 845.7**	**32 532.4**	**34 129.3**	**16.9**	**18.8**	**19.6**	**20.4**	**20.2**
1000 Taxes on income, profits and capital gains	**413.0**	**1 841.6**	**8 329.1**	**11 840.5**	**11 444.6**	**3.9**	**4.4**	**7.5**	**7.4**	**6.8**
1100 Of individuals	99.2	604.1	1 492.8	3 199.9	2 990.7	0.9	1.4	1.3	2.0	1.8
1200 Corporate	219.6	882.9	4 448.7	6 839.1	7 146.7	2.1	2.1	4.0	4.3	4.2
1300 Unallocable between 1100 and 1200	94.2	354.6	2 387.5	1 801.5	1 307.3	0.9	0.8	2.1	1.1	0.8
2000 Social security contributions	**159.6**	**576.8**	**1 494.0**	**2 252.5**	**2 441.4**	**1.5**	**1.4**	**1.3**	**1.4**	**1.4**
2100 Employees	154.0	553.9	1 433.2	2 188.6	2 373.8	1.5	1.3	1.3	1.4	1.4
2200 Employers	5.5	22.8	60.8	63.9	67.6	0.1	0.1	0.1	0.0	0.0
2300 Self-employed or non-employed	0.0	0.0	0.0	0.0	0.0	0.0	0.0	0.0	0.0	0.0
2400 Unallocable between 2100, 2200 and 2300	0.0	0.0	0.0	0.0	0.0	0.0	0.0	0.0	0.0	0.0
3000 Taxes on payroll and workforce	**0.0**	**0.0**	**0.0**	**0.0**	**0.0**	**0.0**	**0.0**	**0.0**	**0.0**	**0.0**
4000 Taxes on property	**109.3**	**554.0**	**898.6**	**1 421.3**	**1 731.7**	**1.0**	**1.3**	**0.8**	**0.9**	**1.0**
4100 Recurrent taxes on immovable property	60.0	302.2	662.4	1 056.9	1 171.4	0.6	0.7	0.6	0.7	0.7
4200 Recurrent taxes on net wealth	0.0	0.0	0.0	0.0	0.0	0.0	0.0	0.0	0.0	0.0
4300 Estate, inheritance and gift taxes	3.4	10.9	39.3	92.2	100.5	0.0	0.0	0.0	0.1	0.1
4400 Taxes on financial and capital transactions	45.9	240.9	196.9	272.1	459.8	0.4	0.6	0.2	0.2	0.3
4500 Non-recurrent taxes	0.0	0.0	0.0	0.0	0.0	0.0	0.0	0.0	0.0	0.0
4600 Other recurrent taxes on property	0.0	0.0	0.0	0.0	0.0	0.0	0.0	0.0	0.0	0.0
5000 Taxes on goods and services	**1 118.7**	**5 041.8**	**11 185.2**	**17 597.4**	**18 629.6**	**10.6**	**12.0**	**10.0**	**11.0**	**11.0**
5100 Taxes on production, sale, transfer, etc	1 074.0	4 789.8	10 532.9	16 515.5	17 449.2	10.2	11.4	9.4	10.3	10.3
5110 General taxes	664.4	3 306.4	8 399.9	13 274.0	14 073.1	6.3	7.9	7.5	8.3	8.3
5111 Value added taxes	664.4	3 306.4	8 399.9	13 274.0	14 073.1	6.3	7.9	7.5	8.3	8.3
5120 Taxes on specific goods and services	409.6	1 483.5	2 133.0	3 241.5	3 376.2	3.9	3.5	1.9	2.0	2.0
5121 Excises	166.0	816.2	1 561.2	2 412.8	2 568.9	1.6	1.9	1.4	1.5	1.5
5200 Taxes on use of goods and perform activities	44.7	251.9	652.3	1 081.9	1 180.4	0.4	0.6	0.6	0.7	0.7
5300 Unallocable between 5100 and 5200	0.0	0.0	0.0	0.0	0.0	0.0	0.0	0.0	0.0	0.0
6000 Other taxes	**-23.4**	**-112.2**	**-61.1**	**-579.3**	**-118.0**	**-0.2**	**-0.3**	**-0.1**	**-0.4**	**-0.1**
Non-wastable tax credits										
Non-wastable tax credits against 1000	0.0	0.0	0.0	175.5	179.6	0.0	0.0	0.0	0.1	0.1
Transfer component	..	..	..	129.7	129.6	..	..	..	0.1	0.1
Tax expenditure component	..	..	..	45.8	50.1	..	..	..	0.0	0.0

.. Not available

Note: More detailed country data and country notes are available in online chapter 5 "Country Tables, 1965-2016": http://dx.doi.org/10.1787/rev_stats-2018-en. Full time series can be accessed at http://oe.cd/full-time-series.

Source: Servicio de Impuestos internos (Chile's Tax Service).

StatLink http://dx.doi.org/10.1787/888933859855

Table 4.10. Chile, tax revenue and % of GDP by level of government and main taxes

	Billion CLP					% of GDP				
	1990	2000	2010	2015	2016	1990	2000	2010	2015	2016
Federal or Central government										
Total tax revenue	**1 579.7**	**6 936.8**	**19 214.8**	**28 257.2**	**29 493.6**	**15.0**	**16.5**	**17.2**	**17.7**	**17.4**
1000 Taxes on income, profits and capital gains	413.0	1 841.6	8 329.1	11 840.5	11 444.6	3.9	4.4	7.5	7.4	6.8
2000 Social security contributions	66.7	232.7	371.4	434.7	483.1	0.6	0.6	0.3	0.3	0.3
3000 Taxes on payroll and workforce	0.0	0.0	0.0	0.0	0.0	0.0	0.0	0.0	0.0	0.0
4000 Taxes on property	59.7	255.4	245.0	379.6	576.8	0.6	0.6	0.2	0.2	0.3
5000 Taxes on goods and services	1 063.7	4 719.3	10 330.4	16 181.7	17 107.1	10.1	11.2	9.3	10.1	10.1
6000 Other taxes	-23.4	-112.2	-61.1	-579.3	-118.0	-0.2	-0.3	-0.1	-0.4	-0.1
State/Regional										
Total tax revenue	..	..	..	..	..	..	..	..	..	..
1000 Taxes on income, profits and capital gains	..	..	..	..	..	..	..	..	..	..
2000 Social security contributions	..	..	..	..	..	..	..	..	..	..
3000 Taxes on payroll and workforce	..	..	..	..	..	..	..	..	..	..
4000 Taxes on property	..	..	..	..	..	..	..	..	..	..
5000 Taxes on goods and services	..	..	..	..	..	..	..	..	..	..
6000 Other taxes	..	..	..	..	..	..	..	..	..	..
Local government										
Total tax revenue	**104.7**	**621.2**	**1 508.3**	**2 457.3**	**2 677.4**	**1.0**	**1.5**	**1.4**	**1.5**	**1.6**
1000 Taxes on income, profits and capital gains	0.0	0.0	0.0	0.0	0.0	0.0	0.0	0.0	0.0	0.0
2000 Social security contributions	0.0	0.0	0.0	0.0	0.0	0.0	0.0	0.0	0.0	0.0
3000 Taxes on payroll and workforce	0.0	0.0	0.0	0.0	0.0	0.0	0.0	0.0	0.0	0.0
4000 Taxes on property	49.6	298.7	653.6	1 041.7	1 154.9	0.5	0.7	0.6	0.7	0.7
5000 Taxes on goods and services	55.0	322.5	854.8	1 415.7	1 522.5	0.5	0.8	0.8	0.9	0.9
6000 Other taxes	0.0	0.0	0.0	0.0	0.0	0.0	0.0	0.0	0.0	0.0
Social Security Funds										
Total tax revenue	**92.8**	**344.0**	**1 122.6**	**1 817.8**	**1 958.4**	**0.9**	**0.8**	**1.0**	**1.1**	**1.2**
1000 Taxes on income, profits and capital gains	0.0	0.0	0.0	0.0	0.0	0.0	0.0	0.0	0.0	0.0
2000 Social security contributions	92.8	344.0	1 122.6	1 817.8	1 958.4	0.9	0.8	1.0	1.1	1.2
3000 Taxes on payroll and workforce	0.0	0.0	0.0	0.0	0.0	0.0	0.0	0.0	0.0	0.0
4000 Taxes on property	0.0	0.0	0.0	0.0	0.0	0.0	0.0	0.0	0.0	0.0
5000 Taxes on goods and services	0.0	0.0	0.0	0.0	0.0	0.0	0.0	0.0	0.0	0.0
6000 Other taxes	0.0	0.0	0.0	0.0	0.0	0.0	0.0	0.0	0.0	0.0

.. Not available

Note: More detailed country data and country notes are available in online chapter 6 "Tax revenues by sub-sectors of general government": http://dx.doi.org/10.1787/rev_stats-2018-en. Full time series can be accessed at http://oe.cd/full-time-series.

Source: Servicio de Impuestos internos (Chile's Tax Service).

StatLink http://dx.doi.org/10.1787/888933859874

Table 4.11. Czech Republic, tax revenue and % of GDP by selected tax category

	Billion CZK					% of GDP				
	1990	2000	2010	2015	2016	1990	2000	2010	2015	2016
Total tax revenue	..	**771.6**	**1 286.9**	**1 532.6**	**1 632.4**	..	**32.4**	**32.5**	**33.3**	**34.2**
1000 Taxes on income, profits and capital gains	..	**175.8**	**259.9**	**329.8**	**361.9**	..	**7.4**	**6.6**	**7.2**	**7.6**
1100 Of individuals	..	99.7	131.7	164.7	183.1	..	4.2	3.3	3.6	3.8
1200 Corporate	..	76.2	128.2	165.1	178.8	..	3.2	3.2	3.6	3.7
1300 Unallocable between 1100 and 1200	..	0.0	0.0	0.0	0.0	..	0.0	0.0	0.0	0.0
2000 Social security contributions	..	**341.5**	**576.0**	**659.7**	**699.6**	..	**14.4**	**14.5**	**14.4**	**14.7**
2100 Employees	..	77.3	116.8	133.9	143.7	..	3.2	2.9	2.9	3.0
2200 Employers	..	220.2	363.1	417.8	444.2	..	9.3	9.2	9.1	9.3
2300 Self-employed or non-employed	..	44.1	96.1	108.1	111.7	..	1.9	2.4	2.4	2.3
2400 Unallocable between 2100, 2200 and 2300	..	0.0	0.0	0.0	0.0	..	0.0	0.0	0.0	0.0
3000 Taxes on payroll and workforce	..	**0.0**	**0.0**	**0.0**	**0.0**	..	**0.0**	**0.0**	**0.0**	**0.0**
4000 Taxes on property	..	**10.9**	**16.4**	**21.9**	**23.4**	..	**0.5**	**0.4**	**0.5**	**0.5**
4100 Recurrent taxes on immovable property	..	4.5	8.8	10.3	10.6	..	0.2	0.2	0.2	0.2
4200 Recurrent taxes on net wealth	..	0.0	0.0	0.0	0.0	..	0.0	0.0	0.0	0.0
4300 Estate, inheritance and gift taxes	..	0.6	0.2	0.0	0.0	..	0.0	0.0	0.0	0.0
4400 Taxes on financial and capital transactions	..	5.8	7.4	11.6	12.8	..	0.2	0.2	0.3	0.3
4500 Non-recurrent taxes	..	0.0	0.0	0.0	0.0	..	0.0	0.0	0.0	0.0
4600 Other recurrent taxes on property	..	0.0	0.0	0.0	0.0	..	0.0	0.0	0.0	0.0
5000 Taxes on goods and services	..	**243.0**	**427.8**	**512.8**	**539.0**	..	**10.2**	**10.8**	**11.2**	**11.3**
5100 Taxes on production, sale, transfer, etc	..	226.4	402.1	487.4	512.7	..	9.5	10.1	10.6	10.8
5110 General taxes	..	141.2	263.5	333.3	353.9	..	5.9	6.6	7.3	7.4
5111 Value added taxes	..	141.2	263.5	333.3	353.9	..	5.9	6.6	7.3	7.4
5120 Taxes on specific goods and services	..	85.1	138.6	154.1	158.7	..	3.6	3.5	3.4	3.3
5121 Excises	..	71.4	138.4	153.8	158.4	..	3.0	3.5	3.3	3.3
5200 Taxes on use of goods and perform activities	..	16.6	25.7	25.5	26.3	..	0.7	0.7	0.6	0.6
5300 Unallocable between 5100 and 5200	..	0.0	0.0	0.0	0.0	..	0.0	0.0	0.0	0.0
6000 Other taxes	..	**0.4**	**0.1**	**0.4**	**0.6**	..	**0.0**	**0.0**	**0.0**	**0.0**
Non-wastable tax credits										
Non-wastable tax credits against 1000	..	0.0	25.7	31.4	32.8	..	0.0	0.6	0.7	0.7
Transfer component	..	..	7.8	8.9	8.6	..	..	0.2	0.2	0.2
Tax expenditure component	..	..	17.9	22.5	24.3	..	..	0.5	0.5	0.5

.. Not available

Note: More detailed country data and country notes are available in online chapter 5 "Country Tables, 1965-2016": http://dx.doi.org/10.1787/rev_stats-2018-en. Full time series can be accessed at http://oe.cd/full-time-series.

Source: Ministry of Finance, Economic Department.

StatLink http://dx.doi.org/10.1787/888933859893

Table 4.12. Czech Republic, tax revenue and % of GDP by level of government and main taxes

	Billion CZK					% of GDP				
	1990	2000	2010	2015	2016	1990	2000	2010	2015	2016
Federal or Central government										
Total tax revenue	..	**423.4**	**687.3**	**846.8**	**906.4**	..	**17.8**	**17.3**	**18.4**	**19.0**
1000 Taxes on income, profits and capital gains	..	175.8	259.9	329.8	361.9	..	7.4	6.6	7.2	7.6
2000 Social security contributions	..	0.0	0.0	0.0	0.0	..	0.0	0.0	0.0	0.0
3000 Taxes on payroll and workforce	..	0.0	0.0	0.0	0.0	..	0.0	0.0	0.0	0.0
4000 Taxes on property	..	6.4	7.6	11.6	12.9	..	0.3	0.2	0.3	0.3
5000 Taxes on goods and services	..	241.0	419.6	505.1	531.1	..	10.1	10.6	11.0	11.1
6000 Other taxes	..	0.1	0.1	0.4	0.6	..	0.0	0.0	0.0	0.0
State/Regional										
Total tax revenue	..	..	..	..	..	..	..	..	..	..
1000 Taxes on income, profits and capital gains	..	..	..	..	..	..	..	..	..	..
2000 Social security contributions	..	..	..	..	..	..	..	..	..	..
3000 Taxes on payroll and workforce	..	..	..	..	..	..	..	..	..	..
4000 Taxes on property	..	..	..	..	..	..	..	..	..	..
5000 Taxes on goods and services	..	..	..	..	..	..	..	..	..	..
6000 Other taxes	..	..	..	..	..	..	..	..	..	..
Local government										
Total tax revenue	..	**6.7**	**17.0**	**18.1**	**18.5**	..	**0.3**	**0.4**	**0.4**	**0.4**
1000 Taxes on income, profits and capital gains	..	0.0	0.0	0.0	0.0	..	0.0	0.0	0.0	0.0
2000 Social security contributions	..	0.0	0.0	0.0	0.0	..	0.0	0.0	0.0	0.0
3000 Taxes on payroll and workforce	..	0.0	0.0	0.0	0.0	..	0.0	0.0	0.0	0.0
4000 Taxes on property	..	4.5	8.7	10.3	10.6	..	0.2	0.2	0.2	0.2
5000 Taxes on goods and services	..	2.0	8.2	7.7	7.9	..	0.1	0.2	0.2	0.2
6000 Other taxes	..	0.3	0.0	0.0	0.0	..	0.0	0.0	0.0	0.0
Social Security Funds										
Total tax revenue	..	**341.5**	**576.0**	**659.7**	**699.6**	..	**14.4**	**14.5**	**14.4**	**14.7**
1000 Taxes on income, profits and capital gains	..	0.0	0.0	0.0	0.0	..	0.0	0.0	0.0	0.0
2000 Social security contributions	..	341.5	576.0	659.7	699.6	..	14.4	14.5	14.4	14.7
3000 Taxes on payroll and workforce	..	0.0	0.0	0.0	0.0	..	0.0	0.0	0.0	0.0
4000 Taxes on property	..	0.0	0.0	0.0	0.0	..	0.0	0.0	0.0	0.0
5000 Taxes on goods and services	..	0.0	0.0	0.0	0.0	..	0.0	0.0	0.0	0.0
6000 Other taxes	..	0.0	0.0	0.0	0.0	..	0.0	0.0	0.0	0.0

.. Not available

Note: More detailed country data and country notes are available in online chapter 6 "Tax revenues by sub-sectors of general government": http://dx.doi.org/10.1787/rev_stats-2018-en. Full time series can be accessed at http://oe.cd/full-time-series.

Source: Ministry of Finance, Economic Department.

StatLink http://dx.doi.org/10.1787/888933859912

Table 4.13. Denmark, tax revenue and % of GDP by selected tax category

	Billion DKK					% of GDP				
	1990	2000	2010	2015	2016	1990	2000	2010	2015	2016
Total tax revenue	**379.8**	**622.0**	**810.5**	**935.1**	**954.2**	**44.4**	**46.9**	**44.8**	**46.1**	**46.2**
1000 Taxes on income, profits and capital gains	**232.6**	**382.3**	**498.5**	**593.7**	**599.4**	**27.2**	**28.8**	**27.5**	**29.3**	**29.0**
1100 Of individuals	205.6	327.8	421.3	516.4	510.2	24.0	24.7	23.3	25.5	24.7
1200 Corporate	14.5	42.1	40.8	55.0	55.6	1.7	3.2	2.3	2.7	2.7
1300 Unallocable between 1100 and 1200	12.5	12.4	36.3	22.2	33.6	1.5	0.9	2.0	1.1	1.6
2000 Social security contributions	**0.1**	**8.4**	**1.8**	**1.4**	**1.2**	**0.0**	**0.6**	**0.1**	**0.1**	**0.1**
2100 Employees	0.1	8.2	0.9	0.8	0.7	0.0	0.6	0.0	0.0	0.0
2200 Employers	0.0	0.2	0.9	0.6	0.5	0.0	0.0	0.1	0.0	0.0
2300 Self-employed or non-employed	0.0	0.0	0.0	0.0	0.0	0.0	0.0	0.0	0.0	0.0
2400 Unallocable between 2100, 2200 and 2300	0.0	0.0	0.0	0.0	0.0	0.0	0.0	0.0	0.0	0.0
3000 Taxes on payroll and workforce	**2.5**	**2.2**	**4.1**	**5.7**	**5.8**	**0.3**	**0.2**	**0.2**	**0.3**	**0.3**
4000 Taxes on property	**16.2**	**20.7**	**33.5**	**38.9**	**38.6**	**1.9**	**1.6**	**1.8**	**1.9**	**1.9**
4100 Recurrent taxes on immovable property	8.9	13.6	24.2	28.1	28.4	1.0	1.0	1.3	1.4	1.4
4200 Recurrent taxes on net wealth	0.9	0.0	0.0	0.0	0.0	0.1	0.0	0.0	0.0	0.0
4300 Estate, inheritance and gift taxes	2.2	2.8	3.6	5.0	4.2	0.3	0.2	0.2	0.2	0.2
4400 Taxes on financial and capital transactions	4.1	4.2	5.7	5.7	5.9	0.5	0.3	0.3	0.3	0.3
4500 Non-recurrent taxes	0.1	0.1	0.0	0.0	0.0	0.0	0.0	0.0	0.0	0.0
4600 Other recurrent taxes on property	0.0	0.0	0.0	0.0	0.0	0.0	0.0	0.0	0.0	0.0
5000 Taxes on goods and services	**128.5**	**205.6**	**269.2**	**291.9**	**305.9**	**15.0**	**15.5**	**14.9**	**14.4**	**14.8**
5100 Taxes on production, sale, transfer, etc	122.5	194.8	249.6	268.9	281.7	14.3	14.7	13.8	13.3	13.6
5110 General taxes	79.9	121.4	170.6	184.9	195.1	9.3	9.1	9.4	9.1	9.4
5111 Value added taxes	71.5	121.4	170.6	184.9	195.1	8.4	9.1	9.4	9.1	9.4
5120 Taxes on specific goods and services	42.6	73.4	79.0	84.0	86.6	5.0	5.5	4.4	4.1	4.2
5121 Excises	38.0	68.7	73.6	79.6	82.0	4.4	5.2	4.1	3.9	4.0
5200 Taxes on use of goods and perform activities	4.4	7.4	14.6	16.1	16.1	0.5	0.6	0.8	0.8	0.8
5300 Unallocable between 5100 and 5200	1.6	3.4	4.9	7.0	8.0	0.2	0.3	0.3	0.3	0.4
6000 Other taxes	**0.0**	**0.4**	**0.2**	**0.3**	**0.3**	**0.0**	**0.0**	**0.0**	**0.0**	**0.0**
Non-wastable tax credits										
Non-wastable tax credits against 1000	..	..	5.0	4.2	4.2	..	..	0.3	0.2	0.2
Transfer component	..	..	0.2	0.2	0.2	..	..	0.0	0.0	0.0
Tax expenditure component	..	..	4.7	4.0	4.0	..	..	0.3	0.2	0.2

.. Not available

Note: More detailed country data and country notes are available in online chapter 5 "Country Tables, 1965-2016": http://dx.doi.org/10.1787/rev_stats-2018-en. Full time series can be accessed at http://oe.cd/full-time-series.

The total tax revenue has been reduced by the amount of any capital transfer that represents uncollected taxes. The capital transfer has been allocated between tax headings in proportion to the reported tax revenue. Therefore, the tax revenue amounts are different to those reported in the detailed country data available in online chapter 5 "Country Tables, 1965-2016".

Source: Danmarks Statistik.

StatLink http://dx.doi.org/10.1787/888933859931

Table 4.14. Denmark, tax revenue and % of GDP by level of government and main taxes

	Billion DKK					% of GDP				
	1990	2000	2010	2015	2016	1990	2000	2010	2015	2016
Federal or Central government										
Total tax revenue	**259.5**	**420.6**	**589.0**	**682.5**	**693.1**	**30.3**	**31.7**	**32.5**	**33.7**	**33.5**
1000 Taxes on income, profits and capital gains	123.7	204.2	305.4	372.9	370.2	14.5	15.4	16.9	18.4	17.9
2000 Social security contributions	0.1	1.4	0.9	0.8	0.7	0.0	0.1	0.1	0.0	0.0
3000 Taxes on payroll and workforce	2.5	2.2	4.1	5.7	5.8	0.3	0.2	0.2	0.3	0.3
4000 Taxes on property	7.5	7.1	9.3	10.8	10.1	0.9	0.5	0.5	0.5	0.5
5000 Taxes on goods and services	125.8	205.3	269.1	291.9	305.8	14.7	15.5	14.9	14.4	14.8
6000 Other taxes	0.0	0.4	0.2	0.3	0.3	0.0	0.0	0.0	0.0	0.0
State/Regional										
Total tax revenue	..	..	..	..	..	..	..	..	..	..
1000 Taxes on income, profits and capital gains	..	..	..	..	..	..	..	..	..	..
2000 Social security contributions	..	..	..	..	..	..	..	..	..	..
3000 Taxes on payroll and workforce	..	..	..	..	..	..	..	..	..	..
4000 Taxes on property	..	..	..	..	..	..	..	..	..	..
5000 Taxes on goods and services	..	..	..	..	..	..	..	..	..	..
6000 Other taxes	..	..	..	..	..	..	..	..	..	..
Local government										
Total tax revenue	**117.6**	**191.7**	**217.3**	**248.8**	**257.6**	**13.8**	**14.4**	**12.0**	**12.3**	**12.5**
1000 Taxes on income, profits and capital gains	108.9	178.1	193.1	220.7	229.2	12.7	13.4	10.7	10.9	11.1
2000 Social security contributions	0.0	0.0	0.0	0.0	0.0	0.0	0.0	0.0	0.0	0.0
3000 Taxes on payroll and workforce	0.0	0.0	0.0	0.0	0.0	0.0	0.0	0.0	0.0	0.0
4000 Taxes on property	8.7	13.6	24.2	28.1	28.4	1.0	1.0	1.3	1.4	1.4
5000 Taxes on goods and services	0.0	0.0	0.0	0.0	0.0	0.0	0.0	0.0	0.0	0.0
6000 Other taxes	0.0	0.0	0.0	0.0	0.0	0.0	0.0	0.0	0.0	0.0
Social Security Funds										
Total tax revenue	**0.0**	**7.1**	**0.9**	**0.5**	**0.5**	**0.0**	**0.5**	**0.1**	**0.0**	**0.0**
1000 Taxes on income, profits and capital gains	0.0	0.0	0.0	0.0	0.0	0.0	0.0	0.0	0.0	0.0
2000 Social security contributions	0.0	7.1	0.9	0.5	0.5	0.0	0.5	0.1	0.0	0.0
3000 Taxes on payroll and workforce	0.0	0.0	0.0	0.0	0.0	0.0	0.0	0.0	0.0	0.0
4000 Taxes on property	0.0	0.0	0.0	0.0	0.0	0.0	0.0	0.0	0.0	0.0
5000 Taxes on goods and services	0.0	0.0	0.0	0.0	0.0	0.0	0.0	0.0	0.0	0.0
6000 Other taxes	0.0	0.0	0.0	0.0	0.0	0.0	0.0	0.0	0.0	0.0

.. Not available

Note: More detailed country data and country notes are available in online chapter 6 "Tax revenues by sub-sectors of general government": http://dx.doi.org/10.1787/rev_stats-2018-en. Full time series can be accessed at http://oe.cd/full-time-series.

The total tax revenue has been reduced by the amount of any capital transfer that represents uncollected taxes. The capital transfer has been allocated between tax headings in proportion to the reported tax revenue. Therefore, the tax revenue amounts are different to those reported in the detailed country data available in online chapter 6 "Tax revenues by sub-sectors of general government".

Source: Danmarks Statistik.

StatLink http://dx.doi.org/10.1787/888933859950

Table 4.15. Estonia, tax revenue and % of GDP by selected tax category

	Billion EUR					% of GDP				
	1990	2000	2010	2015	2016	1990	2000	2010	2015	2016
Total tax revenue	..	**1.9**	**4.9**	**6.9**	**7.3**	..	**31.1**	**33.3**	**33.3**	**33.7**
1000 Taxes on income, profits and capital gains	..	**0.5**	**1.0**	**1.6**	**1.6**	..	**7.7**	**6.6**	**7.8**	**7.5**
1100 Of individuals	..	0.4	0.8	1.2	1.3	..	6.8	5.3	5.7	5.8
1200 Corporate	..	0.1	0.2	0.4	0.4	..	0.9	1.3	2.1	1.7
1300 Unallocable between 1100 and 1200	..	0.0	0.0	0.0	0.0	..	0.0	0.0	0.0	0.0
2000 Social security contributions	..	**0.7**	**1.9**	**2.3**	**2.4**	..	**10.9**	**12.8**	**11.1**	**11.2**
2100 Employees	..	0.0	0.1	0.1	0.1	..	0.0	0.8	0.5	0.5
2200 Employers	..	0.7	1.7	2.2	2.3	..	10.7	11.8	10.5	10.6
2300 Self-employed or non-employed	..	0.0	0.0	0.0	0.0	..	0.2	0.1	0.1	0.1
2400 Unallocable between 2100, 2200 and 2300	..	0.0	0.0	0.0	0.0	..	0.0	0.0	0.0	0.0
3000 Taxes on payroll and workforce	..	**0.0**	**0.0**	**0.0**	**0.0**	..	**0.0**	**0.0**	**0.0**	**0.0**
4000 Taxes on property	..	**0.0**	**0.1**	**0.1**	**0.1**	..	**0.4**	**0.3**	**0.3**	**0.3**
4100 Recurrent taxes on immovable property	..	0.0	0.1	0.1	0.1	..	0.4	0.3	0.3	0.3
4200 Recurrent taxes on net wealth	..	0.0	0.0	0.0	0.0	..	0.0	0.0	0.0	0.0
4300 Estate, inheritance and gift taxes	..	0.0	0.0	0.0	0.0	..	0.0	0.0	0.0	0.0
4400 Taxes on financial and capital transactions	..	0.0	0.0	0.0	0.0	..	0.0	0.0	0.0	0.0
4500 Non-recurrent taxes	..	0.0	0.0	0.0	0.0	..	0.0	0.0	0.0	0.0
4600 Other recurrent taxes on property	..	0.0	0.0	0.0	0.0	..	0.0	0.0	0.0	0.0
5000 Taxes on goods and services	..	**0.7**	**2.0**	**2.9**	**3.2**	..	**12.1**	**13.4**	**14.0**	**14.6**
5100 Taxes on production, sale, transfer, etc	..	0.7	1.9	2.8	3.0	..	11.7	13.0	13.5	13.9
5110 General taxes	..	0.5	1.3	1.9	2.0	..	8.4	8.6	9.1	9.1
5111 Value added taxes	..	0.5	1.3	1.9	2.0	..	8.4	8.5	9.1	9.1
5120 Taxes on specific goods and services	..	0.2	0.7	0.9	1.0	..	3.3	4.4	4.5	4.8
5121 Excises	..	0.2	0.6	0.9	1.0	..	3.0	4.2	4.2	4.6
5200 Taxes on use of goods and perform activities	..	0.0	0.1	0.1	0.1	..	0.4	0.4	0.5	0.7
5300 Unallocable between 5100 and 5200	..	0.0	0.0	0.0	0.0	..	0.0	0.0	0.0	0.0
6000 Other taxes	..	**0.0**	**0.0**	**0.0**	**0.0**	..	**0.0**	**0.0**	**0.0**	**0.0**
Non-wastable tax credits										
Non-wastable tax credits against 1000	..	..	..	..	..	..	..	..	..	..
Transfer component	..	..	..	..	..	..	..	..	..	..
Tax expenditure component	..	..	..	..	..	..	..	..	..	..

.. Not available

Note: More detailed country data and country notes are available in online chapter 5 "Country Tables, 1965-2016": http://dx.doi.org/10.1787/rev_stats-2018-en. Full time series can be accessed at http://oe.cd/full-time-series.

Source: Statistics Estonia.

StatLink http://dx.doi.org/10.1787/888933859969

Table 4.16. Estonia, tax revenue and % of GDP by level of government and main taxes

	Billion EUR					% of GDP				
	1990	2000	2010	2015	2016	1990	2000	2010	2015	2016
Federal or Central government										
Total tax revenue	..	**1.6**	**3.9**	**5.7**	**6.0**	..	**26.3**	**26.7**	**27.4**	**27.8**
1000 Taxes on income, profits and capital gains	..	0.5	1.0	1.6	1.6	..	7.7	6.6	7.8	7.5
2000 Social security contributions	..	0.4	1.0	1.2	1.3	..	6.6	6.8	5.7	5.8
3000 Taxes on payroll and workforce	..	0.0	0.0	0.0	0.0	..	0.0	0.0	0.0	0.0
4000 Taxes on property	..	0.0	0.0	0.0	0.0	..	0.0	0.0	0.0	0.0
5000 Taxes on goods and services	..	0.7	2.0	2.9	3.1	..	12.0	13.3	13.9	14.5
6000 Other taxes	..	0.0	0.0	0.0	0.0	..	0.0	0.0	0.0	0.0
State/Regional										
Total tax revenue	..	..	..	..	..	..	..	..	..	..
1000 Taxes on income, profits and capital gains	..	..	..	..	..	..	..	..	..	..
2000 Social security contributions	..	..	..	..	..	..	..	..	..	..
3000 Taxes on payroll and workforce	..	..	..	..	..	..	..	..	..	..
4000 Taxes on property	..	..	..	..	..	..	..	..	..	..
5000 Taxes on goods and services	..	..	..	..	..	..	..	..	..	..
6000 Other taxes	..	..	..	..	..	..	..	..	..	..
Local government										
Total tax revenue	..	**0.0**	**0.1**	**0.1**	**0.1**	..	**0.5**	**0.5**	**0.3**	**0.3**
1000 Taxes on income, profits and capital gains	..	0.0	0.0	0.0	0.0	..	0.0	0.0	0.0	0.0
2000 Social security contributions	..	0.0	0.0	0.0	0.0	..	0.0	0.0	0.0	0.0
3000 Taxes on payroll and workforce	..	0.0	0.0	0.0	0.0	..	0.0	0.0	0.0	0.0
4000 Taxes on property	..	0.0	0.1	0.1	0.1	..	0.4	0.3	0.3	0.3
5000 Taxes on goods and services	..	0.0	0.0	0.0	0.0	..	0.1	0.1	0.1	0.1
6000 Other taxes	..	0.0	0.0	0.0	0.0	..	0.0	0.0	0.0	0.0
Social Security Funds										
Total tax revenue	..	**0.3**	**0.9**	**1.1**	**1.2**	..	**4.3**	**5.9**	**5.4**	**5.4**
1000 Taxes on income, profits and capital gains	..	0.0	0.0	0.0	0.0	..	0.0	0.0	0.0	0.0
2000 Social security contributions	..	0.3	0.9	1.1	1.2	..	4.3	5.9	5.4	5.4
3000 Taxes on payroll and workforce	..	0.0	0.0	0.0	0.0	..	0.0	0.0	0.0	0.0
4000 Taxes on property	..	0.0	0.0	0.0	0.0	..	0.0	0.0	0.0	0.0
5000 Taxes on goods and services	..	0.0	0.0	0.0	0.0	..	0.0	0.0	0.0	0.0
6000 Other taxes	..	0.0	0.0	0.0	0.0	..	0.0	0.0	0.0	0.0

.. Not available

Note: More detailed country data and country notes are available in online chapter 6 "Tax revenues by sub-sectors of general government": http://dx.doi.org/10.1787/rev_stats-2018-en. Full time series can be accessed at http://oe.cd/full-time-series.

Source: Statistics Estonia.

StatLink http://dx.doi.org/10.1787/888933859988

Table 4.17. Finland, tax revenue and % of GDP by selected tax category

	Billion EUR					% of GDP				
	1990	2000	2010	2015	2016	1990	2000	2010	2015	2016
Total tax revenue	**39.1**	**62.4**	**76.3**	**92.1**	**95.1**	**42.9**	**45.8**	**40.8**	**43.9**	**44.0**
1000 Taxes on income, profits and capital gains	**15.3**	**26.9**	**27.1**	**32.4**	**32.9**	**16.8**	**19.7**	**14.5**	**15.4**	**15.2**
1100 Of individuals	13.6	19.1	22.5	27.8	28.1	14.9	14.0	12.1	13.3	13.0
1200 Corporate	1.8	7.8	4.6	4.5	4.8	1.9	5.7	2.4	2.2	2.2
1300 Unallocable between 1100 and 1200	0.0	0.0	0.0	0.0	0.0	0.0	0.0	0.0	0.0	0.0
2000 Social security contributions	**10.0**	**15.8**	**22.6**	**26.6**	**27.6**	**11.0**	**11.6**	**12.1**	**12.7**	**12.8**
2100 Employees	1.2	2.9	4.7	6.4	6.8	1.3	2.1	2.5	3.0	3.2
2200 Employers	8.1	11.6	16.0	18.2	18.8	8.9	8.5	8.6	8.7	8.7
2300 Self-employed or non-employed	0.7	1.3	1.9	2.0	2.0	0.8	0.9	1.0	1.0	0.9
2400 Unallocable between 2100, 2200 and 2300	0.0	0.0	0.0	0.0	0.0	0.0	0.0	0.0	0.0	0.0
3000 Taxes on payroll and workforce	**0.0**	**0.0**	**0.0**	**0.0**	**0.0**	**0.0**	**0.0**	**0.0**	**0.0**	**0.0**
4000 Taxes on property	**1.0**	**1.5**	**2.1**	**3.0**	**3.1**	**1.1**	**1.1**	**1.1**	**1.4**	**1.4**
4100 Recurrent taxes on immovable property	0.1	0.6	1.2	1.6	1.7	0.1	0.4	0.6	0.8	0.8
4200 Recurrent taxes on net wealth	0.0	0.2	0.0	0.0	0.0	0.0	0.1	0.0	0.0	0.0
4300 Estate, inheritance and gift taxes	0.1	0.4	0.4	0.6	0.5	0.2	0.3	0.2	0.3	0.2
4400 Taxes on financial and capital transactions	0.7	0.4	0.5	0.8	0.9	0.8	0.3	0.3	0.4	0.4
4500 Non-recurrent taxes	0.0	0.0	0.0	0.0	0.0	0.0	0.0	0.0	0.0	0.0
4600 Other recurrent taxes on property	0.0	0.0	0.0	0.0	0.0	0.0	0.0	0.0	0.0	0.0
5000 Taxes on goods and services	**12.7**	**18.1**	**24.3**	**29.8**	**31.2**	**14.0**	**13.3**	**13.0**	**14.2**	**14.4**
5100 Taxes on production, sale, transfer, etc	12.6	17.7	23.5	28.7	30.0	13.8	13.0	12.6	13.7	13.9
5110 General taxes	7.5	10.9	15.5	19.0	19.7	8.3	8.0	8.3	9.1	9.1
5111 Value added taxes	7.5	10.9	15.5	19.0	19.7	8.3	8.0	8.3	9.1	9.1
5120 Taxes on specific goods and services	5.0	6.8	8.0	9.8	10.3	5.5	5.0	4.3	4.7	4.8
5121 Excises	3.8	5.6	6.3	7.7	8.2	4.2	4.1	3.4	3.7	3.8
5200 Taxes on use of goods and perform activities	0.2	0.4	0.8	1.1	1.2	0.2	0.3	0.4	0.5	0.6
5300 Unallocable between 5100 and 5200	0.0	0.0	0.0	0.0	0.0	0.0	0.0	0.0	0.0	0.0
6000 Other taxes	**0.0**	**0.0**	**0.1**	**0.1**	**0.1**	**0.1**	**0.0**	**0.0**	**0.0**	**0.0**
Non-wastable tax credits										
Non-wastable tax credits against 1000	..	..	..	..	..	..	..	..	..	..
Transfer component	..	..	..	..	..	..	..	..	..	..
Tax expenditure component	..	..	..	..	..	..	..	..	..	..

.. Not available

Note: More detailed country data and country notes are available in online chapter 5 "Country Tables, 1965-2016": http://dx.doi.org/10.1787/rev_stats-2018-en. Full time series can be accessed at http://oe.cd/full-time-series.

Source: Bulletin of Statistics; Central Statistical Office (for Central Government revenues); the Annual report of the National Pension Institute and Official Statistics of Finland Series XXIIA published by the Ministry and Social Affairs (for the Social Security and private pension respectively); supplementary information from unpublished sources.

StatLink http://dx.doi.org/10.1787/888933860007

Table 4.18. Finland, tax revenue and % of GDP by level of government and main taxes

	Billion EUR					% of GDP				
	1990	2000	2010	2015	2016	1990	2000	2010	2015	2016
Federal or Central government										
Total tax revenue	**20.7**	**33.1**	**35.0**	**43.3**	**45.3**	**22.7**	**24.3**	**18.7**	**20.7**	**20.9**
1000 Taxes on income, profits and capital gains	7.0	14.0	9.8	12.1	12.7	7.7	10.3	5.2	5.8	5.9
2000 Social security contributions	0.0	0.0	0.0	0.0	0.0	0.0	0.0	0.0	0.0	0.0
3000 Taxes on payroll and workforce	0.0	0.0	0.0	0.0	0.0	0.0	0.0	0.0	0.0	0.0
4000 Taxes on property	0.9	0.9	0.9	1.4	1.4	1.0	0.7	0.5	0.7	0.6
5000 Taxes on goods and services	12.7	18.1	24.3	29.7	31.1	14.0	13.3	13.0	14.2	14.4
6000 Other taxes	0.0	0.0	0.1	0.1	0.1	0.1	0.0	0.0	0.0	0.0
State/Regional										
Total tax revenue	..	..	..	..	..	..	..	..	..	..
1000 Taxes on income, profits and capital gains	..	..	..	..	..	..	..	..	..	..
2000 Social security contributions	..	..	..	..	..	..	..	..	..	..
3000 Taxes on payroll and workforce	..	..	..	..	..	..	..	..	..	..
4000 Taxes on property	..	..	..	..	..	..	..	..	..	..
5000 Taxes on goods and services	..	..	..	..	..	..	..	..	..	..
6000 Other taxes	..	..	..	..	..	..	..	..	..	..
Local government										
Total tax revenue	**8.4**	**13.5**	**18.5**	**21.9**	**22.0**	**9.2**	**9.9**	**9.9**	**10.4**	**10.2**
1000 Taxes on income, profits and capital gains	8.3	12.9	17.3	20.2	20.3	9.1	9.5	9.3	9.7	9.4
2000 Social security contributions	0.0	0.0	0.0	0.0	0.0	0.0	0.0	0.0	0.0	0.0
3000 Taxes on payroll and workforce	0.0	0.0	0.0	0.0	0.0	0.0	0.0	0.0	0.0	0.0
4000 Taxes on property	0.1	0.6	1.2	1.6	1.7	0.1	0.4	0.6	0.8	0.8
5000 Taxes on goods and services	0.0	0.0	0.0	0.0	0.0	0.0	0.0	0.0	0.0	0.0
6000 Other taxes	0.0	0.0	0.0	0.0	0.0	0.0	0.0	0.0	0.0	0.0
Social Security Funds										
Total tax revenue	**10.0**	**15.7**	**22.6**	**26.6**	**27.6**	**11.0**	**11.6**	**12.1**	**12.7**	**12.8**
1000 Taxes on income, profits and capital gains	0.0	0.0	0.0	0.0	0.0	0.0	0.0	0.0	0.0	0.0
2000 Social security contributions	10.0	15.7	22.6	26.6	27.6	11.0	11.6	12.1	12.7	12.8
3000 Taxes on payroll and workforce	0.0	0.0	0.0	0.0	0.0	0.0	0.0	0.0	0.0	0.0
4000 Taxes on property	0.0	0.0	0.0	0.0	0.0	0.0	0.0	0.0	0.0	0.0
5000 Taxes on goods and services	0.0	0.0	0.0	0.0	0.0	0.0	0.0	0.0	0.0	0.0
6000 Other taxes	0.0	0.0	0.0	0.0	0.0	0.0	0.0	0.0	0.0	0.0

.. Not available

Note: More detailed country data and country notes are available in online chapter 6 "Tax revenues by sub-sectors of general government": http://dx.doi.org/10.1787/rev_stats-2018-en. Full time series can be accessed at http://oe.cd/full-time-series.

Source: Bulletin of Statistics; Central Statistical Office (for Central Government revenues); the Annual report of the National Pension Institute and Official Statistics of Finland Series XXIIA published by the Ministry and Social Affairs (for the Social Security and private pension respectively); supplementary information from unpublished sources.

StatLink http://dx.doi.org/10.1787/888933860026

Table 4.19. France, tax revenue and % of GDP by selected tax category

	Billion EUR					% of GDP				
	1990	2000	2010	2015	2016	1990	2000	2010	2015	2016
Total tax revenue	**433.8**	**642.2**	**840.9**	**995.5**	**1 013.1**	**41.2**	**43.4**	**42.1**	**45.3**	**45.5**
1000 Taxes on income, profits and capital gains	**69.6**	**159.5**	**189.7**	**232.7**	**236.3**	**6.6**	**10.8**	**9.5**	**10.6**	**10.6**
1100 Of individuals	46.3	115.2	143.1	186.9	191.0	4.4	7.8	7.2	8.5	8.6
1200 Corporate	23.1	44.3	46.6	45.8	45.4	2.2	3.0	2.3	2.1	2.0
1300 Unallocable between 1100 and 1200	0.3	0.0	0.0	0.0	0.0	0.0	0.0	0.0	0.0	0.0
2000 Social security contributions	**191.1**	**230.2**	**321.3**	**367.6**	**372.4**	**18.1**	**15.6**	**16.1**	**16.7**	**16.7**
2100 Employees	57.3	57.3	77.7	93.1	95.9	5.4	3.9	3.9	4.2	4.3
2200 Employers	118.1	158.3	218.0	246.3	248.7	11.2	10.7	10.9	11.2	11.2
2300 Self-employed or non-employed	15.7	14.6	25.7	28.2	27.7	1.5	1.0	1.3	1.3	1.2
2400 Unallocable between 2100, 2200 and 2300	0.0	0.0	0.0	0.0	0.0	0.0	0.0	0.0	0.0	0.0
3000 Taxes on payroll and workforce	**8.3**	**14.9**	**26.8**	**34.4**	**34.6**	**0.8**	**1.0**	**1.3**	**1.6**	**1.6**
4000 Taxes on property	**27.4**	**46.1**	**73.0**	**92.1**	**94.9**	**2.6**	**3.1**	**3.7**	**4.2**	**4.3**
4100 Recurrent taxes on immovable property	14.8	29.4	50.0	60.4	62.6	1.4	2.0	2.5	2.7	2.8
4200 Recurrent taxes on net wealth	2.6	2.4	4.4	5.2	4.8	0.2	0.2	0.2	0.2	0.2
4300 Estate, inheritance and gift taxes	4.1	6.9	7.7	12.2	12.3	0.4	0.5	0.4	0.6	0.6
4400 Taxes on financial and capital transactions	5.9	7.4	10.8	14.3	15.2	0.6	0.5	0.5	0.7	0.7
4500 Non-recurrent taxes	0.0	0.0	0.0	0.0	0.0	0.0	0.0	0.0	0.0	0.0
4600 Other recurrent taxes on property	0.0	0.0	0.0	0.0	0.0	0.0	0.0	0.0	0.0	0.0
5000 Taxes on goods and services	**123.2**	**165.9**	**208.8**	**241.3**	**247.2**	**11.7**	**11.2**	**10.5**	**11.0**	**11.1**
5100 Taxes on production, sale, transfer, etc	119.2	161.3	202.5	234.3	239.9	11.3	10.9	10.2	10.7	10.8
5110 General taxes	81.3	109.8	140.3	155.7	157.7	7.7	7.4	7.0	7.1	7.1
5111 Value added taxes	80.0	107.1	135.2	151.4	154.2	7.6	7.2	6.8	6.9	6.9
5120 Taxes on specific goods and services	37.9	51.5	62.2	78.6	82.3	3.6	3.5	3.1	3.6	3.7
5121 Excises	26.8	39.7	45.6	56.4	58.6	2.5	2.7	2.3	2.6	2.6
5200 Taxes on use of goods and perform activities	4.0	4.6	6.3	6.9	7.2	0.4	0.3	0.3	0.3	0.3
5300 Unallocable between 5100 and 5200	0.0	0.0	0.0	0.0	0.0	0.0	0.0	0.0	0.0	0.0
6000 Other taxes	**14.1**	**24.1**	**19.5**	**25.5**	**26.0**	**1.3**	**1.6**	**1.0**	**1.2**	**1.2**
Non-wastable tax credits										
Non-wastable tax credits against 1000	..	0.5	17.4	26.7	25.9	..	0.0	0.9	1.2	1.2
Transfer component	..	..	7.9	10.4	11.6	..	..	0.4	0.5	0.5
Tax expenditure component	..	..	9.5	16.2	14.3	..	..	0.5	0.7	0.6

.. Not available

Note: More detailed country data and country notes are available in online chapter 5 "Country Tables, 1965-2016": http://dx.doi.org/10.1787/rev_stats-2018-en. Full time series can be accessed at http://oe.cd/full-time-series.

The total tax revenue has been reduced by the amount of any capital transfer that represents uncollected taxes. The capital transfer has been allocated between tax headings in proportion to the reported tax revenue. Therefore, the tax revenue amounts are different to those reported in the detailed country data available in online chapter 5 "Country Tables, 1965-2016".

Source: General Account of the Administration of finances for the figures of fiscal receipts. OSCE for the figures of Social Security from 1965 to 1969, and ESA for the following years.

StatLink http://dx.doi.org/10.1787/888933860045

Table 4.20. France, tax revenue and % of GDP by level of government and main taxes

	Billion EUR					% of GDP				
	1990	2000	2010	2015	2016	1990	2000	2010	2015	2016
Federal or Central government										
Total tax revenue	**200.1**	**270.3**	**299.6**	**332.5**	**338.1**	**19.0**	**18.3**	**15.0**	**15.1**	**15.2**
1000 Taxes on income, profits and capital gains	69.6	94.4	97.0	120.6	122.7	6.6	6.4	4.9	5.5	5.5
2000 Social security contributions	3.2	5.4	7.6	7.9	8.0	0.3	0.4	0.4	0.4	0.4
3000 Taxes on payroll and workforce	6.2	10.6	4.2	4.8	3.9	0.6	0.7	0.2	0.2	0.2
4000 Taxes on property	8.6	13.4	15.9	23.2	23.0	0.8	0.9	0.8	1.1	1.0
5000 Taxes on goods and services	112.1	143.4	157.2	174.2	179.6	10.6	9.7	7.9	7.9	8.1
6000 Other taxes	0.4	3.1	17.6	1.9	0.8	0.0	0.2	0.9	0.1	0.0
State/Regional										
Total tax revenue	..	..	..	..	..	..	..	..	..	..
1000 Taxes on income, profits and capital gains	..	..	..	..	..	..	..	..	..	..
2000 Social security contributions	..	..	..	..	..	..	..	..	..	..
3000 Taxes on payroll and workforce	..	..	..	..	..	..	..	..	..	..
4000 Taxes on property	..	..	..	..	..	..	..	..	..	..
5000 Taxes on goods and services	..	..	..	..	..	..	..	..	..	..
6000 Other taxes	..	..	..	..	..	..	..	..	..	..
Local government										
Total tax revenue	**40.2**	**64.7**	**89.3**	**131.4**	**136.7**	**3.8**	**4.4**	**4.5**	**6.0**	**6.1**
1000 Taxes on income, profits and capital gains	0.0	0.0	0.1	0.0	0.0	0.0	0.0	0.0	0.0	0.0
2000 Social security contributions	0.0	0.0	0.0	0.0	0.0	0.0	0.0	0.0	0.0	0.0
3000 Taxes on payroll and workforce	1.7	3.9	7.5	9.3	9.7	0.2	0.3	0.4	0.4	0.4
4000 Taxes on property	18.8	32.7	57.1	68.9	71.9	1.8	2.2	2.9	3.1	3.2
5000 Taxes on goods and services	6.0	7.3	23.0	31.0	31.8	0.6	0.5	1.2	1.4	1.4
6000 Other taxes	13.7	20.9	1.6	22.1	23.4	1.3	1.4	0.1	1.0	1.0
Social Security Funds										
Total tax revenue	**190.9**	**305.3**	**450.1**	**528.6**	**534.7**	**18.1**	**20.6**	**22.6**	**24.0**	**24.0**
1000 Taxes on income, profits and capital gains	0.0	65.0	92.7	112.1	113.6	0.0	4.4	4.6	5.1	5.1
2000 Social security contributions	187.9	224.8	313.7	359.7	364.4	17.8	15.2	15.7	16.4	16.4
3000 Taxes on payroll and workforce	0.4	0.4	15.1	20.3	21.0	0.0	0.0	0.8	0.9	0.9
4000 Taxes on property	0.0	0.0	0.0	0.0	0.0	0.0	0.0	0.0	0.0	0.0
5000 Taxes on goods and services	2.5	14.9	28.4	35.9	35.5	0.2	1.0	1.4	1.6	1.6
6000 Other taxes	0.0	0.1	0.2	0.6	0.3	0.0	0.0	0.0	0.0	0.0

.. Not available

Note: More detailed country data and country notes are available in online chapter 6 "Tax revenues by sub-sectors of general government": http://dx.doi.org/10.1787/rev_stats-2018-en. Full time series can be accessed at http://oe.cd/full-time-series.

The total tax revenue has been reduced by the amount of any capital transfer that represents uncollected taxes. The capital transfer has been allocated between tax headings in proportion to the reported tax revenue. Therefore, the tax revenue amounts are different to those reported in the detailed country data available in online chapter 6 "Tax revenues by sub-sectors of general government".

Source: General Account of the Administration of finances for the figures of fiscal receipts. OSCE for the figures of Social Security from 1965 to 1969, and ESA for the following years.

StatLink http://dx.doi.org/10.1787/888933860064

Table 4.21. Germany, tax revenue and % of GDP by selected tax category

	Billion EUR					% of GDP				
	1990	2000	2010	2015	2016	1990	2000	2010	2015	2016
Total tax revenue	**454.8**	**767.0**	**903.2**	**1 127.8**	**1 182.7**	**34.8**	**36.2**	**35.0**	**37.0**	**37.4**
1000 Taxes on income, profits and capital gains	**147.3**	**231.2**	**257.8**	**351.9**	**376.8**	**11.3**	**10.9**	**10.0**	**11.5**	**11.9**
1100 Of individuals	125.3	194.2	219.4	299.8	314.8	9.6	9.2	8.5	9.8	10.0
1200 Corporate	22.0	37.1	38.4	52.1	62.0	1.7	1.8	1.5	1.7	2.0
1300 Unallocable between 1100 and 1200	0.0	0.0	0.0	0.0	0.0	0.0	0.0	0.0	0.0	0.0
2000 Social security contributions	**170.4**	**299.4**	**354.0**	**424.6**	**444.9**	**13.0**	**14.1**	**13.7**	**13.9**	**14.1**
2100 Employees	73.6	131.6	155.3	189.0	199.4	5.6	6.2	6.0	6.2	6.3
2200 Employers	86.7	147.4	167.2	199.2	206.8	6.6	7.0	6.5	6.5	6.5
2300 Self-employed or non-employed	10.2	20.4	31.5	36.5	38.7	0.8	1.0	1.2	1.2	1.2
2400 Unallocable between 2100, 2200 and 2300	0.0	0.0	0.0	0.0	0.0	0.0	0.0	0.0	0.0	0.0
3000 Taxes on payroll and workforce	**0.0**	**0.0**	**0.0**	**0.0**	**0.0**	**0.0**	**0.0**	**0.0**	**0.0**	**0.0**
4000 Taxes on property	**15.3**	**17.5**	**21.0**	**31.1**	**33.4**	**1.2**	**0.8**	**0.8**	**1.0**	**1.1**
4100 Recurrent taxes on immovable property	4.5	8.8	11.3	13.2	13.7	0.3	0.4	0.4	0.4	0.4
4200 Recurrent taxes on net wealth	6.2	0.4	0.0	0.3	0.4	0.5	0.0	0.0	0.0	0.0
4300 Estate, inheritance and gift taxes	1.5	3.0	4.4	6.3	7.0	0.1	0.1	0.2	0.2	0.2
4400 Taxes on financial and capital transactions	3.1	5.2	5.3	11.2	12.4	0.2	0.2	0.2	0.4	0.4
4500 Non-recurrent taxes	0.0	0.0	0.0	0.0	0.0	0.0	0.0	0.0	0.0	0.0
4600 Other recurrent taxes on property	0.0	0.0	0.0	0.0	0.0	0.0	0.0	0.0	0.0	0.0
5000 Taxes on goods and services	**121.6**	**215.3**	**266.1**	**313.3**	**320.6**	**9.3**	**10.2**	**10.3**	**10.3**	**10.1**
5100 Taxes on production, sale, transfer, etc	117.2	208.1	256.9	294.3	301.7	9.0	9.8	10.0	9.7	9.5
5110 General taxes	75.5	140.9	180.5	211.9	219.1	5.8	6.7	7.0	7.0	6.9
5111 Value added taxes	75.5	140.9	180.5	211.9	219.1	5.8	6.7	7.0	7.0	6.9
5120 Taxes on specific goods and services	41.7	67.2	76.1	82.0	82.3	3.2	3.2	2.9	2.7	2.6
5121 Excises	31.2	57.2	63.5	65.3	64.9	2.4	2.7	2.5	2.1	2.1
5200 Taxes on use of goods and perform activities	4.4	7.2	9.2	19.0	18.8	0.3	0.3	0.4	0.6	0.6
5300 Unallocable between 5100 and 5200	0.0	0.0	0.0	0.0	0.0	0.0	0.0	0.0	0.0	0.0
6000 Other taxes	**0.2**	**0.2**	**0.1**	**1.8**	**2.0**	**0.0**	**0.0**	**0.0**	**0.1**	**0.1**
Non-wastable tax credits										
Non-wastable tax credits against 1000	..	39.3	46.3	42.2	42.9	..	1.9	1.8	1.4	1.4
Transfer component	..	..	17.7	15.6	15.7	..	..	0.7	0.5	0.5
Tax expenditure component	..	..	28.6	26.6	27.3	..	..	1.1	0.9	0.9

.. Not available

Note: More detailed country data and country notes are available in online chapter 5 "Country Tables, 1965-2016": http://dx.doi.org/10.1787/rev_stats-2018-en. Full time series can be accessed at http://oe.cd/full-time-series.

Source: Finanzbericht, Bonn; Tax Statistics. Unpublished estimates by the Ministry of Finance.

StatLink http://dx.doi.org/10.1787/888933860083

Table 4.22. Germany, tax revenue and % of GDP by level of government and main taxes

	Billion EUR					% of GDP				
	1990	2000	2010	2015	2016	1990	2000	2010	2015	2016
Federal or Central government										
Total tax revenue	**143.9**	**234.8**	**283.0**	**343.6**	**351.1**	**11.0**	**11.1**	**11.0**	**11.3**	**11.1**
1000 Taxes on income, profits and capital gains	58.2	97.9	104.5	143.8	153.6	4.5	4.6	4.1	4.7	4.9
2000 Social security contributions	0.0	0.0	0.0	0.0	0.0	0.0	0.0	0.0	0.0	0.0
3000 Taxes on payroll and workforce	0.0	0.0	0.0	0.0	0.0	0.0	0.0	0.0	0.0	0.0
4000 Taxes on property	1.2	0.0	0.0	0.3	0.4	0.1	0.0	0.0	0.0	0.0
5000 Taxes on goods and services	84.6	136.9	178.5	199.4	197.2	6.5	6.5	6.9	6.5	6.2
6000 Other taxes	0.0	0.0	0.0	0.0	0.0	0.0	0.0	0.0	0.0	0.0
State/Regional										
Total tax revenue	**97.8**	**172.1**	**190.6**	**259.5**	**279.7**	**7.5**	**8.1**	**7.4**	**8.5**	**8.9**
1000 Taxes on income, profits and capital gains	58.2	88.9	97.6	134.0	143.2	4.5	4.2	3.8	4.4	4.5
2000 Social security contributions	0.0	0.0	0.0	0.0	0.0	0.0	0.0	0.0	0.0	0.0
3000 Taxes on payroll and workforce	0.0	0.0	0.0	0.0	0.0	0.0	0.0	0.0	0.0	0.0
4000 Taxes on property	7.0	8.5	9.7	17.5	19.4	0.5	0.4	0.4	0.6	0.6
5000 Taxes on goods and services	32.6	74.6	83.4	107.9	117.1	2.5	3.5	3.2	3.5	3.7
6000 Other taxes	0.0	0.0	0.0	0.0	0.0	0.0	0.0	0.0	0.0	0.0
Local government										
Total tax revenue	**38.4**	**57.0**	**71.4**	**93.4**	**100.2**	**2.9**	**2.7**	**2.8**	**3.1**	**3.2**
1000 Taxes on income, profits and capital gains	30.9	44.4	55.7	74.0	80.0	2.4	2.1	2.2	2.4	2.5
2000 Social security contributions	0.0	0.0	0.0	0.0	0.0	0.0	0.0	0.0	0.0	0.0
3000 Taxes on payroll and workforce	0.0	0.0	0.0	0.0	0.0	0.0	0.0	0.0	0.0	0.0
4000 Taxes on property	7.2	9.0	11.3	13.2	13.7	0.5	0.4	0.4	0.4	0.4
5000 Taxes on goods and services	0.3	3.4	4.3	5.9	6.3	0.0	0.2	0.2	0.2	0.2
6000 Other taxes	0.2	0.1	0.1	0.2	0.2	0.0	0.0	0.0	0.0	0.0
Social Security Funds										
Total tax revenue	**170.4**	**299.4**	**354.0**	**424.6**	**444.9**	**13.0**	**14.1**	**13.7**	**13.9**	**14.1**
1000 Taxes on income, profits and capital gains	0.0	0.0	0.0	0.0	0.0	0.0	0.0	0.0	0.0	0.0
2000 Social security contributions	170.4	299.4	354.0	424.6	444.9	13.0	14.1	13.7	13.9	14.1
3000 Taxes on payroll and workforce	0.0	0.0	0.0	0.0	0.0	0.0	0.0	0.0	0.0	0.0
4000 Taxes on property	0.0	0.0	0.0	0.0	0.0	0.0	0.0	0.0	0.0	0.0
5000 Taxes on goods and services	0.0	0.0	0.0	0.0	0.0	0.0	0.0	0.0	0.0	0.0
6000 Other taxes	0.0	0.0	0.0	0.0	0.0	0.0	0.0	0.0	0.0	0.0

Note: More detailed country data and country notes are available in online chapter 6 "Tax revenues by sub-sectors of general government": http://dx.doi.org/10.1787/rev_stats-2018-en. Full time series can be accessed at http://oe.cd/full-time-series.

Source: Finanzbericht, Bonn; Tax Statistics. Unpublished estimates by the Ministry of Finance.

StatLink http://dx.doi.org/10.1787/888933860102

Table 4.23. Greece, tax revenue and % of GDP by selected tax category

	Billion EUR					% of GDP				
	1990	2000	2010	2015	2016	1990	2000	2010	2015	2016
Total tax revenue	**11.5**	**47.1**	**72.4**	**64.5**	**67.7**	**25.2**	**33.4**	**32.0**	**36.6**	**38.8**
1000 Taxes on income, profits and capital gains	**2.3**	**12.7**	**15.9**	**14.9**	**15.9**	**5.0**	**9.0**	**7.0**	**8.5**	**9.1**
1100 Of individuals	1.6	6.8	9.0	10.2	10.3	3.6	4.8	4.0	5.8	5.9
1200 Corporate	0.6	5.6	5.7	3.8	4.4	1.4	4.0	2.5	2.2	2.5
1300 Unallocable between 1100 and 1200	0.0	0.2	1.2	0.9	1.2	0.1	0.1	0.5	0.5	0.7
2000 Social security contributions	**3.5**	**14.2**	**24.7**	**18.8**	**19.3**	**7.6**	**10.1**	**10.9**	**10.7**	**11.1**
2100 Employees	1.7	5.6	13.3	11.1	11.6	3.8	4.0	5.9	6.3	6.7
2200 Employers	1.7	6.6	11.5	7.7	7.7	3.8	4.7	5.1	4.4	4.4
2300 Self-employed or non-employed	0.0	2.0	0.0	0.0	0.0	0.0	1.4	0.0	0.0	0.0
2400 Unallocable between 2100, 2200 and 2300	0.0	0.0	0.0	0.0	0.0	0.0	0.0	0.0	0.0	0.0
3000 Taxes on payroll and workforce	**0.1**	**0.0**	**0.0**	**0.0**	**0.0**	**0.2**	**0.0**	**0.0**	**0.0**	**0.0**
4000 Taxes on property	**0.5**	**2.9**	**3.7**	**5.4**	**5.5**	**1.2**	**2.0**	**1.7**	**3.1**	**3.2**
4100 Recurrent taxes on immovable property	0.0	0.2	0.6	3.6	3.7	0.0	0.2	0.2	2.0	2.1
4200 Recurrent taxes on net wealth	0.0	0.1	1.3	1.1	1.1	0.0	0.0	0.6	0.6	0.7
4300 Estate, inheritance and gift taxes	0.1	0.4	0.2	0.1	0.1	0.3	0.3	0.1	0.1	0.1
4400 Taxes on financial and capital transactions	0.4	2.0	1.1	0.5	0.5	0.8	1.5	0.5	0.3	0.3
4500 Non-recurrent taxes	0.0	0.0	0.0	0.0	0.0	0.0	0.0	0.0	0.0	0.0
4600 Other recurrent taxes on property	0.0	0.2	0.6	0.1	0.0	0.0	0.1	0.3	0.0	0.0
5000 Taxes on goods and services	**5.1**	**17.1**	**27.7**	**25.2**	**26.8**	**11.2**	**12.1**	**12.3**	**14.3**	**15.4**
5100 Taxes on production, sale, transfer, etc	4.9	15.6	25.2	21.3	23.1	10.7	11.0	11.2	12.1	13.3
5110 General taxes	3.0	10.1	16.5	13.2	14.6	6.7	7.2	7.3	7.5	8.4
5111 Value added taxes	2.8	9.8	16.0	12.9	14.3	6.2	7.0	7.1	7.3	8.2
5120 Taxes on specific goods and services	1.8	5.4	8.6	8.0	8.4	3.9	3.8	3.8	4.6	4.8
5121 Excises	1.4	4.2	7.6	6.9	7.1	3.0	3.0	3.3	3.9	4.1
5200 Taxes on use of goods and perform activities	0.2	1.3	1.7	3.2	3.2	0.5	0.9	0.7	1.8	1.8
5300 Unallocable between 5100 and 5200	0.0	0.3	0.8	0.7	0.5	0.0	0.2	0.3	0.4	0.3
6000 Other taxes	**0.0**	**0.0**	**0.0**	**0.0**	**0.0**	**0.0**	**0.0**	**0.0**	**0.0**	**0.0**
Non-wastable tax credits										
Non-wastable tax credits against 1000	..	..	..	..	..	..	..	..	..	..
Transfer component	..	..	..	..	..	..	..	..	..	..
Tax expenditure component	..	..	..	..	..	..	..	..	..	..

.. Not available

Note: More detailed country data and country notes are available in online chapter 5 "Country Tables, 1965-2016": http://dx.doi.org/10.1787/rev_stats-2018-en. Full time series can be accessed at http://oe.cd/full-time-series.

The total tax revenue has been reduced by the amount of any capital transfer that represents uncollected taxes. The capital transfer has been allocated between tax headings in proportion to the reported tax revenue. Therefore, the tax revenue amounts are different to those reported in the detailed country data available in online chapter 5 "Country Tables, 1965-2016".

Source: Ministry of Finance, General accounting Office, 20th Directorate of Budget except the heading 2000 provided by the National Statistics Bureau.

StatLink http://dx.doi.org/10.1787/888933860121

Table 4.24. Greece, tax revenue and % of GDP by level of government and main taxes

	Billion EUR					% of GDP				
	1990	2000	2010	2015	2016	1990	2000	2010	2015	2016
Federal or Central government										
Total tax revenue	**7.8**	**32.4**	**46.5**	**44.4**	**47.1**	**17.1**	**23.0**	**20.6**	**25.2**	**27.0**
1000 Taxes on income, profits and capital gains	2.3	12.7	15.9	14.9	15.9	5.0	9.0	7.0	8.4	9.1
2000 Social security contributions	0.0	0.7	1.3	0.7	0.7	0.1	0.5	0.6	0.4	0.4
3000 Taxes on payroll and workforce	0.0	0.0	0.0	0.0	0.0	0.0	0.0	0.0	0.0	0.0
4000 Taxes on property	0.5	2.4	2.1	3.9	3.9	1.2	1.7	0.9	2.2	2.3
5000 Taxes on goods and services	4.9	16.7	27.1	24.9	26.5	10.9	11.8	12.0	14.1	15.2
6000 Other taxes	0.0	0.0	0.0	0.0	0.0	0.0	0.0	0.0	0.0	0.0
State/Regional										
Total tax revenue	..	..	..	..	..	..	..	..	..	..
1000 Taxes on income, profits and capital gains	..	..	..	..	..	..	..	..	..	..
2000 Social security contributions	..	..	..	..	..	..	..	..	..	..
3000 Taxes on payroll and workforce	..	..	..	..	..	..	..	..	..	..
4000 Taxes on property	..	..	..	..	..	..	..	..	..	..
5000 Taxes on goods and services	..	..	..	..	..	..	..	..	..	..
6000 Other taxes	..	..	..	..	..	..	..	..	..	..
Local government										
Total tax revenue	**0.1**	**0.4**	**1.7**	**1.5**	**1.6**	**0.3**	**0.3**	**0.8**	**0.9**	**0.9**
1000 Taxes on income, profits and capital gains	0.0	0.0	0.0	0.0	0.0	0.0	0.0	0.0	0.0	0.0
2000 Social security contributions	0.0	0.0	0.0	0.0	0.0	0.0	0.0	0.0	0.0	0.0
3000 Taxes on payroll and workforce	0.1	0.0	0.0	0.0	0.0	0.2	0.0	0.0	0.0	0.0
4000 Taxes on property	0.0	0.3	1.5	1.4	1.5	0.0	0.2	0.7	0.8	0.9
5000 Taxes on goods and services	0.1	0.1	0.2	0.1	0.1	0.1	0.1	0.1	0.1	0.1
6000 Other taxes	0.0	0.0	0.0	0.0	0.0	0.0	0.0	0.0	0.0	0.0
Social Security Funds										
Total tax revenue	**3.4**	**14.1**	**24.0**	**18.3**	**18.7**	**7.5**	**10.0**	**10.6**	**10.4**	**10.8**
1000 Taxes on income, profits and capital gains	0.0	0.0	0.0	0.0	0.0	0.0	0.0	0.0	0.0	0.0
2000 Social security contributions	3.4	13.6	23.4	18.1	18.6	7.5	9.6	10.4	10.2	10.7
3000 Taxes on payroll and workforce	0.0	0.0	0.0	0.0	0.0	0.0	0.0	0.0	0.0	0.0
4000 Taxes on property	0.0	0.2	0.1	0.0	0.0	0.0	0.1	0.1	0.0	0.0
5000 Taxes on goods and services	0.0	0.3	0.4	0.2	0.1	0.0	0.2	0.2	0.1	0.1
6000 Other taxes	0.0	0.0	0.0	0.0	0.0	0.0	0.0	0.0	0.0	0.0

.. Not available

Note: More detailed country data and country notes are available in online chapter 6 "Tax revenues by sub-sectors of general government": http://dx.doi.org/10.1787/rev_stats-2018-en. Full time series can be accessed at http://oe.cd/full-time-series.

The total tax revenue has been reduced by the amount of any capital transfer that represents uncollected taxes. The capital transfer has been allocated between tax headings in proportion to the reported tax revenue. Therefore, the tax revenue amounts are different to those reported in the detailed country data available in online chapter 6 "Tax revenues by sub-sectors of general government".

Source: Ministry of Finance, General accounting Office, 20th Directorate of Budget except the heading 2000 provided by the National Statistics Bureau.

StatLink http://dx.doi.org/10.1787/888933860140

Table 4.25. Hungary, tax revenue and % of GDP by selected tax category

	Billion HUF					% of GDP				
	1990	2000	2010	2015	2016	1990	2000	2010	2015	2016
Total tax revenue	..	**5 140.6**	**10 145.5**	**13 286.7**	**13 887.8**	..	**38.5**	**37.3**	**38.7**	**39.2**
1000 Taxes on income, profits and capital gains	..	**1 247.4**	**2 098.6**	**2 428.4**	**2 684.6**	..	**9.3**	**7.7**	**7.1**	**7.6**
1100 Of individuals	..	954.7	1 768.8	1 814.9	1 853.4	..	7.2	6.5	5.3	5.2
1200 Corporate	..	292.7	329.7	613.5	831.1	..	2.2	1.2	1.8	2.3
1300 Unallocable between 1100 and 1200	..	0.0	0.0	0.0	0.0	..	0.0	0.0	0.0	0.0
2000 Social security contributions	..	**1 506.8**	**3 184.2**	**4 293.7**	**4 613.9**	..	**11.3**	**11.7**	**12.5**	**13.0**
2100 Employees	..	275.3	1 069.1	1 784.5	1 989.8	..	2.1	3.9	5.2	5.6
2200 Employers	..	1 213.2	2 047.6	2 480.1	2 594.2	..	9.1	7.5	7.2	7.3
2300 Self-employed or non-employed	..	0.9	21.2	0.0	0.0	..	0.0	0.1	0.0	0.0
2400 Unallocable between 2100, 2200 and 2300	..	17.4	46.3	29.1	30.0	..	0.1	0.2	0.1	0.1
3000 Taxes on payroll and workforce	..	**183.4**	**116.0**	**199.3**	**220.8**	..	**1.4**	**0.4**	**0.6**	**0.6**
4000 Taxes on property	..	**89.0**	**312.1**	**438.0**	**391.9**	..	**0.7**	**1.1**	**1.3**	**1.1**
4100 Recurrent taxes on immovable property	..	30.8	92.5	200.9	210.3	..	0.2	0.3	0.6	0.6
4200 Recurrent taxes on net wealth	..	0.0	135.7	136.3	59.8	..	0.0	0.5	0.4	0.2
4300 Estate, inheritance and gift taxes	..	5.5	6.3	7.4	8.3	..	0.0	0.0	0.0	0.0
4400 Taxes on financial and capital transactions	..	52.8	77.6	93.4	113.6	..	0.4	0.3	0.3	0.3
4500 Non-recurrent taxes	..	0.0	0.0	0.0	0.0	..	0.0	0.0	0.0	0.0
4600 Other recurrent taxes on property	..	0.0	0.0	0.0	0.0	..	0.0	0.0	0.0	0.0
5000 Taxes on goods and services	..	**2 081.1**	**4 350.3**	**5 831.4**	**5 882.9**	..	**15.6**	**16.0**	**17.0**	**16.6**
5100 Taxes on production, sale, transfer, etc	..	2 052.4	4 238.8	5 695.6	5 735.5	..	15.4	15.6	16.6	16.2
5110 General taxes	..	1 340.6	3 010.8	4 097.5	4 104.6	..	10.0	11.1	11.9	11.6
5111 Value added taxes	..	1 153.7	2 325.6	3 307.3	3 297.2	..	8.6	8.5	9.6	9.3
5120 Taxes on specific goods and services	..	711.8	1 228.0	1 598.1	1 630.9	..	5.3	4.5	4.7	4.6
5121 Excises	..	533.5	929.9	1 119.2	1 150.6	..	4.0	3.4	3.3	3.2
5200 Taxes on use of goods and perform activities	..	28.7	111.6	135.8	147.4	..	0.2	0.4	0.4	0.4
5300 Unallocable between 5100 and 5200	..	0.0	0.0	0.0	0.0	..	0.0	0.0	0.0	0.0
6000 Other taxes	..	**32.9**	**59.4**	**56.8**	**52.1**	..	**0.2**	**0.2**	**0.2**	**0.1**
Non-wastable tax credits										
Non-wastable tax credits against 1000	..	..	..	..	..	..	..	..	..	..
Transfer component	..	..	..	..	..	..	..	..	..	..
Tax expenditure component	..	..	..	..	..	..	..	..	..	..

.. Not available

Note: More detailed country data and country notes are available in online chapter 5 "Country Tables, 1965-2016": http://dx.doi.org/10.1787/rev_stats-2018-en. Full time series can be accessed at http://oe.cd/full-time-series.

Source: Ministry of Finance, Economic Department.

StatLink http://dx.doi.org/10.1787/888933860159

Table 4.26. Hungary, tax revenue and % of GDP by level of government and main taxes

	Billion HUF					% of GDP				
	1990	2000	2010	2015	2016	1990	2000	2010	2015	2016
Federal or Central government										
Total tax revenue	..	**3 316.0**	**6 391.5**	**8 086.8**	**8 409.9**	..	**24.8**	**23.5**	**23.6**	**23.7**
1000 Taxes on income, profits and capital gains	..	1 230.8	2 064.3	2 311.9	2 551.8	..	9.2	7.6	6.7	7.2
2000 Social security contributions	..	136.6	182.0	148.0	244.4	..	1.0	0.7	0.4	0.7
3000 Taxes on payroll and workforce	..	15.4	103.1	189.1	212.2	..	0.1	0.4	0.6	0.6
4000 Taxes on property	..	29.1	182.8	293.0	236.7	..	0.2	0.7	0.9	0.7
5000 Taxes on goods and services	..	1 878.3	3 799.9	5 102.0	5 126.2	..	14.1	14.0	14.9	14.5
6000 Other taxes	..	25.8	59.4	42.8	38.6	..	0.2	0.2	0.1	0.1
State/Regional										
Total tax revenue	..	..	..	..	..	..	..	..	..	..
1000 Taxes on income, profits and capital gains	..	..	..	..	..	..	..	..	..	..
2000 Social security contributions	..	..	..	..	..	..	..	..	..	..
3000 Taxes on payroll and workforce	..	..	..	..	..	..	..	..	..	..
4000 Taxes on property	..	..	..	..	..	..	..	..	..	..
5000 Taxes on goods and services	..	..	..	..	..	..	..	..	..	..
6000 Other taxes	..	..	..	..	..	..	..	..	..	..
Local government										
Total tax revenue	..	**266.0**	**652.2**	**770.6**	**805.7**	..	**2.0**	**2.4**	**2.2**	**2.3**
1000 Taxes on income, profits and capital gains	..	2.2	0.1	0.0	0.0	..	0.0	0.0	0.0	0.0
2000 Social security contributions	..	0.0	0.0	0.0	0.0	..	0.0	0.0	0.0	0.0
3000 Taxes on payroll and workforce	..	1.2	1.2	0.0	0.0	..	0.0	0.0	0.0	0.0
4000 Taxes on property	..	59.9	129.3	145.0	155.2	..	0.4	0.5	0.4	0.4
5000 Taxes on goods and services	..	202.8	521.6	625.6	650.4	..	1.5	1.9	1.8	1.8
6000 Other taxes	..	0.0	0.0	0.0	0.0	..	0.0	0.0	0.0	0.0
Social Security Funds										
Total tax revenue	..	**1 558.6**	**3 076.2**	**4 389.5**	**4 629.7**	..	**11.7**	**11.3**	**12.8**	**13.1**
1000 Taxes on income, profits and capital gains	..	14.5	34.2	116.5	132.7	..	0.1	0.1	0.3	0.4
2000 Social security contributions	..	1 370.2	3 002.2	4 145.7	4 369.5	..	10.3	11.0	12.1	12.3
3000 Taxes on payroll and workforce	..	166.9	11.7	10.3	8.6	..	1.3	0.0	0.0	0.0
4000 Taxes on property	..	0.0	0.0	0.0	0.0	..	0.0	0.0	0.0	0.0
5000 Taxes on goods and services	..	0.0	28.1	103.1	105.4	..	0.0	0.1	0.3	0.3
6000 Other taxes	..	7.0	0.0	14.0	13.4	..	0.1	0.0	0.0	0.0

.. Not available

Note: More detailed country data and country notes are available in online chapter 6 "Tax revenues by sub-sectors of general government": http://dx.doi.org/10.1787/rev_stats-2018-en. Full time series can be accessed at http://oe.cd/full-time-series.

Source: Ministry of Finance, Economic Department.

StatLink http://dx.doi.org/10.1787/888933860178

Table 4.27. Iceland, tax revenue and % of GDP by selected tax category

	Billion ISK					% of GDP				
	1990	2000	2010	2015	2016	1990	2000	2010	2015	2016
Total tax revenue	**114.9**	**254.6**	**540.3**	**812.0**	**1 265.6**	**30.9**	**36.3**	**33.2**	**36.3**	**51.6**
1000 Taxes on income, profits and capital gains	**34.1**	**101.5**	**239.7**	**381.0**	**429.5**	**9.2**	**14.5**	**14.7**	**17.0**	**17.5**
1100 Of individuals	30.9	88.5	197.3	298.0	337.5	8.3	12.6	12.1	13.3	13.8
1200 Corporate	3.2	8.4	14.6	52.5	62.2	0.9	1.2	0.9	2.4	2.5
1300 Unallocable between 1100 and 1200	0.0	4.6	27.7	30.5	29.9	0.0	0.7	1.7	1.4	1.2
2000 Social security contributions	**3.6**	**19.7**	**63.6**	**79.7**	**85.4**	**1.0**	**2.8**	**3.9**	**3.6**	**3.5**
2100 Employees	0.3	..	..	..	..	0.1	..	..	..	..
2200 Employers	3.3	..	..	..	..	0.9	..	..	..	..
2300 Self-employed or non-employed	0.0	..	..	..	..	0.0	..	..	..	..
2400 Unallocable between 2100, 2200 and 2300	0.0	19.7	63.6	79.7	85.4	0.0	2.8	3.9	3.6	3.5
3000 Taxes on payroll and workforce	**4.1**	**0.2**	**2.8**	**6.6**	**7.4**	**1.1**	**0.0**	**0.2**	**0.3**	**0.3**
4000 Taxes on property	**9.7**	**20.0**	**38.1**	**43.5**	**432.6**	**2.6**	**2.8**	**2.3**	**1.9**	**17.6**
4100 Recurrent taxes on immovable property	4.1	10.1	28.5	34.9	38.7	1.1	1.4	1.8	1.6	1.6
4200 Recurrent taxes on net wealth	2.4	5.2	3.8	0.7	0.4	0.6	0.7	0.2	0.0	0.0
4300 Estate, inheritance and gift taxes	0.2	0.8	2.6	2.9	3.7	0.1	0.1	0.2	0.1	0.2
4400 Taxes on financial and capital transactions	2.9	3.1	2.7	4.3	4.9	0.8	0.4	0.2	0.2	0.2
4500 Non-recurrent taxes	0.0	0.1	0.1	0.4	384.6	0.0	0.0	0.0	0.0	15.7
4600 Other recurrent taxes on property	0.0	0.7	0.3	0.3	0.4	0.0	0.1	0.0	0.0	0.0
5000 Taxes on goods and services	**58.9**	**112.2**	**190.1**	**262.8**	**295.8**	**15.9**	**16.0**	**11.7**	**11.8**	**12.1**
5100 Taxes on production, sale, transfer, etc	56.6	100.7	179.0	250.1	277.1	15.2	14.3	11.0	11.2	11.3
5110 General taxes	37.1	72.7	122.4	183.7	205.4	10.0	10.4	7.5	8.2	8.4
5111 Value added taxes	32.7	72.7	122.4	183.7	205.4	8.8	10.4	7.5	8.2	8.4
5120 Taxes on specific goods and services	19.5	28.0	56.6	66.4	71.7	5.2	4.0	3.5	3.0	2.9
5121 Excises	2.3	23.6	46.7	56.9	61.7	0.6	3.4	2.9	2.5	2.5
5200 Taxes on use of goods and perform activities	2.4	11.6	11.1	12.7	18.8	0.6	1.6	0.7	0.6	0.8
5300 Unallocable between 5100 and 5200	0.0	0.0	0.0	0.0	0.0	0.0	0.0	0.0	0.0	0.0
6000 Other taxes	**4.5**	**1.0**	**6.0**	**38.4**	**14.9**	**1.2**	**0.1**	**0.4**	**1.7**	**0.6**
Non-wastable tax credits										
Non-wastable tax credits against 1000	..	..	..	1.2	1.4	..	..	..	0.1	0.1
Transfer component	..	..	..	1.0	1.2	..	..	..	0.0	0.0
Tax expenditure component	..	..	..	0.2	0.2	..	..	..	0.0	0.0

.. Not available

Note: More detailed country data and country notes are available in online chapter 5 "Country Tables, 1965-2016": http://dx.doi.org/10.1787/rev_stats-2018-en. Full time series can be accessed at http://oe.cd/full-time-series.

Source: Ministry of Finance, Economic Department.

StatLink http://dx.doi.org/10.1787/888933860197

Table 4.28. Iceland, tax revenue and % of GDP by level of government and main taxes

	Billion ISK					% of GDP				
	1990	2000	2010	2015	2016	1990	2000	2010	2015	2016
Federal or Central government										
Total tax revenue	**91.6**	**195.1**	**402.3**	**604.0**	**1 030.2**	**24.7**	**27.8**	**24.7**	**27.0**	**42.0**
1000 Taxes on income, profits and capital gains	19.9	55.5	132.9	210.5	240.8	5.4	7.9	8.2	9.4	9.8
2000 Social security contributions	3.6	19.7	63.6	79.7	85.4	1.0	2.8	3.9	3.6	3.5
3000 Taxes on payroll and workforce	4.1	0.2	2.8	6.6	7.4	1.1	0.0	0.2	0.3	0.3
4000 Taxes on property	6.0	9.9	9.7	8.8	394.1	1.6	1.4	0.6	0.4	16.1
5000 Taxes on goods and services	57.7	108.9	187.4	260.0	287.6	15.5	15.5	11.5	11.6	11.7
6000 Other taxes	0.4	1.0	6.0	38.4	14.9	0.1	0.1	0.4	1.7	0.6
State/Regional										
Total tax revenue	..	..	..	..	..	..	..	..	..	..
1000 Taxes on income, profits and capital gains	..	..	..	..	..	..	..	..	..	..
2000 Social security contributions	..	..	..	..	..	..	..	..	..	..
3000 Taxes on payroll and workforce	..	..	..	..	..	..	..	..	..	..
4000 Taxes on property	..	..	..	..	..	..	..	..	..	..
5000 Taxes on goods and services	..	..	..	..	..	..	..	..	..	..
6000 Other taxes	..	..	..	..	..	..	..	..	..	..
Local government										
Total tax revenue	**23.3**	**59.4**	**138.0**	**208.0**	**235.4**	**6.3**	**8.5**	**8.5**	**9.3**	**9.6**
1000 Taxes on income, profits and capital gains	14.2	46.0	106.8	170.4	188.7	3.8	6.5	6.6	7.6	7.7
2000 Social security contributions	0.0	0.0	0.0	0.0	0.0	0.0	0.0	0.0	0.0	0.0
3000 Taxes on payroll and workforce	0.0	0.0	0.0	0.0	0.0	0.0	0.0	0.0	0.0	0.0
4000 Taxes on property	3.7	10.1	28.4	34.7	38.5	1.0	1.4	1.7	1.6	1.6
5000 Taxes on goods and services	1.2	3.3	2.8	2.8	8.2	0.3	0.5	0.2	0.1	0.3
6000 Other taxes	4.1	0.0	0.0	0.0	0.0	1.1	0.0	0.0	0.0	0.0
Social Security Funds										
Total tax revenue	**0.0**	**0.0**	**0.0**	**0.0**	**0.0**	**0.0**	**0.0**	**0.0**	**0.0**	**0.0**
1000 Taxes on income, profits and capital gains	0.0	0.0	0.0	0.0	0.0	0.0	0.0	0.0	0.0	0.0
2000 Social security contributions	0.0	0.0	0.0	0.0	0.0	0.0	0.0	0.0	0.0	0.0
3000 Taxes on payroll and workforce	0.0	0.0	0.0	0.0	0.0	0.0	0.0	0.0	0.0	0.0
4000 Taxes on property	0.0	0.0	0.0	0.0	0.0	0.0	0.0	0.0	0.0	0.0
5000 Taxes on goods and services	0.0	0.0	0.0	0.0	0.0	0.0	0.0	0.0	0.0	0.0
6000 Other taxes	0.0	0.0	0.0	0.0	0.0	0.0	0.0	0.0	0.0	0.0

.. Not available

Note: More detailed country data and country notes are available in online chapter 6 "Tax revenues by sub-sectors of general government": http://dx.doi.org/10.1787/rev_stats-2018-en. Full time series can be accessed at http://oe.cd/full-time-series.

Source: Ministry of Finance, Economic Department.

StatLink http://dx.doi.org/10.1787/888933860216

Table 4.29. Ireland, tax revenue and % of GDP by selected tax category

	Billion EUR					% of GDP				
	1990	2000	2010	2015	2016	1990	2000	2010	2015	2016
Total tax revenue	**12.3**	**33.3**	**45.3**	**60.6**	**63.7**	**32.4**	**30.8**	**27.0**	**23.1**	**23.3**
1000 Taxes on income, profits and capital gains	**4.7**	**14.6**	**17.5**	**26.0**	**27.5**	**12.3**	**13.4**	**10.5**	**9.9**	**10.1**
1100 Of individuals	4.1	10.6	13.6	19.2	20.1	10.7	9.8	8.1	7.3	7.4
1200 Corporate	0.6	3.9	3.9	6.9	7.4	1.6	3.6	2.4	2.6	2.7
1300 Unallocable between 1100 and 1200	0.0	0.0	0.0	0.0	0.0	0.0	0.0	0.0	0.0	0.0
2000 Social security contributions	**1.7**	**3.9**	**8.4**	**10.2**	**10.7**	**4.6**	**3.6**	**5.0**	**3.9**	**3.9**
2100 Employees	0.6	0.9	3.2	3.5	3.4	1.5	0.9	1.9	1.3	1.3
2200 Employers	1.1	2.8	4.9	6.2	6.7	2.9	2.6	2.9	2.4	2.4
2300 Self-employed or non-employed	0.1	0.2	0.3	0.5	0.6	0.2	0.2	0.2	0.2	0.2
2400 Unallocable between 2100, 2200 and 2300	0.0	0.0	0.0	0.0	0.0	0.0	0.0	0.0	0.0	0.0
3000 Taxes on payroll and workforce	**0.2**	**0.0**	**0.3**	**0.4**	**0.4**	**0.4**	**0.0**	**0.2**	**0.1**	**0.1**
4000 Taxes on property	**0.6**	**1.9**	**2.4**	**3.9**	**3.8**	**1.5**	**1.8**	**1.4**	**1.5**	**1.4**
4100 Recurrent taxes on immovable property	0.3	0.6	1.3	1.9	1.8	0.8	0.5	0.8	0.7	0.7
4200 Recurrent taxes on net wealth	0.0	0.0	0.0	0.2	0.0	0.0	0.0	0.0	0.1	0.0
4300 Estate, inheritance and gift taxes	0.0	0.2	0.2	0.4	0.4	0.1	0.2	0.1	0.2	0.2
4400 Taxes on financial and capital transactions	0.2	1.1	0.8	1.5	1.6	0.6	1.0	0.5	0.6	0.6
4500 Non-recurrent taxes	0.0	0.0	0.0	0.0	0.0	0.0	0.0	0.0	0.0	0.0
4600 Other recurrent taxes on property	0.0	0.0	0.0	0.0	0.0	0.0	0.0	0.0	0.0	0.0
5000 Taxes on goods and services	**5.1**	**12.7**	**16.4**	**19.8**	**20.8**	**13.6**	**11.7**	**9.8**	**7.5**	**7.6**
5100 Taxes on production, sale, transfer, etc	4.9	12.2	15.1	17.8	18.9	13.0	11.2	9.0	6.8	6.9
5110 General taxes	2.5	7.6	10.1	12.0	12.8	6.6	7.1	6.0	4.6	4.7
5111 Value added taxes	2.5	7.6	10.1	12.0	12.8	6.6	7.1	6.0	4.6	4.7
5120 Taxes on specific goods and services	2.4	4.5	5.0	5.9	6.1	6.4	4.2	3.0	2.2	2.2
5121 Excises	2.1	4.4	4.9	5.5	5.8	5.5	4.1	2.9	2.1	2.1
5200 Taxes on use of goods and perform activities	0.2	0.6	1.3	1.9	1.9	0.5	0.5	0.8	0.7	0.7
5300 Unallocable between 5100 and 5200	0.0	0.0	0.0	0.0	0.0	0.0	0.0	0.0	0.0	0.0
6000 Other taxes	**0.0**	**0.0**	**0.0**	**0.0**	**0.0**	**0.0**	**0.0**	**0.0**	**0.0**	**0.0**
Non-wastable tax credits										
Non-wastable tax credits against 1000	..	..	1.1	0.6	0.5	..	..	0.6	0.2	0.2
Transfer component	..	..	0.0	0.0	..	..	..	0.0	0.0	0.0
Tax expenditure component	..	..	1.1	0.6	0.5	..	..	0.6	0.2	0.2

.. Not available

Note: More detailed country data and country notes are available in online chapter 5 "Country Tables, 1965-2016": http://dx.doi.org/10.1787/rev_stats-2018-en. Full time series can be accessed at http://oe.cd/full-time-series.

Source: Annual Report of he Revenue Commissioners, Financial Accounts and National Income and Expenditure Accounts.

StatLink http://dx.doi.org/10.1787/888933860235

Table 4.30. Ireland, tax revenue and % of GDP by level of government and main taxes

	Billion EUR					% of GDP				
	1990	2000	2010	2015	2016	1990	2000	2010	2015	2016
Federal or Central government										
Total tax revenue	**10.1**	**28.7**	**36.9**	**50.3**	**52.4**	**26.7**	**26.5**	**22.0**	**19.2**	**19.2**
1000 Taxes on income, profits and capital gains	4.7	14.6	17.5	26.0	27.5	12.3	13.4	10.5	9.9	10.1
2000 Social security contributions	0.1	0.1	1.5	1.6	1.4	0.2	0.1	0.9	0.6	0.5
3000 Taxes on payroll and workforce	0.2	0.0	0.3	0.4	0.4	0.4	0.0	0.2	0.1	0.1
4000 Taxes on property	0.3	1.3	1.1	2.5	2.5	0.7	1.2	0.6	1.0	0.9
5000 Taxes on goods and services	5.0	12.7	16.4	19.8	20.7	13.1	11.7	9.8	7.5	7.6
6000 Other taxes	0.0	0.0	0.0	0.0	0.0	0.0	0.0	0.0	0.0	0.0
State/Regional										
Total tax revenue	..	..	..	..	..	..	..	..	..	..
1000 Taxes on income, profits and capital gains	..	..	..	..	..	..	..	..	..	..
2000 Social security contributions	..	..	..	..	..	..	..	..	..	..
3000 Taxes on payroll and workforce	..	..	..	..	..	..	..	..	..	..
4000 Taxes on property	..	..	..	..	..	..	..	..	..	..
5000 Taxes on goods and services	..	..	..	..	..	..	..	..	..	..
6000 Other taxes	..	..	..	..	..	..	..	..	..	..
Local government										
Total tax revenue	**0.3**	**0.7**	**1.5**	**1.5**	**1.4**	**0.9**	**0.6**	**0.9**	**0.6**	**0.5**
1000 Taxes on income, profits and capital gains	0.0	0.0	0.0	0.0	0.0	0.0	0.0	0.0	0.0	0.0
2000 Social security contributions	0.0	0.1	0.2	0.1	0.1	0.1	0.1	0.1	0.0	0.0
3000 Taxes on payroll and workforce	0.0	0.0	0.0	0.0	0.0	0.0	0.0	0.0	0.0	0.0
4000 Taxes on property	0.3	0.6	1.3	1.4	1.4	0.8	0.5	0.8	0.5	0.5
5000 Taxes on goods and services	0.0	0.0	0.0	0.0	0.0	0.0	0.0	0.0	0.0	0.0
6000 Other taxes	0.0	0.0	0.0	0.0	0.0	0.0	0.0	0.0	0.0	0.0
Social Security Funds										
Total tax revenue	**1.6**	**3.7**	**6.7**	**8.5**	**9.2**	**4.3**	**3.5**	**4.0**	**3.2**	**3.4**
1000 Taxes on income, profits and capital gains	0.0	0.0	0.0	0.0	0.0	0.0	0.0	0.0	0.0	0.0
2000 Social security contributions	1.6	3.7	6.7	8.5	9.2	4.3	3.5	4.0	3.2	3.4
3000 Taxes on payroll and workforce	0.0	0.0	0.0	0.0	0.0	0.0	0.0	0.0	0.0	0.0
4000 Taxes on property	0.0	0.0	0.0	0.0	0.0	0.0	0.0	0.0	0.0	0.0
5000 Taxes on goods and services	0.0	0.0	0.0	0.0	0.0	0.0	0.0	0.0	0.0	0.0
6000 Other taxes	0.0	0.0	0.0	0.0	0.0	0.0	0.0	0.0	0.0	0.0

.. Not available

Note: More detailed country data and country notes are available in online chapter 6 "Tax revenues by sub-sectors of general government": http://dx.doi.org/10.1787/rev_stats-2018-en. Full time series can be accessed at http://oe.cd/full-time-series.

Source: Annual Report of he Revenue Commissioners, Financial Accounts and National Income and Expenditure Accounts.

StatLink http://dx.doi.org/10.1787/888933860254

Table 4.31. Israel, tax revenue and % of GDP by selected tax category

	Billion ILS					% of GDP				
	1990	2000	2010	2015	2016	1990	2000	2010	2015	2016
Total tax revenue	..	**188.3**	**268.5**	**364.0**	**381.8**	..	**34.9**	**30.7**	**31.3**	**31.3**
1000 Taxes on income, profits and capital gains	..	**74.6**	**78.3**	**113.7**	**120.5**	..	**13.8**	**9.0**	**9.8**	**9.9**
1100 Of individuals	..	54.8	48.2	70.6	75.6	..	10.1	5.5	6.1	6.2
1200 Corporate	..	18.0	23.1	34.7	37.8	..	3.3	2.6	3.0	3.1
1300 Unallocable between 1100 and 1200	..	1.8	6.9	8.4	7.1	..	0.3	0.8	0.7	0.6
2000 Social security contributions	..	**27.6**	**45.3**	**59.6**	**63.5**	..	**5.1**	**5.2**	**5.1**	**5.2**
2100 Employees	..	15.8	27.8	34.7	35.9	..	2.9	3.2	3.0	2.9
2200 Employers	..	8.2	11.4	17.2	19.5	..	1.5	1.3	1.5	1.6
2300 Self-employed or non-employed	..	3.6	6.1	7.6	8.1	..	0.7	0.7	0.7	0.7
2400 Unallocable between 2100, 2200 and 2300	..	0.0	0.0	0.0	0.0	..	0.0	0.0	0.0	0.0
3000 Taxes on payroll and workforce	..	**6.8**	**10.3**	**13.8**	**14.1**	..	**1.3**	**1.2**	**1.2**	**1.2**
4000 Taxes on property	..	**16.9**	**28.8**	**38.7**	**39.4**	..	**3.1**	**3.3**	**3.3**	**3.2**
4100 Recurrent taxes on immovable property	..	11.3	18.8	23.6	24.6	..	2.1	2.1	2.0	2.0
4200 Recurrent taxes on net wealth	..	0.0	0.0	0.0	0.0	..	0.0	0.0	0.0	0.0
4300 Estate, inheritance and gift taxes	..	0.0	0.0	0.0	0.0	..	0.0	0.0	0.0	0.0
4400 Taxes on financial and capital transactions	..	3.2	4.1	6.7	6.6	..	0.6	0.5	0.6	0.5
4500 Non-recurrent taxes	..	2.4	6.0	8.3	8.3	..	0.5	0.7	0.7	0.7
4600 Other recurrent taxes on property	..	0.0	0.0	0.0	0.0	..	0.0	0.0	0.0	0.0
5000 Taxes on goods and services	..	**62.4**	**105.9**	**138.3**	**144.4**	..	**11.6**	**12.1**	**11.9**	**11.8**
5100 Taxes on production, sale, transfer, etc	..	57.9	98.1	128.3	134.4	..	10.7	11.2	11.0	11.0
5110 General taxes	..	49.9	79.9	107.8	112.9	..	9.2	9.2	9.3	9.2
5111 Value added taxes	..	39.8	65.5	90.8	92.0	..	7.4	7.5	7.8	7.5
5120 Taxes on specific goods and services	..	8.0	18.1	20.5	21.6	..	1.5	2.1	1.8	1.8
5121 Excises	..	6.6	15.5	17.6	18.3	..	1.2	1.8	1.5	1.5
5200 Taxes on use of goods and perform activities	..	4.5	7.8	10.0	9.9	..	0.8	0.9	0.9	0.8
5300 Unallocable between 5100 and 5200	..	0.0	0.0	0.0	0.0	..	0.0	0.0	0.0	0.0
6000 Other taxes	..	**0.0**	**0.0**	**0.0**	**0.0**	..	**0.0**	**0.0**	**0.0**	**0.0**
Non-wastable tax credits										
Non-wastable tax credits against 1000	..	..	0.1	1.4	1.3	..	..	0.0	0.1	0.1
Transfer component	..	..	0.1	1.3	1.2	..	..	0.0	0.1	0.1
Tax expenditure component	..	..	0.0	0.1	0.1	..	..	0.0	0.0	0.0

.. Not available

Note: More detailed country data and country notes are available in online chapter 5 "Country Tables, 1965-2016": http://dx.doi.org/10.1787/rev_stats-2018-en. Full time series can be accessed at http://oe.cd/full-time-series.

The data for Israel are supplied by and under the responsibility of the relevant Israeli authorities. The use of such data by the OECD is without prejudice to the status of the Golan Heights, East Jerusalem and Israeli settlements in the West Bank under the terms of international law.

Source: Israel Central Bureau of Statistics and Israel Ministry of Finance.

StatLink http://dx.doi.org/10.1787/888933860273

Table 4.32. Israel, tax revenue and % of GDP by level of government and main taxes

	Billion ILS					% of GDP				
	1990	2000	2010	2015	2016	1990	2000	2010	2015	2016
Federal or Central government										
Total tax revenue	..	**148.0**	**199.8**	**274.9**	**288.1**	..	**27.4**	**22.9**	**23.7**	**23.6**
1000 Taxes on income, profits and capital gains	..	74.6	78.3	113.7	120.5	..	13.8	9.0	9.8	9.9
2000 Social security contributions	..	0.0	0.0	0.0	0.0	..	0.0	0.0	0.0	0.0
3000 Taxes on payroll and workforce	..	6.8	10.3	13.8	14.1	..	1.3	1.2	1.2	1.2
4000 Taxes on property	..	4.8	6.6	10.6	10.7	..	0.9	0.8	0.9	0.9
5000 Taxes on goods and services	..	61.8	104.7	136.8	142.9	..	11.5	12.0	11.8	11.7
6000 Other taxes	..	0.0	0.0	0.0	0.0	..	0.0	0.0	0.0	0.0
State/Regional										
Total tax revenue	..	..	..	..	..	..	..	..	..	..
1000 Taxes on income, profits and capital gains	..	..	..	..	..	..	..	..	..	..
2000 Social security contributions	..	..	..	..	..	..	..	..	..	..
3000 Taxes on payroll and workforce	..	..	..	..	..	..	..	..	..	..
4000 Taxes on property	..	..	..	..	..	..	..	..	..	..
5000 Taxes on goods and services	..	..	..	..	..	..	..	..	..	..
6000 Other taxes	..	..	..	..	..	..	..	..	..	..
Local government										
Total tax revenue	..	**12.7**	**23.4**	**29.5**	**30.2**	..	**2.4**	**2.7**	**2.5**	**2.5**
1000 Taxes on income, profits and capital gains	..	0.0	0.0	0.0	0.0	..	0.0	0.0	0.0	0.0
2000 Social security contributions	..	0.0	0.0	0.0	0.0	..	0.0	0.0	0.0	0.0
3000 Taxes on payroll and workforce	..	0.0	0.0	0.0	0.0	..	0.0	0.0	0.0	0.0
4000 Taxes on property	..	12.1	22.2	28.1	28.7	..	2.2	2.5	2.4	2.4
5000 Taxes on goods and services	..	0.6	1.1	1.4	1.5	..	0.1	0.1	0.1	0.1
6000 Other taxes	..	0.0	0.0	0.0	0.0	..	0.0	0.0	0.0	0.0
Social Security Funds										
Total tax revenue	..	**27.6**	**45.3**	**59.6**	**63.5**	..	**5.1**	**5.2**	**5.1**	**5.2**
1000 Taxes on income, profits and capital gains	..	0.0	0.0	0.0	0.0	..	0.0	0.0	0.0	0.0
2000 Social security contributions	..	27.6	45.3	59.6	63.5	..	5.1	5.2	5.1	5.2
3000 Taxes on payroll and workforce	..	0.0	0.0	0.0	0.0	..	0.0	0.0	0.0	0.0
4000 Taxes on property	..	0.0	0.0	0.0	0.0	..	0.0	0.0	0.0	0.0
5000 Taxes on goods and services	..	0.0	0.0	0.0	0.0	..	0.0	0.0	0.0	0.0
6000 Other taxes	..	0.0	0.0	0.0	0.0	..	0.0	0.0	0.0	0.0

.. Not available

Note: More detailed country data and country notes are available in online chapter 6 "Tax revenues by sub-sectors of general government": http://dx.doi.org/10.1787/rev_stats-2018-en. Full time series can be accessed at http://oe.cd/full-time-series.

The data for Israel are supplied by and under the responsibility of the relevant Israeli authorities. The use of such data by the OECD is without prejudice to the status of the Golan Heights, East Jerusalem and Israeli settlements in the West Bank under the terms of international law.

Source: Israel Central Bureau of Statistics and Israel Ministry of Finance.

StatLink http://dx.doi.org/10.1787/888933860292

Table 4.33. Italy, tax revenue and % of GDP by selected tax category

	Billion EUR					% of GDP				
	1990	2000	2010	2015	2016	1990	2000	2010	2015	2016
Total tax revenue	**265.1**	**503.1**	**671.6**	**712.5**	**716.2**	**36.4**	**40.6**	**41.9**	**43.1**	**42.6**
1000 Taxes on income, profits and capital gains	**96.7**	**166.9**	**219.3**	**226.7**	**229.0**	**13.3**	**13.5**	**13.7**	**13.7**	**13.6**
1100 Of individuals	69.7	124.9	180.2	185.1	184.5	9.6	10.1	11.2	11.2	11.0
1200 Corporate	26.6	34.7	36.7	33.8	36.1	3.7	2.8	2.3	2.0	2.1
1300 Unallocable between 1100 and 1200	0.4	7.3	2.3	7.8	8.3	0.1	0.6	0.1	0.5	0.5
2000 Social security contributions	**87.3**	**143.6**	**209.1**	**214.4**	**215.9**	**12.0**	**11.6**	**13.0**	**13.0**	**12.8**
2100 Employees	16.8	27.3	37.6	39.8	40.0	2.3	2.2	2.3	2.4	2.4
2200 Employers	62.5	99.9	144.3	143.3	144.0	8.6	8.1	9.0	8.7	8.6
2300 Self-employed or non-employed	8.0	16.4	27.2	31.3	31.9	1.1	1.3	1.7	1.9	1.9
2400 Unallocable between 2100, 2200 and 2300	0.0	0.0	0.0	0.0	0.0	0.0	0.0	0.0	0.0	0.0
3000 Taxes on payroll and workforce	**0.9**	**0.0**	**0.0**	**0.0**	**0.0**	**0.1**	**0.0**	**0.0**	**0.0**	**0.0**
4000 Taxes on property	**6.0**	**23.4**	**32.4**	**46.4**	**47.1**	**0.8**	**1.9**	**2.0**	**2.8**	**2.8**
4100 Recurrent taxes on immovable property	0.0	9.4	9.7	25.6	21.7	0.0	0.8	0.6	1.5	1.3
4200 Recurrent taxes on net wealth	0.0	0.0	2.1	0.2	0.4	0.0	0.0	0.1	0.0	0.0
4300 Estate, inheritance and gift taxes	0.4	1.0	0.5	0.7	0.7	0.1	0.1	0.0	0.0	0.0
4400 Taxes on financial and capital transactions	5.6	12.3	17.4	17.4	17.8	0.8	1.0	1.1	1.1	1.1
4500 Non-recurrent taxes	0.0	0.1	0.9	0.3	4.2	0.0	0.0	0.1	0.0	0.3
4600 Other recurrent taxes on property	0.0	0.6	1.9	2.2	2.2	0.0	0.0	0.1	0.1	0.1
5000 Taxes on goods and services	**74.3**	**140.3**	**176.6**	**194.6**	**201.5**	**10.2**	**11.3**	**11.0**	**11.8**	**12.0**
5100 Taxes on production, sale, transfer, etc	67.1	125.7	158.5	172.4	177.0	9.2	10.1	9.9	10.4	10.5
5110 General taxes	38.9	77.5	97.6	101.1	103.0	5.3	6.3	6.1	6.1	6.1
5111 Value added taxes	38.9	77.5	97.6	101.1	103.0	5.3	6.3	6.1	6.1	6.1
5120 Taxes on specific goods and services	28.0	48.3	61.0	71.4	74.0	3.9	3.9	3.8	4.3	4.4
5121 Excises	20.3	31.5	36.4	46.2	48.4	2.8	2.5	2.3	2.8	2.9
5200 Taxes on use of goods and perform activities	4.5	8.5	10.5	11.1	13.4	0.6	0.7	0.7	0.7	0.8
5300 Unallocable between 5100 and 5200	2.7	6.1	7.6	11.0	11.1	0.4	0.5	0.5	0.7	0.7
6000 Other taxes	**0.0**	**27.3**	**31.9**	**28.2**	**20.6**	**0.0**	**2.2**	**2.0**	**1.7**	**1.2**
Non-wastable tax credits										
Non-wastable tax credits against 1000	..	..	0.3	14.7	12.6	..	..	0.0	0.9	0.7
Transfer component	..	..	0.1	6.0	3.7	..	..	0.0	0.4	0.2
Tax expenditure component	..	..	0.2	8.6	8.9	..	..	0.0	0.5	0.5

.. Not available

Note: More detailed country data and country notes are available in online chapter 5 "Country Tables, 1965-2016": http://dx.doi.org/10.1787/rev_stats-2018-en. Full time series can be accessed at http://oe.cd/full-time-series.

Source: Ministero dell'economia e delle finanze; Istituto nazionale di statistica.

StatLink http://dx.doi.org/10.1787/888933860311

Table 4.34. Italy, tax revenue and % of GDP by level of government and main taxes

	Billion EUR					% of GDP				
	1990	2000	2010	2015	2016	1990	2000	2010	2015	2016
Federal or Central government										
Total tax revenue	**168.9**	**280.8**	**357.0**	**378.6**	**389.7**	**23.2**	**22.7**	**22.3**	**22.9**	**23.2**
1000 Taxes on income, profits and capital gains	92.7	154.2	193.6	196.2	198.2	12.7	12.4	12.1	11.9	11.8
2000 Social security contributions	0.0	0.0	0.0	0.0	0.0	0.0	0.0	0.0	0.0	0.0
3000 Taxes on payroll and workforce	0.9	0.0	0.0	0.0	0.0	0.1	0.0	0.0	0.0	0.0
4000 Taxes on property	6.0	12.9	21.0	22.4	26.6	0.8	1.0	1.3	1.4	1.6
5000 Taxes on goods and services	69.3	113.6	142.5	160.0	164.9	9.5	9.2	8.9	9.7	9.8
6000 Other taxes	0.0	0.0	0.0	0.0	0.0	0.0	0.0	0.0	0.0	0.0
State/Regional										
Total tax revenue	..	..	..	..	..	..	..	..	..	..
1000 Taxes on income, profits and capital gains	..	..	..	..	..	..	..	..	..	..
2000 Social security contributions	..	..	..	..	..	..	..	..	..	..
3000 Taxes on payroll and workforce	..	..	..	..	..	..	..	..	..	..
4000 Taxes on property	..	..	..	..	..	..	..	..	..	..
5000 Taxes on goods and services	..	..	..	..	..	..	..	..	..	..
6000 Other taxes	..	..	..	..	..	..	..	..	..	..
Local government										
Total tax revenue	**7.7**	**77.2**	**103.2**	**117.2**	**107.7**	**1.1**	**6.2**	**6.4**	**7.1**	**6.4**
1000 Taxes on income, profits and capital gains	4.0	12.7	25.6	30.5	30.8	0.6	1.0	1.6	1.8	1.8
2000 Social security contributions	0.0	0.0	0.0	0.0	0.0	0.0	0.0	0.0	0.0	0.0
3000 Taxes on payroll and workforce	0.0	0.0	0.0	0.0	0.0	0.0	0.0	0.0	0.0	0.0
4000 Taxes on property	0.0	10.5	11.5	24.0	20.5	0.0	0.8	0.7	1.5	1.2
5000 Taxes on goods and services	3.7	26.7	34.2	34.6	35.8	0.5	2.2	2.1	2.1	2.1
6000 Other taxes	0.0	27.3	31.9	28.2	20.6	0.0	2.2	2.0	1.7	1.2
Social Security Funds										
Total tax revenue	**87.3**	**143.6**	**209.1**	**214.4**	**215.9**	**12.0**	**11.6**	**13.0**	**13.0**	**12.8**
1000 Taxes on income, profits and capital gains	0.0	0.0	0.0	0.0	0.0	0.0	0.0	0.0	0.0	0.0
2000 Social security contributions	87.3	143.6	209.1	214.4	215.9	12.0	11.6	13.0	13.0	12.8
3000 Taxes on payroll and workforce	0.0	0.0	0.0	0.0	0.0	0.0	0.0	0.0	0.0	0.0
4000 Taxes on property	0.0	0.0	0.0	0.0	0.0	0.0	0.0	0.0	0.0	0.0
5000 Taxes on goods and services	0.0	0.0	0.0	0.0	0.0	0.0	0.0	0.0	0.0	0.0
6000 Other taxes	0.0	0.0	0.0	0.0	0.0	0.0	0.0	0.0	0.0	0.0

.. Not available

Note: More detailed country data and country notes are available in online chapter 6 "Tax revenues by sub-sectors of general government": http://dx.doi.org/10.1787/rev_stats-2018-en. Full time series can be accessed at http://oe.cd/full-time-series.

Source: Ministero dell'economia e delle finanze; Istituto nazionale di statistica.

StatLink http://dx.doi.org/10.1787/888933860330

Table 4.35. Japan, tax revenue and % of GDP by selected tax category

	Billion JPY					% of GDP				
	1990	2000	2010	2015	2016	1990	2000	2010	2015	2016
Total tax revenue	**130 842.7**	**136 235.8**	**132 484.3**	**163 533.1**	**164 962.9**	**28.2**	**25.8**	**26.5**	**30.6**	**30.6**
1000 Taxes on income, profits and capital gains	**65 681.6**	**47 398.2**	**40 034.3**	**50 968.7**	**50 447.7**	**14.2**	**9.0**	**8.0**	**9.5**	**9.4**
1100 Of individuals	36 393.6	28 677.3	24 662.7	30 847.1	30 669.6	7.8	5.4	4.9	5.8	5.7
1200 Corporate	29 288.0	18 720.9	15 371.6	20 121.7	19 778.1	6.3	3.5	3.1	3.8	3.7
1300 Unallocable between 1100 and 1200	0.0	0.0	0.0	0.0	0.0	0.0	0.0	0.0	0.0	0.0
2000 Social security contributions	**34 612.6**	**47 968.3**	**54 460.6**	**64 465.2**	**66 614.3**	**7.5**	**9.1**	**10.9**	**12.1**	**12.4**
2100 Employees	13 895.0	19 829.9	23 592.6	28 223.5	29 311.4	3.0	3.8	4.7	5.3	5.4
2200 Employers	16 648.8	22 455.5	24 674.2	29 478.7	30 560.4	3.6	4.2	4.9	5.5	5.7
2300 Self-employed or non-employed	4 068.8	5 682.9	6 193.8	6 763.0	6 742.5	0.9	1.1	1.2	1.3	1.3
2400 Unallocable between 2100, 2200 and 2300	0.0	0.0	0.0	0.0	0.0	0.0	0.0	0.0	0.0	0.0
3000 Taxes on payroll and workforce	**0.0**	**0.0**	**0.0**	**0.0**	**0.0**	**0.0**	**0.0**	**0.0**	**0.0**	**0.0**
4000 Taxes on property	**12 296.3**	**14 294.4**	**12 878.3**	**13 399.7**	**13 772.3**	**2.7**	**2.7**	**2.6**	**2.5**	**2.6**
4100 Recurrent taxes on immovable property	7 098.5	10 413.7	10 225.0	10 005.0	10 165.1	1.5	2.0	2.0	1.9	1.9
4200 Recurrent taxes on net wealth	0.0	0.0	0.0	0.0	0.0	0.0	0.0	0.0	0.0	0.0
4300 Estate, inheritance and gift taxes	1 918.0	1 782.2	1 250.4	1 968.4	2 131.4	0.4	0.3	0.3	0.4	0.4
4400 Taxes on financial and capital transactions	3 279.8	2 098.5	1 402.9	1 426.3	1 475.8	0.7	0.4	0.3	0.3	0.3
4500 Non-recurrent taxes	0.0	0.0	0.0	0.0	0.0	0.0	0.0	0.0	0.0	0.0
4600 Other recurrent taxes on property	0.0	0.0	0.0	0.0	0.0	0.0	0.0	0.0	0.0	0.0
5000 Taxes on goods and services	**17 916.8**	**26 227.2**	**24 730.2**	**34 286.4**	**33 711.0**	**3.9**	**5.0**	**5.0**	**6.4**	**6.3**
5100 Taxes on production, sale, transfer, etc	15 646.5	23 180.2	22 160.4	31 870.7	31 254.2	3.4	4.4	4.4	6.0	5.8
5110 General taxes	5 778.3	12 350.3	12 675.2	22 400.5	21 931.0	1.2	2.3	2.5	4.2	4.1
5111 Value added taxes	5 778.3	12 350.3	12 675.2	22 400.5	21 931.0	1.2	2.3	2.5	4.2	4.1
5120 Taxes on specific goods and services	9 868.2	10 829.9	9 485.2	9 470.2	9 323.2	2.1	2.0	1.9	1.8	1.7
5121 Excises	8 637.2	9 837.0	8 622.4	8 351.2	8 315.9	1.9	1.9	1.7	1.6	1.5
5200 Taxes on use of goods and perform activities	2 270.3	3 047.0	2 569.8	2 415.7	2 456.8	0.5	0.6	0.5	0.5	0.5
5300 Unallocable between 5100 and 5200	0.0	0.0	0.0	0.0	0.0	0.0	0.0	0.0	0.0	0.0
6000 Other taxes	**335.4**	**347.7**	**381.1**	**413.0**	**417.6**	**0.1**	**0.1**	**0.1**	**0.1**	**0.1**
Non-wastable tax credits										
Non-wastable tax credits against 1000	..	..	..	..	..	..	..	..	..	..
Transfer component	..	..	..	..	..	..	..	..	..	..
Tax expenditure component	..	..	..	..	..	..	..	..	..	..

.. Not available

Note: More detailed country data and country notes are available in online chapter 5 "Country Tables, 1965-2016": http://dx.doi.org/10.1787/rev_stats-2018-en. Full time series can be accessed at http://oe.cd/full-time-series.

Source: Tax Bureau, Ministry of Finance.

StatLink http://dx.doi.org/10.1787/888933860349

Table 4.36. Japan, tax revenue and % of GDP by level of government and main taxes

	Billion JPY					% of GDP				
	1990	2000	2010	2015	2016	1990	2000	2010	2015	2016
Federal or Central government										
Total tax revenue	**62 779.7**	**52 720.8**	**43 707.4**	**59 969.4**	**58 956.3**	**13.5**	**10.0**	**8.8**	**11.2**	**10.9**
1000 Taxes on income, profits and capital gains	44 379.1	30 536.2	23 372.1	31 606.8	30 721.4	9.6	5.8	4.7	5.9	5.7
2000 Social security contributions	0.0	0.0	0.0	0.0	0.0	0.0	0.0	0.0	0.0	0.0
3000 Taxes on payroll and workforce	0.0	0.0	0.0	0.0	0.0	0.0	0.0	0.0	0.0	0.0
4000 Taxes on property	4 601.6	3 314.9	2 274.5	3 018.0	3 210.5	1.0	0.6	0.5	0.6	0.6
5000 Taxes on goods and services	13 799.0	18 869.7	18 060.9	25 344.5	25 024.4	3.0	3.6	3.6	4.7	4.6
6000 Other taxes	0.0	0.0	0.0	0.0	0.0	0.0	0.0	0.0	0.0	0.0
State/Regional										
Total tax revenue	..	..	..	..	..	..	..	..	..	..
1000 Taxes on income, profits and capital gains	..	..	..	..	..	..	..	..	..	..
2000 Social security contributions	..	..	..	..	..	..	..	..	..	..
3000 Taxes on payroll and workforce	..	..	..	..	..	..	..	..	..	..
4000 Taxes on property	..	..	..	..	..	..	..	..	..	..
5000 Taxes on goods and services	..	..	..	..	..	..	..	..	..	..
6000 Other taxes	..	..	..	..	..	..	..	..	..	..
Local government										
Total tax revenue	**33 450.4**	**35 546.7**	**34 316.3**	**39 098.5**	**39 392.3**	**7.2**	**6.7**	**6.9**	**7.3**	**7.3**
1000 Taxes on income, profits and capital gains	21 302.5	16 862.0	16 662.3	19 361.9	19 726.3	4.6	3.2	3.3	3.6	3.7
2000 Social security contributions	0.0	0.0	0.0	0.0	0.0	0.0	0.0	0.0	0.0	0.0
3000 Taxes on payroll and workforce	0.0	0.0	0.0	0.0	0.0	0.0	0.0	0.0	0.0	0.0
4000 Taxes on property	7 694.7	10 979.5	10 603.8	10 381.8	10 561.8	1.7	2.1	2.1	1.9	2.0
5000 Taxes on goods and services	4 117.8	7 357.5	6 669.2	8 941.9	8 686.6	0.9	1.4	1.3	1.7	1.6
6000 Other taxes	335.4	347.7	381.1	413.0	417.6	0.1	0.1	0.1	0.1	0.1
Social Security Funds										
Total tax revenue	**34 612.6**	**47 968.3**	**54 460.6**	**64 465.2**	**66 614.3**	**7.5**	**9.1**	**10.9**	**12.1**	**12.4**
1000 Taxes on income, profits and capital gains	0.0	0.0	0.0	0.0	0.0	0.0	0.0	0.0	0.0	0.0
2000 Social security contributions	34 612.6	47 968.3	54 460.6	64 465.2	66 614.3	7.5	9.1	10.9	12.1	12.4
3000 Taxes on payroll and workforce	0.0	0.0	0.0	0.0	0.0	0.0	0.0	0.0	0.0	0.0
4000 Taxes on property	0.0	0.0	0.0	0.0	0.0	0.0	0.0	0.0	0.0	0.0
5000 Taxes on goods and services	0.0	0.0	0.0	0.0	0.0	0.0	0.0	0.0	0.0	0.0
6000 Other taxes	0.0	0.0	0.0	0.0	0.0	0.0	0.0	0.0	0.0	0.0

.. Not available

Note: More detailed country data and country notes are available in online chapter 6 "Tax revenues by sub-sectors of general government": http://dx.doi.org/10.1787/rev_stats-2018-en. Full time series can be accessed at http://oe.cd/full-time-series.

Source: Tax Bureau, Ministry of Finance.

StatLink http://dx.doi.org/10.1787/888933860368

Table 4.37. Korea, tax revenue and % of GDP by selected tax category

	Billion KRW					% of GDP				
	1990	2000	2010	2015	2016	1990	2000	2010	2015	2016
Total tax revenue	**37 261.7**	**136 295.0**	**295 968.0**	**393 559.0**	**430 752.0**	**18.8**	**21.5**	**23.4**	**25.2**	**26.2**
1000 Taxes on income, profits and capital gains	**12 203.5**	**39 254.0**	**82 905.0**	**119 151.0**	**134 503.0**	**6.2**	**6.2**	**6.6**	**7.6**	**8.2**
1100 Of individuals	7 440.4	19 950.0	42 098.0	67 600.0	75 711.0	3.8	3.1	3.3	4.3	4.6
1200 Corporate	4 756.6	19 271.0	40 807.0	51 551.0	58 792.0	2.4	3.0	3.2	3.3	3.6
1300 Unallocable between 1100 and 1200	6.5	33.0	0.0	0.0	0.0	0.0	0.0	0.0	0.0	0.0
2000 Social security contributions	**3 760.0**	**22 759.0**	**69 090.0**	**104 693.0**	**112 658.0**	**1.9**	**3.6**	**5.5**	**6.7**	**6.9**
2100 Employees	1 464.0	8 578.0	28 213.0	44 281.0	48 077.0	0.7	1.4	2.2	2.8	2.9
2200 Employers	1 694.0	9 409.0	30 856.0	47 846.0	51 190.0	0.9	1.5	2.4	3.1	3.1
2300 Self-employed or non-employed	602.0	4 772.0	10 021.0	12 566.0	13 391.0	0.3	0.8	0.8	0.8	0.8
2400 Unallocable between 2100, 2200 and 2300	0.0	0.0	0.0	0.0	0.0	0.0	0.0	0.0	0.0	0.0
3000 Taxes on payroll and workforce	**152.8**	**258.0**	**714.0**	**1 122.0**	**1 293.0**	**0.1**	**0.0**	**0.1**	**0.1**	**0.1**
4000 Taxes on property	**4 388.9**	**16 846.0**	**33 516.0**	**48 625.0**	**49 820.0**	**2.2**	**2.7**	**2.6**	**3.1**	**3.0**
4100 Recurrent taxes on immovable property	980.0	3 385.0	9 270.0	12 486.0	13 095.0	0.5	0.5	0.7	0.8	0.8
4200 Recurrent taxes on net wealth	0.0	0.0	0.0	0.0	0.0	0.0	0.0	0.0	0.0	0.0
4300 Estate, inheritance and gift taxes	353.9	989.0	3 076.0	5 044.0	5 350.0	0.2	0.2	0.2	0.3	0.3
4400 Taxes on financial and capital transactions	2 959.7	11 935.0	21 170.0	31 095.0	31 375.0	1.5	1.9	1.7	2.0	1.9
4500 Non-recurrent taxes	95.3	537.0	0.0	0.0	0.0	0.0	0.1	0.0	0.0	0.0
4600 Other recurrent taxes on property	0.0	0.0	0.0	0.0	0.0	0.0	0.0	0.0	0.0	0.0
5000 Taxes on goods and services	**16 497.5**	**52 271.0**	**99 769.0**	**110 326.0**	**121 197.0**	**8.3**	**8.2**	**7.9**	**7.1**	**7.4**
5100 Taxes on production, sale, transfer, etc	16 023.5	50 023.0	96 573.0	103 254.0	113 644.0	8.1	7.9	7.6	6.6	6.9
5110 General taxes	6 964.4	23 212.0	51 800.0	60 162.0	68 229.0	3.5	3.7	4.1	3.8	4.2
5111 Value added taxes	6 964.4	23 212.0	51 800.0	60 162.0	68 229.0	3.5	3.7	4.1	3.8	4.2
5120 Taxes on specific goods and services	9 059.1	26 811.0	44 773.0	43 092.0	45 415.0	4.6	4.2	3.5	2.8	2.8
5121 Excises	4 923.7	18 155.0	31 340.0	31 857.0	34 762.0	2.5	2.9	2.5	2.0	2.1
5200 Taxes on use of goods and perform activities	473.9	2 248.0	3 196.0	7 072.0	7 553.0	0.2	0.4	0.3	0.5	0.5
5300 Unallocable between 5100 and 5200	0.0	0.0	0.0	0.0	0.0	0.0	0.0	0.0	0.0	0.0
6000 Other taxes	**259.1**	**4 907.0**	**9 974.0**	**9 642.0**	**11 281.0**	**0.1**	**0.8**	**0.8**	**0.6**	**0.7**
Non-wastable tax credits										
Non-wastable tax credits against 1000	..	..	..	..	..	..	..	..	..	..
Transfer component	..	..	..	..	..	..	..	..	..	..
Tax expenditure component	..	..	..	..	..	..	..	..	..	..

.. Not available

Note: More detailed country data and country notes are available in online chapter 5 "Country Tables, 1965-2016": http://dx.doi.org/10.1787/rev_stats-2018-en. Full time series can be accessed at http://oe.cd/full-time-series.

Source: Ministry of Finance and Economy, Ministry of Home Affairs.

StatLink http://dx.doi.org/10.1787/888933860387

Table 4.38. Korea, tax revenue and % of GDP by level of government and main taxes

	Billion KRW					% of GDP				
	1990	2000	2010	2015	2016	1990	2000	2010	2015	2016
Federal or Central government										
Total tax revenue	**27 140.8**	**92 935.0**	**177 718.0**	**217 888.0**	**242 562.0**	**13.7**	**14.6**	**14.0**	**13.9**	**14.8**
1000 Taxes on income, profits and capital gains	11 655.2	35 824.0	75 352.0	106 162.0	121 127.0	5.9	5.6	6.0	6.8	7.4
2000 Social security contributions	0.0	0.0	0.0	0.0	0.0	0.0	0.0	0.0	0.0	0.0
3000 Taxes on payroll and workforce	29.3	0.0	0.0	0.0	0.0	0.0	0.0	0.0	0.0	0.0
4000 Taxes on property	866.3	5 866.0	11 288.0	15 164.0	14 849.0	0.4	0.9	0.9	1.0	0.9
5000 Taxes on goods and services	14 377.5	46 812.0	86 629.0	93 127.0	102 439.0	7.3	7.4	6.8	6.0	6.2
6000 Other taxes	212.5	4 433.0	4 449.0	3 435.0	4 147.0	0.1	0.7	0.4	0.2	0.3
State/Regional										
Total tax revenue	..	..	..	..	..	..	..	..	..	..
1000 Taxes on income, profits and capital gains	..	..	..	..	..	..	..	..	..	..
2000 Social security contributions	..	..	..	..	..	..	..	..	..	..
3000 Taxes on payroll and workforce	..	..	..	..	..	..	..	..	..	..
4000 Taxes on property	..	..	..	..	..	..	..	..	..	..
5000 Taxes on goods and services	..	..	..	..	..	..	..	..	..	..
6000 Other taxes	..	..	..	..	..	..	..	..	..	..
Local government										
Total tax revenue	**6 360.9**	**20 601.0**	**49 160.0**	**70 978.0**	**75 532.0**	**3.2**	**3.2**	**3.9**	**4.5**	**4.6**
1000 Taxes on income, profits and capital gains	548.3	3 430.0	7 553.0	12 989.0	13 376.0	0.3	0.5	0.6	0.8	0.8
2000 Social security contributions	0.0	0.0	0.0	0.0	0.0	0.0	0.0	0.0	0.0	0.0
3000 Taxes on payroll and workforce	123.5	258.0	714.0	1 122.0	1 293.0	0.1	0.0	0.1	0.1	0.1
4000 Taxes on property	3 522.6	10 980.0	22 228.0	33 461.0	34 971.0	1.8	1.7	1.8	2.1	2.1
5000 Taxes on goods and services	2 120.0	5 459.0	13 140.0	17 199.0	18 758.0	1.1	0.9	1.0	1.1	1.1
6000 Other taxes	46.6	474.0	5 525.0	6 207.0	7 134.0	0.0	0.1	0.4	0.4	0.4
Social Security Funds										
Total tax revenue	**3 760.0**	**22 759.0**	**69 090.0**	**104 693.0**	**112 658.0**	**1.9**	**3.6**	**5.5**	**6.7**	**6.9**
1000 Taxes on income, profits and capital gains	0.0	0.0	0.0	0.0	0.0	0.0	0.0	0.0	0.0	0.0
2000 Social security contributions	3 760.0	22 759.0	69 090.0	104 693.0	112 658.0	1.9	3.6	5.5	6.7	6.9
3000 Taxes on payroll and workforce	0.0	0.0	0.0	0.0	0.0	0.0	0.0	0.0	0.0	0.0
4000 Taxes on property	0.0	0.0	0.0	0.0	0.0	0.0	0.0	0.0	0.0	0.0
5000 Taxes on goods and services	0.0	0.0	0.0	0.0	0.0	0.0	0.0	0.0	0.0	0.0
6000 Other taxes	0.0	0.0	0.0	0.0	0.0	0.0	0.0	0.0	0.0	0.0

.. Not available

Note: More detailed country data and country notes are available in online chapter 6 "Tax revenues by sub-sectors of general government": http://dx.doi.org/10.1787/rev_stats-2018-en. Full time series can be accessed at http://oe.cd/full-time-series.

Source: Ministry of Finance and Economy, Ministry of Home Affairs.

StatLink http://dx.doi.org/10.1787/888933860406

Table 4.39. Latvia, tax revenue and % of GDP by selected tax category

	Billion EUR					% of GDP				
	1990	2000	2010	2015	2016	1990	2000	2010	2015	2016
Total tax revenue	..	**2.0**	**5.1**	**7.1**	**7.6**	..	**29.1**	**28.2**	**29.2**	**30.4**
1000 Taxes on income, profits and capital gains	..	**0.5**	**1.3**	**1.8**	**2.0**	..	**7.0**	**7.2**	**7.5**	**8.1**
1100 Of individuals	..	0.4	1.1	1.4	1.6	..	5.5	6.2	5.9	6.4
1200 Corporate	..	0.1	0.2	0.4	0.4	..	1.5	1.0	1.6	1.7
1300 Unallocable between 1100 and 1200	..	0.0	0.0	0.0	0.0	..	0.0	0.0	0.0	0.0
2000 Social security contributions	..	**0.7**	**1.6**	**2.0**	**2.1**	..	**9.8**	**8.7**	**8.3**	**8.3**
2100 Employees	..	0.2	0.4	0.6	0.5	..	2.4	2.2	2.4	2.1
2200 Employers	..	0.5	1.2	1.4	1.5	..	7.3	6.4	5.9	6.1
2300 Self-employed or non-employed	..	0.0	0.0	0.0	0.0	..	0.0	0.1	0.1	0.1
2400 Unallocable between 2100, 2200 and 2300	..	0.0	0.0	0.0	0.0	..	0.0	0.0	0.0	0.0
3000 Taxes on payroll and workforce	..	**0.0**	**0.0**	**0.0**	**0.0**	..	**0.0**	**0.0**	**0.0**	**0.0**
4000 Taxes on property	..	**0.1**	**0.2**	**0.2**	**0.3**	..	**1.1**	**0.9**	**1.0**	**1.1**
4100 Recurrent taxes on immovable property	..	0.1	0.1	0.2	0.2	..	0.9	0.7	0.8	0.9
4200 Recurrent taxes on net wealth	..	0.0	0.0	0.0	0.0	..	0.0	0.0	0.0	0.0
4300 Estate, inheritance and gift taxes	..	0.0	0.0	0.0	0.0	..	0.0	0.0	0.0	0.0
4400 Taxes on financial and capital transactions	..	0.0	0.0	0.0	0.0	..	0.2	0.1	0.2	0.2
4500 Non-recurrent taxes	..	0.0	0.0	0.0	0.0	..	0.0	0.0	0.0	0.0
4600 Other recurrent taxes on property	..	0.0	0.0	0.0	0.0	..	0.0	0.0	0.0	0.0
5000 Taxes on goods and services	..	**0.8**	**2.0**	**3.0**	**3.2**	..	**11.2**	**11.3**	**12.2**	**12.8**
5100 Taxes on production, sale, transfer, etc	..	0.7	1.9	2.8	3.0	..	10.8	10.6	11.5	12.1
5110 General taxes	..	0.5	1.2	1.9	2.1	..	7.0	6.7	7.8	8.3
5111 Value added taxes	..	0.5	1.2	1.9	2.0	..	7.0	6.7	7.7	8.2
5120 Taxes on specific goods and services	..	0.3	0.7	0.9	0.9	..	3.8	3.9	3.6	3.8
5121 Excises	..	0.2	0.6	0.8	0.9	..	3.4	3.6	3.3	3.5
5200 Taxes on use of goods and perform activities	..	0.0	0.1	0.2	0.2	..	0.5	0.7	0.7	0.7
5300 Unallocable between 5100 and 5200	..	0.0	0.0	0.0	0.0	..	0.0	0.0	0.0	0.0
6000 Other taxes	..	**0.0**	**0.0**	**0.0**	**0.0**	..	**0.0**	**0.0**	**0.0**	**0.0**
Non-wastable tax credits										
Non-wastable tax credits against 1000	..	..	..	..	..	..	..	..	..	..
Transfer component	..	..	..	..	..	..	..	..	..	..
Tax expenditure component	..	..	..	..	..	..	..	..	..	..

.. Not available

Note: More detailed country data and country notes are available in online chapter 5 "Country Tables, 1965-2016": http://dx.doi.org/10.1787/rev_stats-2018-en. Full time series can be accessed at http://oe.cd/full-time-series.

Source: Ministry of Finance.

StatLink http://dx.doi.org/10.1787/888933860425

Table 4.40. Latvia, tax revenue and % of GDP by level of government and main taxes

	Billion EUR					% of GDP				
	1990	2000	2010	2015	2016	1990	2000	2010	2015	2016
Federal or Central government										
Total tax revenue	..	**1.0**	**2.5**	**3.7**	**4.0**	..	**14.4**	**13.7**	**15.0**	**16.0**
1000 Taxes on income, profits and capital gains	..	0.2	0.4	0.7	0.8	..	3.1	2.2	2.8	3.1
2000 Social security contributions	..	0.0	0.0	0.0	0.0	..	0.0	0.0	0.0	0.0
3000 Taxes on payroll and workforce	..	0.0	0.0	0.0	0.0	..	0.0	0.0	0.0	0.0
4000 Taxes on property	..	0.0	0.0	0.0	0.0	..	0.2	0.2	0.2	0.2
5000 Taxes on goods and services	..	0.8	2.0	2.9	3.2	..	11.2	11.3	12.1	12.7
6000 Other taxes	..	0.0	0.0	0.0	0.0	..	0.0	0.0	0.0	0.0
State/Regional										
Total tax revenue	..	..	..	..	..	..	..	..	..	..
1000 Taxes on income, profits and capital gains	..	..	..	..	..	..	..	..	..	..
2000 Social security contributions	..	..	..	..	..	..	..	..	..	..
3000 Taxes on payroll and workforce	..	..	..	..	..	..	..	..	..	..
4000 Taxes on property	..	..	..	..	..	..	..	..	..	..
5000 Taxes on goods and services	..	..	..	..	..	..	..	..	..	..
6000 Other taxes	..	..	..	..	..	..	..	..	..	..
Local government										
Total tax revenue	..	**0.3**	**1.0**	**1.4**	**1.5**	..	**4.9**	**5.8**	**5.6**	**5.9**
1000 Taxes on income, profits and capital gains	..	0.3	0.9	1.2	1.2	..	3.9	5.0	4.8	5.0
2000 Social security contributions	..	0.0	0.0	0.0	0.0	..	0.0	0.0	0.0	0.0
3000 Taxes on payroll and workforce	..	0.0	0.0	0.0	0.0	..	0.0	0.0	0.0	0.0
4000 Taxes on property	..	0.1	0.1	0.2	0.2	..	0.9	0.7	0.8	0.9
5000 Taxes on goods and services	..	0.0	0.0	0.0	0.0	..	0.1	0.1	0.1	0.1
6000 Other taxes	..	0.0	0.0	0.0	0.0	..	0.0	0.0	0.0	0.0
Social Security Funds										
Total tax revenue	..	**0.7**	**1.6**	**2.0**	**2.1**	..	**9.8**	**8.7**	**8.3**	**8.3**
1000 Taxes on income, profits and capital gains	..	0.0	0.0	0.0	0.0	..	0.0	0.0	0.0	0.0
2000 Social security contributions	..	0.7	1.6	2.0	2.1	..	9.8	8.7	8.3	8.3
3000 Taxes on payroll and workforce	..	0.0	0.0	0.0	0.0	..	0.0	0.0	0.0	0.0
4000 Taxes on property	..	0.0	0.0	0.0	0.0	..	0.0	0.0	0.0	0.0
5000 Taxes on goods and services	..	0.0	0.0	0.0	0.0	..	0.0	0.0	0.0	0.0
6000 Other taxes	..	0.0	0.0	0.0	0.0	..	0.0	0.0	0.0	0.0

.. Not available

Note: More detailed country data and country notes are available in online chapter 6 "Tax revenues by sub-sectors of general government": http://dx.doi.org/10.1787/rev_stats-2018-en. Full time series can be accessed at http://oe.cd/full-time-series.

Source: Ministry of Finance.

StatLink http://dx.doi.org/10.1787/888933860444

Table 4.41. Lithuania, tax revenue and % of GDP by selected tax category

	Billion EUR					% of GDP				
	1990	2000	2010	2015	2016	1990	2000	2010	2015	2016
Total tax revenue	..	**4.1**	**7.9**	**10.8**	**11.5**	..	**30.8**	**28.3**	**28.9**	**29.8**
1000 Taxes on income, profits and capital gains	..	**1.1**	**1.3**	**2.0**	**2.2**	..	**8.3**	**4.6**	**5.4**	**5.6**
1100 Of individuals	..	1.0	1.0	1.4	1.5	..	7.6	3.6	3.8	4.0
1200 Corporate	..	0.1	0.3	0.6	0.6	..	0.7	1.0	1.5	1.6
1300 Unallocable between 1100 and 1200	..	0.0	0.0	0.0	0.0	..	0.0	0.0	0.0	0.0
2000 Social security contributions	..	**1.3**	**3.3**	**4.3**	**4.7**	..	**9.9**	**11.6**	**11.5**	**12.2**
2100 Employees	..	0.1	0.6	0.9	1.0	..	0.8	2.3	2.3	2.5
2200 Employers	..	1.1	2.1	2.9	3.2	..	8.1	7.5	7.8	8.2
2300 Self-employed or non-employed	..	0.1	0.5	0.5	0.5	..	1.0	1.9	1.5	1.4
2400 Unallocable between 2100, 2200 and 2300	..	0.0	0.0	0.0	0.0	..	0.0	0.0	0.0	0.0
3000 Taxes on payroll and workforce	..	**0.0**	**0.0**	**0.0**	**0.0**	..	**0.0**	**0.0**	**0.0**	**0.0**
4000 Taxes on property	..	**0.1**	**0.1**	**0.1**	**0.1**	..	**0.5**	**0.4**	**0.3**	**0.3**
4100 Recurrent taxes on immovable property	..	0.1	0.1	0.1	0.1	..	0.5	0.4	0.3	0.3
4200 Recurrent taxes on net wealth	..	0.0	0.0	0.0	0.0	..	0.0	0.0	0.0	0.0
4300 Estate, inheritance and gift taxes	..	0.0	0.0	0.0	0.0	..	0.0	0.0	0.0	0.0
4400 Taxes on financial and capital transactions	..	0.0	0.0	0.0	0.0	..	0.0	0.0	0.0	0.0
4500 Non-recurrent taxes	..	0.0	0.0	0.0	0.0	..	0.0	0.0	0.0	0.0
4600 Other recurrent taxes on property	..	0.0	0.0	0.0	0.0	..	0.0	0.0	0.0	0.0
5000 Taxes on goods and services	..	**1.6**	**3.2**	**4.2**	**4.4**	..	**12.1**	**11.5**	**11.4**	**11.5**
5100 Taxes on production, sale, transfer, etc	..	1.6	3.1	4.2	4.4	..	11.6	11.2	11.2	11.3
5110 General taxes	..	1.1	2.2	2.9	3.1	..	8.1	7.8	7.8	7.9
5111 Value added taxes	..	1.0	2.2	2.9	3.0	..	7.5	7.8	7.7	7.8
5120 Taxes on specific goods and services	..	0.5	1.0	1.3	1.3	..	3.5	3.4	3.4	3.4
5121 Excises	..	0.4	0.9	1.2	1.2	..	3.2	3.2	3.1	3.2
5200 Taxes on use of goods and perform activities	..	0.1	0.1	0.1	0.1	..	0.5	0.3	0.2	0.2
5300 Unallocable between 5100 and 5200	..	0.0	0.0	0.0	0.0	..	0.0	0.0	0.0	0.0
6000 Other taxes	..	**0.0**	**0.0**	**0.0**	**0.0**	..	**0.0**	**0.0**	**0.0**	**0.0**
Non-wastable tax credits										
Non-wastable tax credits against 1000	..	..	..	..	..	..	..	..	..	..
Transfer component	..	..	..	..	..	..	..	..	..	..
Tax expenditure component	..	..	..	..	..	..	..	..	..	..

.. Not available

Note: More detailed country data and country notes are available in online chapter 5 "Country Tables, 1965-2016": http://dx.doi.org/10.1787/rev_stats-2018-en. Full time series can be accessed at http://oe.cd/full-time-series.

The total tax revenue has been reduced by the amount of any capital transfer that represents uncollected taxes. The capital transfer has been allocated between tax headings in proportion to the reported tax revenue. Therefore, the tax revenue amounts are different to those reported in the detailed country data available in online chapter 5 "Country Tables, 1965-2016".

Source: Ministry of Finance.

StatLink http://dx.doi.org/10.1787/888933860463

Table 4.42. Lithuania, tax revenue and % of GDP by level of government and main taxes

	Billion EUR					% of GDP				
	1990	2000	2010	2015	2016	1990	2000	2010	2015	2016
Federal or Central government										
Total tax revenue	..	**2.7**	**4.5**	**6.2**	**6.6**	..	**20.3**	**16.0**	**16.7**	**17.0**
1000 Taxes on income, profits and capital gains	..	1.1	1.3	2.0	2.2	..	8.3	4.6	5.4	5.6
2000 Social security contributions	..	0.0	0.0	0.0	0.0	..	0.0	0.0	0.0	0.0
3000 Taxes on payroll and workforce	..	0.0	0.0	0.0	0.0	..	0.0	0.0	0.0	0.0
4000 Taxes on property	..	0.0	0.0	0.0	0.0	..	0.0	0.0	0.0	0.0
5000 Taxes on goods and services	..	1.6	3.2	4.2	4.4	..	12.0	11.4	11.3	11.4
6000 Other taxes	..	0.0	0.0	0.0	0.0	..	0.0	0.0	0.0	0.0
State/Regional										
Total tax revenue	..	..	..	..	..	..	..	..	..	..
1000 Taxes on income, profits and capital gains	..	..	..	..	..	..	..	..	..	..
2000 Social security contributions	..	..	..	..	..	..	..	..	..	..
3000 Taxes on payroll and workforce	..	..	..	..	..	..	..	..	..	..
4000 Taxes on property	..	..	..	..	..	..	..	..	..	..
5000 Taxes on goods and services	..	..	..	..	..	..	..	..	..	..
6000 Other taxes	..	..	..	..	..	..	..	..	..	..
Local government										
Total tax revenue	..	**0.1**	**0.1**	**0.1**	**0.1**	..	**0.6**	**0.5**	**0.4**	**0.4**
1000 Taxes on income, profits and capital gains	..	0.0	0.0	0.0	0.0	..	0.0	0.0	0.0	0.0
2000 Social security contributions	..	0.0	0.0	0.0	0.0	..	0.0	0.0	0.0	0.0
3000 Taxes on payroll and workforce	..	0.0	0.0	0.0	0.0	..	0.0	0.0	0.0	0.0
4000 Taxes on property	..	0.1	0.1	0.1	0.1	..	0.5	0.4	0.3	0.3
5000 Taxes on goods and services	..	0.0	0.0	0.0	0.0	..	0.1	0.1	0.0	0.0
6000 Other taxes	..	0.0	0.0	0.0	0.0	..	0.0	0.0	0.0	0.0
Social Security Funds										
Total tax revenue	..	**1.3**	**3.3**	**4.3**	**4.7**	..	**9.9**	**11.6**	**11.5**	**12.2**
1000 Taxes on income, profits and capital gains	..	0.0	0.0	0.0	0.0	..	0.0	0.0	0.0	0.0
2000 Social security contributions	..	1.3	3.3	4.3	4.7	..	9.9	11.6	11.5	12.2
3000 Taxes on payroll and workforce	..	0.0	0.0	0.0	0.0	..	0.0	0.0	0.0	0.0
4000 Taxes on property	..	0.0	0.0	0.0	0.0	..	0.0	0.0	0.0	0.0
5000 Taxes on goods and services	..	0.0	0.0	0.0	0.0	..	0.0	0.0	0.0	0.0
6000 Other taxes	..	0.0	0.0	0.0	0.0	..	0.0	0.0	0.0	0.0

.. Not available

Note: More detailed country data and country notes are available in online chapter 6 "Tax revenues by sub-sectors of general government": http://dx.doi.org/10.1787/rev_stats-2018-en. Full time series can be accessed at http://oe.cd/full-time-series.

The total tax revenue has been reduced by the amount of any capital transfer that represents uncollected taxes. The capital transfer has been allocated between tax headings in proportion to the reported tax revenue. Therefore, the tax revenue amounts are different to those reported in the detailed country data available in online chapter 6 "Tax revenues by sub-sectors of general government".

Source: Ministry of Finance.

StatLink http://dx.doi.org/10.1787/888933860482

Table 4.43. Luxembourg, tax revenue and % of GDP by selected tax category

	Billion EUR					% of GDP				
	1990	2000	2010	2015	2016	1990	2000	2010	2015	2016
Total tax revenue	**3.7**	**8.5**	**15.0**	**19.3**	**20.2**	**33.5**	**36.9**	**37.4**	**37.1**	**38.1**
1000 Taxes on income, profits and capital gains	**1.5**	**3.1**	**5.5**	**7.0**	**7.4**	**13.5**	**13.5**	**13.6**	**13.5**	**14.0**
1100 Of individuals	0.9	1.6	3.2	4.7	5.0	8.1	6.8	7.9	9.1	9.4
1200 Corporate	0.6	1.5	2.3	2.3	2.5	5.4	6.6	5.8	4.4	4.6
1300 Unallocable between 1100 and 1200	0.0	0.0	0.0	0.0	0.0	0.0	0.0	0.0	0.0	0.0
2000 Social security contributions	**1.0**	**2.2**	**4.4**	**5.6**	**5.8**	**9.2**	**9.6**	**10.8**	**10.7**	**10.9**
2100 Employees	0.4	1.0	2.0	2.5	2.6	3.5	4.3	5.0	4.9	4.9
2200 Employers	0.5	1.0	1.9	2.3	2.4	4.5	4.2	4.7	4.5	4.5
2300 Self-employed or non-employed	0.1	0.3	0.5	0.7	0.7	1.2	1.2	1.2	1.4	1.4
2400 Unallocable between 2100, 2200 and 2300	0.0	0.0	0.0	0.0	0.0	0.0	0.0	0.0	0.0	0.0
3000 Taxes on payroll and workforce	**0.0**	**0.0**	**0.0**	**0.0**	**0.0**	**0.0**	**0.0**	**0.0**	**0.0**	**0.0**
4000 Taxes on property	**0.3**	**0.9**	**1.1**	**1.7**	**1.9**	**2.8**	**3.9**	**2.6**	**3.3**	**3.5**
4100 Recurrent taxes on immovable property	0.0	0.0	0.0	0.0	0.0	0.1	0.1	0.1	0.1	0.1
4200 Recurrent taxes on net wealth	0.2	0.6	0.8	1.3	1.4	1.6	2.7	2.1	2.5	2.7
4300 Estate, inheritance and gift taxes	0.0	0.0	0.1	0.1	0.1	0.1	0.1	0.1	0.1	0.2
4400 Taxes on financial and capital transactions	0.1	0.2	0.2	0.3	0.3	1.0	1.0	0.4	0.6	0.6
4500 Non-recurrent taxes	0.0	0.0	0.0	0.0	0.0	0.0	0.0	0.0	0.0	0.0
4600 Other recurrent taxes on property	0.0	0.0	0.0	0.0	0.0	0.0	0.0	0.0	0.0	0.0
5000 Taxes on goods and services	**0.9**	**2.2**	**4.1**	**5.0**	**5.1**	**7.9**	**9.7**	**10.2**	**9.5**	**9.6**
5100 Taxes on production, sale, transfer, etc	0.8	2.2	4.0	4.9	5.0	7.7	9.6	10.0	9.3	9.4
5110 General taxes	0.4	1.1	2.6	3.4	3.4	4.0	4.9	6.4	6.5	6.4
5111 Value added taxes	0.4	1.1	2.6	3.4	3.4	4.0	4.9	6.4	6.5	6.4
5120 Taxes on specific goods and services	0.4	1.1	1.5	1.5	1.6	3.7	4.7	3.7	2.8	3.1
5121 Excises	0.4	1.0	1.4	1.4	1.4	3.3	4.5	3.5	2.6	2.7
5200 Taxes on use of goods and perform activities	0.0	0.0	0.1	0.1	0.1	0.2	0.1	0.2	0.2	0.1
5300 Unallocable between 5100 and 5200	0.0	0.0	0.0	0.0	0.0	0.0	0.0	0.0	0.0	0.0
6000 Other taxes	**0.0**	**0.0**	**0.0**	**0.0**	**0.0**	**0.1**	**0.1**	**0.1**	**0.1**	**0.1**
Non-wastable tax credits										
Non-wastable tax credits against 1000	..	..	..	0.2	0.2	..	..	..	0.4	0.4
Transfer component	..	..	..	..	..	..	..	..	..	..
Tax expenditure component	..	..	..	..	..	..	..	..	..	..

.. Not available

Note: More detailed country data and country notes are available in online chapter 5 "Country Tables, 1965-2016": http://dx.doi.org/10.1787/rev_stats-2018-en. Full time series can be accessed at http://oe.cd/full-time-series.

Source: General account of the State.

StatLink http://dx.doi.org/10.1787/888933860501

Table 4.44. Luxembourg, tax revenue and % of GDP by level of government and main taxes

	Billion EUR					% of GDP				
	1990	2000	2010	2015	2016	1990	2000	2010	2015	2016
Federal or Central government										
Total tax revenue	**2.4**	**5.8**	**10.1**	**13.2**	**13.7**	**22.1**	**25.3**	**25.2**	**25.3**	**25.9**
1000 Taxes on income, profits and capital gains	1.3	2.6	4.9	6.4	6.7	11.6	11.5	12.1	12.3	12.7
2000 Social security contributions	0.0	0.1	0.1	0.2	0.2	0.1	0.3	0.3	0.3	0.3
3000 Taxes on payroll and workforce	0.0	0.0	0.0	0.0	0.0	0.0	0.0	0.0	0.0	0.0
4000 Taxes on property	0.3	0.9	1.0	1.7	1.8	2.6	3.8	2.5	3.2	3.4
5000 Taxes on goods and services	0.8	2.2	4.1	4.9	5.0	7.7	9.7	10.2	9.4	9.4
6000 Other taxes	0.0	0.0	0.0	0.0	0.0	0.1	0.0	0.0	0.1	0.1
State/Regional										
Total tax revenue	..	..	..	..	..	..	..	..	..	..
1000 Taxes on income, profits and capital gains	..	..	..	..	..	..	..	..	..	..
2000 Social security contributions	..	..	..	..	..	..	..	..	..	..
3000 Taxes on payroll and workforce	..	..	..	..	..	..	..	..	..	..
4000 Taxes on property	..	..	..	..	..	..	..	..	..	..
5000 Taxes on goods and services	..	..	..	..	..	..	..	..	..	..
6000 Other taxes	..	..	..	..	..	..	..	..	..	..
Local government										
Total tax revenue	**0.2**	**0.5**	**0.7**	**0.7**	**0.8**	**2.1**	**2.1**	**1.6**	**1.3**	**1.5**
1000 Taxes on income, profits and capital gains	0.2	0.5	0.6	0.6	0.7	1.9	2.0	1.5	1.2	1.4
2000 Social security contributions	0.0	0.0	0.0	0.0	0.0	0.0	0.0	0.0	0.0	0.0
3000 Taxes on payroll and workforce	0.0	0.0	0.0	0.0	0.0	0.0	0.0	0.0	0.0	0.0
4000 Taxes on property	0.0	0.0	0.0	0.1	0.1	0.2	0.1	0.1	0.1	0.1
5000 Taxes on goods and services	0.0	0.0	0.0	0.0	0.0	0.0	0.0	0.0	0.0	0.0
6000 Other taxes	0.0	0.0	0.0	0.0	0.0	0.0	0.0	0.0	0.0	0.0
Social Security Funds										
Total tax revenue	**1.0**	**2.2**	**4.2**	**5.4**	**5.6**	**9.1**	**9.3**	**10.5**	**10.4**	**10.5**
1000 Taxes on income, profits and capital gains	0.0	0.0	0.0	0.0	0.0	0.0	0.0	0.0	0.0	0.0
2000 Social security contributions	1.0	2.2	4.2	5.4	5.6	9.1	9.3	10.5	10.4	10.5
3000 Taxes on payroll and workforce	0.0	0.0	0.0	0.0	0.0	0.0	0.0	0.0	0.0	0.0
4000 Taxes on property	0.0	0.0	0.0	0.0	0.0	0.0	0.0	0.0	0.0	0.0
5000 Taxes on goods and services	0.0	0.0	0.0	0.0	0.0	0.0	0.0	0.0	0.0	0.0
6000 Other taxes	0.0	0.0	0.0	0.0	0.0	0.0	0.0	0.0	0.0	0.0

.. Not available

Note: More detailed country data and country notes are available in online chapter 6 "Tax revenues by sub-sectors of general government": http://dx.doi.org/10.1787/rev_stats-2018-en. Full time series can be accessed at http://oe.cd/full-time-series.

Source: General account of the State.

StatLink http://dx.doi.org/10.1787/888933860520

Table 4.45. Mexico, tax revenue and % of GDP by selected tax category

	Billion MXN					% of GDP				
	1990	2000	2010	2015	2016	1990	2000	2010	2015	2016
Total tax revenue	**102.0**	**767.2**	**1 716.2**	**2 953.5**	**3 343.3**	**12.1**	**11.5**	**12.8**	**15.9**	**16.6**
1000 Taxes on income, profits and capital gains	**34.7**	**276.5**	**683.6**	**1 230.6**	**1 427.1**	**4.1**	**4.1**	**5.1**	**6.6**	**7.1**
1100 Of individuals	..	..	313.5	609.4	681.8	..	..	2.3	3.3	3.4
1200 Corporate	..	..	246.7	592.4	700.9	..	..	1.8	3.2	3.5
1300 Unallocable between 1100 and 1200	34.7	276.5	123.4	28.7	44.4	4.1	4.1	0.9	0.2	0.2
2000 Social security contributions	**17.2**	**138.2**	**277.5**	**409.2**	**435.0**	**2.0**	**2.1**	**2.1**	**2.2**	**2.2**
2100 Employees	..	..	..	..	..	..	..	..	..	..
2200 Employers	..	..	..	..	..	..	..	..	..	..
2300 Self-employed or non-employed	..	..	..	..	..	..	..	..	..	..
2400 Unallocable between 2100, 2200 and 2300	17.2	138.2	277.5	409.2	435.0	2.0	2.1	2.1	2.2	2.2
3000 Taxes on payroll and workforce	**1.8**	**11.2**	**36.9**	**70.2**	**76.8**	**0.2**	**0.2**	**0.3**	**0.4**	**0.4**
4000 Taxes on property	**1.9**	**14.0**	**39.0**	**57.7**	**63.3**	**0.2**	**0.2**	**0.3**	**0.3**	**0.3**
4100 Recurrent taxes on immovable property	1.0	9.9	25.7	38.0	40.4	0.1	0.1	0.2	0.2	0.2
4200 Recurrent taxes on net wealth	0.0	0.0	0.0	0.0	0.0	0.0	0.0	0.0	0.0	0.0
4300 Estate, inheritance and gift taxes	0.0	0.0	0.0	0.0	0.0	0.0	0.0	0.0	0.0	0.0
4400 Taxes on financial and capital transactions	0.9	4.0	13.2	19.7	22.9	0.1	0.1	0.1	0.1	0.1
4500 Non-recurrent taxes	0.0	0.0	0.0	0.0	0.0	0.0	0.0	0.0	0.0	0.0
4600 Other recurrent taxes on property	0.0	0.0	0.0	0.0	0.0	0.0	0.0	0.0	0.0	0.0
5000 Taxes on goods and services	**44.8**	**319.6**	**651.9**	**1 141.2**	**1 295.7**	**5.3**	**4.8**	**4.9**	**6.2**	**6.4**
5100 Taxes on production, sale, transfer, etc	44.2	310.3	630.1	1 120.6	1 274.7	5.2	4.6	4.7	6.0	6.3
5110 General taxes	26.6	189.6	504.5	707.2	791.7	3.2	2.8	3.8	3.8	3.9
5111 Value added taxes	26.6	189.6	504.5	707.2	791.7	3.2	2.8	3.8	3.8	3.9
5120 Taxes on specific goods and services	17.5	120.7	125.6	413.4	483.0	2.1	1.8	0.9	2.2	2.4
5121 Excises	10.1	86.2	86.1	361.5	420.4	1.2	1.3	0.6	2.0	2.1
5200 Taxes on use of goods and perform activities	0.7	9.3	21.8	20.6	20.9	0.1	0.1	0.2	0.1	0.1
5300 Unallocable between 5100 and 5200	0.0	0.0	0.0	0.0	0.0	0.0	0.0	0.0	0.0	0.0
6000 Other taxes	**1.6**	**7.7**	**27.4**	**44.6**	**45.5**	**0.2**	**0.1**	**0.2**	**0.2**	**0.2**
Non-wastable tax credits										
Non-wastable tax credits against 1000	..	..	40.3	43.8	44.9	..	..	0.3	0.2	0.2
Transfer component	..	..	9.7	1.0	1.1	..	..	0.1	0.0	0.0
Tax expenditure component	..	..	30.6	42.8	43.7	..	..	0.2	0.2	0.2

.. Not available

Note: More detailed country data and country notes are available in online chapter 5 "Country Tables, 1965-2016": http://dx.doi.org/10.1787/rev_stats-2018-en. Full time series can be accessed at http://oe.cd/full-time-series.

Source: Ministry of Finance, Economic Department.

StatLink http://dx.doi.org/10.1787/888933860539

Table 4.46. Mexico, tax revenue and % of GDP by level of government and main taxes

	Billion MXN					% of GDP				
	1990	2000	2010	2015	2016	1990	2000	2010	2015	2016
Federal or Central government										
Total tax revenue	**81.4**	**600.5**	**1 351.5**	**2 374.0**	**2 724.3**	**9.7**	**9.0**	**10.1**	**12.8**	**13.6**
1000 Taxes on income, profits and capital gains	34.7	276.5	683.6	1 230.6	1 427.1	4.1	4.1	5.1	6.6	7.1
2000 Social security contributions	0.0	0.0	0.0	0.0	0.0	0.0	0.0	0.0	0.0	0.0
3000 Taxes on payroll and workforce	0.8	0.0	0.0	0.0	0.0	0.1	0.0	0.0	0.0	0.0
4000 Taxes on property	0.0	0.0	0.0	0.0	0.0	0.0	0.0	0.0	0.0	0.0
5000 Taxes on goods and services	44.6	318.1	645.6	1 116.0	1 268.4	5.3	4.8	4.8	6.0	6.3
6000 Other taxes	1.3	5.9	22.2	27.4	28.8	0.2	0.1	0.2	0.1	0.1
State/Regional										
Total tax revenue	**2.2**	**20.5**	**58.3**	**123.5**	**133.0**	**0.3**	**0.3**	**0.4**	**0.7**	**0.7**
1000 Taxes on income, profits and capital gains	0.0	0.0	0.0	0.0	0.0	0.0	0.0	0.0	0.0	0.0
2000 Social security contributions	0.0	0.0	0.0	0.0	0.0	0.0	0.0	0.0	0.0	0.0
3000 Taxes on payroll and workforce	1.0	11.2	36.8	70.2	76.8	0.1	0.2	0.3	0.4	0.4
4000 Taxes on property	0.9	7.0	13.1	22.5	23.6	0.1	0.1	0.1	0.1	0.1
5000 Taxes on goods and services	0.1	1.3	5.8	24.4	25.9	0.0	0.0	0.0	0.1	0.1
6000 Other taxes	0.2	0.9	2.5	6.5	6.7	0.0	0.0	0.0	0.0	0.0
Local government										
Total tax revenue	**1.3**	**8.0**	**29.0**	**46.7**	**50.9**	**0.1**	**0.1**	**0.2**	**0.3**	**0.3**
1000 Taxes on income, profits and capital gains	0.0	0.0	0.0	0.0	0.0	0.0	0.0	0.0	0.0	0.0
2000 Social security contributions	0.0	0.0	0.0	0.0	0.0	0.0	0.0	0.0	0.0	0.0
3000 Taxes on payroll and workforce	0.0	0.0	0.1	0.0	0.0	0.0	0.0	0.0	0.0	0.0
4000 Taxes on property	1.0	6.9	25.8	35.2	39.6	0.1	0.1	0.2	0.2	0.2
5000 Taxes on goods and services	0.1	0.2	0.5	0.8	1.3	0.0	0.0	0.0	0.0	0.0
6000 Other taxes	0.1	0.9	2.6	10.7	10.0	0.0	0.0	0.0	0.1	0.1
Social Security Funds										
Total tax revenue	**17.2**	**138.2**	**277.5**	**409.2**	**435.0**	**2.0**	**2.1**	**2.1**	**2.2**	**2.2**
1000 Taxes on income, profits and capital gains	0.0	0.0	0.0	0.0	0.0	0.0	0.0	0.0	0.0	0.0
2000 Social security contributions	17.2	138.2	277.5	409.2	435.0	2.0	2.1	2.1	2.2	2.2
3000 Taxes on payroll and workforce	0.0	0.0	0.0	0.0	0.0	0.0	0.0	0.0	0.0	0.0
4000 Taxes on property	0.0	0.0	0.0	0.0	0.0	0.0	0.0	0.0	0.0	0.0
5000 Taxes on goods and services	0.0	0.0	0.0	0.0	0.0	0.0	0.0	0.0	0.0	0.0
6000 Other taxes	0.0	0.0	0.0	0.0	0.0	0.0	0.0	0.0	0.0	0.0

Note: More detailed country data and country notes are available in online chapter 6 "Tax revenues by sub-sectors of general government": http://dx.doi.org/10.1787/rev_stats-2018-en. Full time series can be accessed at http://oe.cd/full-time-series.
Source: Ministry of Finance, Economic Department.

StatLink http://dx.doi.org/10.1787/888933860558

Table 4.47. Netherlands, tax revenue and % of GDP by selected tax category

	Billion EUR					% of GDP				
	1990	2000	2010	2015	2016	1990	2000	2010	2015	2016
Total tax revenue	**104.4**	**166.8**	**227.9**	**255.3**	**272.0**	**39.7**	**36.9**	**35.7**	**37.0**	**38.4**
1000 Taxes on income, profits and capital gains	**33.7**	**43.3**	**63.6**	**70.8**	**74.0**	**12.8**	**9.6**	**9.9**	**10.3**	**10.4**
1100 Of individuals	25.8	25.1	49.0	52.4	50.3	9.8	5.6	7.7	7.6	7.1
1200 Corporate	7.9	18.1	14.6	18.4	23.7	3.0	4.0	2.3	2.7	3.3
1300 Unallocable between 1100 and 1200	0.0	0.0	0.0	0.0	0.0	0.0	0.0	0.0	0.0	0.0
2000 Social security contributions	**39.1**	**64.5**	**82.7**	**96.4**	**103.9**	**14.9**	**14.3**	**12.9**	**14.0**	**14.7**
2100 Employees	24.1	35.3	41.6	48.2	42.0	9.2	7.8	6.5	7.0	5.9
2200 Employers	7.8	18.7	29.4	34.6	36.6	3.0	4.1	4.6	5.0	5.2
2300 Self-employed or non-employed	7.1	10.5	11.7	13.6	25.3	2.7	2.3	1.8	2.0	3.6
2400 Unallocable between 2100, 2200 and 2300	0.0	0.0	0.0	0.0	0.0	0.0	0.0	0.0	0.0	0.0
3000 Taxes on payroll and workforce	**0.0**	**0.0**	**0.0**	**0.0**	**0.0**	**0.0**	**0.0**	**0.0**	**0.0**	**0.0**
4000 Taxes on property	**3.8**	**8.8**	**8.8**	**9.8**	**10.8**	**1.5**	**1.9**	**1.4**	**1.4**	**1.5**
4100 Recurrent taxes on immovable property	1.7	3.1	4.2	6.4	6.6	0.7	0.7	0.7	0.9	0.9
4200 Recurrent taxes on net wealth	0.6	0.8	0.0	0.0	0.0	0.2	0.2	0.0	0.0	0.0
4300 Estate, inheritance and gift taxes	0.5	1.5	1.7	1.6	1.8	0.2	0.3	0.3	0.2	0.3
4400 Taxes on financial and capital transactions	1.0	3.4	2.8	1.8	2.3	0.4	0.8	0.4	0.3	0.3
4500 Non-recurrent taxes	0.0	0.0	0.0	0.0	0.0	0.0	0.0	0.0	0.0	0.0
4600 Other recurrent taxes on property	0.0	0.0	0.0	0.0	0.0	0.0	0.0	0.0	0.0	0.0
5000 Taxes on goods and services	**27.6**	**48.2**	**70.1**	**75.6**	**80.3**	**10.5**	**10.7**	**11.0**	**11.0**	**11.3**
5100 Taxes on production, sale, transfer, etc	25.1	43.6	62.5	67.0	71.6	9.5	9.6	9.8	9.7	10.1
5110 General taxes	17.2	28.9	42.7	44.9	47.9	6.5	6.4	6.7	6.5	6.8
5111 Value added taxes	17.2	28.8	42.7	44.9	47.8	6.5	6.4	6.7	6.5	6.8
5120 Taxes on specific goods and services	7.9	14.7	19.8	22.1	23.7	3.0	3.3	3.1	3.2	3.3
5121 Excises	6.0	13.8	18.4	18.0	19.0	2.3	3.0	2.9	2.6	2.7
5200 Taxes on use of goods and perform activities	2.5	4.6	7.6	8.6	8.7	1.0	1.0	1.2	1.2	1.2
5300 Unallocable between 5100 and 5200	0.0	0.0	0.0	0.0	0.0	0.0	0.0	0.0	0.0	0.0
6000 Other taxes	**0.3**	**0.8**	**1.0**	**0.4**	**0.7**	**0.1**	**0.2**	**0.2**	**0.1**	**0.1**
Non-wastable tax credits										
Non-wastable tax credits against 1000	..	..	..	..	..	..	..	..	..	..
Transfer component	..	..	..	..	..	..	..	..	..	..
Tax expenditure component	..	..	..	..	..	..	..	..	..	..

.. Not available

Note: More detailed country data and country notes are available in online chapter 5 "Country Tables, 1965-2016": http://dx.doi.org/10.1787/rev_stats-2018-en. Full time series can be accessed at http://oe.cd/full-time-series.

Source: Social security contributions and local taxes: Central Bureau of Statistics. Other taxes: Ministry of Finance.

StatLink http://dx.doi.org/10.1787/888933860577

Table 4.48. Netherlands, tax revenue and % of GDP by level of government and main taxes

	Billion EUR					% of GDP				
	1990	2000	2010	2015	2016	1990	2000	2010	2015	2016
Federal or Central government										
Total tax revenue	**61.4**	**95.1**	**135.1**	**146.2**	**156.7**	**23.3**	**21.0**	**21.1**	**21.2**	**22.1**
1000 Taxes on income, profits and capital gains	33.7	43.3	63.6	70.8	74.0	12.8	9.6	9.9	10.3	10.4
2000 Social security contributions	0.0	0.0	0.0	0.0	0.0	0.0	0.0	0.0	0.0	0.0
3000 Taxes on payroll and workforce	0.0	0.0	0.0	0.0	0.0	0.0	0.0	0.0	0.0	0.0
4000 Taxes on property	2.1	5.7	4.6	4.7	5.6	0.8	1.3	0.7	0.7	0.8
5000 Taxes on goods and services	25.3	45.4	66.2	70.2	76.4	9.6	10.0	10.4	10.2	10.8
6000 Other taxes	0.3	0.8	0.8	0.4	0.7	0.1	0.2	0.1	0.1	0.1
State/Regional										
Total tax revenue	..	..	..	..	..	..	..	..	..	..
1000 Taxes on income, profits and capital gains	..	..	..	..	..	..	..	..	..	..
2000 Social security contributions	..	..	..	..	..	..	..	..	..	..
3000 Taxes on payroll and workforce	..	..	..	..	..	..	..	..	..	..
4000 Taxes on property	..	..	..	..	..	..	..	..	..	..
5000 Taxes on goods and services	..	..	..	..	..	..	..	..	..	..
6000 Other taxes	..	..	..	..	..	..	..	..	..	..
Local government										
Total tax revenue	**2.5**	**5.6**	**8.1**	**9.7**	**8.3**	**0.9**	**1.2**	**1.3**	**1.4**	**1.2**
1000 Taxes on income, profits and capital gains	0.0	0.0	0.0	0.0	0.0	0.0	0.0	0.0	0.0	0.0
2000 Social security contributions	0.0	0.0	0.0	0.0	0.0	0.0	0.0	0.0	0.0	0.0
3000 Taxes on payroll and workforce	0.0	0.0	0.0	0.0	0.0	0.0	0.0	0.0	0.0	0.0
4000 Taxes on property	1.7	3.1	4.2	5.0	5.2	0.7	0.7	0.7	0.7	0.7
5000 Taxes on goods and services	0.8	2.5	3.7	4.7	3.2	0.3	0.6	0.6	0.7	0.4
6000 Other taxes	0.0	0.0	0.2	0.0	0.0	0.0	0.0	0.0	0.0	0.0
Social Security Funds										
Total tax revenue	**39.1**	**64.5**	**82.7**	**96.4**	**103.9**	**14.9**	**14.3**	**12.9**	**14.0**	**14.7**
1000 Taxes on income, profits and capital gains	0.0	0.0	0.0	0.0	0.0	0.0	0.0	0.0	0.0	0.0
2000 Social security contributions	39.1	64.5	82.7	96.4	103.9	14.9	14.3	12.9	14.0	14.7
3000 Taxes on payroll and workforce	0.0	0.0	0.0	0.0	0.0	0.0	0.0	0.0	0.0	0.0
4000 Taxes on property	0.0	0.0	0.0	0.0	0.0	0.0	0.0	0.0	0.0	0.0
5000 Taxes on goods and services	0.0	0.0	0.0	0.0	0.0	0.0	0.0	0.0	0.0	0.0
6000 Other taxes	0.0	0.0	0.0	0.0	0.0	0.0	0.0	0.0	0.0	0.0

.. Not available

Note: More detailed country data and country notes are available in online chapter 6 "Tax revenues by sub-sectors of general government": http://dx.doi.org/10.1787/rev_stats-2018-en. Full time series can be accessed at http://oe.cd/full-time-series.

Source: Social security contributions and local taxes: Central Bureau of Statistics. Other taxes: Ministry of Finance.

StatLink http://dx.doi.org/10.1787/888933860596

Table 4.49. New Zealand, tax revenue and % of GDP by selected tax category

	Billion NZD					% of GDP				
	1990	2000	2010	2015	2016	1990	2000	2010	2015	2016
Total tax revenue	**27.5**	**39.8**	**62.3**	**81.5**	**86.6**	**36.2**	**32.5**	**30.3**	**31.6**	**31.6**
1000 Taxes on income, profits and capital gains	**16.4**	**23.9**	**33.5**	**44.7**	**48.1**	**21.6**	**19.5**	**16.3**	**17.3**	**17.6**
1100 Of individuals	13.2	17.1	23.5	30.3	31.9	17.4	14.0	11.4	11.7	11.6
1200 Corporate	1.8	4.9	7.6	11.4	13.5	2.3	4.0	3.7	4.4	4.9
1300 Unallocable between 1100 and 1200	1.4	1.8	2.4	3.0	2.8	1.9	1.5	1.1	1.2	1.0
2000 Social security contributions	**0.0**	**0.0**	**0.0**	**0.0**	**0.0**	**0.0**	**0.0**	**0.0**	**0.0**	**0.0**
2100 Employees	0.0	0.0	0.0	0.0	0.0	0.0	0.0	0.0	0.0	0.0
2200 Employers	0.0	0.0	0.0	0.0	0.0	0.0	0.0	0.0	0.0	0.0
2300 Self-employed or non-employed	0.0	0.0	0.0	0.0	0.0	0.0	0.0	0.0	0.0	0.0
2400 Unallocable between 2100, 2200 and 2300	0.0	0.0	0.0	0.0	0.0	0.0	0.0	0.0	0.0	0.0
3000 Taxes on payroll and workforce	**0.0**	**0.0**	**0.0**	**0.0**	**0.0**	**0.0**	**0.0**	**0.0**	**0.0**	**0.0**
4000 Taxes on property	**1.9**	**2.1**	**4.1**	**5.1**	**5.3**	**2.5**	**1.7**	**2.0**	**2.0**	**1.9**
4100 Recurrent taxes on immovable property	1.7	2.0	4.0	5.0	5.2	2.3	1.7	2.0	1.9	1.9
4200 Recurrent taxes on net wealth	0.0	0.0	0.0	0.0	0.0	0.0	0.0	0.0	0.0	0.0
4300 Estate, inheritance and gift taxes	0.1	0.0	0.0	0.0	0.0	0.1	0.0	0.0	0.0	0.0
4400 Taxes on financial and capital transactions	0.1	0.1	0.1	0.1	0.1	0.1	0.1	0.0	0.0	0.0
4500 Non-recurrent taxes	0.0	0.0	0.0	0.0	0.0	0.0	0.0	0.0	0.0	0.0
4600 Other recurrent taxes on property	0.0	0.0	0.0	0.0	0.0	0.0	0.0	0.0	0.0	0.0
5000 Taxes on goods and services	**9.2**	**13.8**	**24.7**	**31.7**	**33.2**	**12.1**	**11.3**	**12.0**	**12.3**	**12.1**
5100 Taxes on production, sale, transfer, etc	8.7	12.9	23.1	29.6	30.9	11.4	10.5	11.2	11.5	11.3
5110 General taxes	6.2	9.9	19.1	24.6	25.8	8.1	8.1	9.3	9.5	9.4
5111 Value added taxes	6.2	9.9	19.1	24.6	25.8	8.1	8.1	9.3	9.5	9.4
5120 Taxes on specific goods and services	2.5	3.0	4.0	5.0	5.1	3.3	2.5	1.9	1.9	1.9
5121 Excises	1.9	2.1	1.8	2.3	2.2	2.5	1.8	0.9	0.9	0.8
5200 Taxes on use of goods and perform activities	0.5	0.9	1.6	2.1	2.3	0.7	0.7	0.8	0.8	0.8
5300 Unallocable between 5100 and 5200	0.0	0.0	0.0	0.0	0.0	0.0	0.0	0.0	0.0	0.0
6000 Other taxes	**0.0**	**0.0**	**0.0**	**0.0**	**0.0**	**0.0**	**0.0**	**0.0**	**0.0**	**0.0**
Non-wastable tax credits										
Non-wastable tax credits against 1000	..	1.1	2.8	2.4	2.3	..	0.9	1.4	0.9	0.8
Transfer component	..	0.7	1.8	1.1	1.1	..	0.6	0.9	0.4	0.4
Tax expenditure component	..	0.3	1.0	1.3	1.2	..	0.3	0.5	0.5	0.4

.. Not available

Note: More detailed country data and country notes are available in online chapter 5 "Country Tables, 1965-2016": http://dx.doi.org/10.1787/rev_stats-2018-en. Full time series can be accessed at http://oe.cd/full-time-series.

Source: Local Authorities Statistics, Department of Statistics, Wellington.

StatLink http://dx.doi.org/10.1787/888933860615

Table 4.50. New Zealand, tax revenue and % of GDP by level of government and main taxes

	Billion NZD					% of GDP				
	1990	2000	2010	2015	2016	1990	2000	2010	2015	2016
Federal or Central government										
Total tax revenue	**25.8**	**37.5**	**57.9**	**76.0**	**80.8**	**34.0**	**30.7**	**28.1**	**29.4**	**29.5**
1000 Taxes on income, profits and capital gains	16.4	23.9	33.5	44.7	48.1	21.6	19.5	16.3	17.3	17.6
2000 Social security contributions	0.0	0.0	0.0	0.0	0.0	0.0	0.0	0.0	0.0	0.0
3000 Taxes on payroll and workforce	0.0	0.0	0.0	0.0	0.0	0.0	0.0	0.0	0.0	0.0
4000 Taxes on property	0.3	0.1	0.1	0.1	0.1	0.4	0.1	0.0	0.0	0.0
5000 Taxes on goods and services	9.1	13.6	24.3	31.1	32.6	12.0	11.1	11.8	12.1	11.9
6000 Other taxes	0.0	0.0	0.0	0.0	0.0	0.0	0.0	0.0	0.0	0.0
State/Regional										
Total tax revenue	..	..	..	..	..	..	..	..	..	..
1000 Taxes on income, profits and capital gains	..	..	..	..	..	..	..	..	..	..
2000 Social security contributions	..	..	..	..	..	..	..	..	..	..
3000 Taxes on payroll and workforce	..	..	..	..	..	..	..	..	..	..
4000 Taxes on property	..	..	..	..	..	..	..	..	..	..
5000 Taxes on goods and services	..	..	..	..	..	..	..	..	..	..
6000 Other taxes	..	..	..	..	..	..	..	..	..	..
Local government										
Total tax revenue	**1.7**	**2.3**	**4.5**	**5.6**	**5.8**	**2.2**	**1.9**	**2.2**	**2.2**	**2.1**
1000 Taxes on income, profits and capital gains	0.0	0.0	0.0	0.0	0.0	0.0	0.0	0.0	0.0	0.0
2000 Social security contributions	0.0	0.0	0.0	0.0	0.0	0.0	0.0	0.0	0.0	0.0
3000 Taxes on payroll and workforce	0.0	0.0	0.0	0.0	0.0	0.0	0.0	0.0	0.0	0.0
4000 Taxes on property	1.6	2.0	4.0	5.0	5.2	2.0	1.7	2.0	1.9	1.9
5000 Taxes on goods and services	0.1	0.2	0.4	0.6	0.6	0.2	0.2	0.2	0.2	0.2
6000 Other taxes	0.0	0.0	0.0	0.0	0.0	0.0	0.0	0.0	0.0	0.0
Social Security Funds										
Total tax revenue	**0.0**	**0.0**	**0.0**	**0.0**	**0.0**	**0.0**	**0.0**	**0.0**	**0.0**	**0.0**
1000 Taxes on income, profits and capital gains	0.0	0.0	0.0	0.0	0.0	0.0	0.0	0.0	0.0	0.0
2000 Social security contributions	0.0	0.0	0.0	0.0	0.0	0.0	0.0	0.0	0.0	0.0
3000 Taxes on payroll and workforce	0.0	0.0	0.0	0.0	0.0	0.0	0.0	0.0	0.0	0.0
4000 Taxes on property	0.0	0.0	0.0	0.0	0.0	0.0	0.0	0.0	0.0	0.0
5000 Taxes on goods and services	0.0	0.0	0.0	0.0	0.0	0.0	0.0	0.0	0.0	0.0
6000 Other taxes	0.0	0.0	0.0	0.0	0.0	0.0	0.0	0.0	0.0	0.0

.. Not available

Note: More detailed country data and country notes are available in online chapter 6 "Tax revenues by sub-sectors of general government": http://dx.doi.org/10.1787/rev_stats-2018-en. Full time series can be accessed at http://oe.cd/full-time-series.

Source: Local Authorities Statistics, Department of Statistics, Wellington.

StatLink http://dx.doi.org/10.1787/888933860634

Table 4.51. Norway, tax revenue and % of GDP by selected tax category

	Billion NOK					% of GDP				
	1990	2000	2010	2015	2016	1990	2000	2010	2015	2016
Total tax revenue	**301.8**	**631.6**	**1 086.7**	**1 198.2**	**1 207.1**	**40.2**	**41.9**	**41.9**	**38.4**	**38.7**
1000 Taxes on income, profits and capital gains	**106.3**	**284.2**	**512.0**	**475.4**	**458.2**	**14.2**	**18.8**	**19.7**	**15.2**	**14.7**
1100 Of individuals	79.1	152.0	256.5	335.2	332.8	10.5	10.1	9.9	10.8	10.7
1200 Corporate	27.2	132.2	255.5	140.2	125.4	3.6	8.8	9.9	4.5	4.0
1300 Unallocable between 1100 and 1200	0.0	0.0	0.0	0.0	0.0	0.0	0.0	0.0	0.0	0.0
2000 Social security contributions	**79.4**	**132.2**	**243.0**	**325.6**	**330.9**	**10.6**	**8.8**	**9.4**	**10.4**	**10.6**
2100 Employees	25.3	45.2	81.0	112.7	115.4	3.4	3.0	3.1	3.6	3.7
2200 Employers	50.1	79.2	148.1	191.4	193.3	6.7	5.3	5.7	6.1	6.2
2300 Self-employed or non-employed	3.9	7.8	13.9	21.5	22.3	0.5	0.5	0.5	0.7	0.7
2400 Unallocable between 2100, 2200 and 2300	0.0	0.0	0.0	0.0	0.0	0.0	0.0	0.0	0.0	0.0
3000 Taxes on payroll and workforce	**0.0**	**0.0**	**0.0**	**0.0**	**0.0**	**0.0**	**0.0**	**0.0**	**0.0**	**0.0**
4000 Taxes on property	**8.9**	**14.5**	**30.9**	**35.6**	**39.2**	**1.2**	**1.0**	**1.2**	**1.1**	**1.3**
4100 Recurrent taxes on immovable property	2.2	2.8	8.5	12.7	13.7	0.3	0.2	0.3	0.4	0.4
4200 Recurrent taxes on net wealth	5.1	7.7	14.1	14.1	16.7	0.7	0.5	0.5	0.5	0.5
4300 Estate, inheritance and gift taxes	0.4	1.3	2.4	0.3	0.2	0.1	0.1	0.1	0.0	0.0
4400 Taxes on financial and capital transactions	1.1	2.7	5.9	8.4	8.6	0.1	0.2	0.2	0.3	0.3
4500 Non-recurrent taxes	0.0	0.0	0.0	0.0	0.0	0.0	0.0	0.0	0.0	0.0
4600 Other recurrent taxes on property	0.0	0.0	0.0	0.0	0.0	0.0	0.0	0.0	0.0	0.0
5000 Taxes on goods and services	**107.3**	**200.7**	**300.7**	**361.7**	**378.8**	**14.3**	**13.3**	**11.6**	**11.6**	**12.1**
5100 Taxes on production, sale, transfer, etc	102.9	185.9	284.9	342.4	358.8	13.7	12.3	11.0	11.0	11.5
5110 General taxes	56.7	125.0	201.8	256.0	270.1	7.6	8.3	7.8	8.2	8.7
5111 Value added taxes	56.7	124.2	201.2	255.2	269.2	7.6	8.2	7.8	8.2	8.6
5120 Taxes on specific goods and services	46.2	60.9	83.1	86.4	88.8	6.2	4.0	3.2	2.8	2.8
5121 Excises	37.5	54.9	76.3	78.8	79.5	5.0	3.6	2.9	2.5	2.5
5200 Taxes on use of goods and perform activities	4.4	14.8	15.8	19.3	20.0	0.6	1.0	0.6	0.6	0.6
5300 Unallocable between 5100 and 5200	0.0	0.0	0.0	0.0	0.0	0.0	0.0	0.0	0.0	0.0
6000 Other taxes	**0.0**	**0.0**	**0.0**	**0.0**	**0.0**	**0.0**	**0.0**	**0.0**	**0.0**	**0.0**
Non-wastable tax credits										
Non-wastable tax credits against 1000	..	..	1.2	3.0	3.6	..	..	0.0	0.1	0.1
Transfer component	..	..	1.0	2.5	3.0	..	..	0.0	0.1	0.1
Tax expenditure component	..	..	0.3	0.5	0.6	..	..	0.0	0.0	0.0

.. Not available

Note: More detailed country data and country notes are available in online chapter 5 "Country Tables, 1965-2016": http://dx.doi.org/10.1787/rev_stats-2018-en. Full time series can be accessed at http://oe.cd/full-time-series.

Source: Statistics Norway; National Accounts.

StatLink http://dx.doi.org/10.1787/888933860653

Table 4.52. Norway, tax revenue and % of GDP by level of government and main taxes

	Billion NOK					% of GDP				
	1990	2000	2010	2015	2016	1990	2000	2010	2015	2016
Federal or Central government										
Total tax revenue	**165.4**	**536.1**	**938.4**	**1 013.9**	**1 011.7**	**22.1**	**35.6**	**36.2**	**32.5**	**32.4**
1000 Taxes on income, profits and capital gains	50.6	198.4	380.8	314.8	288.9	6.8	13.2	14.7	10.1	9.3
2000 Social security contributions	4.7	132.2	243.0	325.6	330.9	0.6	8.8	9.4	10.4	10.6
3000 Taxes on payroll and workforce	0.0	0.0	0.0	0.0	0.0	0.0	0.0	0.0	0.0	0.0
4000 Taxes on property	3.4	7.0	16.0	13.8	15.4	0.5	0.5	0.6	0.4	0.5
5000 Taxes on goods and services	106.7	198.6	298.6	359.7	376.5	14.2	13.2	11.5	11.5	12.1
6000 Other taxes	0.0	0.0	0.0	0.0	0.0	0.0	0.0	0.0	0.0	0.0
State/Regional										
Total tax revenue	..	..	..	..	..	..	..	..	..	..
1000 Taxes on income, profits and capital gains	..	..	..	..	..	..	..	..	..	..
2000 Social security contributions	..	..	..	..	..	..	..	..	..	..
3000 Taxes on payroll and workforce	..	..	..	..	..	..	..	..	..	..
4000 Taxes on property	..	..	..	..	..	..	..	..	..	..
5000 Taxes on goods and services	..	..	..	..	..	..	..	..	..	..
6000 Other taxes	..	..	..	..	..	..	..	..	..	..
Local government										
Total tax revenue	**61.6**	**95.5**	**148.2**	**184.4**	**195.4**	**8.2**	**6.3**	**5.7**	**5.9**	**6.3**
1000 Taxes on income, profits and capital gains	55.7	85.8	131.2	160.6	169.3	7.4	5.7	5.1	5.2	5.4
2000 Social security contributions	0.0	0.0	0.0	0.0	0.0	0.0	0.0	0.0	0.0	0.0
3000 Taxes on payroll and workforce	0.0	0.0	0.0	0.0	0.0	0.0	0.0	0.0	0.0	0.0
4000 Taxes on property	5.5	7.6	14.9	21.8	23.9	0.7	0.5	0.6	0.7	0.8
5000 Taxes on goods and services	0.4	2.1	2.2	2.0	2.3	0.1	0.1	0.1	0.1	0.1
6000 Other taxes	0.0	0.0	0.0	0.0	0.0	0.0	0.0	0.0	0.0	0.0
Social Security Funds										
Total tax revenue	**74.8**	**0.0**	**0.0**	**0.0**	**0.0**	**10.0**	**0.0**	**0.0**	**0.0**	**0.0**
1000 Taxes on income, profits and capital gains	0.0	0.0	0.0	0.0	0.0	0.0	0.0	0.0	0.0	0.0
2000 Social security contributions	74.6	0.0	0.0	0.0	0.0	10.0	0.0	0.0	0.0	0.0
3000 Taxes on payroll and workforce	0.0	0.0	0.0	0.0	0.0	0.0	0.0	0.0	0.0	0.0
4000 Taxes on property	0.0	0.0	0.0	0.0	0.0	0.0	0.0	0.0	0.0	0.0
5000 Taxes on goods and services	0.2	0.0	0.0	0.0	0.0	0.0	0.0	0.0	0.0	0.0
6000 Other taxes	0.0	0.0	0.0	0.0	0.0	0.0	0.0	0.0	0.0	0.0

.. Not available

Note: More detailed country data and country notes are available in online chapter 6 "Tax revenues by sub-sectors of general government": http://dx.doi.org/10.1787/rev_stats-2018-en. Full time series can be accessed at http://oe.cd/full-time-series.

Source: Statistics Norway; National Accounts.

StatLink http://dx.doi.org/10.1787/888933860672

Table 4.53. Poland, tax revenue and % of GDP by selected tax category

	Billion PLN					% of GDP				
	1990	2000	2010	2015	2016	1990	2000	2010	2015	2016
Total tax revenue	..	**246.0**	**454.0**	**582.4**	**620.6**	..	**32.9**	**31.4**	**32.4**	**33.4**
1000 Taxes on income, profits and capital gains	..	**50.3**	**91.0**	**117.1**	**124.3**	..	**6.7**	**6.3**	**6.5**	**6.7**
1100 Of individuals	..	32.4	62.9	84.0	90.1	..	4.3	4.4	4.7	4.8
1200 Corporate	..	17.9	28.1	33.1	34.2	..	2.4	1.9	1.8	1.8
1300 Unallocable between 1100 and 1200	..	0.0	0.0	0.0	0.0	..	0.0	0.0	0.0	0.0
2000 Social security contributions	..	**96.4**	**156.0**	**223.5**	**236.3**	..	**12.9**	**10.8**	**12.4**	**12.7**
2100 Employees	..	42.4	60.2	88.6	92.7	..	5.7	4.2	4.9	5.0
2200 Employers	..	41.4	65.4	87.6	91.8	..	5.5	4.5	4.9	4.9
2300 Self-employed or non-employed	..	12.6	30.4	47.4	51.8	..	1.7	2.1	2.6	2.8
2400 Unallocable between 2100, 2200 and 2300	..	0.0	0.0	0.0	0.0	..	0.0	0.0	0.0	0.0
3000 Taxes on payroll and workforce	..	**1.6**	**3.7**	**4.0**	**4.2**	..	**0.2**	**0.3**	**0.2**	**0.2**
4000 Taxes on property	..	**10.6**	**19.1**	**24.6**	**25.6**	..	**1.4**	**1.3**	**1.4**	**1.4**
4100 Recurrent taxes on immovable property	..	8.4	16.4	22.2	22.7	..	1.1	1.1	1.2	1.2
4200 Recurrent taxes on net wealth	..	0.0	0.0	0.0	0.0	..	0.0	0.0	0.0	0.0
4300 Estate, inheritance and gift taxes	..	0.2	0.3	0.2	0.3	..	0.0	0.0	0.0	0.0
4400 Taxes on financial and capital transactions	..	2.0	2.4	2.2	2.6	..	0.3	0.2	0.1	0.1
4500 Non-recurrent taxes	..	0.0	0.0	0.0	0.0	..	0.0	0.0	0.0	0.0
4600 Other recurrent taxes on property	..	0.0	0.0	0.0	0.0	..	0.0	0.0	0.0	0.0
5000 Taxes on goods and services	..	**86.9**	**182.0**	**209.7**	**226.1**	..	**11.6**	**12.6**	**11.7**	**12.2**
5100 Taxes on production, sale, transfer, etc	..	84.9	175.2	201.7	218.0	..	11.4	12.1	11.2	11.7
5110 General taxes	..	51.6	109.7	125.8	131.0	..	6.9	7.6	7.0	7.0
5111 Value added taxes	..	51.6	109.7	125.8	131.0	..	6.9	7.6	7.0	7.0
5120 Taxes on specific goods and services	..	33.3	65.5	75.9	87.0	..	4.5	4.5	4.2	4.7
5121 Excises	..	27.2	62.0	70.6	75.6	..	3.6	4.3	3.9	4.1
5200 Taxes on use of goods and perform activities	..	2.0	6.8	8.0	8.1	..	0.3	0.5	0.4	0.4
5300 Unallocable between 5100 and 5200	..	0.0	0.0	0.0	0.0	..	0.0	0.0	0.0	0.0
6000 Other taxes	..	**0.3**	**0.6**	**0.6**	**0.9**	..	**0.0**	**0.0**	**0.0**	**0.1**
Non-wastable tax credits										
Non-wastable tax credits against 1000	..	..	..	..	..	..	..	..	..	..
Transfer component	..	..	..	..	..	..	..	..	..	..
Tax expenditure component	..	..	..	..	..	..	..	..	..	..

.. Not available

Note: More detailed country data and country notes are available in online chapter 5 "Country Tables, 1965-2016": http://dx.doi.org/10.1787/rev_stats-2018-en. Full time series can be accessed at http://oe.cd/full-time-series.

Source: Ministry of Finance, Economic Department.

StatLink http://dx.doi.org/10.1787/888933860691

Table 4.54. Poland, tax revenue and % of GDP by level of government and main taxes

	Billion PLN					% of GDP				
	1990	2000	2010	2015	2016	1990	2000	2010	2015	2016
Federal or Central government										
Total tax revenue	..	**126.9**	**239.2**	**280.9**	**301.2**	..	**17.0**	**16.6**	**15.6**	**16.2**
1000 Taxes on income, profits and capital gains	..	40.0	57.7	71.4	75.2	..	5.3	4.0	4.0	4.0
2000 Social security contributions	..	0.0	0.0	0.0	0.0	..	0.0	0.0	0.0	0.0
3000 Taxes on payroll and workforce	..	1.6	3.7	4.0	4.2	..	0.2	0.3	0.2	0.2
4000 Taxes on property	..	0.0	0.0	0.0	0.0	..	0.0	0.0	0.0	0.0
5000 Taxes on goods and services	..	85.3	177.8	205.5	221.8	..	11.4	12.3	11.4	11.9
6000 Other taxes	..	0.0	0.0	0.0	0.0	..	0.0	0.0	0.0	0.0
State/Regional										
Total tax revenue	..	..	..	..	..	..	..	..	..	..
1000 Taxes on income, profits and capital gains	..	..	..	..	..	..	..	..	..	..
2000 Social security contributions	..	..	..	..	..	..	..	..	..	..
3000 Taxes on payroll and workforce	..	..	..	..	..	..	..	..	..	..
4000 Taxes on property	..	..	..	..	..	..	..	..	..	..
5000 Taxes on goods and services	..	..	..	..	..	..	..	..	..	..
6000 Other taxes	..	..	..	..	..	..	..	..	..	..
Local government										
Total tax revenue	..	**22.7**	**57.1**	**75.1**	**79.8**	..	**3.0**	**4.0**	**4.2**	**4.3**
1000 Taxes on income, profits and capital gains	..	10.3	33.3	45.7	49.0	..	1.4	2.3	2.5	2.6
2000 Social security contributions	..	0.0	0.0	0.0	0.0	..	0.0	0.0	0.0	0.0
3000 Taxes on payroll and workforce	..	0.0	0.0	0.0	0.0	..	0.0	0.0	0.0	0.0
4000 Taxes on property	..	10.6	19.1	24.6	25.6	..	1.4	1.3	1.4	1.4
5000 Taxes on goods and services	..	1.5	4.1	4.1	4.2	..	0.2	0.3	0.2	0.2
6000 Other taxes	..	0.3	0.6	0.6	0.9	..	0.0	0.0	0.0	0.1
Social Security Funds										
Total tax revenue	..	**96.4**	**156.0**	**223.5**	**236.3**	..	**12.9**	**10.8**	**12.4**	**12.7**
1000 Taxes on income, profits and capital gains	..	0.0	0.0	0.0	0.0	..	0.0	0.0	0.0	0.0
2000 Social security contributions	..	96.4	156.0	223.5	236.3	..	12.9	10.8	12.4	12.7
3000 Taxes on payroll and workforce	..	0.0	0.0	0.0	0.0	..	0.0	0.0	0.0	0.0
4000 Taxes on property	..	0.0	0.0	0.0	0.0	..	0.0	0.0	0.0	0.0
5000 Taxes on goods and services	..	0.0	0.0	0.0	0.0	..	0.0	0.0	0.0	0.0
6000 Other taxes	..	0.0	0.0	0.0	0.0	..	0.0	0.0	0.0	0.0

.. Not available

Note: More detailed country data and country notes are available in online chapter 6 "Tax revenues by sub-sectors of general government": http://dx.doi.org/10.1787/rev_stats-2018-en. Full time series can be accessed at http://oe.cd/full-time-series.

Source: Ministry of Finance, Economic Department.

StatLink http://dx.doi.org/10.1787/888933860710

Table 4.55. Portugal, tax revenue and % of GDP by selected tax category

	Billion EUR					% of GDP				
	1990	2000	2010	2015	2016	1990	2000	2010	2015	2016
Total tax revenue	**14.8**	**39.9**	**54.7**	**61.9**	**63.7**	**26.5**	**31.1**	**30.4**	**34.4**	**34.3**
1000 Taxes on income, profits and capital gains	**3.8**	**11.7**	**14.6**	**18.8**	**18.3**	**6.8**	**9.1**	**8.1**	**10.4**	**9.9**
1100 Of individuals	2.4	6.9	9.6	13.1	12.6	4.2	5.4	5.4	7.3	6.8
1200 Corporate	1.2	4.7	4.9	5.6	5.7	2.1	3.7	2.7	3.1	3.1
1300 Unallocable between 1100 and 1200	0.3	0.0	0.1	0.0	0.0	0.5	0.0	0.0	0.0	0.0
2000 Social security contributions	**4.0**	**10.2**	**15.5**	**16.2**	**16.9**	**7.2**	**7.9**	**8.6**	**9.0**	**9.1**
2100 Employees	1.5	4.3	6.7	7.0	7.2	2.6	3.3	3.7	3.9	3.9
2200 Employers	2.4	5.9	8.8	9.2	9.7	4.3	4.6	4.9	5.1	5.2
2300 Self-employed or non-employed	0.1	0.0	0.0	0.0	0.0	0.3	0.0	0.0	0.0	0.0
2400 Unallocable between 2100, 2200 and 2300	0.0	0.0	0.0	0.0	0.0	0.0	0.0	0.0	0.0	0.0
3000 Taxes on payroll and workforce	**0.0**	**0.0**	**0.0**	**0.0**	**0.0**	**0.0**	**0.0**	**0.0**	**0.0**	**0.0**
4000 Taxes on property	**0.4**	**1.5**	**1.9**	**2.3**	**2.4**	**0.7**	**1.1**	**1.1**	**1.3**	**1.3**
4100 Recurrent taxes on immovable property	0.1	0.5	1.1	1.5	1.5	0.2	0.4	0.6	0.9	0.8
4200 Recurrent taxes on net wealth	0.0	0.0	0.0	0.0	0.0	0.0	0.0	0.0	0.0	0.0
4300 Estate, inheritance and gift taxes	0.1	0.1	0.0	0.0	0.0	0.1	0.1	0.0	0.0	0.0
4400 Taxes on financial and capital transactions	0.2	0.9	0.8	0.8	0.9	0.3	0.7	0.5	0.4	0.5
4500 Non-recurrent taxes	0.0	0.0	0.0	0.0	0.0	0.0	0.0	0.0	0.0	0.0
4600 Other recurrent taxes on property	0.0	0.0	0.0	0.0	0.0	0.0	0.0	0.0	0.0	0.0
5000 Taxes on goods and services	**6.6**	**16.1**	**22.0**	**23.8**	**25.2**	**11.7**	**12.5**	**12.2**	**13.3**	**13.6**
5100 Taxes on production, sale, transfer, etc	6.4	15.6	21.2	22.8	24.0	11.5	12.2	11.8	12.7	12.9
5110 General taxes	2.9	9.7	13.5	15.4	15.8	5.2	7.6	7.5	8.5	8.5
5111 Value added taxes	2.9	9.7	13.5	15.4	15.8	5.2	7.6	7.5	8.5	8.5
5120 Taxes on specific goods and services	3.5	5.9	7.7	7.5	8.2	6.3	4.6	4.3	4.2	4.4
5121 Excises	2.1	4.5	5.7	5.2	5.8	3.7	3.5	3.1	2.9	3.1
5200 Taxes on use of goods and perform activities	0.1	0.4	0.7	1.0	1.1	0.2	0.3	0.4	0.6	0.6
5300 Unallocable between 5100 and 5200	0.0	0.1	0.0	0.0	0.1	0.0	0.0	0.0	0.0	0.1
6000 Other taxes	**0.0**	**0.3**	**0.5**	**0.7**	**0.7**	**0.1**	**0.2**	**0.3**	**0.4**	**0.4**
Non-wastable tax credits										
Non-wastable tax credits against 1000	..	..	..	..	..	..	..	..	..	..
Transfer component	..	..	..	..	..	..	..	..	..	..
Tax expenditure component	..	..	..	..	..	..	..	..	..	..

.. Not available

Note: More detailed country data and country notes are available in online chapter 5 "Country Tables, 1965-2016": http://dx.doi.org/10.1787/rev_stats-2018-en. Full time series can be accessed at http://oe.cd/full-time-series.

Source: Instituto Nacionale de Estatistica; Conta do Estado, Contas de Gerência dos Fundos e Serviços Autonomos da Administraçao Central; Estatisticas das Financas publicas; Relatorio do Instituto de Gestao Financeira da Seguranta Social, Contas de Gerência das Regioes Autonomas da Madeira e dos Atores.

StatLink http://dx.doi.org/10.1787/888933860729

Table 4.56. Portugal, tax revenue and % of GDP by level of government and main taxes

	Billion EUR					% of GDP				
	1990	2000	2010	2015	2016	1990	2000	2010	2015	2016
Federal or Central government										
Total tax revenue	**9.8**	**27.8**	**36.5**	**45.2**	**46.3**	**17.6**	**21.6**	**20.3**	**25.1**	**25.0**
1000 Taxes on income, profits and capital gains	3.6	11.1	13.6	17.5	17.0	6.4	8.7	7.5	9.7	9.2
2000 Social security contributions	0.0	1.3	1.9	5.3	5.6	0.0	1.0	1.1	3.0	3.0
3000 Taxes on payroll and workforce	0.0	0.0	0.0	0.0	0.0	0.0	0.0	0.0	0.0	0.0
4000 Taxes on property	0.1	0.3	0.2	0.2	0.2	0.1	0.2	0.1	0.1	0.1
5000 Taxes on goods and services	6.1	14.8	20.3	21.5	22.9	10.9	11.5	11.3	12.0	12.3
6000 Other taxes	0.0	0.3	0.5	0.7	0.7	0.1	0.2	0.3	0.4	0.4
State/Regional										
Total tax revenue	..	..	..	..	..	..	..	..	..	..
1000 Taxes on income, profits and capital gains	..	..	..	..	..	..	..	..	..	..
2000 Social security contributions	..	..	..	..	..	..	..	..	..	..
3000 Taxes on payroll and workforce	..	..	..	..	..	..	..	..	..	..
4000 Taxes on property	..	..	..	..	..	..	..	..	..	..
5000 Taxes on goods and services	..	..	..	..	..	..	..	..	..	..
6000 Other taxes	..	..	..	..	..	..	..	..	..	..
Local government										
Total tax revenue	**0.8**	**2.5**	**3.6**	**4.5**	**4.6**	**1.5**	**2.0**	**2.0**	**2.5**	**2.5**
1000 Taxes on income, profits and capital gains	0.2	0.6	1.1	1.2	1.3	0.4	0.4	0.6	0.7	0.7
2000 Social security contributions	0.0	0.0	0.0	0.0	0.0	0.0	0.0	0.0	0.0	0.0
3000 Taxes on payroll and workforce	0.0	0.0	0.0	0.0	0.0	0.0	0.0	0.0	0.0	0.0
4000 Taxes on property	0.3	1.2	1.7	2.1	2.1	0.6	0.9	0.9	1.2	1.2
5000 Taxes on goods and services	0.3	0.7	0.8	1.1	1.2	0.5	0.6	0.5	0.6	0.6
6000 Other taxes	0.0	0.0	0.0	0.0	0.0	0.0	0.0	0.0	0.0	0.0
Social Security Funds										
Total tax revenue	**4.0**	**9.4**	**14.4**	**12.1**	**12.4**	**7.2**	**7.3**	**8.0**	**6.7**	**6.7**
1000 Taxes on income, profits and capital gains	0.0	0.0	0.0	0.0	0.0	0.0	0.0	0.0	0.0	0.0
2000 Social security contributions	4.0	8.8	13.5	10.9	11.4	7.2	6.9	7.5	6.0	6.1
3000 Taxes on payroll and workforce	0.0	0.0	0.0	0.0	0.0	0.0	0.0	0.0	0.0	0.0
4000 Taxes on property	0.0	0.0	0.0	0.0	0.0	0.0	0.0	0.0	0.0	0.0
5000 Taxes on goods and services	0.0	0.5	0.8	1.2	1.0	0.0	0.4	0.5	0.7	0.5
6000 Other taxes	0.0	0.0	0.0	0.0	0.0	0.0	0.0	0.0	0.0	0.0

.. Not available

Note: More detailed country data and country notes are available in online chapter 6 "Tax revenues by sub-sectors of general government": http://dx.doi.org/10.1787/rev_stats-2018-en. Full time series can be accessed at http://oe.cd/full-time-series.

Source: Instituto Nacionale de Estatistica; Conta do Estado, Contas de Gerência dos Fundos e Serviços Autonomos da Administraçao Central; Estatisticas das Financas publicas; Relatorio do Instituto de Gestao Financeira da Seguranta Social, Contas de Gerência das Regioes Autonomas da Madeira e dos Atores.

StatLink http://dx.doi.org/10.1787/888933860748

Table 4.57. Slovak Republic, tax revenue and % of GDP by selected tax category

	Billion EUR					% of GDP				
	1990	2000	2010	2015	2016	1990	2000	2010	2015	2016
Total tax revenue	..	**10.6**	**19.0**	**25.4**	**26.3**	..	**33.6**	**28.1**	**32.2**	**32.4**
1000 Taxes on income, profits and capital gains	..	**2.2**	**3.6**	**5.5**	**5.7**	..	**6.9**	**5.3**	**7.0**	**7.0**
1100 Of individuals	..	1.1	1.8	2.5	2.7	..	3.3	2.6	3.1	3.3
1200 Corporate	..	0.8	1.7	2.9	2.8	..	2.6	2.5	3.7	3.5
1300 Unallocable between 1100 and 1200	..	0.3	0.2	0.2	0.2	..	1.0	0.2	0.2	0.2
2000 Social security contributions	..	**4.4**	**8.2**	**10.9**	**11.4**	..	**14.0**	**12.1**	**13.8**	**14.1**
2100 Employees	..	0.9	2.1	2.4	2.6	..	2.9	3.1	3.1	3.3
2200 Employers	..	2.9	4.6	6.3	6.5	..	9.0	6.8	8.0	8.0
2300 Self-employed or non-employed	..	0.7	1.5	2.2	2.3	..	2.1	2.2	2.7	2.9
2400 Unallocable between 2100, 2200 and 2300	..	0.0	0.0	0.0	0.0	..	0.0	0.0	0.0	0.0
3000 Taxes on payroll and workforce	..	**0.0**	**0.0**	**0.0**	**0.0**	..	**0.0**	**0.0**	**0.0**	**0.0**
4000 Taxes on property	..	**0.2**	**0.3**	**0.3**	**0.3**	..	**0.6**	**0.4**	**0.4**	**0.4**
4100 Recurrent taxes on immovable property	..	0.1	0.3	0.3	0.3	..	0.5	0.4	0.4	0.4
4200 Recurrent taxes on net wealth	..	0.0	0.0	0.0	0.0	..	0.0	0.0	0.0	0.0
4300 Estate, inheritance and gift taxes	..	0.0	0.0	0.0	0.0	..	0.0	0.0	0.0	0.0
4400 Taxes on financial and capital transactions	..	0.0	0.0	0.0	0.0	..	0.1	0.0	0.0	0.0
4500 Non-recurrent taxes	..	0.0	0.0	0.0	0.0	..	0.0	0.0	0.0	0.0
4600 Other recurrent taxes on property	..	0.0	0.0	0.0	0.0	..	0.0	0.0	0.0	0.0
5000 Taxes on goods and services	..	**3.8**	**6.8**	**8.5**	**8.7**	..	**12.2**	**10.1**	**10.8**	**10.7**
5100 Taxes on production, sale, transfer, etc	..	3.6	6.3	7.8	8.0	..	11.5	9.3	9.9	9.8
5110 General taxes	..	2.2	4.2	5.4	5.4	..	6.9	6.2	6.9	6.7
5111 Value added taxes	..	2.2	4.2	5.4	5.4	..	6.9	6.2	6.9	6.7
5120 Taxes on specific goods and services	..	1.5	2.1	2.4	2.5	..	4.6	3.1	3.1	3.1
5121 Excises	..	1.0	1.9	2.1	2.2	..	3.1	2.9	2.7	2.7
5200 Taxes on use of goods and perform activities	..	0.2	0.4	0.5	0.6	..	0.7	0.6	0.7	0.7
5300 Unallocable between 5100 and 5200	..	0.0	0.1	0.2	0.2	..	0.0	0.2	0.2	0.2
6000 Other taxes	..	**0.0**	**0.0**	**0.0**	**0.0**	..	**0.0**	**0.0**	**0.0**	**0.0**
Non-wastable tax credits										
Non-wastable tax credits against 1000	..	..	0.3	0.3	0.3	..	..	0.4	0.3	0.3
Transfer component	..	..	..	..	..	..	..	..	..	..
Tax expenditure component	..	..	..	..	..	..	..	..	..	..

.. Not available

Note: More detailed country data and country notes are available in online chapter 5 "Country Tables, 1965-2016": http://dx.doi.org/10.1787/rev_stats-2018-en. Full time series can be accessed at http://oe.cd/full-time-series.

Source: Ministry of Finance.

StatLink http://dx.doi.org/10.1787/888933860767

Table 4.58. Slovak Republic, tax revenue and % of GDP by level of government and main taxes

	Billion EUR					% of GDP				
	1990	2000	2010	2015	2016	1990	2000	2010	2015	2016
Federal or Central government										
Total tax revenue	..	**6.2**	**10.3**	**14.1**	**14.5**	..	**19.5**	**15.3**	**17.9**	**17.8**
1000 Taxes on income, profits and capital gains	..	2.2	3.6	5.5	5.7	..	6.9	5.3	7.0	7.0
2000 Social security contributions	..	0.1	0.2	0.3	0.3	..	0.3	0.3	0.3	0.3
3000 Taxes on payroll and workforce	..	0.0	0.0	0.0	0.0	..	0.0	0.0	0.0	0.0
4000 Taxes on property	..	0.1	0.0	0.0	0.0	..	0.2	0.0	0.0	0.0
5000 Taxes on goods and services	..	3.8	6.5	8.3	8.5	..	12.1	9.7	10.6	10.5
6000 Other taxes	..	0.0	0.0	0.0	0.0	..	0.0	0.0	0.0	0.0
State/Regional										
Total tax revenue	..	..	..	..	..	..	..	..	..	..
1000 Taxes on income, profits and capital gains	..	..	..	..	..	..	..	..	..	..
2000 Social security contributions	..	..	..	..	..	..	..	..	..	..
3000 Taxes on payroll and workforce	..	..	..	..	..	..	..	..	..	..
4000 Taxes on property	..	..	..	..	..	..	..	..	..	..
5000 Taxes on goods and services	..	..	..	..	..	..	..	..	..	..
6000 Other taxes	..	..	..	..	..	..	..	..	..	..
Local government										
Total tax revenue	..	**0.1**	**0.5**	**0.5**	**0.5**	..	**0.5**	**0.8**	**0.7**	**0.6**
1000 Taxes on income, profits and capital gains	..	0.0	0.0	0.0	0.0	..	0.0	0.0	0.0	0.0
2000 Social security contributions	..	0.0	0.0	0.0	0.0	..	0.0	0.0	0.0	0.0
3000 Taxes on payroll and workforce	..	0.0	0.0	0.0	0.0	..	0.0	0.0	0.0	0.0
4000 Taxes on property	..	0.1	0.3	0.3	0.3	..	0.4	0.4	0.4	0.4
5000 Taxes on goods and services	..	0.0	0.3	0.2	0.2	..	0.0	0.4	0.2	0.2
6000 Other taxes	..	0.0	0.0	0.0	0.0	..	0.0	0.0	0.0	0.0
Social Security Funds										
Total tax revenue	..	**4.3**	**7.9**	**10.6**	**11.2**	..	**13.7**	**11.7**	**13.4**	**13.8**
1000 Taxes on income, profits and capital gains	..	0.0	0.0	0.0	0.0	..	0.0	0.0	0.0	0.0
2000 Social security contributions	..	4.3	7.9	10.6	11.2	..	13.7	11.7	13.4	13.8
3000 Taxes on payroll and workforce	..	0.0	0.0	0.0	0.0	..	0.0	0.0	0.0	0.0
4000 Taxes on property	..	0.0	0.0	0.0	0.0	..	0.0	0.0	0.0	0.0
5000 Taxes on goods and services	..	0.0	0.0	0.0	0.0	..	0.0	0.0	0.0	0.0
6000 Other taxes	..	0.0	0.0	0.0	0.0	..	0.0	0.0	0.0	0.0

.. Not available

Note: More detailed country data and country notes are available in online chapter 6 "Tax revenues by sub-sectors of general government": http://dx.doi.org/10.1787/rev_stats-2018-en. Full time series can be accessed at http://oe.cd/full-time-series.

Source: Ministry of Finance.

StatLink http://dx.doi.org/10.1787/888933860786

Table 4.59. Slovenia, tax revenue and % of GDP by selected tax category

	Billion EUR					% of GDP				
	1990	2000	2010	2015	2016	1990	2000	2010	2015	2016
Total tax revenue	..	**6.9**	**13.4**	**14.1**	**14.7**	..	**36.6**	**36.9**	**36.4**	**36.5**
1000 Taxes on income, profits and capital gains	..	**1.3**	**2.7**	**2.5**	**2.8**	..	**6.8**	**7.4**	**6.6**	**6.8**
1100 Of individuals	..	1.0	2.0	2.0	2.1	..	5.5	5.6	5.1	5.2
1200 Corporate	..	0.2	0.7	0.6	0.6	..	1.1	1.8	1.5	1.6
1300 Unallocable between 1100 and 1200	..	0.0	0.0	0.0	0.0	..	0.1	0.0	0.0	0.0
2000 Social security contributions	..	**2.6**	**5.4**	**5.6**	**5.8**	..	**13.9**	**14.8**	**14.4**	**14.5**
2100 Employees	..	1.4	2.8	2.9	3.0	..	7.7	7.7	7.5	7.5
2200 Employers	..	1.0	2.1	2.1	2.2	..	5.3	5.7	5.5	5.5
2300 Self-employed or non-employed	..	0.2	0.5	0.6	0.6	..	0.9	1.5	1.4	1.4
2400 Unallocable between 2100, 2200 and 2300	..	0.0	0.0	0.0	0.0	..	0.0	0.0	0.0	0.0
3000 Taxes on payroll and workforce	..	**0.3**	**0.0**	**0.0**	**0.0**	..	**1.5**	**0.1**	**0.1**	**0.0**
4000 Taxes on property	..	**0.1**	**0.2**	**0.2**	**0.3**	..	**0.6**	**0.6**	**0.6**	**0.6**
4100 Recurrent taxes on immovable property	..	0.1	0.2	0.2	0.2	..	0.4	0.5	0.5	0.5
4200 Recurrent taxes on net wealth	..	0.0	0.0	0.0	0.0	..	0.0	0.0	0.0	0.0
4300 Estate, inheritance and gift taxes	..	0.0	0.0	0.0	0.0	..	0.0	0.0	0.0	0.0
4400 Taxes on financial and capital transactions	..	0.0	0.0	0.0	0.0	..	0.1	0.1	0.1	0.1
4500 Non-recurrent taxes	..	0.0	0.0	0.0	0.0	..	0.1	0.0	0.0	0.0
4600 Other recurrent taxes on property	..	0.0	0.0	0.0	0.0	..	0.0	0.0	0.0	0.0
5000 Taxes on goods and services	..	**2.6**	**5.0**	**5.7**	**5.8**	..	**13.8**	**13.8**	**14.6**	**14.3**
5100 Taxes on production, sale, transfer, etc	..	2.5	4.8	5.3	5.4	..	13.1	13.2	13.6	13.4
5110 General taxes	..	1.6	2.9	3.2	3.3	..	8.7	8.1	8.3	8.2
5111 Value added taxes	..	1.6	2.9	3.2	3.3	..	8.5	8.1	8.3	8.2
5120 Taxes on specific goods and services	..	0.8	1.9	2.1	2.1	..	4.4	5.1	5.3	5.2
5121 Excises	..	0.6	1.6	1.6	1.7	..	3.1	4.3	4.2	4.1
5200 Taxes on use of goods and perform activities	..	0.1	0.2	0.4	0.4	..	0.6	0.6	1.0	0.9
5300 Unallocable between 5100 and 5200	..	0.0	0.0	0.0	0.0	..	0.0	0.0	0.0	0.0
6000 Other taxes	..	**0.0**	**0.0**	**0.0**	**0.0**	..	**0.0**	**0.0**	**0.0**	**0.0**
Non-wastable tax credits										
Non-wastable tax credits against 1000	..	..	..	..	..	..	..	..	..	..
Transfer component	..	..	..	..	..	..	..	..	..	..
Tax expenditure component	..	..	..	..	..	..	..	..	..	..

.. Not available

Note: More detailed country data and country notes are available in online chapter 5 "Country Tables, 1965-2016": http://dx.doi.org/10.1787/rev_stats-2018-en. Full time series can be accessed at http://oe.cd/full-time-series.

Source: Statistical Office of the Republic of Slovenia.

StatLink http://dx.doi.org/10.1787/888933860805

Table 4.60. Slovenia, tax revenue and % of GDP by level of government and main taxes

	Billion EUR					% of GDP				
	1990	2000	2010	2015	2016	1990	2000	2010	2015	2016
Federal or Central government										
Total tax revenue	..	**3.8**	**6.5**	**7.2**	**7.5**	..	**20.2**	**18.0**	**18.4**	**18.5**
1000 Taxes on income, profits and capital gains	..	0.9	1.6	1.5	1.7	..	4.8	4.3	3.9	4.2
2000 Social security contributions	..	0.0	0.1	0.1	0.1	..	0.1	0.2	0.2	0.2
3000 Taxes on payroll and workforce	..	0.3	0.0	0.0	0.0	..	1.5	0.1	0.1	0.0
4000 Taxes on property	..	0.0	0.0	0.0	0.0	..	0.1	0.0	0.0	0.0
5000 Taxes on goods and services	..	2.6	4.9	5.5	5.7	..	13.7	13.5	14.3	14.1
6000 Other taxes	..	0.0	0.0	0.0	0.0	..	0.0	0.0	0.0	0.0
State/Regional										
Total tax revenue	..	..	..	..	..	..	..	..	..	..
1000 Taxes on income, profits and capital gains	..	..	..	..	..	..	..	..	..	..
2000 Social security contributions	..	..	..	..	..	..	..	..	..	..
3000 Taxes on payroll and workforce	..	..	..	..	..	..	..	..	..	..
4000 Taxes on property	..	..	..	..	..	..	..	..	..	..
5000 Taxes on goods and services	..	..	..	..	..	..	..	..	..	..
6000 Other taxes	..	..	..	..	..	..	..	..	..	..
Local government										
Total tax revenue	..	**0.5**	**1.5**	**1.4**	**1.4**	..	**2.7**	**4.0**	**3.5**	**3.5**
1000 Taxes on income, profits and capital gains	..	0.4	1.1	1.0	1.1	..	2.0	3.1	2.6	2.6
2000 Social security contributions	..	0.0	0.0	0.0	0.0	..	0.0	0.0	0.0	0.0
3000 Taxes on payroll and workforce	..	0.0	0.0	0.0	0.0	..	0.0	0.0	0.0	0.0
4000 Taxes on property	..	0.1	0.2	0.2	0.3	..	0.6	0.6	0.6	0.6
5000 Taxes on goods and services	..	0.0	0.1	0.1	0.1	..	0.1	0.3	0.2	0.2
6000 Other taxes	..	0.0	0.0	0.0	0.0	..	0.0	0.0	0.0	0.0
Social Security Funds										
Total tax revenue	..	**2.6**	**5.3**	**5.5**	**5.8**	..	**13.8**	**14.7**	**14.3**	**14.3**
1000 Taxes on income, profits and capital gains	..	0.0	0.0	0.0	0.0	..	0.0	0.0	0.0	0.0
2000 Social security contributions	..	2.6	5.3	5.5	5.8	..	13.8	14.7	14.3	14.3
3000 Taxes on payroll and workforce	..	0.0	0.0	0.0	0.0	..	0.0	0.0	0.0	0.0
4000 Taxes on property	..	0.0	0.0	0.0	0.0	..	0.0	0.0	0.0	0.0
5000 Taxes on goods and services	..	0.0	0.0	0.0	0.0	..	0.0	0.0	0.0	0.0
6000 Other taxes	..	0.0	0.0	0.0	0.0	..	0.0	0.0	0.0	0.0

.. Not available

Note: More detailed country data and country notes are available in online chapter 6 "Tax revenues by sub-sectors of general government": http://dx.doi.org/10.1787/rev_stats-2018-en. Full time series can be accessed at http://oe.cd/full-time-series.

Source: Statistical Office of the Republic of Slovenia.

StatLink http://dx.doi.org/10.1787/888933860824

Table 4.61. Spain, tax revenue and % of GDP by selected tax category

	Billion EUR					% of GDP				
	1990	2000	2010	2015	2016	1990	2000	2010	2015	2016
Total tax revenue	**103.7**	**214.7**	**337.4**	**362.8**	**371.2**	**31.6**	**33.2**	**31.2**	**33.6**	**33.2**
1000 Taxes on income, profits and capital gains	**31.8**	**60.7**	**93.8**	**102.9**	**104.5**	**9.7**	**9.4**	**8.7**	**9.5**	**9.3**
1100 Of individuals	22.5	41.1	73.2	77.5	79.4	6.9	6.4	6.8	7.2	7.1
1200 Corporate	9.1	19.6	20.6	25.4	25.1	2.8	3.0	1.9	2.4	2.2
1300 Unallocable between 1100 and 1200	0.1	0.0	0.0	0.0	0.0	0.0	0.0	0.0	0.0	0.0
2000 Social security contributions	**36.7**	**74.9**	**128.4**	**122.6**	**126.8**	**11.2**	**11.6**	**11.9**	**11.4**	**11.3**
2100 Employees	6.0	12.1	20.3	18.7	19.5	1.8	1.9	1.9	1.7	1.7
2200 Employers	26.4	53.9	89.8	87.8	91.4	8.0	8.3	8.3	8.1	8.2
2300 Self-employed or non-employed	4.4	8.8	18.3	16.1	15.9	1.3	1.4	1.7	1.5	1.4
2400 Unallocable between 2100, 2200 and 2300	0.0	0.0	0.0	0.0	0.0	0.0	0.0	0.0	0.0	0.0
3000 Taxes on payroll and workforce	**0.0**	**0.0**	**0.0**	**0.0**	**0.0**	**0.0**	**0.0**	**0.0**	**0.0**	**0.0**
4000 Taxes on property	**5.7**	**13.9**	**22.6**	**28.1**	**28.6**	**1.7**	**2.2**	**2.1**	**2.6**	**2.6**
4100 Recurrent taxes on immovable property	1.5	4.0	9.7	12.6	12.7	0.5	0.6	0.9	1.2	1.1
4200 Recurrent taxes on net wealth	0.6	1.4	0.7	1.9	2.0	0.2	0.2	0.1	0.2	0.2
4300 Estate, inheritance and gift taxes	0.4	1.4	2.4	2.8	2.7	0.1	0.2	0.2	0.3	0.2
4400 Taxes on financial and capital transactions	2.5	6.0	8.1	7.2	7.5	0.8	0.9	0.7	0.7	0.7
4500 Non-recurrent taxes	0.6	1.1	1.8	3.5	3.7	0.2	0.2	0.2	0.3	0.3
4600 Other recurrent taxes on property	0.0	0.0	0.0	0.0	0.0	0.0	0.0	0.0	0.0	0.0
5000 Taxes on goods and services	**29.4**	**64.3**	**90.5**	**107.3**	**109.2**	**9.0**	**10.0**	**8.4**	**9.9**	**9.8**
5100 Taxes on production, sale, transfer, etc	26.7	58.2	83.2	99.1	100.9	8.2	9.0	7.7	9.2	9.0
5110 General taxes	16.6	37.9	56.3	68.7	71.1	5.1	5.9	5.2	6.4	6.4
5111 Value added taxes	16.3	37.9	56.0	68.5	70.9	5.0	5.9	5.2	6.3	6.3
5120 Taxes on specific goods and services	10.1	20.4	26.9	30.4	29.8	3.1	3.2	2.5	2.8	2.7
5121 Excises	6.0	17.7	23.5	25.4	25.3	1.8	2.7	2.2	2.4	2.3
5200 Taxes on use of goods and perform activities	2.6	6.1	7.3	8.2	8.3	0.8	0.9	0.7	0.8	0.7
5300 Unallocable between 5100 and 5200	0.1	0.0	0.0	0.0	0.0	0.0	0.0	0.0	0.0	0.0
6000 Other taxes	**0.0**	**0.0**	**0.5**	**0.2**	**0.2**	**0.0**	**0.0**	**0.0**	**0.0**	**0.0**
Non-wastable tax credits										
Non-wastable tax credits against 1000	..	0.0	1.9	1.1	1.8	..	0.0	0.2	0.1	0.2
Transfer component	..	..	1.2	0.6	0.9	..	..	0.1	0.1	0.1
Tax expenditure component	..	..	0.7	0.6	0.9	..	..	0.1	0.1	0.1

.. Not available

Note: More detailed country data and country notes are available in online chapter 5 "Country Tables, 1965-2016": http://dx.doi.org/10.1787/rev_stats-2018-en. Full time series can be accessed at http://oe.cd/full-time-series.

The total tax revenue has been reduced by the amount of any capital transfer that represents uncollected taxes. The capital transfer has been allocated between tax headings in proportion to the reported tax revenue. Therefore, the tax revenue amounts are different to those reported in the detailed country data available in online chapter 5 "Country Tables, 1965-2016".

Source: Informacion Estatistica del Ministerio de Hacienda (for national taxes). Cuentas de las Administraciones Publicas (for local taxes and social security) both published by Secretaria General Tecnica del Ministerio de Hacienda.

StatLink http://dx.doi.org/10.1787/888933860843

Table 4.62. Spain, tax revenue and % of GDP by level of government and main taxes

	Billion EUR					% of GDP				
	1990	2000	2010	2015	2016	1990	2000	2010	2015	2016
Federal or Central government										
Total tax revenue	**53.7**	**105.2**	**136.4**	**155.0**	**154.6**	**16.4**	**16.3**	**12.6**	**14.4**	**13.8**
1000 Taxes on income, profits and capital gains	29.5	51.6	61.0	62.7	61.0	9.0	8.0	5.6	5.8	5.5
2000 Social security contributions	0.4	2.2	3.4	3.4	3.4	0.1	0.3	0.3	0.3	0.3
3000 Taxes on payroll and workforce	0.0	0.0	0.0	0.0	0.0	0.0	0.0	0.0	0.0	0.0
4000 Taxes on property	0.4	0.3	0.1	1.2	1.1	0.1	0.1	0.0	0.1	0.1
5000 Taxes on goods and services	23.4	51.0	71.4	87.7	88.9	7.2	7.9	6.6	8.1	7.9
6000 Other taxes	0.0	0.0	0.5	0.1	0.1	0.0	0.0	0.0	0.0	0.0
State/Regional										
Total tax revenue	**5.0**	**16.5**	**43.6**	**50.9**	**54.5**	**1.5**	**2.5**	**4.0**	**4.7**	**4.9**
1000 Taxes on income, profits and capital gains	0.4	5.5	27.6	34.6	37.6	0.1	0.9	2.5	3.2	3.4
2000 Social security contributions	0.0	0.0	0.0	0.0	0.0	0.0	0.0	0.0	0.0	0.0
3000 Taxes on payroll and workforce	0.0	0.0	0.0	0.0	0.0	0.0	0.0	0.0	0.0	0.0
4000 Taxes on property	3.0	7.8	10.1	10.5	10.8	0.9	1.2	0.9	1.0	1.0
5000 Taxes on goods and services	1.6	3.2	5.9	5.7	6.1	0.5	0.5	0.5	0.5	0.5
6000 Other taxes	0.0	0.0	0.0	0.0	0.0	0.0	0.0	0.0	0.0	0.0
Local government										
Total tax revenue	**8.1**	**19.5**	**30.8**	**36.0**	**36.8**	**2.5**	**3.0**	**2.9**	**3.3**	**3.3**
1000 Taxes on income, profits and capital gains	1.9	3.5	5.2	5.6	5.8	0.6	0.5	0.5	0.5	0.5
2000 Social security contributions	0.0	0.0	0.0	0.0	0.0	0.0	0.0	0.0	0.0	0.0
3000 Taxes on payroll and workforce	0.0	0.0	0.0	0.0	0.0	0.0	0.0	0.0	0.0	0.0
4000 Taxes on property	2.3	5.8	12.4	16.4	16.7	0.7	0.9	1.1	1.5	1.5
5000 Taxes on goods and services	3.9	10.1	13.3	13.9	14.3	1.2	1.6	1.2	1.3	1.3
6000 Other taxes	0.0	0.0	0.0	0.1	0.0	0.0	0.0	0.0	0.0	0.0
Social Security Funds										
Total tax revenue	**36.4**	**72.6**	**125.1**	**119.2**	**123.4**	**11.1**	**11.2**	**11.6**	**11.0**	**11.0**
1000 Taxes on income, profits and capital gains	0.0	0.0	0.0	0.0	0.0	0.0	0.0	0.0	0.0	0.0
2000 Social security contributions	36.4	72.6	125.1	119.2	123.4	11.1	11.2	11.6	11.0	11.0
3000 Taxes on payroll and workforce	0.0	0.0	0.0	0.0	0.0	0.0	0.0	0.0	0.0	0.0
4000 Taxes on property	0.0	0.0	0.0	0.0	0.0	0.0	0.0	0.0	0.0	0.0
5000 Taxes on goods and services	0.0	0.0	0.0	0.0	0.0	0.0	0.0	0.0	0.0	0.0
6000 Other taxes	0.0	0.0	0.0	0.0	0.0	0.0	0.0	0.0	0.0	0.0

Note: More detailed country data and country notes are available in online chapter 6 "Tax revenues by sub-sectors of general government": http://dx.doi.org/10.1787/rev_stats-2018-en. Full time series can be accessed at http://oe.cd/full-time-series.

The total tax revenue has been reduced by the amount of any capital transfer that represents uncollected taxes. The capital transfer has been allocated between tax headings in proportion to the reported tax revenue. Therefore, the tax revenue amounts are different to those reported in the detailed country data available in online chapter 6 "Tax revenues by sub-sectors of general government".

Source: Informacion Estatistica del Ministerio de Hacienda (for national taxes). Cuentas de las Administraciones Publicas (for local taxes and social security) both published by Secretaria General Tecnica del Ministerio de Hacienda.

StatLink http://dx.doi.org/10.1787/888933860862

Table 4.63. Sweden, tax revenue and % of GDP by selected tax category

	Billion SEK					% of GDP				
	1990	2000	2010	2015	2016	1990	2000	2010	2015	2016
Total tax revenue	**756.0**	**1 166.0**	**1 521.3**	**1 809.4**	**1 940.0**	**49.5**	**49.0**	**43.2**	**43.1**	**44.0**
1000 Taxes on income, profits and capital gains	**314.8**	**475.3**	**539.7**	**649.8**	**698.9**	**20.6**	**20.0**	**15.3**	**15.5**	**15.9**
1100 Of individuals	291.1	387.5	423.9	525.9	578.4	19.1	16.3	12.0	12.5	13.1
1200 Corporate	23.7	87.8	115.8	123.9	120.5	1.5	3.7	3.3	3.0	2.7
1300 Unallocable between 1100 and 1200	0.0	0.0	0.0	0.0	0.0	0.0	0.0	0.0	0.0	0.0
2000 Social security contributions	**205.9**	**307.0**	**384.7**	**404.9**	**438.9**	**13.5**	**12.9**	**10.9**	**9.6**	**10.0**
2100 Employees	0.8	63.1	89.2	108.4	113.3	0.1	2.7	2.5	2.6	2.6
2200 Employers	196.9	237.5	288.4	291.6	321.4	12.9	10.0	8.2	6.9	7.3
2300 Self-employed or non-employed	8.1	5.6	7.5	5.1	5.1	0.5	0.2	0.2	0.1	0.1
2400 Unallocable between 2100, 2200 and 2300	0.0	0.8	-0.4	-0.2	-1.0	0.0	0.0	0.0	0.0	0.0
3000 Taxes on payroll and workforce	**18.7**	**50.1**	**107.5**	**194.1**	**203.4**	**1.2**	**2.1**	**3.1**	**4.6**	**4.6**
4000 Taxes on property	**26.6**	**39.9**	**36.5**	**43.9**	**46.3**	**1.7**	**1.7**	**1.0**	**1.0**	**1.1**
4100 Recurrent taxes on immovable property	8.9	23.3	26.4	32.4	33.4	0.6	1.0	0.8	0.8	0.8
4200 Recurrent taxes on net wealth	3.2	8.2	0.0	0.0	0.0	0.2	0.3	0.0	0.0	0.0
4300 Estate, inheritance and gift taxes	1.4	2.5	0.0	0.0	0.0	0.1	0.1	0.0	0.0	0.0
4400 Taxes on financial and capital transactions	13.1	5.8	10.1	11.4	12.8	0.9	0.2	0.3	0.3	0.3
4500 Non-recurrent taxes	0.0	0.0	0.0	0.0	0.0	0.0	0.0	0.0	0.0	0.0
4600 Other recurrent taxes on property	0.0	0.0	0.0	0.0	0.0	0.0	0.0	0.0	0.0	0.0
5000 Taxes on goods and services	**188.7**	**288.8**	**446.1**	**509.2**	**544.4**	**12.4**	**12.1**	**12.7**	**12.1**	**12.4**
5100 Taxes on production, sale, transfer, etc	181.6	281.4	429.7	490.4	524.7	11.9	11.8	12.2	11.7	11.9
5110 General taxes	112.4	199.6	326.7	382.7	409.4	7.4	8.4	9.3	9.1	9.3
5111 Value added taxes	112.4	197.5	322.6	378.8	405.0	7.4	8.3	9.2	9.0	9.2
5120 Taxes on specific goods and services	69.2	81.8	103.0	107.7	115.3	4.5	3.4	2.9	2.6	2.6
5121 Excises	55.3	70.3	91.5	91.6	95.5	3.6	3.0	2.6	2.2	2.2
5200 Taxes on use of goods and perform activities	7.1	7.4	16.4	18.8	19.7	0.5	0.3	0.5	0.4	0.4
5300 Unallocable between 5100 and 5200	0.0	0.0	0.0	0.0	0.0	0.0	0.0	0.0	0.0	0.0
6000 Other taxes	**1.3**	**1.5**	**1.4**	**1.4**	**2.2**	**0.1**	**0.1**	**0.0**	**0.0**	**0.0**
Non-wastable tax credits										
Non-wastable tax credits against 1000	..	..	..	..	..	..	..	..	..	..
Transfer component	..	..	..	..	..	..	..	..	..	..
Tax expenditure component	..	..	..	..	..	..	..	..	..	..

.. Not available

Note: More detailed country data and country notes are available in online chapter 5 "Country Tables, 1965-2016": http://dx.doi.org/10.1787/rev_stats-2018-en. Full time series can be accessed at http://oe.cd/full-time-series.

Source: Monthly reports of central Government Revenues (unpublished) National Audit Bureau, Stockholm. Local Government Finance (SOS), Tax assessment statistics (SOS) , National Central Bureau of Statistics, Stockholm.National Accounts (Statistical Reports), National Bureau of Statistics, Stockholm.

StatLink http://dx.doi.org/10.1787/888933860881

Table 4.64. Sweden, tax revenue and % of GDP by level of government and main taxes

	Billion SEK					% of GDP				
	1990	2000	2010	2015	2016	1990	2000	2010	2015	2016
Federal or Central government										
Total tax revenue	**383.9**	**699.1**	**795.2**	**927.3**	**1 014.1**	**25.1**	**29.4**	**22.6**	**22.1**	**23.0**
1000 Taxes on income, profits and capital gains	94.7	139.0	16.9	14.1	29.3	6.2	5.8	0.5	0.3	0.7
2000 Social security contributions	54.8	180.2	201.2	180.7	205.0	3.6	7.6	5.7	4.3	4.7
3000 Taxes on payroll and workforce	18.7	50.1	107.5	194.1	203.4	1.2	2.1	3.1	4.6	4.6
4000 Taxes on property	26.6	39.9	22.4	27.9	29.9	1.7	1.7	0.6	0.7	0.7
5000 Taxes on goods and services	187.8	288.5	445.8	509.1	544.3	12.3	12.1	12.7	12.1	12.4
6000 Other taxes	1.3	1.5	1.4	1.4	2.2	0.1	0.1	0.0	0.0	0.0
State/Regional										
Total tax revenue	..	..	..	..	..	..	..	..	..	..
1000 Taxes on income, profits and capital gains	..	..	..	..	..	..	..	..	..	..
2000 Social security contributions	..	..	..	..	..	..	..	..	..	..
3000 Taxes on payroll and workforce	..	..	..	..	..	..	..	..	..	..
4000 Taxes on property	..	..	..	..	..	..	..	..	..	..
5000 Taxes on goods and services	..	..	..	..	..	..	..	..	..	..
6000 Other taxes	..	..	..	..	..	..	..	..	..	..
Local government										
Total tax revenue	**221.0**	**336.3**	**537.0**	**651.7**	**685.9**	**14.5**	**14.1**	**15.3**	**15.5**	**15.6**
1000 Taxes on income, profits and capital gains	220.1	336.3	522.9	635.7	669.6	14.4	14.1	14.9	15.1	15.2
2000 Social security contributions	0.0	0.0	0.0	0.0	0.0	0.0	0.0	0.0	0.0	0.0
3000 Taxes on payroll and workforce	0.0	0.0	0.0	0.0	0.0	0.0	0.0	0.0	0.0	0.0
4000 Taxes on property	0.0	0.0	14.1	15.9	16.3	0.0	0.0	0.4	0.4	0.4
5000 Taxes on goods and services	0.9	0.0	0.0	0.0	0.0	0.1	0.0	0.0	0.0	0.0
6000 Other taxes	0.0	0.0	0.0	0.0	0.0	0.0	0.0	0.0	0.0	0.0
Social Security Funds										
Total tax revenue	**151.1**	**126.8**	**183.5**	**224.1**	**233.9**	**9.9**	**5.3**	**5.2**	**5.3**	**5.3**
1000 Taxes on income, profits and capital gains	0.0	0.0	0.0	0.0	0.0	0.0	0.0	0.0	0.0	0.0
2000 Social security contributions	151.1	126.8	183.5	224.1	233.9	9.9	5.3	5.2	5.3	5.3
3000 Taxes on payroll and workforce	0.0	0.0	0.0	0.0	0.0	0.0	0.0	0.0	0.0	0.0
4000 Taxes on property	0.0	0.0	0.0	0.0	0.0	0.0	0.0	0.0	0.0	0.0
5000 Taxes on goods and services	0.0	0.0	0.0	0.0	0.0	0.0	0.0	0.0	0.0	0.0
6000 Other taxes	0.0	0.0	0.0	0.0	0.0	0.0	0.0	0.0	0.0	0.0

.. Not available

Note: More detailed country data and country notes are available in online chapter 6 "Tax revenues by sub-sectors of general government": http://dx.doi.org/10.1787/rev_stats-2018-en. Full time series can be accessed at http://oe.cd/full-time-series.

Source: Monthly reports of central Government Revenues (unpublished) National Audit Bureau, Stockholm. Local Government Finance (SOS), Tax assessment statistics (SOS) , National Central Bureau of Statistics, Stockholm.National Accounts (Statistical Reports), National Bureau of Statistics, Stockholm.

StatLink http://dx.doi.org/10.1787/888933860900

Table 4.65. Switzerland, tax revenue and % of GDP by selected tax category

	Billion CHF					% of GDP				
	1990	2000	2010	2015	2016	1990	2000	2010	2015	2016
Total tax revenue	**85.1**	**126.8**	**161.9**	**180.4**	**183.0**	**23.7**	**27.6**	**26.6**	**27.6**	**27.8**
1000 Taxes on income, profits and capital gains	**40.0**	**55.9**	**73.7**	**83.7**	**85.2**	**11.2**	**12.2**	**12.1**	**12.8**	**12.9**
1100 Of individuals	27.7	37.6	51.3	55.9	56.8	7.7	8.2	8.4	8.5	8.6
1200 Corporate	6.3	11.2	16.2	19.3	20.7	1.8	2.4	2.7	3.0	3.1
1300 Unallocable between 1100 and 1200	6.1	7.1	6.2	8.5	7.7	1.7	1.6	1.0	1.3	1.2
2000 Social security contributions	**19.9**	**30.6**	**38.3**	**43.9**	**44.4**	**5.5**	**6.7**	**6.3**	**6.7**	**6.7**
2100 Employees	9.3	14.3	17.5	20.4	20.6	2.6	3.1	2.9	3.1	3.1
2200 Employers	9.3	14.3	17.6	20.4	20.6	2.6	3.1	2.9	3.1	3.1
2300 Self-employed or non-employed	1.3	2.0	3.2	3.2	3.2	0.4	0.4	0.5	0.5	0.5
2400 Unallocable between 2100, 2200 and 2300	0.0	0.0	0.0	0.0	0.0	0.0	0.0	0.0	0.0	0.0
3000 Taxes on payroll and workforce	**0.0**	**0.0**	**0.0**	**0.0**	**0.0**	**0.0**	**0.0**	**0.0**	**0.0**	**0.0**
4000 Taxes on property	**7.6**	**12.2**	**12.3**	**13.0**	**13.3**	**2.1**	**2.7**	**2.0**	**2.0**	**2.0**
4100 Recurrent taxes on immovable property	0.4	0.7	1.0	1.1	1.2	0.1	0.2	0.2	0.2	0.2
4200 Recurrent taxes on net wealth	3.4	5.2	7.0	8.0	8.4	0.9	1.1	1.2	1.2	1.3
4300 Estate, inheritance and gift taxes	0.9	1.2	1.0	1.1	1.1	0.2	0.3	0.2	0.2	0.2
4400 Taxes on financial and capital transactions	2.2	4.3	2.4	1.9	1.5	0.6	0.9	0.4	0.3	0.2
4500 Non-recurrent taxes	0.0	0.0	0.0	0.0	0.0	0.0	0.0	0.0	0.0	0.0
4600 Other recurrent taxes on property	0.6	0.8	0.9	0.9	0.9	0.2	0.2	0.2	0.1	0.1
5000 Taxes on goods and services	**17.5**	**27.8**	**37.1**	**39.0**	**39.2**	**4.9**	**6.1**	**6.1**	**6.0**	**5.9**
5100 Taxes on production, sale, transfer, etc	16.0	25.3	32.2	33.7	33.7	4.5	5.5	5.3	5.1	5.1
5110 General taxes	9.9	16.9	21.0	22.7	22.7	2.8	3.7	3.4	3.5	3.4
5111 Value added taxes	9.9	16.6	20.6	22.3	22.3	2.8	3.6	3.4	3.4	3.4
5120 Taxes on specific goods and services	6.1	8.3	11.1	10.9	10.9	1.7	1.8	1.8	1.7	1.7
5121 Excises	4.6	6.8	8.3	8.0	8.1	1.3	1.5	1.4	1.2	1.2
5200 Taxes on use of goods and perform activities	1.6	2.5	4.9	5.3	5.5	0.4	0.6	0.8	0.8	0.8
5300 Unallocable between 5100 and 5200	0.0	0.0	0.0	0.0	0.0	0.0	0.0	0.0	0.0	0.0
6000 Other taxes	**0.1**	**0.2**	**0.6**	**0.8**	**0.9**	**0.0**	**0.0**	**0.1**	**0.1**	**0.1**
Non-wastable tax credits										
Non-wastable tax credits against 1000	..	..	..	..	..	..	..	..	..	..
Transfer component	..	..	..	..	..	..	..	..	..	..
Tax expenditure component	..	..	..	..	..	..	..	..	..	..

.. Not available

Note: More detailed country data and country notes are available in online chapter 5 "Country Tables, 1965-2016": http://dx.doi.org/10.1787/rev_stats-2018-en. Full time series can be accessed at http://oe.cd/full-time-series.

Source: Financial Statistics, Federal Finance Administration.

StatLink http://dx.doi.org/10.1787/888933860919

Table 4.66. Switzerland, tax revenue and % of GDP by level of government and main taxes

	Billion CHF					% of GDP				
	1990	2000	2010	2015	2016	1990	2000	2010	2015	2016
Federal or Central government										
Total tax revenue	**29.0**	**46.9**	**59.2**	**64.4**	**64.4**	**8.1**	**10.2**	**9.7**	**9.8**	**9.8**
1000 Taxes on income, profits and capital gains	10.9	17.0	22.7	26.8	26.8	3.0	3.7	3.7	4.1	4.1
2000 Social security contributions	0.0	0.0	0.0	0.0	0.0	0.0	0.0	0.0	0.0	0.0
3000 Taxes on payroll and workforce	0.0	0.0	0.0	0.0	0.0	0.0	0.0	0.0	0.0	0.0
4000 Taxes on property	2.1	4.1	2.2	1.7	1.3	0.6	0.9	0.4	0.3	0.2
5000 Taxes on goods and services	16.0	25.7	34.3	36.0	36.2	4.5	5.6	5.6	5.5	5.5
6000 Other taxes	0.0	0.0	0.0	0.0	0.1	0.0	0.0	0.0	0.0	0.0
State/Regional										
Total tax revenue	**21.3**	**28.9**	**39.9**	**44.5**	**45.7**	**6.0**	**6.3**	**6.5**	**6.8**	**6.9**
1000 Taxes on income, profits and capital gains	16.4	21.8	30.9	34.3	35.1	4.6	4.7	5.1	5.3	5.3
2000 Social security contributions	0.0	0.0	0.0	0.0	0.0	0.0	0.0	0.0	0.0	0.0
3000 Taxes on payroll and workforce	0.0	0.0	0.0	0.0	0.0	0.0	0.0	0.0	0.0	0.0
4000 Taxes on property	3.5	5.0	6.3	7.1	7.6	1.0	1.1	1.0	1.1	1.1
5000 Taxes on goods and services	1.4	2.1	2.7	2.9	2.8	0.4	0.4	0.4	0.4	0.4
6000 Other taxes	0.0	0.0	0.0	0.2	0.2	0.0	0.0	0.0	0.0	0.0
Local government										
Total tax revenue	**14.9**	**20.5**	**24.6**	**27.5**	**28.5**	**4.2**	**4.5**	**4.0**	**4.2**	**4.3**
1000 Taxes on income, profits and capital gains	12.7	17.1	20.2	22.6	23.3	3.5	3.7	3.3	3.5	3.5
2000 Social security contributions	0.0	0.0	0.0	0.0	0.0	0.0	0.0	0.0	0.0	0.0
3000 Taxes on payroll and workforce	0.0	0.0	0.0	0.0	0.0	0.0	0.0	0.0	0.0	0.0
4000 Taxes on property	2.0	3.1	3.8	4.2	4.4	0.6	0.7	0.6	0.6	0.7
5000 Taxes on goods and services	0.1	0.1	0.1	0.1	0.1	0.0	0.0	0.0	0.0	0.0
6000 Other taxes	0.1	0.2	0.6	0.6	0.6	0.0	0.0	0.1	0.1	0.1
Social Security Funds										
Total tax revenue	**19.9**	**30.6**	**38.3**	**43.9**	**44.4**	**5.5**	**6.7**	**6.3**	**6.7**	**6.7**
1000 Taxes on income, profits and capital gains	0.0	0.0	0.0	0.0	0.0	0.0	0.0	0.0	0.0	0.0
2000 Social security contributions	19.9	30.6	38.3	43.9	44.4	5.5	6.7	6.3	6.7	6.7
3000 Taxes on payroll and workforce	0.0	0.0	0.0	0.0	0.0	0.0	0.0	0.0	0.0	0.0
4000 Taxes on property	0.0	0.0	0.0	0.0	0.0	0.0	0.0	0.0	0.0	0.0
5000 Taxes on goods and services	0.0	0.0	0.0	0.0	0.0	0.0	0.0	0.0	0.0	0.0
6000 Other taxes	0.0	0.0	0.0	0.0	0.0	0.0	0.0	0.0	0.0	0.0

Note: More detailed country data and country notes are available in online chapter 6 "Tax revenues by sub-sectors of general government": http://dx.doi.org/10.1787/rev_stats-2018-en. Full time series can be accessed at http://oe.cd/full-time-series.

Source: Financial Statistics, Federal Finance Administration.

StatLink http://dx.doi.org/10.1787/888933860938

Table 4.67. Turkey, tax revenue and % of GDP by selected tax category

	Billion TRY					% of GDP				
	1990	2000	2010	2015	2016	1990	2000	2010	2015	2016
Total tax revenue	**0.1**	**40.3**	**287.9**	**586.7**	**660.0**	**14.5**	**23.6**	**24.8**	**25.1**	**25.3**
1000 Taxes on income, profits and capital gains	**0.0**	**11.9**	**61.3**	**119.1**	**139.6**	**4.9**	**7.0**	**5.3**	**5.1**	**5.4**
1100 Of individuals	0.0	9.0	40.4	85.8	96.6	3.9	5.2	3.5	3.7	3.7
1200 Corporate	0.0	2.9	20.9	33.4	43.0	1.0	1.7	1.8	1.4	1.6
1300 Unallocable between 1100 and 1200	0.0	0.0	0.0	0.0	0.0	0.0	0.0	0.0	0.0	0.0
2000 Social security contributions	**0.0**	**7.5**	**71.7**	**170.3**	**190.2**	**2.9**	**4.4**	**6.2**	**7.3**	**7.3**
2100 Employees	0.0	2.7	26.9	64.2	72.8	1.1	1.6	2.3	2.7	2.8
2200 Employers	0.0	3.6	39.4	95.1	107.9	1.6	2.1	3.4	4.1	4.1
2300 Self-employed or non-employed	0.0	1.2	5.4	11.0	9.5	0.2	0.7	0.5	0.5	0.4
2400 Unallocable between 2100, 2200 and 2300	0.0	0.0	0.0	0.0	0.0	0.0	0.0	0.0	0.0	0.0
3000 Taxes on payroll and workforce	**0.0**	**0.0**	**0.0**	**0.0**	**0.0**	**0.0**	**0.0**	**0.0**	**0.0**	**0.0**
4000 Taxes on property	**0.0**	**1.3**	**11.7**	**28.6**	**31.9**	**0.3**	**0.7**	**1.0**	**1.2**	**1.2**
4100 Recurrent taxes on immovable property	0.0	0.2	2.7	5.9	6.7	0.0	0.1	0.2	0.3	0.3
4200 Recurrent taxes on net wealth	0.0	0.0	0.0	0.0	0.0	0.0	0.0	0.0	0.0	0.0
4300 Estate, inheritance and gift taxes	0.0	0.0	0.2	0.4	0.6	0.0	0.0	0.0	0.0	0.0
4400 Taxes on financial and capital transactions	0.0	1.1	8.8	22.3	24.5	0.3	0.6	0.8	1.0	0.9
4500 Non-recurrent taxes	0.0	0.0	0.0	0.0	0.0	0.0	0.0	0.0	0.0	0.0
4600 Other recurrent taxes on property	0.0	0.0	0.0	0.0	0.0	0.0	0.0	0.0	0.0	0.0
5000 Taxes on goods and services	**0.0**	**16.9**	**137.3**	**260.0**	**287.9**	**4.1**	**9.9**	**11.8**	**11.1**	**11.0**
5100 Taxes on production, sale, transfer, etc	0.0	16.3	131.9	250.3	277.6	4.0	9.6	11.4	10.7	10.6
5110 General taxes	0.0	9.7	62.5	121.1	130.8	2.9	5.7	5.4	5.2	5.0
5111 Value added taxes	0.0	9.7	62.5	121.1	130.8	2.7	5.7	5.4	5.2	5.0
5120 Taxes on specific goods and services	0.0	6.6	69.3	129.2	146.8	1.1	3.9	6.0	5.5	5.6
5121 Excises	0.0	4.7	57.3	105.9	120.4	0.1	2.8	4.9	4.5	4.6
5200 Taxes on use of goods and perform activities	0.0	0.6	5.4	9.7	10.4	0.1	0.3	0.5	0.4	0.4
5300 Unallocable between 5100 and 5200	0.0	0.0	0.0	0.0	0.0	0.0	0.0	0.0	0.0	0.0
6000 Other taxes	**0.0**	**2.7**	**5.9**	**8.7**	**10.4**	**2.4**	**1.6**	**0.5**	**0.4**	**0.4**
Non-wastable tax credits										
Non-wastable tax credits against 1000	..	..	..	..	..	..	..	..	..	..
Transfer component	..	..	..	..	..	..	..	..	..	..
Tax expenditure component	..	..	..	..	..	..	..	..	..	..

.. Not available

Note: More detailed country data and country notes are available in online chapter 5 "Country Tables, 1965-2016": http://dx.doi.org/10.1787/rev_stats-2018-en. Full time series can be accessed at http://oe.cd/full-time-series.

Source: Bulletin of national accounts and the Budget revenue Bulletin.

StatLink http://dx.doi.org/10.1787/888933860957

Table 4.68. Turkey, tax revenue and % of GDP by level of government and main taxes

	Billion TRY					% of GDP				
	1990	2000	2010	2015	2016	1990	2000	2010	2015	2016
Federal or Central government										
Total tax revenue	**0.1**	**29.1**	**189.4**	**359.9**	**405.8**	**10.4**	**17.1**	**16.3**	**15.4**	**15.6**
1000 Taxes on income, profits and capital gains	0.0	10.5	54.6	104.7	122.5	4.3	6.2	4.7	4.5	4.7
2000 Social security contributions	0.0	0.0	0.0	0.0	0.0	0.0	0.0	0.0	0.0	0.0
3000 Taxes on payroll and workforce	0.0	0.0	0.0	0.0	0.0	0.0	0.0	0.0	0.0	0.0
4000 Taxes on property	0.0	0.9	8.1	20.2	22.2	0.3	0.5	0.7	0.9	0.9
5000 Taxes on goods and services	0.0	15.2	124.0	231.2	256.2	3.6	8.9	10.7	9.9	9.8
6000 Other taxes	0.0	2.5	2.7	3.8	4.9	2.2	1.5	0.2	0.2	0.2
State/Regional										
Total tax revenue	..	..	..	..	..	..	..	..	..	..
1000 Taxes on income, profits and capital gains	..	..	..	..	..	..	..	..	..	..
2000 Social security contributions	..	..	..	..	..	..	..	..	..	..
3000 Taxes on payroll and workforce	..	..	..	..	..	..	..	..	..	..
4000 Taxes on property	..	..	..	..	..	..	..	..	..	..
5000 Taxes on goods and services	..	..	..	..	..	..	..	..	..	..
6000 Other taxes	..	..	..	..	..	..	..	..	..	..
Local government										
Total tax revenue	**0.0**	**3.6**	**26.8**	**56.5**	**64.0**	**1.3**	**2.1**	**2.3**	**2.4**	**2.5**
1000 Taxes on income, profits and capital gains	0.0	1.4	6.7	14.4	17.0	0.6	0.8	0.6	0.6	0.7
2000 Social security contributions	0.0	0.0	0.0	0.0	0.0	0.0	0.0	0.0	0.0	0.0
3000 Taxes on payroll and workforce	0.0	0.0	0.0	0.0	0.0	0.0	0.0	0.0	0.0	0.0
4000 Taxes on property	0.0	0.3	3.6	8.4	9.7	0.0	0.2	0.3	0.4	0.4
5000 Taxes on goods and services	0.0	1.7	13.3	28.7	31.8	0.5	1.0	1.1	1.2	1.2
6000 Other taxes	0.0	0.2	3.2	5.0	5.5	0.2	0.1	0.3	0.2	0.2
Social Security Funds										
Total tax revenue	**0.0**	**7.5**	**71.7**	**170.3**	**190.2**	**2.9**	**4.4**	**6.2**	**7.3**	**7.3**
1000 Taxes on income, profits and capital gains	0.0	0.0	0.0	0.0	0.0	0.0	0.0	0.0	0.0	0.0
2000 Social security contributions	0.0	7.5	71.7	170.3	190.2	2.9	4.4	6.2	7.3	7.3
3000 Taxes on payroll and workforce	0.0	0.0	0.0	0.0	0.0	0.0	0.0	0.0	0.0	0.0
4000 Taxes on property	0.0	0.0	0.0	0.0	0.0	0.0	0.0	0.0	0.0	0.0
5000 Taxes on goods and services	0.0	0.0	0.0	0.0	0.0	0.0	0.0	0.0	0.0	0.0
6000 Other taxes	0.0	0.0	0.0	0.0	0.0	0.0	0.0	0.0	0.0	0.0

.. Not available

Note: More detailed country data and country notes are available in online chapter 6 "Tax revenues by sub-sectors of general government": http://dx.doi.org/10.1787/rev_stats-2018-en. Full time series can be accessed at http://oe.cd/full-time-series.

Source: Bulletin of national accounts and the Budget revenue Bulletin.

StatLink http://dx.doi.org/10.1787/888933860976

Table 4.69. United Kingdom, tax revenue and % of GDP by selected tax category

	Billion GBP					% of GDP				
	1990	2000	2010	2015	2016	1990	2000	2010	2015	2016
Total tax revenue	**202.4**	**358.7**	**512.9**	**609.6**	**644.7**	**32.9**	**32.9**	**32.3**	**32.2**	**32.7**
1000 Taxes on income, profits and capital gains	**79.6**	**142.2**	**192.6**	**214.8**	**230.1**	**12.9**	**13.1**	**12.1**	**11.3**	**11.7**
1100 Of individuals	59.5	104.1	147.0	168.9	176.6	9.7	9.6	9.3	8.9	9.0
1200 Corporate	20.1	38.1	45.6	46.0	53.4	3.3	3.5	2.9	2.4	2.7
1300 Unallocable between 1100 and 1200	0.0	0.0	0.0	0.0	0.0	0.0	0.0	0.0	0.0	0.0
2000 Social security contributions	**34.5**	**60.3**	**97.3**	**114.1**	**121.9**	**5.6**	**5.5**	**6.1**	**6.0**	**6.2**
2100 Employees	13.3	24.2	38.7	44.5	47.3	2.2	2.2	2.4	2.3	2.4
2200 Employers	20.0	34.0	55.9	66.5	71.4	3.2	3.1	3.5	3.5	3.6
2300 Self-employed or non-employed	1.2	2.0	2.8	3.1	3.2	0.2	0.2	0.2	0.2	0.2
2400 Unallocable between 2100, 2200 and 2300	0.0	0.0	0.0	0.0	0.0	0.0	0.0	0.0	0.0	0.0
3000 Taxes on payroll and workforce	**0.0**	**0.0**	**0.0**	**0.0**	**0.0**	**0.0**	**0.0**	**0.0**	**0.0**	**0.0**
4000 Taxes on property	**16.5**	**41.1**	**61.8**	**76.6**	**81.4**	**2.7**	**3.8**	**3.9**	**4.0**	**4.1**
4100 Recurrent taxes on immovable property	13.5	30.6	50.0	58.2	60.3	2.2	2.8	3.2	3.1	3.1
4200 Recurrent taxes on net wealth	0.0	0.0	0.0	0.0	0.0	0.0	0.0	0.0	0.0	0.0
4300 Estate, inheritance and gift taxes	1.3	2.2	2.6	4.4	4.8	0.2	0.2	0.2	0.2	0.2
4400 Taxes on financial and capital transactions	1.8	8.4	9.1	13.8	16.0	0.3	0.8	0.6	0.7	0.8
4500 Non-recurrent taxes	0.0	0.0	0.0	0.1	0.3	0.0	0.0	0.0	0.0	0.0
4600 Other recurrent taxes on property	0.0	0.0	0.0	0.0	0.0	0.0	0.0	0.0	0.0	0.0
5000 Taxes on goods and services	**62.8**	**113.3**	**158.3**	**201.1**	**208.1**	**10.2**	**10.4**	**10.0**	**10.6**	**10.6**
5100 Taxes on production, sale, transfer, etc	59.4	108.3	150.8	193.6	200.5	9.7	9.9	9.5	10.2	10.2
5110 General taxes	34.1	64.3	95.9	129.4	133.9	5.5	5.9	6.0	6.8	6.8
5111 Value added taxes	34.1	64.3	95.9	129.4	133.9	5.5	5.9	6.0	6.8	6.8
5120 Taxes on specific goods and services	25.3	44.0	54.9	64.2	66.6	4.1	4.0	3.5	3.4	3.4
5121 Excises	19.7	37.3	45.4	47.3	47.9	3.2	3.4	2.9	2.5	2.4
5200 Taxes on use of goods and perform activities	3.4	5.0	7.4	7.4	7.6	0.6	0.5	0.5	0.4	0.4
5300 Unallocable between 5100 and 5200	0.0	0.0	0.0	0.0	0.0	0.0	0.0	0.0	0.0	0.0
6000 Other taxes	**9.0**	**0.0**	**0.0**	**0.0**	**0.0**	**1.5**	**0.0**	**0.0**	**0.0**	**0.0**
Non-wastable tax credits										
Non-wastable tax credits against 1000	7.5	4.7	30.1	30.8	30.1	1.2	0.4	1.9	1.6	1.5
Transfer component	0.5	3.4	23.7	27.4	26.7	0.1	0.3	1.5	1.4	1.4
Tax expenditure component	7.0	1.2	6.5	3.4	3.4	1.1	0.1	0.4	0.2	0.2

Note: More detailed country data and country notes are available in online chapter 5 "Country Tables, 1965-2016": http://dx.doi.org/10.1787/rev_stats-2018-en. Full time series can be accessed at http://oe.cd/full-time-series.

Source: National Income and Expenditure; Central Statistical Office; Annual reports of Her Majesty's Revenue and Customs.

StatLink http://dx.doi.org/10.1787/888933860995

Table 4.70. United Kingdom, tax revenue and % of GDP by level of government and main taxes

	Billion GBP					% of GDP				
	1990	2000	2010	2015	2016	1990	2000	2010	2015	2016
Federal or Central government										
Total tax revenue	**151.9**	**282.1**	**386.4**	**462.5**	**488.1**	**24.7**	**25.9**	**24.3**	**24.4**	**24.8**
1000 Taxes on income, profits and capital gains	79.6	142.2	192.6	214.8	230.1	12.9	13.1	12.1	11.3	11.7
2000 Social security contributions	0.0	0.0	0.0	0.0	0.0	0.0	0.0	0.0	0.0	0.0
3000 Taxes on payroll and workforce	0.0	0.0	0.0	0.0	0.0	0.0	0.0	0.0	0.0	0.0
4000 Taxes on property	11.4	26.9	35.5	46.6	50.0	1.9	2.5	2.2	2.5	2.5
5000 Taxes on goods and services	60.9	112.9	158.3	201.1	208.0	9.9	10.4	10.0	10.6	10.6
6000 Other taxes	0.0	0.0	0.0	0.0	0.0	0.0	0.0	0.0	0.0	0.0
State/Regional										
Total tax revenue	..	..	..	..	..	..	..	..	..	..
1000 Taxes on income, profits and capital gains	..	..	..	..	..	..	..	..	..	..
2000 Social security contributions	..	..	..	..	..	..	..	..	..	..
3000 Taxes on payroll and workforce	..	..	..	..	..	..	..	..	..	..
4000 Taxes on property	..	..	..	..	..	..	..	..	..	..
5000 Taxes on goods and services	..	..	..	..	..	..	..	..	..	..
6000 Other taxes	..	..	..	..	..	..	..	..	..	..
Local government										
Total tax revenue	**14.1**	**14.2**	**26.2**	**29.9**	**31.4**	**2.3**	**1.3**	**1.7**	**1.6**	**1.6**
1000 Taxes on income, profits and capital gains	0.0	0.0	0.0	0.0	0.0	0.0	0.0	0.0	0.0	0.0
2000 Social security contributions	0.0	0.0	0.0	0.0	0.0	0.0	0.0	0.0	0.0	0.0
3000 Taxes on payroll and workforce	0.0	0.0	0.0	0.0	0.0	0.0	0.0	0.0	0.0	0.0
4000 Taxes on property	5.1	14.2	26.2	29.9	31.4	0.8	1.3	1.7	1.6	1.6
5000 Taxes on goods and services	0.0	0.0	0.0	0.0	0.0	0.0	0.0	0.0	0.0	0.0
6000 Other taxes	9.0	0.0	0.0	0.0	0.0	1.5	0.0	0.0	0.0	0.0
Social Security Funds										
Total tax revenue	**34.5**	**60.3**	**97.3**	**114.1**	**121.9**	**5.6**	**5.5**	**6.1**	**6.0**	**6.2**
1000 Taxes on income, profits and capital gains	0.0	0.0	0.0	0.0	0.0	0.0	0.0	0.0	0.0	0.0
2000 Social security contributions	34.5	60.3	97.3	114.1	121.9	5.6	5.5	6.1	6.0	6.2
3000 Taxes on payroll and workforce	0.0	0.0	0.0	0.0	0.0	0.0	0.0	0.0	0.0	0.0
4000 Taxes on property	0.0	0.0	0.0	0.0	0.0	0.0	0.0	0.0	0.0	0.0
5000 Taxes on goods and services	0.0	0.0	0.0	0.0	0.0	0.0	0.0	0.0	0.0	0.0
6000 Other taxes	0.0	0.0	0.0	0.0	0.0	0.0	0.0	0.0	0.0	0.0

.. Not available

Note: More detailed country data and country notes are available in online chapter 6 "Tax revenues by sub-sectors of general government": http://dx.doi.org/10.1787/rev_stats-2018-en. Full time series can be accessed at http://oe.cd/full-time-series.

Source: National Income and Expenditure; Central Statistical Office; Annual reports of Her Majesty's Revenue and Customs.

StatLink http://dx.doi.org/10.1787/888933861014

Table 4.71. United States, tax revenue and % of GDP by selected tax category

	Billion USD					% of GDP				
	1990	2000	2010	2015	2016	1990	2000	2010	2015	2016
Total tax revenue	**1 552.4**	**2 900.5**	**3 515.8**	**4 754.0**	**4 821.5**	**26.0**	**28.2**	**23.5**	**26.2**	**25.9**
1000 Taxes on income, profits and capital gains	**701.7**	**1 453.9**	**1 491.5**	**2 309.5**	**2 313.1**	**11.7**	**14.1**	**10.0**	**12.7**	**12.4**
1100 Of individuals	584.7	1 224.5	1 224.5	1 923.6	1 945.2	9.8	11.9	8.2	10.6	10.4
1200 Corporate	117.0	229.3	267.0	385.8	367.9	2.0	2.2	1.8	2.1	2.0
1300 Unallocable between 1100 and 1200	0.0	0.0	0.0	0.0	0.0	0.0	0.0	0.0	0.0	0.0
2000 Social security contributions	**397.0**	**683.1**	**917.8**	**1 128.7**	**1 159.2**	**6.6**	**6.6**	**6.1**	**6.2**	**6.2**
2100 Employees	173.9	305.6	406.4	503.5	519.6	2.9	3.0	2.7	2.8	2.8
2200 Employers	204.1	343.2	462.1	564.0	576.7	3.4	3.3	3.1	3.1	3.1
2300 Self-employed or non-employed	19.0	34.4	49.3	61.3	62.8	0.3	0.3	0.3	0.3	0.3
2400 Unallocable between 2100, 2200 and 2300	0.0	0.0	0.0	0.0	0.0	0.0	0.0	0.0	0.0	0.0
3000 Taxes on payroll and workforce	**0.0**	**0.0**	**0.0**	**0.0**	**0.0**	**0.0**	**0.0**	**0.0**	**0.0**	**0.0**
4000 Taxes on property	**180.3**	**295.2**	**462.1**	**513.0**	**533.9**	**3.0**	**2.9**	**3.1**	**2.8**	**2.9**
4100 Recurrent taxes on immovable property	161.5	254.7	435.0	479.4	499.8	2.7	2.5	2.9	2.6	2.7
4200 Recurrent taxes on net wealth	0.0	0.0	0.0	0.0	0.0	0.0	0.0	0.0	0.0	0.0
4300 Estate, inheritance and gift taxes	15.8	35.6	19.5	25.4	25.5	0.3	0.3	0.1	0.1	0.1
4400 Taxes on financial and capital transactions	0.0	0.0	0.0	0.0	0.0	0.0	0.0	0.0	0.0	0.0
4500 Non-recurrent taxes	0.0	0.0	0.0	0.0	0.0	0.0	0.0	0.0	0.0	0.0
4600 Other recurrent taxes on property	3.0	4.8	7.5	8.3	8.5	0.1	0.0	0.1	0.0	0.0
5000 Taxes on goods and services	**273.5**	**468.4**	**644.4**	**802.8**	**815.3**	**4.6**	**4.6**	**4.3**	**4.4**	**4.4**
5100 Taxes on production, sale, transfer, etc	235.2	404.1	542.1	682.5	693.1	3.9	3.9	3.6	3.8	3.7
5110 General taxes	125.6	221.4	294.4	364.6	373.5	2.1	2.2	2.0	2.0	2.0
5111 Value added taxes	0.0	0.0	0.0	0.0	0.0	0.0	0.0	0.0	0.0	0.0
5120 Taxes on specific goods and services	109.6	182.7	247.6	317.9	319.7	1.8	1.8	1.7	1.8	1.7
5121 Excises	65.0	108.6	145.3	156.3	157.6	1.1	1.1	1.0	0.9	0.8
5200 Taxes on use of goods and perform activities	38.2	64.3	102.3	120.4	122.2	0.6	0.6	0.7	0.7	0.7
5300 Unallocable between 5100 and 5200	0.0	0.0	0.0	0.0	0.0	0.0	0.0	0.0	0.0	0.0
6000 Other taxes	**0.0**	**0.0**	**0.0**	**0.0**	**0.0**	**0.0**	**0.0**	**0.0**	**0.0**	**0.0**
Non-wastable tax credits										
Non-wastable tax credits against 1000	6.2	36.5	171.9	157.2	165.6	0.1	0.4	1.1	0.9	0.9
Transfer component	4.4	26.9	101.8	113.9	121.1	0.1	0.3	0.7	0.6	0.7
Tax expenditure component	1.8	9.6	70.1	43.4	44.6	0.0	0.1	0.5	0.2	0.2

Note: More detailed country data and country notes are available in online chapter 5 "Country Tables, 1965-2016": http://dx.doi.org/10.1787/rev_stats-2018-en. Full time series can be accessed at http://oe.cd/full-time-series.

Source: Federal estimates are derived from the US Budget, the Final Monthly Treasury Statement and the Annual Report of the US Treasury Department. The State and Local estimates are derived from Government Finances, published by the Bureau of the Census.

StatLink http://dx.doi.org/10.1787/888933861033

Table 4.72. United States, tax revenue and % of GDP by level of government and main taxes

	Billion USD					% of GDP				
	1990	2000	2010	2015	2016	1990	2000	2010	2015	2016
Federal or Central government										
Total tax revenue	**632.2**	**1 316.6**	**1 288.6**	**2 036.7**	**2 028.8**	**10.6**	**12.8**	**8.6**	**11.2**	**10.9**
1000 Taxes on income, profits and capital gains	569.7	1 201.3	1 176.7	1 876.3	1 871.7	9.5	11.7	7.9	10.4	10.1
2000 Social security contributions	0.0	0.0	0.0	0.0	0.0	0.0	0.0	0.0	0.0	0.0
3000 Taxes on payroll and workforce	0.0	0.0	0.0	0.0	0.0	0.0	0.0	0.0	0.0	0.0
4000 Taxes on property	11.6	28.1	15.1	20.2	20.0	0.2	0.3	0.1	0.1	0.1
5000 Taxes on goods and services	50.9	87.3	96.8	140.2	137.0	0.9	0.8	0.6	0.8	0.7
6000 Other taxes	0.0	0.0	0.0	0.0	0.0	0.0	0.0	0.0	0.0	0.0
State/Regional										
Total tax revenue	**309.7**	**547.6**	**724.1**	**919.4**	**934.8**	**5.2**	**5.3**	**4.8**	**5.1**	**5.0**
1000 Taxes on income, profits and capital gains	120.2	231.0	282.0	392.7	399.1	2.0	2.2	1.9	2.2	2.1
2000 Social security contributions	0.0	0.0	0.0	0.0	0.0	0.0	0.0	0.0	0.0	0.0
3000 Taxes on payroll and workforce	0.0	0.0	0.0	0.0	0.0	0.0	0.0	0.0	0.0	0.0
4000 Taxes on property	10.1	17.6	18.1	20.0	20.5	0.2	0.2	0.1	0.1	0.1
5000 Taxes on goods and services	179.4	299.0	424.0	506.6	515.2	3.0	2.9	2.8	2.8	2.8
6000 Other taxes	0.0	0.0	0.0	0.0	0.0	0.0	0.0	0.0	0.0	0.0
Local government										
Total tax revenue	**213.6**	**353.2**	**585.3**	**669.3**	**698.7**	**3.6**	**3.4**	**3.9**	**3.7**	**3.8**
1000 Taxes on income, profits and capital gains	11.9	21.6	32.8	40.5	42.3	0.2	0.2	0.2	0.2	0.2
2000 Social security contributions	0.0	0.0	0.0	0.0	0.0	0.0	0.0	0.0	0.0	0.0
3000 Taxes on payroll and workforce	0.0	0.0	0.0	0.0	0.0	0.0	0.0	0.0	0.0	0.0
4000 Taxes on property	158.6	249.4	428.9	472.8	493.3	2.7	2.4	2.9	2.6	2.6
5000 Taxes on goods and services	43.1	82.1	123.6	156.0	163.1	0.7	0.8	0.8	0.9	0.9
6000 Other taxes	0.0	0.0	0.0	0.0	0.0	0.0	0.0	0.0	0.0	0.0
Social Security Funds										
Total tax revenue	**397.0**	**683.1**	**917.8**	**1 128.7**	**1 159.2**	**6.6**	**6.6**	**6.1**	**6.2**	**6.2**
1000 Taxes on income, profits and capital gains	0.0	0.0	0.0	0.0	0.0	0.0	0.0	0.0	0.0	0.0
2000 Social security contributions	397.0	683.1	917.8	1 128.7	1 159.2	6.6	6.6	6.1	6.2	6.2
3000 Taxes on payroll and workforce	0.0	0.0	0.0	0.0	0.0	0.0	0.0	0.0	0.0	0.0
4000 Taxes on property	0.0	0.0	0.0	0.0	0.0	0.0	0.0	0.0	0.0	0.0
5000 Taxes on goods and services	0.0	0.0	0.0	0.0	0.0	0.0	0.0	0.0	0.0	0.0
6000 Other taxes	0.0	0.0	0.0	0.0	0.0	0.0	0.0	0.0	0.0	0.0

Note: More detailed country data and country notes are available in online chapter 6 "Tax revenues by sub-sectors of general government": http://dx.doi.org/10.1787/rev_stats-2018-en. Full time series can be accessed at http://oe.cd/full-time-series.

Source: Federal estimates are derived from the US Budget, the Final Monthly Treasury Statement and the Annual Report of the US Treasury Department. The State and Local estimates are derived from Government Finances, published by the Bureau of the Census.

StatLink http://dx.doi.org/10.1787/888933861052

4.2. Memorandum tables

Table 4.73 shows different sources for financing social benefits, beyond compulsory social security contributions reported in section 4.1. In addition, this table shows also data on other taxes, on voluntary contributions to government and on compulsory contributions to private sector.

Table 4.74 shows social security contributions and payroll taxes paid by government. During the revision of the Interpretative Guide in 1984, the question arose of how to treat taxes paid by government. The two most prominent examples of such taxes are social security contributions and payroll taxes paid by government in respect of its employees. After a long discussion it was decided that the data shown in this publication should continue to include taxes paid by government (see §5 of the Interpretative Guide in annex A).

Whilst it was recognised that for certain purposes (e.g. to show the cash flow to the government sector from the private sector) it would be appropriate to eliminate taxes paid by one sector of government to another or tax payments between different units of the same sector of government, the view was taken that to record tax flows in the context of the economy as a whole required that taxes paid by government should be included in the data. This treatment ensures that the different resource flows of an economy, including the calculation of the output of government, are measured consistently in after-tax units. Nevertheless, it was decided that data on identifiable taxes paid by government should be separately identified in a memorandum item and this is the purpose of the country tables which follow.

The data that are reproduced in the following tables refer to actual compulsory payments made by general government in respect of their employees. Fictive, voluntary and imputed contributions are excluded from these data. The definitions of social security contributions, payroll taxes and general government are those set out in §35 to §41, §42 and §3 to §4 of the Interpretative Guide. Information on the other taxes paid by government (namely property taxes and consumption taxes) is not available in most countries, although it is believed that in all countries taxes based upon payroll are the most important taxes paid by government. In many cases, the data are estimates and are not always constructed on a basis consistent with that used in the main tables.

Table 4.73. Financing of social security benefits

National currency

	Currency	Total					2016				
		1990	2000	2010	2015	2016	Social security contributions	Other taxes	Voluntary contributions to government	Compulsory contributions to private sector	**Total**
Australia	Million AUD	0.0	0.0	0.0	0.0	0.0	..	..	..	..	**0.0**
Austria	Million EUR	17.9	30.7	41.8	50.2	52.0	51.7	0.0	0.3	0.0	**52.0**
Belgium	Million EUR	24.1	40.1	67.3	71.0	71.0	57.9	13.0	0.1	0.0	**71.0**
Canada	Million CAD	29.7	53.1	76.8	96.4	98.9	98.9	0.0	0.0	0.0	**98.9**
Chile	Million CLP	487.7	2 598.4	6 902.7	11 166.9	12 090.2	2 441.4	0.0	0.0	9 648.8	**12 090.2**
Czech Republic	Million CZK	..	345.5	582.8	666.9	707.1	699.6	0.0	0.4	7.1	**707.1**
Denmark	Million DKK	9.5	26.5	22.9	19.1	19.0	1.2	0.0	14.8	3.0	**19.0**
Estonia	Million EUR	..	0.7	1.9	2.7	2.8	2.4	0.0	0.0	0.4	**2.8**
Finland	Million EUR	11.1	16.9	23.5	27.6	28.6	27.6	0.0	0.3	0.6	**28.6**
France	Million EUR	194.1	312.9	461.2	540.6	546.8	375.2	171.6	0.0	0.0	**546.8**
Germany	Million EUR	184.9	328.9	369.8	444.1	464.7	444.9	0.0	8.8	11.0	**464.7**
Greece	Million EUR	3.5	14.3	24.7	18.8	19.3	19.3	0.0	0.0	0.0	**19.3**
Hungary	Million HUF	..	1 759.3	3 539.6	4 588.7	4 932.2	4 613.9	317.1	1.2	0.0	**4 932.2**
Iceland	Million ISK	37.6	95.3	236.5	317.5	471.8	85.4	108.6	0.0	277.9	**471.8**
Ireland	Million EUR	1.7	3.9	8.4	10.2	10.7	10.7	0.0	0.0	0.0	**10.7**
Israel	Million ILS	..	27.6	54.4	94.8	102.5	63.5	0.0	0.0	39.0	**102.5**
Italy	Million EUR	87.3	144.1	209.7	215.1	216.7	215.9	0.0	0.8	0.0	**216.7**
Japan	Billion JPY	34.6	48.0	54.5	64.5	66.6	66.6	0.0	0.0	0.0	**66.6**
Korea	Billion KRW	3.8	22.8	69.1	104.7	112.7	112.7	0.0	0.0	0.0	**112.7**
Latvia	Million EUR	..	0.7	1.6	2.1	2.2	2.1	0.1	0.0	0.0	**2.2**
Lithuania	Million EUR	..	1.4	3.4	4.5	4.9	4.7	0.0	0.0	0.2	**4.9**
Luxembourg	Million EUR	1.0	2.2	4.4	5.6	5.8	5.8	0.0	0.0	0.0	**5.8**
Mexico	Million MXN	21.0	205.6	423.6	616.1	659.8	435.0	0.0	0.0	224.8	**659.8**
Netherlands	Million EUR	45.0	101.6	..	..	..	103.9	0.0	0.0	..	**..**
New Zealand	Million NZD	0.0	0.0	0.0	0.0	0.0	..	..	..	..	**0.0**
Norway	Million NOK	79.7	132.2	243.0	325.6	330.9	330.9	0.0	0.0	0.0	**330.9**
Poland	Million PLN	..	96.4	156.0	223.5	236.3	236.3	0.0	0.0	0.0	**236.3**
Portugal	Million EUR	4.1	10.6	16.2	17.2	17.7	16.9	0.8	0.0	0.0	**17.7**
Slovak Republic	Million EUR	..	4.4	8.9	11.3	11.9	11.4	0.0	0.0	0.4	**11.9**
Slovenia	Million EUR	..	2.6	5.4	5.6	5.8	5.8	0.0	0.0	0.0	**5.8**
Spain	Million EUR	36.7	76.0	129.7	124.6	128.7	127.5	0.0	1.1	0.0	**128.7**
Sweden	Million SEK	205.9	315.1	399.6	421.5	456.9	438.9	0.0	18.0	0.0	**456.9**
Switzerland	Million CHF	41.9	64.8	90.5	104.9	106.9	44.5	7.6	0.0	54.8	**106.9**
Turkey	Million TRY	0.0	7.5	71.7	170.3	190.2	190.2	0.0	0.0	0.0	**190.2**
United Kingdom	Million GBP	45.7	76.7	128.2	144.6	149.9	121.9	0.0	25.9	2.1	**149.9**
United States	Million USD	408.7	705.7	979.6	1 203.6	1 241.4	1 159.2	0.0	82.2	0.0	**1 241.4**

.. Not available

StatLink http://dx.doi.org/10.1787/888933861071

Table 4.74. Social security contributions and payroll taxes paid by government

National currency

		Total					2016				
	Currency	1990	2000	2010	2015	2016	Federal or Central government	State/Regional	Local government	Social security Funds	**Total**
Australia[1]	Million AUD	0.1	0.3	0.6	0.8	0.8	0.0	0.0	0.0	0.0	**0.8**
Austria	Million EUR	1.3	2.9	5.6	6.6	6.9	2.6	2.0	2.0	0.3	**6.9**
Belgium	Million EUR	1.8	3.1	5.3	7.4	7.5	0.7	2.4	4.0	0.4	**7.5**
Canada	Million CAD	..	6.4	10.2	12.4	12.5	1.5	6.8	4.2	0.0	**12.5**
Chile	Million CLP	..	54.6	190.0	269.3	299.0	221.4	..	76.8	0.7	**299.0**
Czech Republic	Million CZK	..	34.2	55.8	80.5	85.1	39.8	..	44.3	1.0	**85.1**
Denmark	Million DKK	0.0	0.0	0.0	0.0	0.0	..	..	..	..	**0.0**
Estonia	Million EUR	..	0.2	0.5	0.7	0.8	0.5	..	0.3	0.0	**0.8**
Finland	Million EUR	1.9	3.8	5.6	6.2	6.1	1.1	..	4.9	0.1	**6.1**
France	Million EUR	23.4	36.3	53.7	60.1	60.8	15.0	..	22.7	23.0	**60.8**
Germany	Million EUR	13.6	16.5	20.8	23.7	24.8	2.2	7.9	11.7	3.0	**24.8**
Greece	Million EUR	0.1	1.7	3.6	2.6	2.7	2.3	..	0.0	0.3	**2.7**
Hungary	Million HUF	..	367.0	544.9	697.4	739.5	572.0	..	164.6	2.9	**739.5**
Iceland	Million ISK	..	..	..	..	..	..	..	..	..	**..**
Ireland	Million EUR	0.1	0.4	1.2	1.4	1.5	0.5	..	1.0	0.0	**1.5**
Israel	Million ILS	..	4.1	6.7	9.3	9.9	7.9	..	2.0	0.0	**9.9**
Italy	Million EUR	..	36.7	50.6	49.3	49.9	0.0	..	0.0	49.9	**49.9**
Japan	Billion JPY	2.0	2.9	3.0	3.4	3.5	0.9	..	2.6	0.0	**3.5**
Korea	Billion KRW	..	..	..	..	..	..	..	..	..	**..**
Latvia	Million EUR	..	0.0	0.2	0.3	0.2	..	..	..	..	**0.2**
Lithuania	Million EUR	..	0.4	0.7	0.8	0.9	0.5	..	0.4	0.0	**0.9**
Luxembourg	Million EUR	0.3	0.3	0.5	0.6	0.7	0.6	..	0.0	0.0	**0.7**
Mexico	Million MXN	3.0	44.9	103.4	145.3	150.4	150.4	0.0	0.0	0.0	**150.4**
Netherlands	Million EUR	0.3	2.0	0.0	0.0	0.0	..	..	..	..	**0.0**
New Zealand	Million NZD	0.0	0.0	0.0	0.0	0.0	..	..	..	..	**0.0**
Norway	Million NOK	17.9	36.7	77.6	112.4	113.0	51.8	..	61.2	0.0	**113.0**
Poland	Million PLN	..	11.6	18.6	24.7	25.3	10.2	..	14.6	0.5	**25.3**
Portugal	Million EUR	0.0	0.2	0.0	0.0	0.0	..	..	..	..	**0.0**
Slovak Republic	Million EUR	..	0.6	1.3	1.7	1.8	1.1	..	0.7	0.0	**1.8**
Slovenia	Million EUR	..	0.3	0.6	0.6	0.6	0.4	..	0.2	0.0	**0.6**
Spain	Million EUR	4.0	9.6	18.5	18.8	19.2	2.2	11.8	4.6	0.5	**19.2**
Sweden	Million SEK	69.3	101.6	136.7	164.3	177.6	40.4	..	137.2	0.0	**177.6**
Switzerland	Million CHF	1.5	1.9	2.8	3.2	3.3	0.5	1.8	0.9	0.0	**3.3**
Turkey	Million TRY	0.0	3.6	39.4	95.1	107.9	107.9	..	0.0	0.0	**107.9**
United Kingdom	Million GBP	4.1	6.0	11.7	12.4	13.2	8.4	..	4.8	0.0	**13.2**
United States	Million USD	28.9	44.1	71.6	75.2	76.8	26.8	50.3	0.0	0.0	**76.8**

.. Not available

1. For Australia, the total differs from the sum of the four levels of government. The difference is due to a multi-jurisdictional (University) sector specific to this country. This sector contains units where jurisdiction is shared between two or more governments, or where classification of a unit to a jurisdiction is otherwise unclear. The main type of units currently falling into this category is public universities.

StatLink http://dx.doi.org/10.1787/888933861090

Annex A.
The OECD Classification of Taxes and Interpretative Guide

Table of Contents

A.1 The OECD Classification of Taxes

1. 1000 Taxes on income, profits and capital gains
    - 1100 Taxes on income, profits and capital gains of individuals
        - 1110 On income and profits
        - 1120 On capital gains
    - 1200 Corporate taxes on income, profits and capital gains
        - 1210 On income and profits
        - 1220 On capital gains
    - 1300 Unallocable as between 1100 and 1200
2. 2000 Social security contributions
    - 2100 Employees
    - 2110 On a payroll basis
    - 2120 On an income tax basis
    - 2200 Employers
        - 2210 On a payroll basis
        - 2220 On an income tax basis
    - 2300 Self-employed or non-employed
        - 2310 On a payroll basis
        - 2320 On an income tax basis
    - 2400 Unallocable as between 2100, 2200 and 2300
        - 2410 On a payroll basis
        - 2420 On an income tax basis
3. 3000 Taxes on payroll and workforce
4. 4000 Taxes on property
    - 4100 Recurrent taxes on immovable property
        - 4110 Households
        - 4120 Other
    - 4200 Recurrent taxes on net wealth
        - 4210 Individual
        - 4220 Corporate
    - 4300 Estate, inheritance and gift taxes
        - 4310 Estate and inheritance taxes
        - 4320 Gift taxes
    - 4400 Taxes on financial and capital transactions

4500 Other non-recurrent taxes on property

4510 On net wealth

4520 Other non-recurrent taxes

4600 Other recurrent taxes on property

5. 5000 Taxes on goods and services

5100 Taxes on production, sale, transfer, leasing and delivery of goods and rendering of services

5110 General taxes

5111 Value added taxes

5112 Sales taxes

5113 Turnover and other general taxes on goods and services

5120 Taxes on specific goods and services

5121 Excises

5122 Profits of fiscal monopolies

5123 Customs and import duties

5124 Taxes on exports

5125 Taxes on investment goods

5126 Taxes on specific services

5127 Other taxes on international trade and transactions

5128 Other taxes on specific goods and services

5130 Unallocable as between 5110 and 5120

5200 Taxes on use of goods, or on permission to use goods or perform activities

5210 Recurrent taxes

5211Paid by households in respect of motor vehicles

5212 Paid by others in respect of motor vehicles

5213 Other recurrent taxes

5220 Non-recurrent taxes

5300 Unallocable as between 5100 and 5200

6. 6000 Other taxes

6100 Paid solely by business

6200 Paid by other than business or unidentifiable

A.2 Coverage

General criteria

1. In the OECD classification the term "taxes" is confined to compulsory unrequited payments to general government. Taxes are unrequited in the sense that benefits provided by government to taxpayers are not normally in proportion to their payments.

2. The term "tax" does not include fines, penalties and compulsory loans paid to government. Borderline cases between tax and non-tax revenues in relation to certain fees and charges are discussed in §11–14.

3. General government consists of the central administration, agencies whose operations are under its effective control, state and local governments and their administrations, certain social security schemes and autonomous governmental entities, excluding public enterprises. This definition of government follows that of the 2008 *System of National Accounts* (SNA).[1] In that publication, the general government sector and its sub-sectors are defined in Chapter 4, paragraphs 4.117 to 4.165.

4. Extra-budgetary units are part of the general government system. These are general government entities with individual budgets that are not fully covered by the main or general budget. These entities operate under the authority or control of a central, state, or local government. Extra-budgetary entities may have their own revenue sources, which may be supplemented by grants (transfers) from the general budget or from other sources. Even though their budgets may be subject to approval by the legislature, similar to that of budgetary accounts, they have discretion over the volume and composition of their spending. Such entities may be established to carry out specific government functions, such as road construction, or the nonmarket production of health or education services. Budgetary arrangements vary widely across countries, and various terms are used to describe these entities, but they are often referred to as "extra-budgetary funds" or "decentralised agencies."

5. Compulsory payments to supra-national bodies and their agencies are no longer included as taxes as from 1998, with some exceptions. However, custom duties collected by EU member states on behalf of the European Union are still identified as memorandum items and included in overall tax revenue amounts in the country tables (Chapter 4) of the country in which they are collected. (See §99). In countries where the church forms part of general government church taxes are included, provided they meet the criteria set out in §1 above. As the data refer to receipts of general government, levies paid to non-government bodies, welfare agencies or social insurance schemes outside general government, trade unions or trade associations, even where such levies are compulsory, are excluded. Compulsory payments to general government earmarked for such bodies are, however, included, provided that the government is not simply acting in an agency capacity.[2] Profits from fiscal monopolies are distinguished from those of other public enterprises and are treated as taxes because they reflect the exercise of the taxing power of the state by the use of monopoly powers (see §65–67), as are profits received by the government from the purchase and sale of foreign exchange at different rates (see §74).

6. Taxes paid by governments (e.g., social security contributions and payroll taxes paid by governments in their capacity as an employer, consumption taxes on their purchases or taxes on their property) are not excluded from the data provided. However,

where it is possible to identify the amounts of revenue involved,[3] they are shown in Chapter 4.2 of this Report.

7. The relationship between this classification and that of the System of National Accounts (SNA) is set out in Sections A.9 and A.11 below. Because of the differences between the two classifications, the data shown in national accounts are sometimes calculated or classified differently from the practice set out in this guide. These and other differences are mentioned where appropriate (e.g., in §30 below) but it is not possible to refer to all of them. There may also be some differences between this classification and that employed domestically by certain national administrations (e.g., see §12 below), so that OECD and national statistics data may not always be consistent: any such differences, however, are likely to be very slight in terms of amounts of revenues involved.

Social security contributions

8. Compulsory social security contributions, as defined in §39, and paid to general government, are treated here as tax revenues. Being compulsory payments to general government they clearly resemble taxes. They may, however, differ from other taxes in that the receipt of social security benefits depends, in most countries, upon appropriate contributions having been made, although the size of the benefits is not necessarily related to the amount of the contributions. Better comparability between countries is obtained by treating social security contributions as taxes, but they are listed under a separate heading so that they can be distinguished in any analysis.

9. The strict dividing line between tax revenues (compulsory unrequited payments to general government) and non-tax compulsory payments (NTCPs) (payments that are either requited or made to other institutions) is clearly defined. However, within the range of different compulsory payments to governments existing across countries, it is not always straightforward in practice to decide whether specific payments are either taxes or NTCPs. For example, compulsory pension savings that are controlled by general government and that accumulate on an individual account earning a market return or a rate that compensates for inflation would at first sight be categorised as NTCPs as opposed to taxes. However, even these payments might still be 'unrequited' and therefore classify as taxes instead of NTCPs (for example if these pension savings are not paid out when the taxpayer dies before reaching the pension age and the funds are then used to provide a minimum pension to all taxpayers that are insured). These issues result in the social security revenue figures reported for most countries being based on the premise that all types of compulsory payments to general government are judged to some extent to have a re-distributional element. It should be noted that this conclusion is based on a typically broad interpretation of the term 'unrequited' in the tax definition.

10. Social security contributions which are either voluntary or not payable to general government (see §1) are not treated as taxes, though in some countries, as indicated in the country footnotes, there are difficulties in completely eliminating voluntary contributions and certain compulsory payments to the private sector from the revenue figures. Imputed social security contributions are also not treated as taxes.

Fees, user charges and licence fees

11. Apart from vehicle licence fees, which are universally regarded as taxes, it is not easy to distinguish between those fees and user charges which are to be treated as taxes and those which are not, since, whilst a fee or charge is levied in connection with a

specific service or activity, the strength of the link between the fee and the service provided may vary considerably, as may the relation between the amount of the fee and the cost of providing the service. Where the recipient of a service pays a fee clearly related to the cost of providing the service, the levy may be regarded as requited and under the definition of §1 would not be considered as a tax. In the following cases, however, a levy could be considered as 'unrequited':

a) where the charge greatly exceeds the cost of providing the service;

b) where the payer of the levy is not the receiver of the benefit (e.g., a fee collected from slaughterhouses to finance a service which is provided to farmers);

c) where government is not providing a specific service in return for the levy which it receives even though a licence may be issued to the payer (e.g., where the government grants a hunting, fishing or shooting licence which is not accompanied by the right to use a specific area of government land);

d) where benefits are received only by those paying the levy but the benefits received by each individual are not necessarily in proportion to his payments (e.g., a milk marketing levy paid by dairy farmers and used to promote the consumption of milk).

12. In marginal cases, however, the application of the criteria set out in §1 can be particularly difficult. The solution adopted — given the desirability of international uniformity and the relatively small amounts of revenue usually involved — is to follow the predominant practice among tax administrations rather than to allow each country to adopt its own view as to whether such levies are regarded as taxes or as non-tax revenue.[4]

13. A list of the main fees and charges in question and their normal[5] treatment in this publication is as follows:

Non-tax revenues:	court fees; driving licence fees; harbour fees; passport fees; radio and television licence fees where public authorities provide the service.
Taxes within heading 5200:	permission to perform such activities as distributing films; hunting, fishing and shooting; providing entertainment or gambling facilities; selling alcohol or tobacco; permission to own dogs or to use or own motor vehicles or guns; severance taxes.

14. In practice it may not always be possible to isolate tax receipts from non-tax revenue receipts when they are recorded together. If it is estimated that the bulk of the receipts derive from non-tax revenues, the whole amount involved is treated as a non-tax revenue; otherwise, such government receipts are included and classified according to the rules provided in §32 below.

Royalties

15. The ownership of subsoil assets in the form of deposits of minerals or fossil fuels (coal, oil, or natural gas) depends upon the way in which property rights are defined by law and also on international agreements in the case of deposits below international waters. In some cases, either the ground below which the mineral deposits are located, the deposits themselves or both may belong to a local or central government unit.

16. In such cases, these general government units may grant leases to other institutional units that permit them to extract these deposits over a specified period of time in return for a payment or series of payments. These payments are often described as 'royalties' but they are essentially rent that accrues to owners of natural resources in

return for putting these assets at the disposal of other units for specified periods of time. The rent may take the form of periodic payments of fixed amounts, irrespective of the rate of extraction, or, more commonly, they may be a function of the quantity, volume, or value of the asset extracted. Enterprises engaged in exploration on government land may make payments to general government units in exchange for the right to undertake test drilling or otherwise investigate the existence and location of subsoil assets. Such payments are also recorded as rents even though no extraction may take place. These payments are therefore classified as non-tax revenues.

17. The same principles apply when other institutional units are granted leases that permit them to fell timber in natural forests on land owned by general government units. These payments are also classified as non-tax revenues.

18. These rents or royalties paid to general government should not be confused with taxes on income and profits, severance taxes, business licenses, or other taxes. If the payments are levied on the profits from the extraction activity, then they should be classified as taxes on incomes, profits and gains (1000). In addition, any severance payments that are imposed on the extraction of minerals and fossil fuels from reserves owned privately or by another government should be classified as taxes. Payments related to the gross value of production should be classified as other taxes on goods and services (5128). Payments for a license or permit to conduct extraction operations should be classified as taxes on use of goods and on permission to use goods or perform activities (5213).

Fines and penalties

19. In principle, fines and penalties charged on overdue taxes or penalties imposed for the attempted evasion of taxes should not be recorded as tax revenues. However it may not be possible to separate payments of fines or other penalties from the revenues from the taxes to which they relate. In this case the fines and penalties relating to a particular tax are recorded together with the revenues from that tax and fines and penalties paid with revenue from unidentifiable taxes are classified as other taxes in Category 6000. Fines not relating to tax offences (e.g., for parking offences), or not identifiable as relating to tax offences, are also not treated as tax revenues.

A.3 Basis of reporting

Accrual reporting

20. The data reported in this publication for recent years are predominantly recorded on an accrual basis, i.e. recorded at the time that the tax liability was created. Further information is provided in the footnotes to the country table in Chapter 4 of the Report.

21. However, data for earlier years are still predominantly recorded on a cash basis, i.e. at the time at which the payment was received by government. Thus, for example, taxes withheld by employers in one year but paid to the government in the following year and taxes due in one year but actually paid in the following year are both included in the receipts of the second year. Corrective transactions, such as refunds, repayments and drawbacks, are deducted from gross revenues of the period in which they are made.

22. Data on tax revenues are recorded without offsets for the administrative expenses connected with tax collection. Similarly, where the proceeds of tax are used to subsidise particular members of the community, the subsidy is not deducted from the yield of the

tax, though the tax may be shown net of subsidies in the national records of some countries.

23. As regards fiscal monopolies (heading 5122), only the amount actually transferred to the government is included in government revenues. However, if any expenditures of fiscal monopolies are considered to be government expenditures (e.g., social expenditures undertaken by fiscal monopolies at the direction of the government) they are added back for the purpose of arriving at tax revenue figures (see §65 below).

The distinction between tax and expenditure provisions[6]

24. Because this publication is concerned only with the revenue side of government operations, no account being taken of the expenditure side, a distinction has to be made between tax and expenditure provisions. Normally there is no difficulty in making this distinction as expenditures are made outside the tax system and the tax accounts and under legislation separate from the tax legislation. In borderline cases, cash flow is used to distinguish between tax provisions and expenditure provisions. Insofar as a provision affects the flow of tax payments from the taxpayer to the government, it is regarded as a tax provision and is taken into account in the data shown in this publication. A provision which does not affect this flow is seen as an expenditure provision and is disregarded in the data recorded in this publication.

25. Tax allowances, exemptions and deductions against the tax base clearly affect the amount of tax paid to the government and are therefore considered as tax provisions. At the other extreme, those subsidies which cannot be offset against tax liability and which are clearly not connected with the assessment process, do not reduce tax revenues as recorded in this publication. Tax credits are amounts deductible from tax payable (as distinct from deductions from the tax base). Two types of tax credits are distinguished, those (referred to here as wastable tax credits) which are limited to the amount of the tax liability and therefore cannot give rise to a payment by the authorities to the taxpayer, and those (referred to as non-wastable tax credits) which are not so limited, so that the excess of the credit over the tax liability can be paid to the taxpayer.[7] A wastable tax credit, like a tax allowance, clearly affects the amount of tax paid to the government, and is therefore considered as a tax provision. The practice followed for non-wastable tax credits[8] is to distinguish between the 'tax expenditure component',[9] which is that portion of the credit that is used to reduce or eliminate a taxpayer's liability, and the 'transfer component', which is the portion that exceeds the taxpayer's liability and is paid to that taxpayer. Reported tax revenues should be reduced by the amount of the tax expenditure component but not by the amount of the transfer component. In addition, the amounts of the tax expenditure and transfer components should be reported as memorandum items in the country tables. Countries that are unable to distinguish between the tax expenditure and transfer components should indicate whether or not the tax revenues have been reduced by the total of these components, and provide any available estimates of the amounts of the two components. Further information is given in Chapter 1 of the Report, which illustrates the effect of alternative treatments of non-wastable tax credits on tax to GDP.

Calendar and fiscal years

26. National authorities whose fiscal years do not correspond to the calendar year show data, where possible, on a calendar year basis to permit maximum comparability with the data of other countries. There remain a few countries where data refer to fiscal

years. For these the GDP data used in the comparative tables also correspond to the fiscal years.

A.4 General classification criteria

The main classification criteria

27. The classification of receipts among the main headings (1000, 2000, 3000, 4000, 5000 and 6000) is generally governed by the base on which the tax is levied: 1000 income, profits and capital gains; 2000 and 3000 earnings, payroll or number of employees; 4000 property; 5000 goods and services; 6000 multiple bases, other bases or unidentifiable bases. Where a tax is calculated on more than one base, the receipts are, where possible, split among the various headings (see §32 and §81). The headings 4000 and 5000 cover not only taxes where the tax base is the property, goods or services themselves but also certain related taxes. Thus, taxes on the transfer of property are included in 4400[10] and taxes on the use of goods or on permission to perform activities in 5200. In headings 4000 and 5000 a distinction is made in certain sub-headings between recurrent and non-recurrent taxes: recurrent taxes are defined as those levied at regular intervals (usually annually) and non-recurrent taxes are levied once and for all (see also §47 to §50, §53, §54 and §79 for particular applications of this distinction).

28. Earmarking of a tax for specific purposes does not affect the classification of tax receipts. However, as explained in §39 on the classification of social security contributions, the conferment of an entitlement to social benefits is crucial to the definition of the 2000 main heading.

29. The way that a tax is levied or collected (e.g., by use of stamps) does not affect classification.

Classification of taxpayers

30. In certain sub-headings distinctions are made between different categories of taxpayers. These distinctions vary from tax to tax:

a) Between individuals and corporations in relation to income and net wealth taxes

The basic distinction is that corporation income taxes, as distinct from individual income taxes, are levied on the corporation as an entity, not on the individuals who own it, and without regard to the personal circumstances of these individuals. The same distinction applies to net wealth taxes on corporations and those on individuals. Taxes paid on the profits of partnerships and the income of institutions, such as life insurance or pension funds, are classified according to the same rule. They are classified as corporate taxes (1200) if they are charged on the partnership or institution as an entity without regard to the personal circumstances of the owners. Otherwise, they are treated as individual taxes (1100). Usually, there is different legislation for the corporation taxes and for the individual taxes.[11] The distinction made here between individuals and corporations does not follow the sector classification between households, enterprises, and so on of the System of National Accounts for income and outlay accounts. The SNA classification requires certain unincorporated businesses[12] to be excluded from the household sector and included with non-financial enterprises and financial institutions. The tax on the profits of these businesses, however, cannot always be separated from the tax on the other income of their owners, or can be separated only on an arbitrary basis. No attempt at this separation is made here and the whole of the individual income tax is shown together without regard to the nature of the income chargeable.

b) Between households and others in relation to taxes on immovable property

Here the distinction is that adopted by the SNA for the production and consumption expenditure accounts. The distinction is between households as consumers (i.e. excluding non-incorporated business) on the one hand and producers on the other hand. However, taxes on dwellings occupied by households, whether paid by owner-occupiers, tenants or landlords, are classified under households. This follows the common distinction made between taxes on domestic property versus taxes on business property. Some countries are not, however, in a position to make this distinction.

c) Between households and others in relation to motor vehicle licences

Here the distinction is between households as consumers on the one hand and producers on the other, as in the production and consumption expenditure accounts of the SNA.

d) Between business and others in relation to the residual taxes (6000)

The distinction is the same as in c) above between producers on the one hand and households as consumers on the other hand. Taxes which are included under the heading 6000 because they involve more than one tax base or because the tax base does not fall within any of the previous categories but which are identifiable as levyable only on producers and not on households are included under 'business'. The rest of the taxes which are included under the heading 6000 are shown as 'other' or non-identified.

Surcharges

31. Receipts from surcharges in respect of particular taxes are usually classified with the receipts from the relevant tax whether or not the surcharge is temporary. If, however, the surcharge has a characteristic which would render it classifiable in a different heading of the OECD list, receipts from the surcharge are classified under that heading separately from the relevant tax.

Unidentifiable tax receipts and residual sub-headings

32. . A number of cases arise where taxes cannot be identified as belonging entirely to a heading or sub-heading of the OECD classification and the following practices are applied in such cases:

a) The heading is known, but it is not known how receipts should be allocated between sub-headings: receipts are classified in the appropriate residual sub-heading (1300, 2400, 4520, 4600, 5130, 5300 or 6200).

b) It is known that the bulk of receipts from a group of taxes (usually local taxes) is derived from taxes within a particular heading or sub-heading, but some of the taxes in the group whose amount cannot be precisely ascertained may be classifiable in other headings or sub-headings: receipts are shown in the heading or sub-heading under which most of the receipts fall.

c) Neither the heading nor sub-heading of a tax (usually local) can be identified: the tax is classified in 6200 unless it is known that it is a tax on business in which case it is classified in 6100.

A.5 Commentaries on items of the list

1000 — Taxes on income, profits and capital gains

33. This heading covers taxes levied on the net income or profits (i.e. gross income minus allowable tax reliefs) of individuals and enterprises. Also covered are taxes levied on the capital gains of individuals and enterprises, and gains from gambling.

34. Included in the heading are:

a) taxes levied predominantly on income or profits, though partially on other bases. Taxes on various bases which are not predominantly income or profits are classified according to the principles laid down in §32 and §81;

b) taxes on property, which are levied on a presumed or estimated income as part of an income tax (see also §47(a), (c) and (d));

c) compulsory payments to social security fund contributions that are levied on income but do not confer an entitlement to social benefits. When such contributions do confer an entitlement to social benefits, they are included in heading 2000 (see §39);

d) receipts from integrated scheduler income tax systems are classified as a whole in this heading, even though certain of the scheduler taxes may be based upon gross income and may not take into account the personal circumstances of the taxpayer.

35. The main subdivision of this heading is between levies on individuals (1100) and those on corporate enterprises (1200). Under each subdivision a distinction is made between taxes on income and profits (1110 and 1210), and taxes on capital gains (1120 and 1220). If certain receipts cannot be identified as appropriate to either 1100 or 1200, or if in practice this distinction cannot be made (e.g., because there are no reliable data on the recipients of payments from which withholding taxes are deducted) they are classified in 1300 as not-allocable.

Treatment of credits under imputation systems

36. Under imputation systems of corporate income tax, a company's shareholders are wholly or partly relieved of their liability to income tax on dividends paid by the company out of income or profits liable to corporate income tax. In countries with such systems,[13] part of the tax on the company's profits is available to provide relief against the shareholders' own tax liability. The relief to the shareholder takes the form of a tax credit, the amount of which may be less than, equal to, or more than the shareholder's overall tax liability. If the tax credit exceeds this tax liability the excess may be payable to the shareholder. As this type of tax credit is an integral part of the imputation system of corporate income tax, any payment to the shareholders is treated as a repayment of tax and not as expenditure (compare the treatment of other tax credits described in §25).

37. As the tax credit under imputation systems (even when exceeding tax liability) is to be regarded as a tax provision, the question arises whether it should be deducted from individual income tax receipts (1110) or corporate income tax receipts (1210). In this Report, the full amount of corporate income tax paid is shown under 1210 and no imputed tax is included under 1110. Thus, the full amount of the credit reduces the amount of 1110 whether the credit results in a reduction of personal income tax liability or whether an actual refund is made because the credit exceeds the income tax liability.

(Where, however, such tax credits are deducted from corporation tax in respect of dividends paid to corporations the amounts are deducted from the receipts of 1210).

1120 and 1220 — Taxes on capital gains

38. These sub-headings comprise taxes imposed on capital gains, 1120 covering those levied on the gains of individuals and 1220 those levied on the gains of corporate enterprises, where receipts from such taxes can be separately identified. In many countries this is not the case and the receipts from such taxes are then classified with those from the income tax. Heading 1120 also includes taxes on gains from gambling.

2000 — Social security contributions

39. Classified here are all compulsory payments that confer an entitlement to receive a (contingent) future social benefit. Such payments are usually earmarked to finance social benefits and are often paid to institutions of general government that provide such benefits. However, such earmarking is not part of the definition of social security contributions and is not required for a tax to be classified here. However, conferment of an entitlement is required for a tax to be classified under this heading. So, levies on income or payroll that are earmarked for social security funds but do not confer an entitlement to benefit are excluded from this heading and shown under personal income taxes (1100) or taxes on payroll and workforce (3000). Taxes on other bases, such as goods and services, which are earmarked for social security benefits are not shown here but are classified according to their respective bases because they generally confer no entitlement to social security benefits.

40. Contributions for the following types of social security benefits would, *inter alia*, be included: unemployment insurance benefits and supplements, accident, injury and sickness benefits, old-age, disability and survivors' pensions, family allowances, reimbursements for medical and hospital expenses or provision of hospital or medical services. Contributions may be levied on both employees and employers.

41. Contributions may be based on earnings or payroll ('on a payroll basis') or on net income after deductions and exemptions for personal circumstances ('on an income tax basis'), and the revenues from the two bases should be separately identified if possible. However, where contributions to a general social security scheme are on a payroll basis, but the contributions of particular groups (such as the self-employed) cannot be assessed on this basis and net income is used as a proxy for gross earnings, the receipts may still be classified as being on a payroll basis. In principle, this heading excludes voluntary contributions paid to social security schemes. When separately identifiable these are shown in the memorandum item on the financing of social security benefits. In practice, however, they cannot always be separately identified from compulsory contributions, in which case they are included in this heading.

42. Contributions to social insurance schemes which are not institutions of general government and to other types of insurance schemes, provident funds, pension funds, friendly societies or other saving schemes are not considered as social security contributions. Provident funds are arrangements under which the contributions of each employee and of the corresponding employer on his/her behalf are kept in a separate account earning interest and withdrawable under specific circumstances. Pension funds are separately organised schemes negotiated between employees and employers and carry provisions for different contributions and benefits, sometimes more directly tied to salary levels and length of service than under social security schemes. When contributions to

these schemes are compulsory or quasi-compulsory (e.g., by virtue of agreement with professional and union organisations) they are shown in the memorandum item (refer to Chapter 4.2 of the Report).

43. Contributions by government employees and by governments in respect of their employees, to social security schemes classified within general government are included in this heading. Contributions to separate schemes for government employees, which can be regarded as replacing general social security schemes, are also regarded as taxes.[14] Where, however, a separate scheme is not seen as replacing a general scheme and has been negotiated between the government, in its role as an employer, and its employees, it is not regarded as social security and contributions to it are not regarded as taxes, even though the scheme may have been established by legislation.

44. This heading excludes 'imputed' contributions, which correspond to social benefits paid directly by employers to their employees or former employees or to their representatives (e.g., when employers are legally obliged to pay sickness benefits for a certain period).

45. Contributions are divided into those of employees (2100), employers (2200), and self-employed or non-employed (2300), and then further sub-divided according to the basis on which they are levied. Employees are defined for this purpose as all persons engaged in activities of business units, government bodies, private non-profit institutions, or other paid employment, except the proprietors and their unpaid family members in the case of unincorporated businesses. Members of the armed forces are included, irrespective of the duration and type of their service, if they contribute to social security schemes. The contributions of employers are defined as their payments on account of their employees to social security schemes. Where employees or employers are required to continue the payment of social security contributions when the employee becomes unemployed these contributions, data permitting, are shown in 2100 and 2200 respectively. Accordingly, the sub-heading 2300 is confined to contributions paid by the self-employed and by those outside of the labour force (e.g., disabled or retired individuals).

3000 — Taxes on payroll and workforce

46. These consist of taxes payable by enterprises assessed either as a proportion of the wages or salaries paid or as a fixed amount per person employed. They do not include compulsory social security contributions paid by employers or any taxes paid by employees themselves out of their wages or salaries

4000 — Taxes on property

47. This heading covers recurrent and non-recurrent taxes on the use, ownership or transfer of property. These include taxes on immovable property or net wealth, taxes on the change of ownership of property through inheritance or gift and taxes on financial and capital transactions. The following kinds of tax are excluded from this heading:

- *a)* taxes on capital gains resulting from the sale of a property (1120 or 1220);
- *b)* taxes on the use of goods or on permission to use goods or perform activities (5200); see §76;
- *c)* taxes on immovable property levied on the basis of a presumed net income which take into account the personal circumstances of the taxpayer. They are classified

as income taxes along with taxes on income and capital gains derived from property (1100);

d) taxes on the use of property for residence, where the tax is payable by either proprietor or tenant and the amount payable is a function of the user's personal circumstances (pay, dependants, and so on). They are classified as taxes on income (1100);

e) taxes on building in excess of permitted maximum density, taxes on the enlargement, construction or alteration of certain buildings beyond a permitted value and taxes on building construction. They are classified as taxes on permission to perform activities (5200);

f) taxes on the use of one's own property for special trading purposes like selling alcohol, tobacco, meat or for exploitation of land resources (e.g., United States severance taxes). They are classified as taxes on permission to perform activities (5200).

4100 — Recurrent taxes on immovable property

48. This sub-heading covers taxes levied regularly in respect of the use or ownership of immovable property.

- these taxes are levied on land and buildings;
- they can be in the form of a percentage of an assessed property value based on a national rental income, sales price, or capitalised yield; or in terms of other characteristics of real property, (for example size or location) from which a presumed rent or capital value can be derived.
- such taxes can be levied on proprietors, tenants, or both. They can also be paid by one level of government to another level of government in respect of property under the jurisdiction of the latter.
- debts are not taken into account in the assessment of these taxes, and they differ from taxes on net wealth in this respect.

49. Taxes on immovable property are further sub-divided into those paid by households (4110) and those paid by other entities (4120), according to the criteria set out in §30(*b*) above.

4200 — Recurrent taxes on net wealth

50. This sub-heading covers taxes levied regularly (in most cases annually) on net wealth, i.e. taxes on a wide range of movable and immovable property, net of debt. It is sub-divided into taxes paid by individuals (4210) and taxes paid by corporate enterprises (4220) according to the criteria set out in §30(*a*) above. If separate figures exist for receipts paid by institutions, the tax payments involved are added to those paid by corporations.

4300 — Estate, inheritance and gift taxes

51. This sub-heading is divided into taxes on estates and inheritances (4310) and taxes on gifts (4320).[15] Estate taxes are charged on the amount of the total estate whereas inheritance taxes are charged on the shares of the individual recipients; in addition the latter may take into account the relationship of the individual recipients to the deceased.

4400 — Taxes on financial and capital transactions

52. This sub-heading comprises, *inter alia*, taxes on the issue, transfer, purchase and sale of securities, taxes on cheques, and taxes levied on specific legal transactions such as validation of contracts and the sale of immovable property. The heading does not include:

- *a)* taxes on the use of goods or property or permission to perform certain activities (5200);
- *b)* fees paid to cover court charges, charges for birth, marriage or death certificates, which are normally regarded as non-tax revenues (see §11);
- *c)* taxes on capital gains (1000);
- *d)* recurrent taxes on immovable property (4100);
- *e)* recurrent taxes on net wealth (4200);
- *f)* once-and-for-all levies on property or wealth (4500).

4500 — Other non-recurrent taxes on property16

53. This sub-heading covers once-and-for-all, as distinct from recurrent, levies on property. It is divided into taxes on net wealth (4510) and other non-recurrent taxes on property (4520). Heading 4510 would include taxes levied to meet emergency expenditures, or for redistribution purposes. Heading 4520 would cover taxes levied to take account of increases in land value due to permission given to develop or provision of additional local facilities by general government, any taxes on the revaluation of capital and once-and-for-all taxes on particular items of property.

4600 — Other recurrent taxes on property

54. These rarely exist in OECD member countries, but the heading would include taxes on goods such as cattle, jewellery, windows, and other external signs of wealth.

5000 — Taxes on goods and services

55. All taxes and duties levied on the production, extraction, sale, transfer, leasing or delivery of goods, and the rendering of services (5100), or in respect of the use of goods or permission to use goods or to perform activities (5200) are included here. The heading thus covers:

- *a)* multi-stage cumulative taxes;
- *b)* general sales taxes — whether levied at manufacture/production, wholesale or retail level;
- *c)* value-added taxes;
- *d)* excises;
- *e)* taxes levied on the import and export of goods;
- *f)* taxes levied in respect of the use of goods and taxes on permission to use goods, or perform certain activities;
- *g)* taxes on the extraction, processing or production of minerals and other products.

56. Borderline cases between this heading and heading 4000 (taxes on property) and 6100 (other taxes on business) are referred to in §47, §52 and §78. Residual sub-headings (5300) and (5130) cover tax receipts which cannot be allocated between 5100 and 5200 and between 5110 and 5120, respectively; see §32.

5100 — Taxes on the production, sale, transfer, leasing and delivery of goods and rendering of services

57. This sub-heading consists of all taxes, levied on transactions in goods and services on the basis of their intrinsic characteristics (e.g., value, weight of tobacco, strength of alcohol, and so on) as distinct from taxes imposed on the use of goods, or permission to use goods or perform activities, which fall under 5200.

5110 — General taxes on goods and services

58. This sub-heading includes all taxes, other than import and export duties (5123 and 5124), levied on the production, leasing, transfer, delivery or sales of a wide range of goods and/or the rendering of a wide range of services, irrespective of whether they are domestically produced or imported and irrespective of the stage of production or distribution at which they are levied. It thus covers value-added taxes, sales taxes and multi-stage cumulative taxes. Receipts from border adjustments in respect of such taxes when goods are imported are added to gross receipts for this category, and repayments of such taxes when goods are exported are deducted. These taxes are subdivided into 5111 value-added taxes, 5112 sales taxes, 5113 turnover and other general taxes on goods and services.

59. Borderline cases arise between this heading and taxes on specific goods (5120) when taxes are levied on a large number of goods, for example, the United Kingdom purchase tax (repealed in 1973) and the Japanese commodity tax (repealed in 1988). In conformity with national views, the former United Kingdom purchase tax is classified as a general tax (5112) and the former Japanese commodity tax as excises (5121).

5111 — Value-added taxes

60. All general consumption taxes charged on value-added are classified in this sub-heading, irrespective of the method of deduction and the stages at which the taxes are levied. In practice, all OECD countries with value-added taxes normally allow immediate deduction of taxes on purchases by all but the final consumer and impose tax at all stages. In some countries the heading may include certain taxes, such as those on financial and insurance activities, either because receipts from them cannot be identified separately from those from the value-added tax, or because they are regarded as an integral part of the value-added tax, even though similar taxes in other countries might be classified elsewhere (e.g., 5126 as taxes on services or 4400 as taxes on financial and capital transactions).

5112 — Sales taxes

61. All general taxes levied at one stage only, whether at manufacturing or production, wholesale or retail stage are classified here.

5113 — Turnover and other general taxes on goods and services

62. These are multi-stage cumulative taxes and taxes where elements of consumption taxes are combined with multistage taxes. These taxes are levied each time a transaction takes place without deduction for taxes paid on inputs. Multi-stage taxes can be combined with elements of value-added or sales taxes.

5120 — Taxes on specific goods and services

63. Excises, profits generated and transferred from fiscal monopolies, and customs and imports duties as well as taxes on exports, foreign exchange transactions, investment goods and betting stakes and special taxes on services, which do not form part of a general tax of 5110, are included in this category.

5121 — Excises

64. Excises are taxes levied as a product specific unit tax on a predefined limited range of goods. Excises are usually levied at differentiated rates on nonessential or luxury goods, alcoholic beverages, tobacco, and energy. Excises may be imposed at any stage of production or distribution and are usually assessed as a specific charge per unit based on characteristics by reference to the value, weight, strength, or quantity of the product. Included are special taxes on individual products such as sugar, sugar beets, matches, and chocolates; taxes levied at varying rates on a certain range of goods; and taxes levied on tobacco goods, alcoholic drinks, motor fuels, and hydrocarbon oils. If a tax collected principally on imported goods also applies, or would apply, under the same law to comparable domestically produced goods, then the revenue from this tax is classified as arising from excises rather than from import duties. This principle applies even if there is no comparable domestic production or no possibility of such production. Taxes on the use of utilities such as water, electricity, gas, and energy are regarded as excises rather than taxes on specific services (5126). Excises exclude those taxes that are levied as general taxes on goods and services (5110); profits of fiscal monopolies (5122); customs and other import duties (5123); or taxes on exports (5124).

5122 — Profits of fiscal monopolies

65. This sub-heading covers that part of the profits of fiscal monopolies which is transferred to general government or which is used to finance any expenditures considered to be government expenditures (see §23). Amounts are shown when they are transferred to general government or used to make expenditures considered to be government expenditures.

66. Fiscal monopolies reflect the exercise of the taxing power of government by the use of monopoly powers. Fiscal monopolies are non-financial public enterprises exercising a monopoly in most cases over the production or distribution of tobacco, alcoholic beverages, salt, matches, playing cards and petroleum or agricultural products (i.e. on the kind of products which are likely to be, alternatively or additionally, subject to the excises of 5121), to raise the government revenues which in other countries are gathered through taxes on dealings in such commodities by private business units. The government monopoly may be at the production stage or, as in the case of government-owned and controlled liquor stores, at the distribution stage.

67. Fiscal monopolies are distinguished from public utilities such as rail transport, electricity, post offices, and other communications, which may enjoy a monopoly or

quasi-monopoly position but where the primary purpose is normally to provide basic services rather than to raise revenue for government. Transfers from such other public enterprises to the government are considered as non-tax revenues. The traditional concept of fiscal monopoly is not generally extended to include state lotteries, the profits of which are usually accordingly regarded as non-tax revenues. However, they can be included as tax revenues if the prime reason for their operation is to raise revenues to finance government expenditure. Fiscal monopoly profits are distinguished from export and import monopoly profits (5127) transferred from marketing boards or other enterprises dealing with international trade.

5123 — Customs and other import duties

68. Taxes, stamp duties and surcharges restricted by law to imported products are included here. Also included are levies on imported agricultural products which are imposed in member countries of the European Union and amounts paid by certain of these countries under the Monetary Compensation Accounts (MCA) system.[16] Starting from 1998, customs duties collected by European Union member states on behalf of the European Union are no longer reported under this heading in the country tables (in Chapter 4 of the Report). Excluded here are taxes collected on imports as part of a general tax on goods and services, or an excise applicable to both imported and domestically produced goods.

5124 — Taxes on exports

69. In the 1970s, export duties were levied in Australia, Canada and Portugal as a regular measure and they have been used in Finland for counter-cyclical purposes. Some member countries of the European Union pay, as part of the MCA system, a levy on exports (see note 16 to §68). Where these amounts are identifiable, they are shown in this heading. This heading does not include repayments of general consumption taxes or excises or customs duties on exported goods, which should be deducted from the gross receipts under 5110, 5121 or 5123, as appropriate.

5125 — Taxes on investment goods

70. This sub-heading covers taxes on investment goods, such as machinery. These taxes may be imposed for a number of years or temporarily for counter-cyclical purposes. Taxes on industrial inputs which are also levied on consumers [e.g., the Swedish energy tax which is classified under (5121)] are not included here.

5126 — Taxes on specific services

71. All taxes assessed on the payment for specific services, such as taxes on insurance premiums, banking services, gambling and betting stakes (e.g., from horse races, football pools, lottery tickets), transport, entertainment, restaurant and advertising charges, fall into this category. Taxes levied on the gross income of companies providing the service (e.g., gross insurance premiums or gambling stakes received by the company) are also classified under this heading. Tax revenues from bank levies and payments to deposit insurance and financial stability schemes are provisionally included here for the 2012 edition. The detailed classification is set out in §108.

72. Excluded from this sub-heading are:

a) taxes on services forming part of a general tax on goods and services (5110);

b) taxes on electricity, gas and energy (5121 as excises);

c) taxes on individual gains from gambling (1120 as taxes on capital gains of individuals and non-corporate enterprises) and lump-sum taxes on the transfer of private lotteries or on the permission to set up lotteries (5200);[17]

d) taxes on cheques and on the issue, transfer or redemption of securities (4400 as taxes on financial and capital transactions).

5127 — Other taxes on international trade and transactions

73. This sub-heading covers revenue received by the government from the purchase and sale of foreign exchange at different rates. When the government exercises monopoly powers to extract a margin between the purchase and sales price of foreign exchange, other than to cover administrative costs, the revenue derived constitutes a compulsory levy exacted in indeterminate proportions from both purchaser and seller of foreign exchange. It is the common equivalent of an import duty and export duty levied in a single exchange rate system or of a tax on the sale or purchase of foreign exchange. Like the profits of fiscal monopolies and import or export monopolies transferred to government, it represents the exercise of monopoly powers for tax purposes and is included in tax revenues.

74. The sub-heading covers also the profits of export or import monopolies, which do not however exist in OECD countries, taxes on purchase or sale of foreign exchange, and any other taxes levied specifically on international trade or transactions.

5128 — Other taxes on specific goods and services

75. This item includes taxes on the extraction of minerals, fossil fuels and other exhaustible resources from deposits owned privately or by another government together with any other unidentifiable receipts from taxes on specific goods and services. Taxes on the extraction of exhaustible resources are usually a fixed amount per unit of quality or weight, but can be a percentage of value. The taxes are recorded when the resources are extracted. Payments from the extraction of exhaustible resources from deposits owned by the government unit receiving the payment are classified as rent.

5200 — Taxes on use of goods or on permission to use goods or perform activities

76. This sub-heading covers taxes which are levied in respect of the use of goods as distinct from taxes on the goods themselves. Unlike the latter taxes – reported under 5100 –, they are not assessed on the value of the goods but usually as fixed amounts. Taxes on permission to use goods or to perform activities are also included here, as are pollution taxes not based upon the value of particular goods. It is sometimes difficult to distinguish between compulsory user charges and licence fees which are regarded as taxes and those which are excluded as non-tax revenues. The criteria which are employed are noted in §11–12.

77. Although the sub-heading refers to the 'use' of goods, registration of ownership rather than use may be what generates liability to tax, so that the taxes of this heading may apply to the ownership of animals or goods rather than their use (e.g., race horses, dogs and motor vehicles) and may apply even to unusable goods (e.g., unusable motor vehicles or guns).

78. Borderline cases arise with:

a) taxes on the permission to perform business activities which are levied on a combined income, payroll or turnover base and, accordingly, are classified following the rules in §81;

b) taxes on the ownership or use of property of headings 4100, 4200 and 4600. The heading 4100 is confined to taxes on the ownership or tenancy of immovable property and – unlike the taxes of 5200 – they are related to the value of the property. The net wealth taxes and taxes on chattels of 4200 and 4600 respectively are confined to the ownership rather than the use of assets, apply to groups of assets rather than particular goods and again are related to the value of the assets,

5210 — Recurrent taxes on use of goods and on permission to use goods or perform activities

79. The principal characteristic of taxes classified here is that they are levied at regular intervals and that they are usually fixed amounts. The most important item in terms of revenue receipts is vehicle licence taxes. This sub-heading also covers taxes on permission to hunt, shoot, fish or to sell certain products and taxes on the ownership of dogs and on the performance of certain services, provided that they meet the criteria set out in §11–12. The sub-divisions of 5210 are user taxes on motor vehicles paid by households (5211) and those paid by others (5212). Sub-heading 5213 covers dog licences and user charges for permission to perform activities such as selling meat or liquor when the levies are on a recurring basis. It also covers recurrent general licences for hunting, shooting and fishing where the right to carry out these activities is not granted as part of a normal commercial transaction (e.g., the granting of the licence is not accompanied by the right to use a specific area which is owned by government).

5220 — Non-recurrent taxes on use of goods and on permission to use goods or perform activities

80. This section covers non-recurrent taxes levied on the use of goods or on permission to use goods or perform activities and taxes levied each time goods are used. It includes taxes levied on the emission or discharge into the environment of noxious gases, liquids or other harmful substances.

- Payments for tradable emission permits issued by governments under cap and trade schemes should be recorded here at the time the emissions occur. No revenue should be recorded for permits that governments issue free of charge. The accrual basis of recording means that there can be a timing difference between the cash being received by government for the permits and the time the emission occurs. In the national accounts, this timing gives rise to a financial liability for government during the period.
- Payments made for the collection and disposal of waste or noxious substances by public authorities should be excluded as they constitute a sale of services to enterprises.

81. Other taxes falling under heading 5200 that are not levied recurrently are also included here. Thus, once-and-for-all payments for permission to sell liquor or tobacco or to set up betting shops are included provided they meet the criteria set out in §11–12.

6000 — Other taxes

82. Taxes levied on a base, or bases, other than those described under headings 1000, 3000, 4000 and 5000, or on bases of which cannot be considered to be related to any one of these headings, are included here. Where taxes are levied on a multiple base and it is possible to estimate the receipts related to each base the separate amounts are included under the appropriate headings. If separate amounts cannot be estimated and it is known that most of the receipts are derived from one base, the whole of the receipts are classified according to that base. Otherwise, they are classified here. Other revenues included here are presumptive taxes not included elsewhere in the classification system, taxes on individuals in the form of a poll tax or capitation tax, stamp taxes not related to financial and capital transactions nor falling exclusively on a single category of transaction, expenditure taxes where personal deductions or exemptions are applied and unidentifiable tax receipts. A subdivision is made between taxes levied wholly or predominantly on business (6100) and those levied on others (6200).

A.6 Conciliation with National Accounts

83. This section of the tables provides a re-conciliation between the OECD calculation of total tax revenues and the total of all taxes and social contributions paid to general government as recorded in the country's National Accounts. Where the country is a member of the European Union (EU), the comparison is between the OECD calculation of total tax revenues and the sum of tax revenues and social contributions recorded in the combination of the general government and the institutions of the EU sectors of the National Accounts.

A.7 Memorandum item on the financing of social security benefits

84. In view of the varying relationship between taxation and social security contributions and the cases referred to in §39 to §45, a memorandum item collects together all payments earmarked for social security-type benefits, other than voluntary payments to the private sector. Data are presented as follows (refer Chapter 4.2 of the Report):

a) Taxes of 2000 series.

b) Taxes earmarked for social security benefits.

c) Voluntary contributions to the government.

d) Compulsory contributions to the private sector.

Guidance on the breakdown of (a) to (d) above is provided in §39 to §45.

A.8 Memorandum item on identifiable taxes paid by government

85. Identifiable taxes actually paid by government are presented in a memorandum item classified by the main headings of the OECD classification of taxes. In the vast majority of countries, only social security contributions and payroll taxes paid by government can be identified. These are, however, usually the most important taxes paid by governments (refer to Chapter 4.2 of the Report).

A.9 Relation of OECD classification of taxes to national accounting systems

86. A system of national accounts (SNA) seeks to provide a coherent framework for recording and presenting the main flows relating respectively to production, consumption, accumulation and external transactions of a given economic area, usually a country or a

major region within a country. Government revenues are an important part of the transactions recorded in SNA. The final version of the 2008 SNA was jointly published by five international organisations: the United Nations, the International Monetary Fund, the European Union, the Organisation for Economic Co-operation and Development, and the World Bank in August 2009. The *System* is a comprehensive, consistent and flexible set of macroeconomic accounts. It is designed for use in countries with market economies, whatever their stage of economic development, and also in countries in transition to market economies. The important parts of the SNA's conceptual framework and its definitions of the various sectors of the economy have been reflected in the OECD's classification of taxes.

87. There are, however, some differences between the OECD classification of taxes and SNA concepts that are listed below. They arise because the aim of the former is to provide the maximum disaggregation of statistical data on what are generally regarded as taxes by tax administrations.

a) OECD includes compulsory social security contributions paid to general government in total tax revenues. Imputed and voluntary contributions plus those paid to private funds are not treated as taxes (§8 and §10 above);

b) there are different points of view on whether or not some levies and fees are classified as taxes (§11 and §12 above);

c) OECD excludes imputed taxes or subsidies resulting from the operation of official multiple exchange rates or from the central bank paying a rate of interest on required reserves that is different from other market rates;

d) there are differences in the treatment of non-wastable tax credits

88. As noted in §1 and §2, headings 1000 to 6000 of the OECD list of taxes cover all unrequited payments to general government, other than compulsory loans and fines. Such unrequited payments including fines, but excluding compulsory loans can be obtained from adding together the following figures in the 2008 SNA

- value-added type taxes (D.211);
- taxes and duties on imports, excluding VAT (D.212);
- export taxes (D.213);
- taxes on products, excluding VAT, import and export taxes (D.214);
- other taxes on production (D.29);
- taxes on income (D.51);
- other current taxes (D.59);
- social contributions (D.61), excluding voluntary contributions;
- capital taxes (D.91).

A.10 The OECD classification of taxes and the International Monetary Fund (GFS) system

89. The coverage and valuation of tax revenues in the GFS system and the 2008 SNA are very similar. Therefore, the differences between the OECD classification and that of the 2008 SNA (see §87 above) also apply to the GFS. In addition the International

Monetary Fund subdivides the OECD 5000 heading into section IV (Domestic Taxes on Goods and Services) and section V (Taxes on International Trade and Transactions). This reflects the fact that while the latter usually yield insignificant amounts of revenue in OECD countries, this is not the case in many non-OECD countries.

A.11 Comparison of the OECD classification of taxes with other international classifications

90. The table below describes an item by item comparison of the OECD classification of taxes and the classifications used in the following:

a) System of National Accounts (2008 SNA);

b) European System of Accounts (2010 ESA);

c) IMF *Government Finance Statistics Manual* (GFSM2014).

91. These comparisons represent those that would be expected to apply in the majority of cases. However in practice some flexibility should be used in their application. This is because in particular cases, countries can adopt varying approaches to the classification of revenues in National Accounts.

OECD Classification					2008 SNA	2010 ESA	GFSM2014
1000				Taxes on income, profits and capital gains			
	1100			Individuals			
		1110		Income and profits	D51-8.61a	D51A	1111
		1120		Capital gains	D51-8.61c, d	D51C, D	1111
	1200			Corporations			
		1210		Income and profits	D51-8.61b	D51B	1112
		1220		Capital gains	D51-8.61c	D51C	1112
	1300			Unallocable as between 1100 and 1200			1113
2000				Social security contributions			
	2100			Employees	D613-8.85	D613	1211
	2200			Employers	D611-8.83	D611	1212
	2300			Self-employed, non-employed	D613-8.85	D613	1213
	2400			Unallocable as between 2100, 2200 and 2300			1214
3000				Taxes on payroll and workforce	D29-7.97a	D29C	112
4000				Taxes on property			
	4100			Recurrent taxes on immovable property			
		4110		Households	D59-8.63a	D59A	1131
		4120		Other	D29-7.97b	D29A	1131
	4200			Recurrent net wealth taxes			
		4210		Individual	D59-8.63b	D59A	1132
		4220		Corporations	D59-8.63b	D59A	1132
	4300			Estate, inheritance and gift taxes			
		4310		Estate and inheritance taxes	D91-10.207b	D91A	1133
		4320		Gift taxes	D91-10.207b	D91A	1133
	4400			Taxes on financial and capital transactions	D59-7.96d; D29-7.97e	D214B, C	114114; 1161
	4500			Other non-recurrent taxes on property	D91-10.207a	D91B	1135
	4600			Other recurrent taxes on property	D59-8.63c	D59A	1136
5000				Taxes on goods and services			
	5100			Taxes on production, sale and transfer of goods and services			
		5110		General taxes on goods and services			
			5111	Value-added taxes	D211-7.89	D211; D29G	11411
			5112	Sales taxes	D2122-7.94a; D214-7.96a	D21224; D214I	11412
			5113	Other general taxes on goods and services	D214-7.96a	D214I	11413
		5120		Taxes on specific goods and services			
			5121	Excises	D2122-7.94b; D214-7.96b	D21223; D214A, B, D	1142
			5122	Profits of fiscal monopolies	D214-7.96e	D214J	1143
			5123	Customs and other import duties	D2121-7.93	D2121; D21221, 2	1151
			5124	On exports	D213-7.95a	D214K	1152-4
			5125	On investment goods			
			5126	On specific services	D2122-7.94c; D214-7.96c	D21225; D214E, F, G, H; D29F	1144; 1156
			5127	Other taxes on international trade and transactions	D2122-7.94d D29-7.95b D29-7.97g D59-8.64d	D21226; D29D; D59E	1153; 1155-6
			5128	Other taxes on specific goods and services			1146
		5130		Unallocable between 5110 and 5120			
	5200			Taxes on use of goods and on permission to use goods or			

				perform activities			
		5210		Recurrent taxes on use of goods and on permission to use goods or perform activities			
			5211	Motor vehicle taxes households	D59-8.64c	D59D	11451
			5212	Motor vehicles taxes others	D29-7.97d	D214D; D29B	11451
			5213	Other recurrent taxes on use of goods and on permission to use goods or perform activities	D29-7.97c, d, f D59-8.64c	D29B, E, F; D59D	11452
		5220		Non-recurrent taxes on permission to use goods or perform activities			11452
	5300			Unallocable as between 5100 and 5200			
6000				Other taxes			
	6100			Payable solely by business			1161
	6200			Payable by other than business, or unidentifiable	D59-8.64a, b	D59B, C	1162

A.12 Attribution of tax revenues by sub-sectors of general government

92. The OECD classification requires a breakdown of tax revenues by sub-sectors of government. The definition of each sub-sector and the criteria to be used to attribute tax revenues between these sub-sectors are set out below. They follow the guidance of the 2008 SNA and GFSM 2014.

Sub-sectors of general government to be identified

a) Central government

93. The central government sub-sector includes all governmental departments, offices, establishments and other bodies which are agencies or instruments of the central authority whose competence extends over the whole territory, with the exception of the administration of social security funds. Central government therefore has the authority to impose taxes on all resident and non-resident units engaged in economic activities within the country.

b) State, provincial or regional government

94. This sub-sector consists of intermediate units of government exercising a competence at a level below that of central government. It includes all such units operating independently of central government in a part of a country's territory encompassing a number of smaller localities, with the exception of the administration of social security funds. In unitary countries, regional governments may be considered to have a separate existence where they have substantial autonomy to raise a significant proportion of their revenues from sources within their control and their officers are independent of external administrative control in the actual operation of the unit's activities.

95. At present, federal countries comprise the majority of cases where revenues attributed to intermediate units of government are identified separately. Spain is the only unitary country in this position. In the remaining unitary countries, regional revenues are included with those of local governments.

c) Local government

96. This sub-sector includes all other units of government exercising an independent competence in part of the territory of a country, with the exception of the administration

of social security funds. It encompasses various urban and/or rural jurisdictions (e.g., local authorities, municipalities, cities, boroughs, districts).

d) Social security funds

97. Social security funds form a separate sub-sector of general government. The social security sub-sector is defined in the 2008 SNA by the following extracts from paragraphs 4.124 to 4.126 and 4.147:

"Social security schemes are social insurance schemes covering the community as a whole or large section of the community that are imposed and controlled by government units. The schemes cover a wide variety of programmes, providing benefits in cash or in kind for old age, invalidity or death, survivors, sickness and maternity, work injury, unemployment, family allowance, health care, etc. There is not necessarily a direct link between the amount of the contribution paid by an individual and the benefits he or she may receive." (Paragraph 4.124).

"When social security schemes are separately organised from the other activities of government units and hold their assets and liabilities separately from the latter and engage in financial transactions on their own account they qualify as institutional units that are described as social security funds." (Paragraph 4.125).

"The amounts raised, and paid out, in social security contributions and benefits may be deliberately varied in order to achieve objectives of government policy that have no direct connection with the concept of social security as a scheme to provide social benefits to members of the community. They may be raised or lowered in order to influence the level of aggregate demand in the economy, for example. Nevertheless, so long as they remain separately constituted funds, they must be treated as separate institutional units in the SNA. (Paragraph 4.126).

"The social security funds sub-sector (of general government) consists of the social security funds operating at all levels of government. Such funds are social insurance schemes covering the community as a whole or large section of the community that are imposed by government units." (Paragraph 4.147).

98. This definition of social security funds is followed in the OECD classification with the two following exceptions which are excluded

- Schemes imposed by government and operated by bodies outside the general government sector, as defined in §3 of this manual; and
- Schemes to which all contributions are voluntary.

Supra-national Authorities

99. This sub-sector covers the revenue-raising operations of supra-national authorities within a country. In practice, the only relevant supra-national authority in the OECD area is that of the institutions of the European Union (EU). As from 1998, supra-national authorities are no longer included in the *Revenue Statistics*, to achieve consistency with the SNA definition of general government which excludes them. For example, income taxes and social security contributions collected by European Institutions and paid by European civil servants who are resident of EU member countries should not be included. However the specific levies paid by the member states of the EU continue to be included in total tax revenues and they are shown under this heading.

Criteria to be used for the attribution of tax revenues

100. When a government collects taxes and pays them over in whole or in part to other governments, it is necessary to determine whether the revenues should be considered to be those of the collecting government which it distributes to others as grants, or those of the beneficiary governments which the collecting government receives and passes on only as their agent. The criteria to be used in the attribution of revenues are set out in §101 to §104 which replicate paragraphs 3.70 to 3.73 from the 2008 SNA.

101. In general, a tax is attributed to the government unit that

a) exercises the authority to impose the tax (either as a principal or through the delegated authority of the principal),

b) has final discretion to set and vary the rate of the tax

102. Where an amount is collected by one government for and on behalf of another government, and the latter government has the authority to impose the tax, and set and vary its rate, then the former is acting as an agent for the latter and the tax is reassigned. Any amount retained by the collecting government as a collection charge should be treated as a payment for a service. Any other amount retained by the collecting government, such as under a tax-sharing arrangement, should be treated as a current grant. If the collecting government was delegated the authority to set and vary the rate, then the amount collected should be treated as tax revenue of this government.

103. Where different governments jointly and equally set the rate of a tax and jointly and equally decide on the distribution of the proceeds, with no individual government having ultimate overriding authority, then the tax revenues are attributed to each government according to its respective share of the proceeds. If an arrangement allows one government unit to exercise ultimate overriding authority, then all of the tax revenue is attributed to that unit.

104. There may also be the circumstance where a tax is imposed under the constitutional or other authority of one government, but other governments individually set the tax rate in their jurisdictions. The proceeds of the tax generated in each respective government's jurisdiction are attributed as tax revenues of that government.

Levies paid by member states of the European Union

105. The levies paid by the member states of the EU take the form specific levies which include

a) custom duties and levies on agricultural goods (5123),

b) gross monetary compensation accounts (5123 if relating to imports and 5124 if relating to exports); and

c) Steel, coal, sugar and milk levies (5128).

106. The custom duties collected by member states on behalf of the EU are recorded

- on a gross of collection fee basis;
- using figures adjusted so that duties are shown on a 'final destination' as opposed to a 'country of first entry' basis where such adjustments can be made. These adjustments concern in particular duties collected at important (sea) ports. Although the EU duties are collected by the authorities of the country of first

entry, when possible these duties should be excluded from the revenue of the collecting country and be included in the revenue of the country of final destination

107. This is the specific EU levy that most clearly conforms to the attribution criterion described in §99 above. Consequently as from 1998, these amounts are footnoted as a memorandum item to the EU member state country tables (in Chapter 4) and no longer shown under heading 5123. However the figures are included in the total tax revenue figures on the top line for all the relevant years shown in the tables.

A.13 Provisional classification of revenues from bank levies and payments to deposit insurance and financial stability schemes

108. The OECD have adopted the following interim approach to reporting revenue from bank levies plus deposit insurance and stability fees for the 2012 and subsequent editions of *OECD Revenue Statistics*. It is recommended that the amounts should be recorded under category 5126.

- Compulsory payments of stability fees, bank levies and deposit insurance should generally be treated as tax revenues where the payments are made to General Government and allocated to the governments' consolidated or general funds so that the Government is free to make immediate use of the money for the purposes that it chooses. This principle would apply regardless of whether the Government is promising to make payments to guarantee the banks' customer deposits in some future contingency.
- If the compulsory payments are made to general government and placed in funds that are earmarked to be entirely channelled back to the sector of the economy that comprises the companies that are subject to the payment, they would still generally be treated as tax revenues on the grounds that the funds would be available for the government and would reduce its budget deficit, the fee is unrequited for an individual entity and the amounts raised could be unrelated to any eventual pay out to depositors or expenditure on wider support for the financial sector.
- Payments to made to the smaller long-standing schemes for insuring 'retail' deposits, where the payment levels are consistent with the costs of insurance should be classified as fee for service.
- Any payments which involve governments realising the assets of a failed institution or receiving a priority claim on its assets in liquidation in order to fund payments of compensation to customers for their lost deposits would be treated as a fee for a service as opposed to tax revenues.
- Compulsory payments that are made to funds operated outside the government sector and non-state institutions backed by the deposit takers and all payments to voluntary schemes should not be treated as tax revenues.

Notes

1. All references to SNA are to the 2008 edition.

2. See section A.12 of this guide for a discussion of the concept of agency capacity.

3. It is usually possible to identify amounts of social security contributions and payroll taxes, but not other taxes paid by government.

4. If, however, a levy which is considered as non-tax revenue by most countries is regarded as a tax — or raises substantial revenue — in one or more countries, the amounts collected are footnoted at the end of the relevant country tables, even though the amounts are not included in total tax revenues.

5. Names, however, can frequently be misleading. For example, though a passport fee would normally be considered a non-tax revenue, if a supplementary levy on passports (as is the case in Portugal) were imposed in order to raise substantial amounts of revenue relative to the cost of providing the passport, the levy would be regarded as a tax under 5200.

6. A more detailed explanation of this distinction can be found in the special feature, 'Current issues in reporting tax revenues', in the 2001 edition of the *Revenue Statistics*.

7. Sometimes the terms 'non-refundable' and 'refundable' are used, but it may be considered illogical to talk of 'refundable' when nothing has been paid.

8. A different treatment, however, is accorded to non-wastable tax credits under imputation systems of corporate income tax (§36–38).

9. This is not strictly a true tax expenditure in the formal sense. Such tax expenditures require identification of a benchmark tax system for each country or, preferably, a common international benchmark. In practice it has not been possible to reach agreement on a common international benchmark.

10. Unless based on the profit made on a sale, in which case they would be classified as capital gains taxes under 1120 or 1220.

11. In some countries the same legislation applies to both individual and corporate enterprises for particular taxes on income. However, the receipts from such taxes are usually allocable between individuals and enterprises and can therefore be shown in the appropriate sub-heading.

12. For example, "...sufficiently self-contained and independent that they behave in the same way as corporations.......(including) keeping a complete set of accounts" (2008 SNA, section 4.44).

13. In Canada — a country also referred to as having an imputation system — the (wastable) tax credit for the shareholder is in respect of domestic corporation tax deemed to have been paid whether or not a corporation tax liability has arisen. As there is no integral connection between the corporation tax liability and the credit given against income tax under such systems, these credits for dividends are treated, along with other tax credits, on the lines described in §25.

14. This may also apply where a scheme for government employees existed prior to the introduction of a general social security scheme.

15. In the 2008 SNA these are regarded as capital transfers and not as taxes (see section A.8).

16. This is the system by which the European Union adjusts for differences between the exchange rates used to determine prices under the Common Market Agricultural Policy and actual exchange rates. Payments under the system may relate to imports or exports and where these amounts are separately identifiable they are shown under the appropriate heading (5123 or 5124). In this Report, these amounts are shown gross (i.e. without deducting any subsidies paid out under the MCA system).

17. Transfers of profits of State lotteries are regarded as non-tax revenues (see also §67).

ORGANISATION FOR ECONOMIC CO-OPERATION AND DEVELOPMENT

The OECD is a unique forum where governments work together to address the economic, social and environmental challenges of globalisation. The OECD is also at the forefront of efforts to understand and to help governments respond to new developments and concerns, such as corporate governance, the information economy and the challenges of an ageing population. The Organisation provides a setting where governments can compare policy experiences, seek answers to common problems, identify good practice and work to co-ordinate domestic and international policies.

The OECD member countries are: Australia, Austria, Belgium, Canada, Chile, the Czech Republic, Denmark, Estonia, Finland, France, Germany, Greece, Hungary, Iceland, Ireland, Israel, Italy, Japan, Korea, Latvia, Lithuania, Luxembourg, Mexico, the Netherlands, New Zealand, Norway, Poland, Portugal, the Slovak Republic, Slovenia, Spain, Sweden, Switzerland, Turkey, the United Kingdom and the United States. The European Union takes part in the work of the OECD.

OECD Publishing disseminates widely the results of the Organisation's statistics gathering and research on economic, social and environmental issues, as well as the conventions, guidelines and standards agreed by its members.

OECD PUBLISHING, 2, rue André-Pascal, 75775 PARIS CEDEX 16
(23 2018 48 1 P) ISBN 978-92-64-30878-7 – 2018

www.ingramcontent.com/pod-product-compliance
Lightning Source LLC
Chambersburg PA
CBHW061212240926
51846CB00006B/1199